Appalachia Inside Out

VOLUME 2

Culture and Custom

Appalachia Inside Out

A Sequel to *Voices from the Hills*

VOLUME 2

Culture and Custom

Editors

Robert J. Higgs
Ambrose N. Manning
Jim Wayne Miller

Associate Editors

Laura L. Higgs
Cindy Hyder Tipton
Annie H. Michal
Douglas Powell

The University of Tennessee Press • Knoxville

To the pioneers of modern Appalachian consciousness:

Harriette Arnow
Harry Caudill
Wilma Dykeman
Loyal Jones
James Still
Jesse Stuart
Cratis Williams

Cartoons by Tony Feathers.

LIBRARY OF CONGRESS CATALOGING IN PUBLICATION DATA

Appalachia inside out / editors, Robert J. Higgs, Ambrose N. Manning, Jim Wayne Miller;
    associate editors, Laura L. Higgs [et al.] —1st ed.
                p.   cm.
      "A sequel to Voices from the hills."
      Includes bibliographical references and index.
      Contents: v.1. Conflict and change—v.2. Culture and custom.
      ISBN 0-87049-873-8 v. 1 (cloth: alk paper)
      ISBN 0-87049-874-6 v. 1 (pbk: alk. paper)
      ISBN 0-87049-875-4 v. 2 (cloth: alk paper)
      ISBN 0-87049-876-2 v. 2 (pbk: alk. paper)
    1. Mountain life—Appalachian Region, Southern—Literary collections.
    2. American literature—Appalachian Region, Southern.
    3. Appalachian Region, Southern—Civilization.
    I. Higgs, Robert J., 1932-   . II. Manning, Ambrose N. III. Miller, Jim Wayne.
PS554.A65 1995
810.8'0327568—dc20   94-18718
                                                CIP

Contents

Volume 2

Culture and Custom

Introduction

The great constant in Appalachian history has been change, and for this reason we chose for volume 1 of *Appalachia Inside Out* the title *Conflict and Change.* But in the midst of change, certain defining features of Appalachian culture have persisted—folklore, humor, language, religion. Hence we call volume 2 *Culture and Custom.*

Just as we cannot define precisely where Appalachia begins and ends geographically, neither can we say exactly where the culture and customs of the region begin and end. The same is true of the region's literature and criticism. This linkage between "inside" and "outside" seems in keeping with some current critical theory. The title, *Appalachia Inside Out,* also refers to an effort to look not only at the visible Appalachia but also at underlying influences and at the relationships in the region between the dark and the light, the ugly and the beautiful, the upside down and the right side up, the "antisigodlin" and the "plumb straight," and at angles in between. Though there is considerable overlap between what Henry Shapiro calls the "otherness" of the myth of Appalachia and the otherness of the myth of progress of mid-America, each offers a valuable critique of the other.

Like the issues of gender and ethnicity, the question of region has also entered the debate over what constitutes the canon of American, and even southern, literature. *Appalachia Inside Out* engages this issue of region which major American literature texts fail substantially to address, focusing as they usually do upon major authors and literary movements. It is our belief that, if self-knowledge is the goal of humanistic learning, literature should reflect some understanding of the self not only in the abstract but also on native or familiar ground.

How long the culture and customs of Appalachia will remain identifiable is an open question which we consider in the final chapter of this volume. But if Appalachia becomes indistinguishable from American life in other parts of the country, if it loses its "otherness," there still would be a need for knowledge of the history of Appalachia. Should Appalachia prove to be the invention of a rather small group of people, as Shapiro has argued, then we still would want to know why that invention could not prevail. Inventions, like grass and trees, compete for light. What we finally seek, to paraphrase Joseph Campbell, are good inventions to live by. The Appalachian myth or invention may die harder than we expect, if it dies at all; for, as the chapter on religion illustrates, it is a myth old indeed—a myth in which people are bound to a bountiful but stubborn earth, on the one hand, and to a loving and punishing God on the other, forever beyond our reach but forever compelling, even among the luxuries of civilization and progress.

We extend thanks to the staff of the Charles Sherrod Library at East Tennessee State University, especially Dr. Fred Borchuck, head librarian, and Beth Hogan of Interlibrary Loan, for supporting this project in innumerable ways. We are grateful, too, for the support of Jean Haskell Speer, director of the Center for Appalachian Studies and Services, ETSU, and of Dr. Styron Harris, chair, Department of English, ETSU.

A special tribute goes to Deanna Bryant, who not only typed both volumes on disks but also served as factotum for the project, coordinating editing, permissions, typing, and rewriting tasks. If there was one point at which all the aspects of such a huge undertaking came together, it was Deanna's desk. Despite the constant workload imposed upon Deanna, from her there never was heard a discouraging word. She kept a faithful and reliable hand on the helm throughout the voyage. We are grateful for her professional service and her inspiration. Hers is a truly pioneering spirit, appropriate to this task.

Chapter 1

Family and Community

Introduction

Like other Americans, Appalachians have often responded to conflicting forces in a changing land by migrating. But another facet of
the region's cultural heritage is represented by those who have
stayed in place, creating a sense of continuity in the face of perpetual change, a solid ground on which to make one's stand, for
better or worse, with the accumulated experience of generations
to draw on. While those who have resolved to remain may have
done so against considerable odds, resisting the same pressures
which have drawn others away, both expatriate and die-hard share
a respect and love for not only the land but for family and community as well.

A sense of place is not purely geographical—it is not a mere attachment to landscape. Commitment to locale comes also through
relationships with other people. And though personal relationships
are not always positive—sometimes the effect of others is to hone
and temper—the family nevertheless provides the framework,
sure or shaky, upon which community life is built.

The sense of family and community in the succession of generations thus provides a strong link in the continuity of Appalachian
life, uniting the living and the dead. This sense of family and community is also a point upon which some of the negative stereotyp-
ing of mountaineers rests, as seen in the chapter in volume I on
"Feuds and Violence." Appalachian texts are richly complex, often
paradoxical and difficult to read. Even constant elements such as
family and community require careful scrutiny.

Jane Wilson Joyce

Jane Wilson Joyce was born in Kingsport, Tennessee, and educated in Pennsylvania and Texas. Her chapbook, *The Quilt Poems* (1984), originally published by Mill Springs Press, has been reissued by Gnomon Press in a volume entitled *Quilt Pieces* (1991). Gnomon is also the publisher of *Beyond the Blue Mountains* (1992). A professor of classics at Centre College, Danville, Kentucky, Joyce is the translator of Lucan's *Pharsalia* (1993).

Hooked Album Quilt, 1870

Mama, I finished your quilt
but my heart wasn't in it
like yours was
so my work stands out—
plain crochet, thin and poor
alongside of yours.

I watched you
cut up the uniforms
they shipped home from Virginia,
sliding your big scissorblades
up the trouserlegs
like a doctor
slicing open a boot
when the leg inside is broken.

You sat, skeins striping
your black skirt
green, yellow, red,
tugging heavy yarns
through the dense weave of dull cloth
strand by strand,
shearing them down
just so: 33 squares
you worked this way,
never saying a word
that wasn't bright,

From *Quilt Pieces,* Gnomon Press, 1991. Reprinted by permission of the publisher.

while the blisters came up on your hand,
broke, and wept.

I finished the quilt—
counterpane, you called it—
rolled it up and packed it away
in the cedar chest in the attic,
touching the rounded bunches
of cat-tails, tulips,
the one sunflower,
repeating fields of moss rose.
Why would you want to sleep
under such a weight
of remembering.

Gurney Norman

Gurney Norman is one of the leading writers of Southern Appalachia. Born in Grundy, Virginia, he grew up in Hazard in the eastern Kentucky coalfields. He was educated at the University of Kentucky and at Stanford University, where, as a Wallace Stegner Fellow, he studied short-story writing with Frank O'Connor.

Norman is the author of *Divine Right's Trip,* which was first published in segments in *The Last Whole Earth Catalog* (1971) and of *Kinfolks: The Wilgus Stories* (1977), a book of short stories including "Fat Monroe," which was made into a movie featuring Ned Beatty. He is also the author of narratives for three documentary programs on Kentucky and Appalachian history for Kentucky Educational Television. Professor of English at the University of Kentucky, he is also an instructor for the Hindman Settlement School Appalachian Writers Workshop conducted annually at Hindman, Kentucky. Norman is noted as much as a teacher of writing as he is as an author.

"Fat Monroe" has been made into a film by the same name featuring Ned Beatty. Both story and film realistically depict persistent themes dealing with family life in Appalachia: the rite marking the young person's passage into adulthood; the often fragile and ambiguous relationship between parent and child, and between father and mother as well; and the trickery which seems almost irrepressible in many Appalachians, fictional and real.

Fat Monroe

The boy walked on the right side of the road the first mile or two, trying to hitch a ride home after seeing the show in town.

But it was late Saturday afternoon and most of the folks from his end of the county who'd been to town that day had already gone on home.

Only two cars passed him in two miles and they didn't even slow down.

So finally he gave up trying to thumb, crossed the narrow pike to the higher shoulder where the walking was better, and stepped out at his best pace toward home.

But then he didn't get a hundred yards before a dusty pickup rattled past him, slowed, stopped, then came flying down the highway backwards, straddling the white dividing line.

"Well hurry up there boy!" shouted a big fat man with a cigar between his teeth. "I'm losing air in both front tires, running out of gas plus an airplane's going to land here any minute now. Come on!"

The boy was already running but at the sound of the man's hoarse voice he ran faster. He knew better than to believe that about the airplane but he glanced into the sky anyway as he climbed on the running board. And for something to do in the awkward first moment in the cab, he craned his neck and through the windshield looked at the sky again.

"Take either one of those seats there you want, old timer," the fat man said, shifting gears as the old truck started rolling. "I wouldn't want you to be uncomfortable."

There was so much junk on the seat and the floor the boy barely found room for himself, and that was on the point of a spring sticking through the cotton wadding and imitation leather of the seat. Around him were tools and parts of two or three old motors, a chainsaw and a can of gasoline, some steel cable and a great coil of thick rope on the floor. The boy glanced at the man curiously, then out at the sky again. Finally he settled back with his feet propped on a tool box.

"Well, what is it?" the fat man asked.

"What's what?" asked Wilgus.

"Your name. What is it? Puddintane?"

"Wilgus Collier," said the boy.

"How was that again?" said the man. He cupped his hand to his ear and leaned in Wilgus' direction. "This old truck makes so much noise I don't hear good."

"Wilgus Collier."

The fat man nodded. "Monroe Short. That's what I thought you said. But I wonder if that's actually right. I mean, could your name be Short Monroe and you just got confused?"

Wilgus grinned. "My name's Wilgus Collier," he said.

From *Kinfolks: The Wilgus Stories,* Gnomon Press, 1977. Reprinted by permission of the publisher.

"Just like that, eh? Monroe Short and that's all?"

"Wilgus Collier's my name. I don't have a middle name."

The fat man shook his head and sucked his teeth. "Well," he said. "Either way, it's a poor out for a name. What I mean, it's not any name you'd go around bragging about. Why don't you change it, call yourself Monroe, or Stepinfetchit or something?"

Wilgus laughed out loud this time. "Oh, I'll just keep it like it is."

The fat man shrugged. "Well," he said. "It's a free country. How about a cigar?"

He reached into a box of cigars next to his leg and took out three or four. He put all but one into his shirt pocket, then held the one out for Wilgus.

Wilgus said he didn't smoke.

"That's all right," said the fat man. "Take it home and give it to your mommy. Or sell it to somebody if nothing else. That's something you ought to learn, Short Collier, don't never turn down a free cigar. Besides, it would be a kindness to me if you took it."

"Well, okay," said Wilgus, and he held out his hand. "Give me one then."

Looking very solemn and earnest, the man put the good cigar in his shirt pocket with the others, then took the frayed, soggy one out of his mouth and ceremoniously stuck it in Wilgus' hand.

"Yes sir," he said. "I learned a long time ago about not taking stuff that's free. It's like I said to my wives, I got 'em all together one day . . . but you probably don't want to hear that story. Tell me, Monroe, how many wives you got? Five? Six?"

Wilgus said he didn't have any. "I ain't but eight," he said. "And my name ain't Monroe, neither. It's Wilgus."

"Eight! Is that all the old you are? Why Wilgus Short, I had you figured to be up around twenty-five or thirty somewhere."

Wilgus said, "You did not. You're teasing. Here, take this old cigar back, I don't want it."

The man slammed on the brakes. Wilgus pitched forward, along with most of the tools and equipment. He would have hurt himself if he hadn't got his free hand up to catch himself on the dashboard.

"Don't *want* it!" the fat man exclaimed. "How come you to take it if you don't want it?"

Wilgus was too shaken to answer. Nervously he glanced at the man. Then he shoved the chainsaw around so he could sit back down as the truck began to pick up speed again. The cigar had fallen to the floor.

"Oh Lord," the fat man moaned. He wiped his face with the palm of his hand. "Oh Lordy me, why did I ever pick up this boy?" Looking at Wilgus, his lower lip drooping, he said, "You've hurt my feelings bad, boy. You really have."

And two big tears welled out of the corners of his eyes and rolled down his puffy cheeks.

Wilgus didn't have anything to say.

"You have, now," the fat man sniffed. "You really have. There I give you a nice cigar and then you tell me you don't want it anymore."

"I didn't go to hurt your feelings," said Wilgus. "But I don't really think I did."

"Listen at him," sighed the fat man. "Accusing me of telling lies. Oh Lord above, why did I ever pick up such a boy?"

"I didn't call you no liar," said Wilgus. "You're just making all that stuff up."

"You know," said the fat man. He sat up a little straighter now. "You know, Short Wilgus, I had a suspicion you was going to turn out to be mean. I didn't want to say anything about it, but I could tell, three or four miles ago, I could see it in those eyes of yours. Mean, just plain m-e-a-n mean. I don't know what else to do with you but report you. Whose boy are you?"

"Glen Collier's."

"Glen Collier's what?"

"His *boy*," said Wilgus. "He's my daddy."

"You know," said the fat man. "It seems to me like I've heard of Glen Collier. Ain't he that fishing worm salesman from over on Leatherwood?"

Wilgus didn't have anything to say. He refused to even look at the man. They were passing familiar places now, within a mile or two of his house, and Wilgus stared out the window, wishing he was already home.

"If he don't sell fishing worms, what *does* he do? Talk to me now, Short Wilgus, let's get all this said while we've got the chance."

"Daddy loads coal for the Harlowe brothers when there's work."

"And your mommy? How does he treat your mommy?"

"Daddy's real good to us," said Wilgus.

"Well that ain't the way I heard it," said the fat man, and he clucked his tongue and shook his head knowingly.

"What do you mean?" Wilgus asked.

"Somebody told me your daddy drunk whiskey, played all his money away on cards, laid out on the weekends and that when he *would* come home. . . ."

"That's not so. My daddy's good."

"How often does he beat your mommy up?"

"My daddy's *good*."

"That ain't the way I heard it," said the fat man. "I heard he beat on you and was too sorry to work and that him and your mommy fit one another all the time, that they just fit and throwed things and rassled all over the floor. And that she went out with boy friends and he went out with girl friends and left you at the house all by yourself without anything to eat and no coal for the stove. Now me, I don't blame you for hating a man like that. If *my* daddy had ever treated me like that. . . ."

"None of that's so!" Wilgus cried. "I *like* my mommy and I *like* my daddy, and that's the last thing I'm going to say. And I'm going to tell him on you too if you don't hush."

"But *why*, Wilgus? *Why* do you like them? That's the point?"

"Because I just do," said Wilgus. "They're my mommy and daddy ain't they?"

"I don't know," said the fat man. "Are they?"

He broke into such violent laughter then the truck started swerving back and forth across the road. Great tears rolled down his puffy cheeks. His eyes seemed to roll back inside his head as he tossed his head, laughing.

"Oh me," he groaned. "Oh Lordy me, what a boy this is."

But gradually the fat man's laughter became a fit of hoarse coughing. He rocked back and forth, clutching the steering wheel with both hands, sucking for air, turning red in the face from the effort. "Hit me on the back, boy, hit me on the back. Hit me on the back, I'm dying."

Wilgus watched him anxiously, trying to understand what he was supposed to do.

"Hit me on the back, Short Wilgus. Quick!"

"Do you really want me to?" Wilgus yelled above the noise.

"Oh Lord yes, hit me, hit me, I'm dying."

Wilgus wanted to hit him. He wanted very much to hit the fat man, hard, in the face, on the head. He wanted to pick up one of the heavy wrenches from the floor and hit him hard enough to kill him. He slapped him once on his thick neck. He made a fist and struck him on his enormous back, then again and again. He hit him on the shoulder and along the neck. With both hands he beat the fat man with all his might, pounding him about the neck and back and shoulders.

Wilgus was crying now.

"Whoa! Whoa!" someone shouted into the truck. "Whoa there tiger, take it easy."

The voice belonged to Wilgus' father. In a sudden cloud of dust the truck had veered off the highway onto the narrow dirt lane that led to Wilgus' house. They'd driven right into the yard and stopped at the edge of the coal pile, where his father stood with a bucket in his hand, grinning.

"He's a pure-god wildcat, this 'un is," the fat man said as he clambered out of the truck to shake Glen's hand. "You've raised you a tough 'un there now Glen, I declare you have."

Laughing, Wilgus' father glanced into the truck where his son sat wiping his eyes. He was a lanky, thin-muscled man with a miner's cap on, and no shirt. The galluses of his faded overalls lay against his bare, pale miner's skin.

Wilgus' father looked strange without a shirt on. It was strange to see him in the daytime without coal dust on his face. He was clean and shaved, and he'd got a haircut somewhere that day. His father looked so different that in some ways Wilgus didn't recognize him. The light refracting off the windshield seemed to curve him. It even made his words, his voice, sound curved.

"Aye god, don't I know it," Glen said, shaking his head and smiling proudly. "You've got to watch out for that Wilgus. He'll beat your ears off if you ain't careful."

"He like to beat me to pieces," said the fat man. "All I did was to allow what a scoundrel you are and *pow,* he lit in on me till I thought I was a goner."

"He's my defender, that boy is," said Glen.

And Glen took his old friend Monroe Short by the arm and led him away, talking and laughing about the old days.

Wilgus sat in the truck, watching them.

Then he jumped out and ran across the dusty yard to the house, where his mother was.

Victor Depta

Victor Depta (the unusual name comes from his Czech grandparents) was born in the coalfields of southern West Virginia in 1939, in Logan County, at Accoville on Buffalo Creek, where, in 1972, the collapse of a Pittston Coal slurry dam ravaged the narrow valley and killed 125 people, including one of his uncles and five of his uncle's children. "The destruction of Buffalo Creek," said Depta, "is a horrible, realistic illustration of my feelings for the area, which are sympathy and rage." Depta graduated from Man High School (West Virginia) in 1956 and then served four years in the U.S. Navy. He received a B.A. in English from Marshall University in 1965; an M.A. in creative writing from San Francisco State University in 1968; and a Ph.D. in American literature from Ohio University in 1972. He is currently a professor of English at the University of Tennessee at Martin.

Juke Boxes

Up in the hollow, my brother folds his arms across his chest and leans in the doorway, something like a crowbar.

Now I've seen guys whose eyes were empty as snail shells, a mouth like a horseshoe nailed to a post, hands like an ax blade stuck in a car door. Those are the ones I don't hang around with much, including my brother.

Why don't you talk to him? Mom asks. You ought to talk to him. I *did* talk to him. I even hugged him once when he was slobbery drunk. I felt so sorry for him, and he melted in my arms like a corpse moaning in my ear, then backed off looking wild. Afterwards he would stomp out of the room when I came in, or glare like he hated me, the crazy hillbilly.

From *A Doorkeeper in the House,* Ion Books, 1993. Reprinted by permission of the publisher.

His motorcycle's high. He screams juke boxes at night down the road,
flaking purple and red scars, hoping for a man to love him but hating
cocks. He screams and screams like a shredded face in a windshield.

Stephen L. Fisher

Steve Fisher was born and raised in Charleston, West Virginia. He received
a B.A. from Wake Forest University and an M.A. and Ph.D. from Tulane
University. Since 1971 he has been a member of the Department of Political Science at Emory and Henry College, Emory, Virginia, serving as department chair on three different occasions, for a total of ten years; at present
he is Hawthorne Professor. He has been the recipient of numerous research grants and of awards for exceptional teaching in the Faculty Scholars Programs at the University of Kentucky and, twice, at Emory and Henry
College. He received the 1994 Outstanding Faculty Award presented by
the Virginia Council of Higher Education. He is editor of *Fighting Back in
Appalachia: Traditions of Resistance and Change* (1993).

Life with Father:
Reflections on Class Analysis

I

There is no private domain of a person's life that is not political and there is no political issue that is not ultimately
personal. The old barriers have fallen.
                                        —Charlotte Bunch

Not to be able to come to one's own truth or not to use it
in one's writing . . . robs one of drive, of conviction, limits
potential stature.
                                        —Tillie Olsen

My father died of alcoholism in 1976. The four years preceding his death
were painful ones for me. We fought constantly, mainly over politics, and I
watched in horror as the man who had once seemed so strong grew helpless
and incoherent. The sense of loss I felt at his death was mixed with relief and

From *Appalachian Journal* 11 (Autumn–Winter 1983–84), © *Appalachian Journal*/Appala-
    chian State University. Used with permission.

guilt. Throughout the funeral and its immediate aftermath, I was the "man" he had taught me to be—no tears, in control, able to tuck it all away and get on with my life. Or so I thought.

In the following years, I experienced some rough emotional times. I'm not sure what role my father's death played in this, but it gradually became very important to me to gain a better understanding of his life and our relationship. Things came to a head several summers ago when, after listening to me talk on a number of occasions about my father, a friend asked, "Don't you have a single happy memory of time spent with him?" "Of course," I said, "there was. . . ." But I stopped; I couldn't, at that moment, think of one. I was stunned, and I came for the first time to acknowledge that I had, at least during parts of my life, hated my father. I was ashamed, angry, scared. How could I have felt that way about a man who had worked so hard to give me so much?

This essay, using insights from Richard Sennett and Jonathan Cobb's *The Hidden Injuries of Class,*[1] explores how class analysis provides a partial answer to that question. A *partial* answer, because this essay raises as many questions as it answers—questions which point to serious deficiencies in class analysis and expose the power of patriarchy in shaping our lives.

This is a very personal essay. I use my own and my father's lives as data. I do so because I've come to believe increasingly that only the willingness to share private, and sometimes painful, experience enables us to create a collective description of the world that is truly ours. I have been taught most of my life to separate or withhold the "personal" from my professional life, my politics, my relationships with others. The feminist movement, with its insistence that "the personal is political," has helped me to see how this separation makes us powerless and denies us the integrity of work and life which can be found only in an emotional and intellectual connectedness within ourselves and with each other. I'm not fully convinced that the personal *is* wholly political—that there are no necessary distinctions between public and private, personal and political. But I am convinced that the personal and the political are interrelated in important and intriguing ways often hidden to us by liberal, professional, class, and sexist ideologies and practices, and that the personal and the political are analogous to one another along certain axes of power and privilege.

II

. . . no more urgent business in a life can exist than establishing a sense of personal dignity—if forces beyond one's control call the dignity into question from the time one is a schoolchild, it becomes a prior question to power and possession, and indeed a reason why power and possession are sought at all.

—Richard Sennett and Jonathan Cobb

> This is gonna sound square, but my kid is my imprint. He
> is my freedom. . . . This is why I work. Every time I see a
> young guy walk by with a shirt and tie and dressed up real
> sharp, I'm looking at my kid, you know? That's it.
> —Mike LeFevre, quoted in Studs Terkel, *Working*

My father spent all his life in Charleston, West Virginia. His first job was pumping gas in the afternoons during high school. After graduation he worked behind the cigar counter at a local drug store and then on the road as a salesman for Beechnut. He tried to enlist in the army after Pearl Harbor, but the aftereffects of a childhood disease kept him home. He put in for defense work and was hired by Union Carbide in 1942. He stayed there for over twenty-five years. He never talked about his work, and to this day no one in my family has a clear idea of what he did. He handled chemicals, but, since his formal education ended with high school, his job offered little challenge or major responsibility. He let us know he didn't like his work, and I remember his once saying he hated it. What made him really angry was watching new employees with college degrees being given jobs or responsibilities he wanted.

In 1949, my father answered a newspaper ad and took on a second job, as a part-time salesman for Nationwide Insurance. He worked at night out of an office in the basement of our home. It was a job he liked (at least in comparison to the one at Carbide), for it provided some degree of freedom and responsibility. He talked of quitting Carbide, but he thought the risk was too great. He wasn't sure he could make enough money from selling insurance to provide a comfortable lifestyle for his family and send his kids (my younger sister and me) to college. So he worked at two jobs most of the rest of his life, and we began to acquire, a step at a time, all the trappings of the American dream—a house in the suburbs, wall-to-wall carpets, the kids off to college, a color television, and, finally, a second car. Then, around 1970, his Carbide pension assured and his children through school, he quit Carbide and sold insurance full-time. For the next few years, before his drinking got way out of hand, he almost doubled the salary he had made at Carbide.

My father and I spent little time together, and we were never very close. He always seemed to be angry. He had little patience, and I could never predict when he would yell at me, chide me, shame me. I grew up fearing him. I had trouble figuring out what I was supposed to do to make him happy. At times the signals were "be a real man like me." I still remember: "Big boys don't cry or kiss their fathers good night." "Are you a coward? Fight, don't run from that bully." "Why are you always so sick?" "You're so clumsy— you can't even put a nail in the wall." Yet he never told me how to express love if I couldn't kiss him, never took the time to teach me to fight, never showed me how to work with my hands. More frequently, the signals were "be different from me": "study," "get good grades," "go to college," "make a lot of money." Although no one from either side of my family had ever been to college, it was always assumed that I would go. He worked hard to make sure I went in style. While I held various odd jobs during the summers, he didn't want me to work during the school year. He bought me a used car, paid fraternity dues, sent me spending money. He wanted me to become a doctor or lawyer ("that's where the money and status is"), but a college professor seemed to satisfy him. Without his working two jobs, one of which he despised, I don't know if I would be teaching college today.

But, rather than gratitude, what he got from me was anger. Anger over his increasing racism: "We were talking down at the plant and decided that nigger King got what he deserved." Anger over his seeming willingness to sacrifice me as cannon fodder: "I know there is something wrong with that war in Vietnam, but you've got to go if called." Anger over his unwillingness to argue rationally or to admit he was wrong: "All I know, Steve, is the Bible says. . . ." Anger over his view of mountain people: "I didn't help you get a Ph.D. just so you could study hillbillies." He would bait me, push me, until I would argue, search for ways to let him know he was still in charge. I dreaded trips home.

This pattern of father's sacrifice and son's betrayal is apparently not uncommon, especially among American blue-collar families struggling to make it into the frayed white-collar class. What went on between my father and me, say Sennett and Cobb, grew out of his struggle to achieve some sense of personal dignity and self-worth. For, in American society today, being able to provide a reasonably comfortable lifestyle does not in itself necessarily provide a source of dignity. Workers such as my father are often plagued by self-doubt, by feelings of powerlessness, by a shame at not being able to advance farther.

The key to dignity in American society, with its focus on individuality and standing out from the crowd, is to possess a sense of freedom or independence. But class checks that freedom. How can one see himself as free or special when he must take orders at work, is passed over again and again for promotion, must punch a clock each morning with hundreds of other workers? In cultures with strong working-class traditions, or a sense of working-class solidarity, working men and women get from each other the respect as equals that they may not get from those who command them. But there is little such solidarity in the United States, and individual workers frequently take on themselves the burden of responsibility for their situation. When the idea of natural equality ("all men are created equal") coexists in a society with actual social inequality (class distinctions), the result is the crippling of the self-image and the dignity of those who are placed in socially determined and socially evaluated subordinate positions.

What then does it mean to be free in our class society? For many like my father, it involves moving toward a position where one gives orders, where one controls situations, where one has access to a greater set of roles in life. These workers believe that what gives them the tools to achieve this freedom is knowledge acquired through formal education. This faith in education leads them not only to accept the power of the educated to rule them, but also to believe that their own situation is deserved since they lack precious educational credentials. Much of my father's anger, as he watched college-educated people being given positions he wanted, was directed not at Carbide, not at a class system that had denied him opportunities and now had him boxed in, but at himself. He had, in his mind, failed. He had come so far, but not far enough. He brought his anger and shame home.

If the circumstances of class limited my father's freedom in comparison to that of educated people, how was he to create freedom for himself—that is, how was he to shape the actions open to him so that, in his own mind, he could feel as though he were acting from choice rather than necessity? The route he took was that of personal sacrifice. He chose to sacrifice his time, his energy, his life so as to give his children the material means to move away from him. He could see himself acting as a free man when he could think of himself as choosing to sacrifice. Feeling inadequate and unfulfilled in demonstrating his worth at work, thinking he was working for the good of someone else made the performance legitimate for him (i.e., gave him a sense of self-worth). He was sacrificing so that I would be better armed, less vulnerable than he. Through his sacrifice, I was getting an education so that I would be what he was not—free! Freedom to my father meant joining one of the professions: as Sennett and Cobb explain, the power of professionals lies in their ability to give or withhold knowledge, so that they are in positions that, by and large, aren't questioned by others—they are "authorities" themselves, "authorities" unto themselves. I never received much overt pressure from my father about career choices, but he clearly wanted me to be a professional. He was asking me to take his life not as a model but as a warning.

Such sacrifice, say Sennett and Cobb, takes the form of a contract. The sacrifice is future-oriented, but the sacrificer is also making demands in the present on those for whom he is sacrificing. My father believed that his sacrifice for his family gave him the right to expect his family to act as he wished. Taking away some of our freedom was legitimate, he thought, because he was denying himself out of love for us. Thus my mother couldn't return to work after the children started school—that would cheapen the sacrifice. My sister could not date boys from working-class (as opposed to middle-class) backgrounds. I was to be obedient, grateful, humbled by his sacrifice. I was not to make mistakes, be weak, embarrass him, make him doubt his sacrifice.

Betrayal was inevitable. I never agreed to the contract, and this led to resentment, guilt, and feelings of being manipulated. His sacrifice (i.e., working two jobs) meant that he had little time for me, and I interpreted that as a lack of caring, a lack of love. His "freedom" impinged upon mine. Where was I to get a sense of self-worth? He was always dissatisfied with me; it really couldn't have been any other way. Every act became a test of whether the sacrifice was worth it. Given the extent of the sacrifice, I was always falling short. Even good grades weren't enough, for my father had ambivalent feelings about education. Education was necessary for "freedom," but educated men didn't do "real" work, weren't "real" men. Thus the mixed signals described above. I couldn't win; but then neither could he.

A middle-class father may pass off the tensions of his work by thinking he is doing it for his children, but in the process he needn't necessarily desire that they rise to a higher class and leave him behind. For working-class fathers like mine, the whole point of sacrificing revolves about the expectation that the children will become unlike them. In this sense, my father's sacrifice was successful. I got the education, and I became different from him. But this did not end his vulnerability. I may have become better armed, but my father did so only by proxy. My success did not end in his own life the social conditions that made him question his self-worth. In fact, in one way, it made him more vulnerable. Now, through my education, I had the power to look down upon him, to shame him. He encouraged me to desert his past—to leave him behind—and I did. His sacrifice succeeded in transforming my life, and he then became a burden to me, an embarrassment. He feared that would happen; he sensed that it did. So he would pick fights with me, flaunt his racism, let me know who was boss. Every fight with me was a battle for his personal worth.

The most serious of all our fights occurred when I told him I would refuse to go to Vietnam if drafted. My mother had warned me that that piece of information would give him a heart attack, and she wasn't far from wrong. He yelled, he threatened, and finally, he pleaded. I went away convinced that this was another sign he didn't love me, that he didn't care if I died in an immoral war. But he was fighting for his life. If I had gone to jail or run off to Canada, that would have made his sacrifice, his life, meaningless. How could he have justified it to his friends? How could he have justified it to himself? How arrogant I must have seemed to him! I had it all—everything that he didn't have that he thought necessary for freedom—and I was going to voluntarily give it up. But I never had to make the choice—I slid through on graduate deferments. I guess one could argue that, to some extent, his sacrifice helped me get to graduate school and made possible the deferments that kept me out of the war.

My father felt betrayal on another level. As Sennett and Cobb make clear, the theme of sacrifice and receiving ingratitude in return stretches beyond the home to the more general awareness workingmen have of their class position in America. Workingmen feel that the anxieties they have taken upon themselves and the tensions they have to bear give them a claim to societal respect. But ingratitude is the return they feel from society, too. In particular, society's provision of welfare aid to those who don't work strikes workers as a direct repudiation of the sacrificial contract. My father was obsessed with the notion of welfare "chiselers." Of what value was his sacrifice for his family and children, if people who he believed were refusing to sacrifice could get aid and sympathy from society? To my father, such people were the incarnation of evil, the denial of anything a decent man does; for, if not, then what was his life all about? This was the source of much of his anger against blacks. He made a distinction between "good" blacks and "bad"—"good" blacks being those he saw living and thinking like himself, and "bad" being the stereotypical welfare chiselers who appealed to a government contemptuous of the worker. To him, all welfare chiselers were blacks, but not all blacks were welfare chiselers.

Sacrifice, say Sennett and Cobb, legitimizes a person's view of himself as an individual with the right to feel anger. But it is anger of a peculiar, focused sort:

> In setting you off as an individual, a virtuous person compared to less forceful others, self-denial makes possible the ultimate perversion of love; it permits you to practice that most insidious and devastating form of self-righteousness where you, oppressed, in your anger turn on others who are also oppressed rather than on those intangible, invisible, impersonal forces that have made you all vulnerable.[2]

My father had played by all the rules and by 1970 had much to be proud of. He had quit Carbide and was making good money selling insurance full-time, he had achieved the outwards signs of material prosperity, and his sacrifice had led to his son's Ph.D. Why then did he still feel defenseless? Why hadn't he earned his son's and society's respect? Why did he still feel a need to prove his self-worth, and what was to be his source of dignity now? What had his life been about? Alcohol was probably as good a way as any to avoid facing those questions.

Sennett and Cobb's use of class analysis doesn't provide all the answers necessary for understanding my father's life and our relationship. The reasons behind his racism, his drinking, his attitudes toward work, his relationship with me are complex and many-sided and can't be fully explained by any single factor. Nevertheless, class analysis holds important truths. How many of us, however lucky (or better armed), do not carry, though perhaps less vividly, the same marks of class as my father, do not feel somehow judged as he did? How many of us do not fall back on the need to justify ourselves with "the claim of at least a fancied sacrifice for others, if not the genuine sacrifice that is," for my father and the people Sennett and Cobb interviewed, "the solitary remnant of the assertion of self?"[3] How many of our lives aren't infected with the fear of being summoned before some hidden bar of judgment and being found inadequate?

My father's sacrifice did not "free" me from such a fear. I may be less vulnerable than he, but I have been, as he was, haunted by self-doubt and motivated by a search for dignity. For much of my life, my struggle for a sense of dignity centered around the relationship with my father. I wanted and needed to find ways to please him, to make him proud of me, but I never seemed able to do so. Now, I search for dignity in the classroom as I identify and nurture the responsive few, so as to feel I am doing some good, am reaching and helping someone. Unfulfilled in the classroom, I turn to political work, driven by the belief that here I can truly contribute to the common good, can sacrifice to help make others' lives better. I have my own sacrificial contracts—with my students, with society at large. And, of course, with those contracts come frustrations, disappointments, betrayals.

Thus the wounds of class are transferred from generation to generation. My father loved me, but he feared that what he had to give for love depended on his standing in the larger world. In this way, the social class system, an abstract condition far removed from our daily lives, came between us. It shaped, for the worse, the ways in which we lived our lives together, the ways in which we expressed our love, the ways we related to those around us. It shaped and shapes, for the worse, the way I am now.

The injuries of class are slow to heal, and they can leave ugly scars. But the road to healing begins with proper diagnosis, with the understanding of how our personal troubles are intimately connected to the historical structures in which the milieu of our everyday lives is organized. Coming to understand how my father and I were, in many ways, victims of class has begun my healing process. It is changing the ways I think and feel about my father; the ways I think, feel, and act about myself, my work, my relationships with others. It is, in a real sense, helping me to become free.

III

Since the notion of class assumes that women are merely subsumed under either the dominant males of the ruling class, or the oppressed males of the working class, it has perhaps only been natural that class analysis, male created, has taken precedence over a sexual analysis.

—Adrienne Rich

Our first responsibility as radicals is to create a knowledge, individual and then social, that what we are doing is not good enough. Then we must imagine something better. That defines us as people who offer our fellow citizens a meaningful choice about how we can define and live our lives.

—William Appleton Williams

When I decided to write this piece, I was convinced that in class analysis I had found the theoretical framework I needed to explain the family dynamics that had shaped me into who I am. But something is missing. Where are my mother and sister in this story? True, this essay presents a social-psychological explanation of a father-son relationship, so it seems only natural that my mother and sister wouldn't play key roles. But why is this a story about my father? Why should I assume that my relationship with him encompasses the whole of the family relationship that shaped me? In other words, why did I seek dignity only from my father rather than from my mother or my father and mother? Do the dynamics of class account for this, or do we need an additional frame of reference? If we shift the focus from father-son (from the dynamics of male vulnerability in a class struggle for dignity) to intrafamily social-psychological relationships, we begin to see the limitations of class and the importance of gender as analytical tools.

I wrote above that the key to dignity in American society is to possess a sense of freedom and independence and that class limits that freedom. It limited my father's, it limits mine. But how would my mother and sister write that? Would they view class as the primary check on their freedom? If my father had been of a different class, would my mother have been allowed to return to work, my sister free to date boys from varying class backgrounds? My father wanted me to be a professional, that was the road to freedom. But he never talked about my sister becoming a lawyer or a doctor. How was she to be free? What was his contract with her?

I am not, at this point in time, able to tell my mother's and sister's stories. When I think about *my* relationship with them, I come up only with questions. But these questions are enough to make it clear that, while their stories no doubt would contain some of the themes I've elaborated, they would be much different from mine. Why, for example, did my sister, after giving birth to Jennifer, tell our mother that this was the first thing she had ever done that she felt I had been proud of? Why do I remember so little about the relationship with my mother? Why were her views on my physique, my school performance, my career choice, the war, or race not important to me? Why am I just now coming even to recognize, much less appreciate, the sacrifices she made for me? What was the nature of our contract?

Class analysis doesn't provide convincing answers to these questions. Nor does it adequately explain why my father was so concerned that I not cry or kiss him, that I fight rather than run, that I be a "real" man—advice that led me to spend a good part of my life unable to express any emotion except anger. Class, indeed, came between my father and me, but there was something we shared. Maleness. My father couldn't find dignity at work nor could I find it from him, but we still operated in a world that guaranteed us both power over women and the privileges and sense of dignity associated with it.

I cannot fully understand the family dynamics that shaped me until I know my mother's and sister's stories, until I come to grips with the ways in which patriarchy affects our lives, conditions our responses. In order to understand issues of power, subordination, freedom, and dignity in our society, we must struggle to discover the ways in which gender systems and class systems are interconnected. This struggle requires new, reshaped, not added on, categories and frames of reference.

There is something else missing from my understanding of my relationship with my father: any hint of how it could have been different. Class analysis is a critically important explanatory tool; it has helped me better understand my own life. But now that I understand some of what went on, what can I do about it? Even if I had understood it at the time, what could I have done? Class analysis provides few clues in this regard—not only in terms of reconstructing personal relationships, but also in terms of reconstructing society. Jean Bethke Elshtain poses the problem quite well:

> Marx's category "class" can be adopted variously depending upon one's reconstructive aims. As a powerful tool of social analysis, a category neces-

sary in any critical assessment of social reality, class is inescapable. But as a basis for a theory of political renewal in contemporary America, class has limited critical purchase. Americans do not see themselves primarily as members of a class even as they are aware of what the Marxist would call "class-divisions" in the larger social order and in their personal lives.[4]

Elshtain is one of a number of scholars critical of the American social order who have recently called attention to the limits of class analysis. Their basic charge is that much of Marxist theory and politics cuts people off from their past, their folkways, and their group identities. They claim that actual social movements in the United States have sprung not from class consciousness and a radical rupture with tradition, as many Marxists insist, but rather from buried cultural themes from the past. These "populists" present a host of studies that reveal how farmers and factory workers have drawn on a range of ethnic, kinship, religious, and other traditional relations in fighting back and in developing collective consciousness, and how the origins of feminist consciousness in different periods of American history have grown directly out of traditional structures and ideologies that women have reshaped for radical purposes. Yet the populists have their own blinders. They disregard the ways in which traditional understandings and values are often racist and sexist, are used to justify inequality, and serve to bind people to the status quo. Moreover, culturally held traditions have often been easily adapted to ruling-class purposes and have led more often than not to "flashes of independent political anger" rather than to sustained efforts at social and political change.

I see no easy path out of the woods. Class analysis is a crucial piece of the puzzle of how to change the way we are on both a personal and societal level. But it is only one piece. There is a constant debate on the Left over what the other pieces of the puzzle are and how to put them together. Much of this debate is insular and as out of touch with American life as the prescriptions coming out of the conservative and liberal camps these days. There are hopeful signs: cultural Marxism, with its focus on social-psychological issues, and radical social history, which is revealing the particular mechanisms that shape political consciousness. But transcending the American forms of class and gender oppression will require what Adrienne Rich calls "a quantum leap" of the imagination. And it is Rich and other feminist thinkers who are currently doing the kind of political writing that will move us in that direction. They are grappling boldly with questions of personal and political change in an effort to carve alternative visions that can provide us with the energy and courage to work for transformations that we won't live to see realized. As Rich puts it:

> I believe we must cope courageously and practically . . . with the here and now, our feet on this ground where we now live. But nothing less than the most radical imagination will carry us beyond this place, beyond the mere struggle for survival, to that lucid recognition of our possibilities which will keep us impatient, and unresigned to mere survival.[5]

Notes

This is a personal essay that has been a long time in the writing. A number of friends have contributed in a wide variety of ways to this project. I'm aware that I have not followed all of their suggestions, but this essay is better because of their advice and support. Thanks to the members of my men's group (Larry Harley, Rick O'Neil, Eric Reese, Rees Shearer); my colleagues in the Southern Mountain Research Collective (Alan Banks, Jim Foster, Doug Gamble, Bill Horton); Jamie Cohen; Nancy Garretson; Nina Gregg; Robin Gregg; Barry O'Connell; Lucy Phenix; and Jerry Williamson. Sally Maggard has played a special role in this endeavor, first by helping me come to grips with my feelings about my father and then by offering an extensive critique of an early draft of this essay. Her insights helped me better understand the limitations of class and the importance of gender as analytical tools in explaining my family relationships, and the discussion of this in part 3 relies heavily upon her critique.

1. Richard Sennett and Jonathan Cobb, *The Hidden Injuries of Class* (New York: Vintage, 1973). Sennett and Cobb center their analysis around interviews with residents of Boston's blue-collar neighborhoods and their children in suburbia. See also William E. Connolly, *Appearance and Reality in Politics* (Cambridge, England: Cambridge UP, 1981), 63–89.
2. Sennett and Cobb, *Hidden Injuries* 140.
3. Murray Kempton, "Blue Collar Blues," *New York Review of Books,* 8 Feb. 1973, p. 12.
4. Jean Bethke Elshtain, *Public Man, Private Woman: Women in Social and Political Thought* (Princeton: Princeton UP, 1981), 344.
5. Adrienne Rich, *On Lies, Secrets, and Silence: Selected Prose, 1966–1978* (New York: Norton, 1979), 273.

Parks Lanier, Jr.

Parks Lanier, Jr., has Appalachian ancestors from northern Georgia and far Western North Carolina. Born in Athens, Georgia, he is related to Sidney Lanier, whose novel *Tiger Lilies* (1867) drew early portraits of mountain people. President of the Appalachian Writers Association from 1990 to 1994, he edited *The Poetics of Appalachian Space* (1991). He enjoys writing poetry and critical essays and is professor of English at Radford College.

The Legacy

After the funeral
we sit at the table eating the meal
of cold regret. Potatoes are boiled hard.
On the shelf are chickens and chocolate cakes,
pans and pans of bread past cooled, but no wine
reminds us. Faithfully we bend and eat,
fast unremembering her who fed us
whether she who cooked was hungry or not,
she, dying, whose last words to me were, "Go
home, there are three fruit pies hidden
in a bowl for you. Eat them all."
Knowing they would be the last made them sweet
to the taste of memory this food lacks.

The Spinning Wheel

The mother of us all has passed this down,
Her spinning wheel that none of us can use
Or needs to use, but yet we cling to it
Like some worn talisman. It leans beside
The television set and gathers dust,
And once I saw across the wheel itself
A spider's web hung out to catch the wind
Where nothing ever moved and no wind blew.
The spinner has returned, I thought, and casts
New threads much finer than the ones she spun
When last she sat, and said her work was done.

The Doctor's Saddlebag

His bag is creased by time and gnawed by mice,
But all the bottles it contained are snug
And labeled in his hand, medicinal
Yet kindly and concerned. He took them all
The night he rode ten miles through rain and snow
To help a baby far beyond his help,
Then both were dead and buried on the hill

From *Appalachian Writers' Association Chapbook Series* (Blacksburg, VA), no. 1 (1982). The poems are reprinted by permission of the author.

Behind the church where once we walked and read
The scattered stones among the flowers strewn
And faded by the wind, all silk that could not die.
This was the legacy he left behind,
This leather satchel tossed upon a shelf
And never touched because its healing herbs
Were useless for the man who could not heal himself.

The Photograph Album

A hundred years of nameless faces here
Peer out at me and ask why they should sit
Lit by artificial light, wear dark suits,
Boots that pinch, hats sure not to be in style
While purchasing cheap immortality,
Facsimiles of life at lower rates.

Commensurate with vanity and pride,
Alongside the starched frills and furbelows,
Calicos and mustachios come demands
And pleas to be remembered, to be named,
Claimed each time I turn the pages of these dead
Fled into the realm against which they inveigh.

I am the mirror into which they stare,
And they the image of my own despair.

Ronnie Day

Ronnie Day was born and raised on a farm in Laurel County in southeastern Kentucky and educated at Cumberland College and Texas Christian University. He is professor of history and chair of the History Department at East Tennessee State University.

In the following essay, Day focuses on the impact of poverty and economic conditions on the people he knew in Eastern Kentucky. The problems of identity Day noted in the early seventies remain with him, as he states in an addendum to the original essay.

Pride and Poverty: An Impressionistic View of the Family in the Cumberlands of Appalachia

Of all the various mountain ranges in the eastern United States, none has a more colorful history than the Cumberlands. Describing a shallow arc through Kentucky, Virginia, Tennessee, and Alabama, these western outposts of the Southern Appalachians have become synonymous with feuds and "moonshine," pride and poverty. They have given the American heritage Li'l Abner and Sergeant York; and they have contributed their fair share to the "hillbilly" mythology, country music, and mountain culture in general.

The outsider is presented with two diametrically opposite views of the mountain people of the Cumberlands. One is the romantic portrayal of fiction and film. John Fox, Jr., in *The Trail of the Lonesome Pine*, saw the mountaineer much as Sir Walter Scott had envisioned the medieval knight:

> They were Unionists because of the Revolution, as they were Americans in the beginning because of the spirit of the Covenanter. They live like the pioneers; the axe and the rifle are still their weapons and they still have the same fight with nature. This feud business is a matter of clan-loyalty that goes back to Scotland. They argue this way: You are my friend or my kinsman, your quarrel is my quarrel, and whoever hits you, hits me. If you are in trouble, I must not testify against you. If you are an officer, you must not arrest me; you must send me a kindly request to come into court. If I'm innocent and it's perfectly convenient—why maybe I'll come!

And in *A Cumberland Vendetta*:

> The Stetsons had a good strain of Anglo-Saxon blood, and owned valley lands; the Lewallens kept store, and made "moonshine"; so kindred and debtors and kindred and tenants were arrayed with one or the other leader, and gradually the retainers of both settled on one or the other side of the river. In time of hostility the Cumberland came to be the boundary between life and death for the dwellers on each shore. It was feudalism born again.

A second view, brutally sobering and more contemporary, is that of the Cumberlands as a depressed area—a rural slum with even the beautiful mountains raped and ruined by the strip-miners' bulldozers. In *The Longest Mile,* one of the very best of the works with a sociological flavor, Dr. Rena Gazaway describes life in one of the many hollows tucked away out of sight in the Cumberlands. What Jerzy Kosinski wrote in *The Painted Bird* of the

From "Pride and Poverty: An Impressionistic View of the Family in the Cumberlands of Appalachia," *Appalachia: Family Patterns in Transition,* ed. Emmett M. Essin III (Johnson City: East Tennessee State UP, 1975). Reprinted by permission of the author.

ignorance and poverty of Central Europe cannot surpass the conditions in "Duddie's Branch," Kentucky. Houses are shanties unfit for human habitation; toilet and washing facilities are nonexistent; food is mostly government surplus ("commodities"); and drinking water is usually contaminated— where, in effect, almost every descriptive phrase conjures up the image of filth and squalor. The English language is as rich in adjectives to describe poverty as the poverty-stricken are poor. For these, however, substitute the image from a conversation recorded by Bruce and Nancy Roberts in *Where Time Stood Still.* "Joanie," the mountain woman related to a public health officer, "had so much trouble breathin' awhile back, it gave me a real fright. I tried reachin' down into the back of her throat an' you know, I just scraped out gobs and gobs of worms."

Which view, then, is correct? That of the rugged, chivalric knight of the hills? Or that of the wretched, illiterate recipient of some type of government dole? To a certain degree, each view contains some truth. The Cumberland mountaineer can have no pretensions to noble ancestry such as those which flourished in the antebellum South, nourished on Scott's novels and catered to by genealogists who could supply a coat of arms for every household. Rather the Cumberland mountaineer was, by his very name, as Harry Caudill wrote in *Night Comes to the Cumberlands,* marked "as the son of a penniless laborer whose forebears, in turn, had been more often than not simply serfs." Indeed, the Cumberlands were settled by a people as mongrel as the hounds gracing the porch of every mountain cabin—border Scot hyphenated English hyphenated Irish, an Anglo-Saxon, Viking, Celtic mixture. In the Old World they had lived in a no-man's-land, and the struggle to survive the to-and-fro passage of armies and raiding bands bred into them an independence, a fierce and fatalistic acceptance of violence as a way of life, which not even the sophistication of the twentieth century can dampen. So, while the mountain culture was not an American transplant of "Camelot," there was—and is today—a "Code of the Hills"; a sense of what is fair and honorable, and which, when violated—as, of course, it is on occasion—incurs the grave disapproval of the community. The code, however, was not an inheritance of medieval chivalry, but rather a product of the frontier. For, when the rewards and restraints of civilization are absent, the individual stands alone. His honor, his courage, his "word," as the mountain people put it, reside in him alone and are for that reason highly valued. Several years ago, for example, a sheriff of a Cumberland county turned bully—"a man who you had to be afraid of," folks said—which in hill parlance means someone will have to kill him. In time, he was lured up a "holler" and recalled with a high-powered rifle fired from ambush. "I know he got exactly what he deserved," declared one deeply religious mountain woman, "but I just don't approve of how it was done."

Vestiges of the code still linger, therefore, despite the fact that the woman who made that comment on the murdered sheriff is, in terms of material things, a member of the American middle class. Which leads to the second image of the Cumberlands as an Appalachian ghetto. For a century, industrial civilization—with all its blessings and curses—passed the mountains by; it reached the West Coast and jumped the Pacific to Japan; it transformed the United States into the wealthiest nation in the world. Still the mountaineer lived much as he had before. But when civilization hit, crept through the gaps and spread up the hollows and creeks like the tentacles of a giant octopus, it hit with a vengeance. All around the mountaineer as he shot squirrels, or made whiskey, beneath stunted hillside corn where his woman and children worked with grub-hoes, was a wealth of timber and coal great enough to dazzle Solomon. Both, and especially the coal, were vital to industrial civilization, and the giant corporate powers, both American and foreign, moved into the Cumberlands. Before long, they owned them. Competition to the mountaineer became how much whiskey he could drink and still stand or who could bag the first squirrel; but against corporate wealth and corporate lawyers, he was helpless. All is fair in love, war, and industrial ethics—and so the mountaineer was legally, if not morally, disinherited from his patrimony; while mountain coal stoked the fires of American production, he was reduced to the status of an industrial serf, bound as firmly to the company and treated worse than John of Cayworth, peasant, Battle Abbey, thirteenth century.

From that moment on, coal ruled, or, more appropriately, those who owned coal ruled; and the mountaineer of the Cumberland Plateau was welded to the whims of such distant places as Pittsburgh, Gary, and London, England. During a "boom" he thrived (at least by mountain standards); during a "bust" he starved. Mountain culture had always been primitive, and the effect of the invasion of the outside world upon that way of life was to superimpose the worst aspects of the modern civilization. While the wealth lasted, the mountaineer shared in it the least, and that at the price of watching the mountains destroyed and the streams polluted (strip-mining today is supplying the *coup d'grace* to the Cumberlands). In the beginning, no doubt, some of the companies recognized a community obligation, but as the ups and downs of the industry continued, and the slag heaps grew larger and larger, that sense of obligation was smothered in the palls of coal dust rising from the valleys. Since the companies had the only taxable wealth necessary to support the necessities of modern life, and controlled politics, mountain people went without education, health care—all of the amenities of life in the twentieth century. Only the Great Depression, the "New Deal" policies, and the militant wars of the United Mine Workers broke the political stranglehold, and, even then, the only remedy of those who would aid the mountain people was to usher in the Welfare State. Thus originated the prevalent view of the Cumberland Plateau: a shack standing on some creek a stone's throw from prosperous middle-class people traveling the highway, the inevitable broken washing machine sitting on the porch, and the inhabitants living on some type of welfare ("relief").

The effect of the twentieth century on the family of the Cumberland Plateau has thus been double-edged. Some—merchants in the county seats, the more prosperous farmers, educated professionals—have adapted to the new conditions and live as comfortably as their counterparts outside the Plateau. The others, functionally illiterate, poor beyond even urban ghetto standards, live a miserable existence out of sight in the numerous hollows.

Yet there are certain characteristics, certain ways of behaving—including the mountain dialect which is spoken—which mark a family, whether well-off or poor, as a child of the Cumberlands. The family still reflects some of the characteristics which so impressed John Fox, Jr., nearly a century ago. It is patriarchal; no woman would dare usurp the authority of the husband and father, even if he (as is often the case up the hollows) does nothing whatsoever to support the family. Even an inclination on the part of the hill-woman to be assertive brings derision on that husband who happens to be so unfortunate; for a man "bossed" by his woman is considered less than a man. Even today, see a hill-family walking, and the man will always be leading the way, the wife following behind him. Or in one of the fundamentalist churches on the Sunday the preacher chooses the status of women for his topic—which, put simply, is rearing children, obeying her husband, and not meddling in church affairs—the loudest "amens" will come from the women.

Hand in hand with the patriarchy goes the old clan-like family loyalty. A family, prosperous or on welfare, is expected to take care of its own. Adversity is not an unexpected calamity but an accepted routine. The family endures it as one, whether it is sickness, a murder indictment against a son, or the illegitimate pregnancy of a daughter. Not to do so brings the strongest disapprobation from one's neighbors. Thus a son kills his father in a drunken brawl, and the family, while never approving, defends the son before the legal authorities. Or a father of the affluent class sends his pregnant daughter to a distant home for unwed mothers and, as a result, incurs the contempt of the community. Or a son who dares place his parents in a nursing home, or refuses in any way to support them, is universally condemned.

The fierce independence of the mountain people reinforces this clannishness. "We'll get along all right," one often hears a family remark, despite a near-hopeless situation. As a result, authority of any type is still resented. More often than not, an elected judge must be more of a diplomat and arbitrator than a legal official resting his case on the cold letter of the statutory law. Any sheriff must walk a thin line between what the mountaineer accepts as fair and that which he resents as "bullying." No official or clerk must "smart off" to the more self-sufficient mountaineer on pain of being taught a rude lesson in hill manners. Even the man on welfare considers the agencies supporting him as enemies and his existence as continual warfare to outsmart the bureaucrats and so "draw" his checks. Indeed, outsmarting the welfare official and maintaining his independence is little different from his ancestors' eluding the revenuer in the golden age of moonshining.

Nor is it merely the fear of outside authority which causes the mountain family to stand as one on the defensive. Isolated while the world changes so radically about them, the mountain folk are different and are made bitterly aware of that difference. The moment one utters a word, he is branded; for mountain English at its best is three hundred years out of date. (At its worst, it is little more than a sequence of guttural grunts). Families may communicate well with single words, such as "reckon," which can mean an assent, a refusal, or simply a neutral stance, but which the outsider cannot understand. And while one dialect is as good as another, be it mountain or Bostonian—Cuba, for example, does not have an *r,* according to the *Oxford English Dictionary*— the mountaineer is taught that he is inferior and ignorant and the other learned and superior. A clerk in a northern city exhibits this superiority when he has a mountaineer repeat a simple request in order to savor the rustic flavor even at the expense of embarrassing the customer. Fear of the outside world breeds both contempt and resentment. Anything different from what he had known in the narrow confines of the mountains excites derision as being "quare"; a city dude hunter decked in red or yellow would be "quare," as would be a married couple who maintained separate bedrooms, and the list could go on and on. Resentment and defensiveness border almost on paranoia. Practically any mountain family can repeat the story of some local person who went north and came back "putting on 'airs'"—too good, that is, to speak to common folk. A genuine outsider is cross-examined as to his biases about mountain folk, and, should he slip, he had best move quickly back to "furrin" parts. And a returning native who has been to any degree successful is watched as carefully as a chicken hawk watches the coop, for the slightest betrayal that he "thinks he's bet'ern his raisin'."

Nevertheless, these locked-in castaways of American life are extremely patriotic. Next only to loyalty to kin is their loyalty to the United States. Reasons for war matter little, the enemy not at all—most are aware only that "they went across the water." But it is a well-known fact that mountain boys volunteered in the world wars of the century, volunteered in such numbers and fought so well that the mountains suffered a higher proportional kill-ratio than other parts of the nation. On occasion, this loyalty can border on the absurd. Some years ago, social workers entered one of the coal-mining counties and began to organize the miners. They were promptly branded Communists. A politician—and an attorney for coal interests—running for high state office, came on a statewide television broadcast, literally wrapped himself in the American flag, and wept because of love of his country. Should these Communists call in Russian tanks to support them, he threatened, then he would call in Governor Wallace's "army" and drive them from the mountains. (The governor from Alabama would no doubt be a little surprised to find that he led an army). Even though he had shared little in its blessings, to the mountaineer, at least until very recently, the American Way is not to be questioned.

The mountain values linger on, in both the affluent and the poor. They are, of course, waning and will eventually disappear. Television and radio, good highways, telephones, and the like, are opening the mountains to middle-class culture. Middle-class culture is already taking root among the economically well-off, while poverty has already practically destroyed mountain culture among the rest. The value placed on work is a good example. The affluent, proud of their achievement, value work as one of the highest virtues. A young man "sowing his oats" will have much of his activity excused if he is known as a hard worker. The poverty-stricken, on the other hand, are by and large reconciled to their life of deprivation, rationalizing that they "are better off than some"—the some remaining unidentified—and think it simply stupid to work when they can draw from the government. To them, they are more intelligent for being able to exist, if one can call it existence, without working; to their more affluent neighbors, they are "sorry" and "worthless."

ॐ

Looking back over what I wrote nearly two decades ago, I find that my perspective has changed somewhat. For one thing, relative youth has given way to late middle age, and I have had the ensuing interval to wrestle further with what it means to be a "hillbilly." For another, during the same period, some excellent work has been published on the region and its culture—among the best being Margaret Ripley Wolfe's *Kingsport Tennessee: A Planned American City* (1987) and Allen W. Batteau's *The Invention of Appalachia* (1990). Finally, for the past five years I have been working in the papers—editing a diary from World War II and preparing to write a biography of another son of Appalachia, Mack Morriss, a World War II combat correspondent, a novelist and writer, and a well-known radio commentator who was a life-long resident of Elizabethton, Tennessee.

Reconstructing the life of Mack Morriss has been the greatest influence. I have tried to retrace his path through World War II and, in so doing, I have developed an intimate connection with many people and a number of cultures of the Solomon Islands in the South Pacific. Today, of course, the Solomon Islands would be classified as "Third World," but this is a description so broad that, like "Appalachia," it has no real value. Batteau's remark that "'Appalachia' is a frame of reference, not a fact," can—and should—be applied to the use of "Third World." Nonetheless, I have been struck by the similarities between the Solomon Islands today and the small patch of southeastern Kentucky where I grew up fifty years ago. The outside world invaded both areas at roughly the same time—World War II struck the Solomons in the early 1940s, and REA and passable roads arrived in southeastern Kentucky in the late 1940s. Numerous "cargo cults" sprang up in the Solomons and the rest of the South Pacific whose prophets foretold the return of the American LSTs bringing a wealth of Western goods; a mountain preacher is on record thanking God equally for Jesus Christ and REA. The real distinction, it seems to me, is between the affluent who can afford to embrace modernity and the poor who can't. When I was growing up, this distinction was marked by who could afford a car and an indoor bathroom. In the Solomon Islands today, the same distinction is marked by who can afford a fiberglass canoe and a Japanese-made outboard motor. Economic status is the key to distinguishing between areas within what is called Appalachia and peoples living within any one of the areas. So, in response to CBS's "Twentieth Century" production of February 23, 1964, which was devoted to the poverty in Clay County, Kentucky (the county adjoining the one where I grew up, in fact only a couple of miles from my home), Morriss could write, "I've never been to Clay County, Kentucky, and after seeing Twentieth Century's presentation I'm not ever going, if I can help it." Yet Morriss considered himself to be Appalachian and devoted a considerable amount of his talent to trying to define what it meant to be Appalachian.

Did he—or I—ever come to a satisfactory conclusion? I think not. The dominant culture defines reality for the rest—CBS's view of things is respected as authority, that of the mountain preacher who gave thanks for Jesus and REA in the same breath is regarded as merely quaint by the charitable and as ridiculous by the not-so-charitable. What makes it so difficult for those of us who carry a trace of the mountain preacher in our make-up is that the dominant view is itself schizophrenic. In the same response to the "Twentieth Century" broadcast in 1964, Morriss noticed this peculiarity: "We alternately seem to swing, as a regional group, from one image to another in the eyes of much of the rest of the nation," he wrote:

> Sometimes we are a proud, fiercely independent people in whose blood runs the strain of giants—Daniel Boone, Davy Crockett, Abe Lincoln, Cordell Hull. We are resourceful, shrewd, courageous, picturesque— naïve perhaps but appealing types, whether we wear a coonskin cap or the slouch hat of a Jed Clampett. Then, again, we find ourselves shorn of the phony glamour and we're not the Beverly Hillbillies but just hillbillies—poor, ignorant, shiftless, degenerate, substandard citizens who are written off by one of the world's most eminent historians as "little better than barbarians." This swing from one extreme to the other occurs with remarkable regularity, almost rhythmic over the years, and is enough to set up a sort of schizophrenia—as a matter of fact, I think it has, in us and in the rest of the country regarding us—which may explain the popularity of the "Beverly Hillbillies."

What more can be said? I am still wrestling with what it means to be a hillbilly—and still trying to understand Mack Morriss's wrestling with the same intellectual problem.

Bennie Lee Sinclair

Bennie Lee Sinclair, poet laureate of South Carolina, is author of the following books of poems: *Little Chicago Suite* (1971), *The Arrowhead Scholar* (1978), *Lord of Springs* (1990), and *The Endangered, New and Selected Poems* (1992). She is the recipient of the Winthrop Award, the Appalachian Writers Association Book-of-the-Year Award, the Stephen Vincent Benét Narrative Poem Award, and a Best American Short Story Citation. A novel, *The Lynching* (1991), is based on the story of Willie Earl, who was lynched in Greenville County, South Carolina, in 1947.

Decoration Day

This first Sunday in June, this green
first Sabbath of June, has long been designated
for the cleaning of graves. Each program
is the same: everyone brings rake, hoe, some
flowers, and, after preaching, climbs

this stubbled hill to find wiregrass
and weeds have taken ground since June's
first Sunday past; wild vines
and briars choke the rose and dahlia
left of last year's tending.

Each pilgrim as of age assumes his role:
the old knead deeply in ancestral
dust, upending spiny threats upon
their own sure home, while those of lesser
urgency resolve themselves unmossing faded

elegiacs. It is the young who take
no part. Escaping one by one to ride
the afternoon, they do not hear the gentle chime
of hand-tool hitting rock; this knelling
for green bones as well as brittle.

Breece D'J Pancake

Born in Kanawha County, West Virginia, Breece D'J Pancake earned his B.A. from Marshall University, Huntington, West Virginia. After teaching at military academies, he attended graduate school at the University of Virginia from 1976 until 1979, when he died from a self-inflicted gunshot wound. His reputation derives largely from the recognition gained following the posthumous publication of *The Stories of Breece D'J Pancake* (1983), which earned a Pulitzer Prize nomination. These tales, set in rural West Virginia, rendered Appalachia as a bleak, rugged region and revealed the coarser aspects of humanity. He has been compared to Hemingway for his spare, direct style and is particularly noted for the sensitivity of his characterizations. John Casey, who wrote the afterword to *The Stories of Breece D'J Pancake,* says, "A lot of people miss him and miss what he would have gone on to write."

First Day of Winter

Hollis sat by his window all night, staring at his ghost in glass, looking for some way out of the tomb Jake had built for him. Now he could see the first blue blur of morning growing behind bare tree branches, and beyond them the shadows of the farm. The work was done: silos stood full of corn, hay bales rose to the barn's roof, and the slaughter stock had gone to market; it was work done for figures in a bank, for debts, and now corn stubble leaned in the fields among stacks of fodder laced with frost. He could hear his parents shuffling about downstairs for their breakfast; his old mother giggling, her mind half gone from blood too thick in her veins; his father, now blind and coughing. He had told Jake on the phone, they'll live a long time. Jake would not have his parents put away like furniture. Hollis asked Jake to take them into his parsonage at Harpers Ferry; the farm was failing. Jake would not have room: the parsonage was too modest, his family too large.

He went downstairs for coffee. His mother would not bathe, and the warm kitchen smelled of her as she sat eating oatmeal with his father. The lids of the blind man's eyes hung half closed and he had not combed his hair; it stuck out in tufts where he had slept on it.

"Cer'al's hot." His mother giggled, and the crescent of her mouth made a weak grin. "Your daddy's burnt his mouth."

"I ain't hungry." Hollis poured his coffee, leaned against the sink.

The old man turned his head a little toward Hollis, bits of meal stuck to his lips. "You going hunting like I asked?"

Hollis sat his cup in the sink. "Thought I'd work on the car. We can't be with no way to town all winter because you like squirrel meat."

The old man ate his cereal, staring ahead. "Won't be Thanksgiving without wild game."

"Won't be Thanksgiving till Jake and Milly gets here," she said.

"They said last night they ain't coming down," his father said, and the old woman looked at Hollis dumbly.

"I got to work on the car," Hollis said, and went toward the door.

"Car's been setting too long," the old woman yelled. "You be careful of snakes."

Outside, the air was sharp, and when the wind whipped against his face, he gasped. The sky was low, gray, and the few Angus he had kept from market huddled near the feeder beside the barn. He threw them some hay, brought his tool chest from the barn, began to work on the car. He got in to see if it would start, ground it. As he sat behind the wheel, door open, he watched his father come down from the porch with his cane. The engine's grinding echoed through the hollows, across the hills.

Hollis's knuckles were bloody, scraped under the raised hood, and they stung as he turned the key harder, gripped the wheel. His father's cane tapped through the frosty yard, the still of December, and came closer to Hollis. The blind man's mouth was shut against the cold, the dark air so close to his face, and Hollis stopped trying the engine, got out.

"You can tell she's locking up." The blind man faced him.

"This ain't a tractor." Hollis walked around, looked under the hood, saw the hairline crack along one side of the engine block.

His father's cane struck the fender, and he stood still and straight beside his son. Hollis saw his father's fingers creeping along the grille, holding him steady. "She sounded locked up," he said again.

"Yeah." Hollis edged the man aside, shut the hood. He didn't have the tools to pull the engine, and had no engine to replace it. "Maybe Jake'll loan you the money for a new car."

"No," the old man said. "We'll get by without bothering Jake."

"Put it on the cuff? Do you think the bank would give us another nickel?"

"Jake has too much to worry with as it is."

"I asked him to take you-all last night."

"Why?"

"I asked him and Molly to take you in and he said no. I'm stuck here. I can't make my own way for fighting a losing battle with this damn farm."

"Farming's making your way."

"Hell."

"Everybody's trying for something better anymore. When everybody's going one way, it's time to turn back." He rationalized in five directions.

In the faded morning the land looked scarred. The first snows had already come, melted, and seated the hills with a heavy frost the sun could not soften. Cold winds had peeled away the last clinging oak leaves, left the hills a quiet gray-brown that sloped into the valley on either side.

He saw the old man's hair bending in the wind.

"Come on inside, you'll catch cold."

"You going hunting like I asked?"
"I'll go hunting."

As he crossed the last pasture heading up toward the ridges, Hollis felt a sinking in his gut, a cold hunger. In the dry grass he shuffled toward the fence line to the rising ridges and high stand of oaks. He stopped at the fence, looked down on the valley and the farm. A little at a time Jake had sloughed everything to him, and now that his brother was away, just for this small moment, Hollis was happier.

He laid down his rifle, crossed the fence, and took it up again. He headed deeper into the oaks, until they began to mingle with the yellow pine along the ridge. He saw no squirrels, but sat on a stump with oaks on all sides, their roots and bottom trunk brushed clean by squirrel tails. He grew numb with waiting, with cold; taking a nickel from his pocket, he raked it against the notched stock, made the sound of a squirrel cutting nuts. Soon enough he saw a flick of tail, the squirrel's body hidden by the tree trunk. He tossed a small rock beyond the tree, sent it stirring and rattling the leaves, watched as the squirrel darted to the broadside trunk. Slowly, he raised his rifle, and when the echoes cleared from the far hills across the valley, the squirrel fell. He field-dressed it, and the blood dried cold on his hands; then he moved up the ridge toward the pine thicket, stopping every five minutes to kill until the killing drained him and his game bag weighed heavily at his side.

He rested against a tree near the thicket, stared into its dark wavings of needles and branches; there, almost blended with the red needles, lay a fox. He watched it without moving, and thought of Jake, hidden, waiting for him to break, to move. In a fit of meanness, he snapped his rifle to his shoulder and fired. When he looked again the fox was gone, and he caught a glimpse of its white-tipped tail drifting through the piney darkness.

Hollis dropped his gun, sat against the tree, and, when the wind snatched at his throat, fumbled to button his collar. He felt old and tired, worn and beaten, and he thought of what Jake had said about the state home he wanted the folks in. They starve them, he said, and they mistreat them, and in the end they smother them. For a moment, Hollis wondered what it would be like to smother them, and in the same moment caught himself, laughing; but a darkness had covered him, and he pulled his gloves on to hide the blood on his hands. He stumbled up, and, grabbing his gun, ran between trees to the clearing nearest the fence, and when he crossed into the pasture felt again a light mist of sweat on his face, a calming.

He crossed the fields and fences, slogged across the bottoms and up to the house. Inside, his mother sat in the tiny back room, listening, with the husband, to quiet music on the radio. She came to Hollis, and he saw in her wide-set eyes a fear and knowledge—and he knew she could see what insanity had driven him to.

He handed her the squirrels, dressed and skinned, from his game bag, and went to wash his hands. From the corner of his eye, he saw her, saw as she dropped the squirrels into soaking brine, saw her hand go up to her mouth, saw her lick a trace of blood and smile.

Sitting at the table, he looked down at his empty plate, waiting for the grace, and when it was said, passed the plate of squirrel. He had taken for himself only the forequarters and liver, leaving the meaty hinds and saddles.

"Letter come from Jake." The old man held a hindquarter, gnawed at it.

"And pitchers of them." His mother got up, came back with a handful of snapshots.

"He done fine for himself. Lookee at the pretty church and the children," she said.

The church was yellow brick and low, stained windows. In the picture Jake stood holding a baby, his baby girl, named after their mother. His face was squinted with a smile. The old woman poked a withered finger into the picture. "That's my Mae Ellen," she said. "That's my favorite."

"Shouldn't have favorites." His father laid down the bones.

"Well, you got to face that he done fine for himself."

Hollis looked out the window; the taste of liver, a taste like acorns, coated his mouth with cold grease. "Coming snow," he said.

His father laughed. "Can't feel it."

"Jake says they're putting a little away now. Says the church is right nice people."

"They ain't putting away enough to hear him tell it."

"Now," she said, "he's done fine, just let it be."

When the meal was finished, Hollis pushed back his chair. "I asked Jake to help by taking you-all in; he said no."

The old man turned away; Hollis saw tears in his blind eyes, and that his body shook from crying. He wagged his head again and again. The old woman scowled, and she took up the plates, carried them to the sink. When she came back, she bent over Hollis.

"What'd you figure he'd say? He's worked like an ox and done good, but he can't put us all up."

The old man was still crying, and she went to him, helped him from the chair. He was bent with age, with crying, and he raised himself slowly, strung his flabby arm around the woman's waist. He turned to Hollis. "How could you do such a goddamned thing as that?"

"We'll take our nap," she said. "We need our rest."

Hollis went to the yard, to where his car stood, looked again at the cracked block. He ran his hand along the grille where the old man's hands had cleared away dust. The wind took his breath, beat on him, and the first light flecks of ice bounced from the fenders. The land lay brittle, open, and dead.

He went back to the house, and in the living room stretched out on the couch. Pulling the folded quilt to his chest, he held it there like a pillow against himself. He heard the cattle lowing to be fed, heard the soft rasp of his father's crying breath, heard his mother's broken humming of a hymn. He lay that way in the graying light and slept.

The sun was blackened with snow, and the valley closed in quietly with humming, quietly as an hour of prayer.

Jo Carson

In Johnson City, Tennessee, Jo Carson learned the art of storytelling from her family of raconteurs. A poet, playwright, and essayist, Carson also writes short stories and works for children. Carson has delighted audiences across the country and in Europe with readings from her works both in person and as a commentator on National Public Radio's "All Things Considered." Carson's *Daytrips* (1989) received the Kesselring Award for best play of the year by a new playwright and has had successful runs in Los Angeles and New York. Her acclaimed *Stories I Ain't Told Nobody Yet* (1989) is a collection of performance material used in her one-woman shows. Her play, *A Preacher with a Horse to Ride* (1990), which centers on Theodore Dreiser's 1931 investigation of Kentucky coal strikes, won a Rogers L. Stevens Award in 1993 and was published in 1994. She has also written a play called *The Bear Facts,* which won an NEA Playwriting Fellowship in 1993, featuring Davy Crockett's encounter with bears. Her most recent publication is *The Great Shaking* (1994), a children's book about the New Madrid earthquakes of 1811–12.

"Lightning" is typical Jo Carson as it reveals the eternal presence of family and home, a theme central to all her work.

Lightning

She was so frightened that she frightened me,
Grandmother who kept her doors locked
and her kips pursed against transgression.
I lay in the middle of her living room floor
called in from play or up from sleep, a storm;
my face pressed against the scratchy rug
so when lightning did come in the window
it might not notice me. It never came

but it had come to get great aunt Rebecca.
I knew that story from the other half the family,
Grandma told it, said twice ball lightning
chased her sister down the same Virginia hill
into the house, into her room, into her bed,
said it rolled all over Rebecca,
said both times Rebecca almost died.

From *Appalachian Journal* 14.4, © *Appalachian Journal*/Appalachian State University. Used with permission.

Her sons asked why she didn't tell the truth.
Grandma said she saw no reason
to ruin a good story by sticking to facts.
The facts were—the sons didn't disagree—
ball lightning ran over Rebecca twice,
it just never came into the house.

By the time I knew Rebecca, she looked
as though she'd been run over
and the ball lightning was more impressive
than a husband who drank too much.
Rebecca said "if you feel a powerful tingling,
you're in trouble."

So I lay in the living room floor at home
and tried to distinguish fear from tingling
between the bone jarrings of a summer thunder storm.
My father picked me up, carried me with him.
"You've been listening to your grandmothers."

And we sat on the front stoop, me in his lap,
and after each great crash and bolt of lightning
he tempted God to make me laugh. "You missed us!"
he would holler, "if you want to scare us,
you have to get closer than that!"

Harriette Simpson Arnow

Harriette Simpson Arnow was born in Wayne County, Kentucky. The daughter of teachers, she attended Berea College in Berea, Kentucky, and earned her B.S. at the University of Louisville. She began her Kentucky trilogy with the publication of *Mountain Path* (1936). *Hunter's Horn* (1949) is the second book of the trilogy, and *The Dollmaker* (1954), the best known, is the third. It was runner-up for the 1955 National Book Award and experienced a renewal of popularity following its film adaptation in 1984. Arnow also captured the essence of rural life in the Cumberland in two nonfiction works, *Seedtime on the Cumberland* (1960) and *Flowering of the Cumberland* (1963). Arnow was also the author of several short stories that were published in the 1930s and contributed articles and reviews to various magazines. She died in 1986 in Ann Arbor, Michigan.

Sandra Ballard, author of the introduction to the Arnow selection, holds a Ph.D. in English from the University of Tennessee. She is currently working on a biography of Harriette Arnow and teaches English at Carson-Newman College in Jefferson City, Tennessee.

Introduction to "The Washerwoman's Day"
Sandra Ballard

"Washerwoman's Day," written in 1934 or 1935, was the story that earned for twenty-eight-year-old Harriette L. Simpson her first money as a writer. Robert Penn Warren was the editor of the old *Southern Review* who accepted this story for the Winter 1936 issue and paid her twenty-five dollars. Although it was the first story for which she earned cash, it was not the first story she had written, nor the first she published. After moving in 1934 from Kentucky to Cincinnati, she worked at a number of odd jobs—waitress, clerk, typist—to support herself as a writer.

Primarily a short-story writer in the late 1930s, she placed two stories prior to "Washerwoman's Day" in "little literary magazines": "Marigolds and Mules" in *Kosmos: Dynamic Stories of Today* (1934) and "A Mess of Pork" in *The New Talent* (1935). Those small publications, she explained, paid only in "free copies" and the "glory" of writers seeing their work in print. In her case, however, the reward was greater because the 1935 story prompted a letter from a New York editor, Harold Strauss, who wondered if she had considered writing a novel. With this encouragement, the year 1936 became very productive and satisfying for Harriette Simpson (who would not publish under the name Harriette Arnow until 1939, when she married Chicago journalist Harold Arnow). At the outset of 1936 she sold her first story to a prestigious journal, and by the end of the year, she saw the release of her first novel *Mountain Path,* published by Covici-Friede, John Steinbeck's publisher at the time.

"Washerwoman's Day" became Arnow's best-known short story after it was anthologized in several editions of the revolutionary New Critical textbook by Cleanth Brooks, John Purser, and Robert Penn Warren, *An Approach to Literature* (1939, 1952), and in the *Anthology of Stories from "The Southern Review"* (1953). As with many of her stories and her early novels, it is set in the region she knew best, the hills of south-central Kentucky.

Told from the point of view of Jane, a naive but observant first-person narrator, this ironic story exposes a youngster's early encounter with a pious community's notions of "respectability." The story lends itself to analysis of the class structure of the small community, in which the Ladies' Aid Society wields merciless power in the name of charity. The interactions within the community of women reveal human inequities underlined by poverty and hypocrisy.

The sanctimonious reaction of characters to an impoverished woman's death introduces a thematic situation which received fuller treatment in Arnow's later fiction. In her second novel, *Hunter's Horn* (1949), Lureenie Cramer is the poor neighbor whose death (during an excruciating childbirth scene) was due in part to her pride, which prevented her from admitting that her husband had deserted the family and that she and her children were starving. "Washerwoman's Day" also prefigures scenes from Arnow's best-known work, *The Dollmaker* (1954), in which the character of Gertie Nevels endures the pious pronouncements of her mother about how to live according to "God's will," and more importantly, according to the neighbors' opinions. In each episode, scripture-quoting characters self-righteously ignore any responsibility they might assume for the poverty and pain of an individual in their community.

The short story "Washerwoman's Day" continues to move us because the naiveté of the narrator, who reports more than she understands, does not cloud the perceptive reader's interpretations of adult behavior. Jane's limited understanding of what she has observed leads readers to question a community's responsibility to an individual.

The Washerwoman's Day

"It was pneumonia all right, but the lye maybe had something to do with it," Granma said.

Mama shifted Joie to her other breast. "Ollie Rankin ought to have had more sense," she said.

"She didn't know the old fool would take off her shoes and scrub the kitchen barefooted."

"Can I go to the funeral," I said.

"Be quiet," Mama said. "Her shoes were new, and she maybe thought to save them. The poor fool, her legs were swollen purple to her waist, Molly Hardwick said."

"If that Laurie Mae were fit to go into a decent house. They say that baby is exactly like Perce. . . ."

Mama looked at me. Granma hushed. "Can I go to the funeral?" I said.

"No," Mama said. "It does make it unhandy. I guess we'll have to get a nigger from Canetown, but I don't like niggers about."

"I always said I'd rather have black trash than white trash any day. . . ."

From *Southern Review* 1 (Winter 1936): 522–27. Reprinted by permission of the copyright holders, Marcella J. Arnow and Thomas Louis Arnow.

"Did she walk home without her shoes? Susie Chrisman said she did, and there was snow and. . . ."

"Hush, Jane," Mama said. "You'll be late to school."

"Spell *vegetation*," Granma said.

"V-e-g-e-t-a-t-i-o-n," I spelled.

"Wear your overshoes," Mama said.

"Don't go about the funeral," Granma said.

"The Ladies Aid are burying her. Susie Chrisman said her father. . . ."

"Don't argue," Mama said, and Granma tapped her cane.

I ran all the way to school. I thought all morning, and at noon I said, "Miss Rankin, my little brother Joie was croupy this morning and Mama forgot."

"What?"

"To write a note of excuse for me to go to the funeral. Susie Chrisman is going."

"Are you sure your mother wanted you to go?"

"Yes, ma'am. Clarie Bolin has always done our washing. Mama said I should go out of respect for the dead and the Ladies Aid . . . if she was poor white trash. I know my spelling."

"You may go at one-thirty," she said.

Susie and I held hands and ran fast down the sidewalk from the school. We laughed as we ran, for it was good to be out of school and there was a snow promise in the air and Christmas was only two weeks away. At the foot of the hill we stopped. "It's not proper to run all the way to a funeral," Susie said.

"No," I said. "Did they undertake her?"

"No. My father said it was a waste of good money to undertake poor people in cold weather. He sold the Ladies Aid the coffin, though."

"Is it true about the roses?"

Susie skipped twice before she remembered and was proper again. "Yes. The Ladies Aid sent all the way to Lexington. Two dozen white roses, and it the dead of winter. They cost three dollars . . . and her the washerwoman, Papa said."

Inside the church Mrs. Hyden was singing a solo. Her mouth was very wide open, and while we tiptoed to the second row from the back she held the word *dew* until it seemed she would not let it go until we sat down. I was embarrassed and in my haste stumbled over Susie. Susie tittered. When we were seated, Mrs. Hyden sang on about the dew on the roses and the voice she heard.

Susie nudged me. "Laurie Mae don't look so nice. That coat Mrs. Harvey gave her don't fit so good."

I craned my head down the aisle to see. Laurie Mae sat alone in the front row before her mother's coffin. Beside her was a long bundle wrapped in a piece of dirty brown blanket. "Mama said, 'She'll have her nerve to bring that baby.' The Ladies' Aid'll be mad," Susie whispered.

"Mama said the baby looked like Mr. Perce Burton," I said.

"On account of Laurie Mae was a hired girl there last year."

Something jerked my pigtail. I looked around. Mrs. John Crabtree set her lips tight together and looked hard at me. She was president of The Ladies Aid, and Mrs. Ollie Rankin sat with her. I nudged Susie, and we were still. Reverend Lipscomb read The Beatitudes and prayed. While he prayed Susie and I raised our heads and looked at all the people. Susie pinched me. Laurie Mae didn't have her head bowed at her own mother's funeral. "Isn't she awful," Susie whispered.

Then the choir sang "Lord, I'm coming home." Then Reverend Lipscomb preached the funeral. I was glad he made it so short. He talked about what the Bible meant when it said things like the poor and the meek shall inherit the earth. He explained that the poor must be hard working and patient and righteous. He said that righteousness had this day been shown by the ladies of the church in their beautiful putting away of the dead. I thought his words were so wonderful that I would remember them.

He said that man was made to err, and that the dead woman had been no different from the world of men, but he hoped that God in His divine mercy and goodness and infinite wisdom would look down on her and forgive her sins and take her to His bosom. He hoped that the one of the living nearest and dearest to the dead would profit by the affliction that God in His almighty wisdom had seen fit to lay upon her, and change the path of her ways and walk henceforth with uprightness and decency. "He means Laurie Mae," Susie whispered.

"She's not even crying," I said.

He finished and the choir sang. Then Miss Virginia played the piano, and we all walked around and looked at Clarie Bolin and the white roses and Laurie Mae. "Didn't she look ugly," Susie whispered when we were back in our seats.

"She looked mad," I said, and didn't want to whisper any more. It was no longer fun. I wondered why the dead woman looked the way she did with her teeth clamped tight together and her thin blue lips drawn back a little ways. She looked, I thought, as if she had just come back from a long fight, and had lost in the fight. I wished in a dim sort of way that she could know The Ladies Aid had spent three dollars for white roses. I thought it would have made her feel better.

Susie's father wheeled the coffin down the aisle. The rollers made a little squeaking as they rolled over the carpet, and the white roses quivered until one pale petal slipped loose and fell behind the coffin. Laurie Mae sat and looked straight in front of her until the coffin was going through the door into the vestibule. She got up then, and took the ragged bundle from the seat and laid it carefully on her arm, and walked slowly down the aisle. All the ladies looked at her and the bundle, but she did not look at anything.

When the coffin was in the vestibule Mrs. Crabtree and Mrs. Rankin started whispering. We turned around to listen. "Not so much as a thank-you for all we've done," Mrs. Crabtree said.

"As soon as I heard that she was dead I went right up there into that hut," Mrs. Rankin said.

Mrs. Hyden and some other ladies left their places in the choir and joined them. Mrs. Hyden leaned over me to talk to Mrs. Crabtree and I could feel her fat breasts on my shoulder. "What about the roses?" she said. "You're not going to send them to the cemetery?"

"No," Mrs. Crabtree said. "I had thought we might give Laurie Mae some and keep the others for the sewing circle tomorrow afternoon."

"What would Laurie Mae do with roses?" Susie's mother said.

"We could give her just a few. . . . I think maybe we ought to."

"I'll go see to it," Mrs. Crabtree said, and got up.

We followed her to the church door, where men were carrying the coffin down the high steps. Susie's father had taken away the roses and stood holding them all bundled in his hands. Mrs. Crabtree took them. She looked at the flowers and arranged them in a neat bouquet. When she had finished arranging them, she turned the bouquet round and round and looked at it. She saw the rose with the petal missing and took it out. Then she took out five others.

Laurie Mae stood on the top step watching the men carry down the coffin. For a moment it looked as if they were going to drop it and Susie and I held our breaths. Mrs. Crabtree tapped Laurie Mae on the shoulder. "Here are some roses," she said, and handed her the six roses. "Reverend Lipscomb will drive you to the cemetery in his buggy."

Laurie Mae took the roses and did not say anything. She waited until the coffin was down and in the hearse, and then went to the buggy. Susie and I watched to see how she would manage. Reverend Lipscomb hadn't come out of the church, and no one offered to help her into the buggy. She tried first to step in it with the roses and the baby and almost fell over into the muddy road. Then she laid the baby and the roses on the seat and climbed in.

Susie and I followed the hearse and buggy. The grave was on the far side of the cemetery away from the road where there were no fine big tombstones, and the weeds and grass from the summer stood high and brown. We walked up to the edge of the grave and stood while the coffin was lowered, and Reverend Lipscomb said a short prayer.

The others went away then, and left us to watch the men throw the yellow dirt in. Laurie Mae stood behind us a few feet away and watched the men, too. "She means to put the roses on the grave," Susie whispered.

Laurie Mae didn't do that. When the men were finished she turned and started home. "Let's go after her and ask to see the baby," Susie said.

"Mama wouldn't want me to be seen talking with her," I said, and hung back until Susie ran past me calling, "We want to see the baby, Laurie Mae."

The girl stopped and laid the roses on the ground and with her free hand unwrapped the bundle. We stood without saying anything and looked at the baby. I didn't think it was a pretty baby. Its head was too big with the veins showing in its face. "Doesn't it ever cry?" Susie asked.

"No," Laurie Mae said. "He hardly ever cries." Her voice sounded hoarse and rusty as if she had not used it in a long time. She wrapped the baby up again, and picked up the roses.

"Don't you think they're pretty roses," I said.

"They cost three dollars," Susie said.

"Three dollars," Laurie Mae said, and stopped and looked at the flowers.

We thought she would be pleased to know The Ladies Aid had spent so much. Her voice sounded full of something else. We didn't know what it was. "Three dollars is a lot of money," Susie said.

"I know," Laurie Mae said. "It's a lot of money."

We left her then, for she could walk but slowly with the baby and the roses. Susie left me at the cemetery gate for she went one way and I another. I slipped behind the concrete pillars of the gate and waited. I wanted to see Laurie Mae. I thought that now she was alone she might cry. I wanted to see her cry.

She came out of the gate and looked all around; up and down the road, and at the nearest houses, and up into the snowy sky. When she saw no one she laid the baby on the ground, and took the white roses one by one and threw them in the yellow mud of the road. She pushed them out of sight with her foot and raked the mud over them, and then she picked up the baby.

Rita Quillen

Rita Quillen was born and raised in Hiltons, Virginia, where her father's family has lived for five generations. She received her undergraduate and M.A. degrees at East Tennessee State University, where her master's thesis provided the background for her book *Looking for Native Ground: Contemporary Appalachian Poetry* (1989). She is also the author of *October Dusk* (1987), a collection of her own poems. A versatile writer, her poetry, fiction, and reviews have appeared in a wide variety of publications. Within a few years she has become a leading Appalachian poet and critical evaluator of poetry.

October Dusk

the evening dark
falls all around me
its warm breath
casts a shadow on my face

sitting on my front steps
I am a candle flame
drawing moths and mosquitoes
holding the moment in my cupped hands

"October Dusk" from *October Dusk* (Seven Buffaloes Press, 1987). Reprinted by permission of the author. "Woman Writer" printed by permission of the author.

he sits quietly by me
memories of the day's work
swift moving color shared
like fall leaves in the yard

the potatoes from the garden
lie scattered in the grass
tomorrow we will sort them
and store them for winter

his hand rests on my neck
as he slowly stands
he offers the other dirty hand
to help me up

our eyes meet in the fading light
we go inside
surrendering to night
the smell of earth still strong

Woman Writer

Spending the days attending Bodily Functions
our own and everyone else's
gives us a handicap.
Words crawl into the laundry basket
hide among the socks
circle and scream in the toilet
hang in the closet and beg
for freedom.
While my son warms in my arms
a line that could make me famous
leaps up in my face
spits and leaves by the back door.
I cannot throw down my baby
and chase into the air
I am too tired anyway
too tired.
I dream words that have magic
I dream lines that make my heart
beat faster in the heat of recognition.

Today
a poem becomes a morning song

a psalm almost
but dies after a few verses
drowned in the everyday,
the creeping cynicism that
my daylight words are not androgynous
enough, not homogenous enough
for the editors anyway.
A lost poem swirling down
blurred like the face
of a childhood friend
lands at someone's doorstep.
Next morning
a woman opens the door
and steps on the poem.
Writhing, gasping words
try to cry out
get off the page.
Her children came to hover
just watch and wait.

Lynn Champion,

Charles O. Jackson,

Mary Richards, and Others

Generally, Appalachian literature is taught as a self-contained unit reflective of a particular region of the United States, but increasingly scholars are looking at comparative approaches in which classics of Appalachian writing are paired with those of other cultures, in the interest of self-knowledge. The focus can be broad or narrow. The Appalachian Humanities Education Program which follows illustrates the possibilities of the study of a single theme, that of community, and the works which may be used to amplify several aspects of that theme. The program was sponsored in 1985 by the College of Liberal Arts at the University of Tennessee at Knoxville under a grant from the National Endowment of the Humanities. Dr. Lynn Champion, then director of Community Outreach Programs for the college, authored both the planning and the implementation grants and served as project director. Dr. Charles O. Jackson, as humanist coordinator, was responsible for insuring the humanities content for the program. Dr. Jackson developed questions to encourage readers to think about books as they related to the overall theme. In addition to Dr. Jackson, three other persons contributed to the reading guide: Dr. Mary Richards edited it; and Annelle Foutch and Angie LeClercq conducted research on book selections, supplementary readings, and other materials. Other members of the planning committee included Peter Garvie, Anne Kraus, Bonnie Ledbetter, Dr. Thomas Pruitt, and Dr. J. W. Williamson. Although not official members of the planning committee, Wilma Dykeman, Dr. James S. Greene III, Loyal Jones, Dr. Parks Lanier, Dr. Jim Wayne Miller, Dr. John Stephenson, and Shirley Underwood, contributed richly to the program through their knowledge of literature and Appalachian culture.

Ridge to Ridge, Ocean to Ocean: The Theme of Community in Appalachian Literature and World Classics

Theme: Boundaries of Community

Appalachia is a region of opposites: imposing mountains, green hills, lush forests, rushing streams juxtaposed against gashed hillsides, scattered refuse, and apparent poverty. Until the 1920s, Appalachia was primarily an agricultural region composed of small, self-sufficient farms. Industrialism and coal mining destroyed this simple form of community as they did in parts of England during the Industrial Revolution. The rural economy was disrupted when the people moved to towns to find work. The adjustment to this new, stressful way of life was extremely difficult for families who had been poor but self-reliant. The following works illustrate the problems faced by families as they tried to adjust and prosper in an alien, dehumanizing environment.

Dickens's Hard Times

In 1854, the year Charles Dickens wrote *Hard Times*, England is in the midst of the Industrial Revolution. The factories, and the coal mines that provide the energy for them, dominate the lives of rich and poor alike. Those with more money and education, such as Thomas Gradgrind and Josiah Bounderby, try to justify exploiting the workers by adopting certain theories of economic and human behavior. Laborers and the land are destroyed by the overwhelming power of industry. This novel provides fascinating insights into family relationships, as individuals attempt to adjust to life in an industrial town.

This information was first published in the fall of 1985 by the College of Liberal Arts at the University of Tennessee, Knoxville, as a program guide for participants enrolled in the Appalachian Humanities Education Program funded by the National Endowment for the Humanities. The title of the guide was "A Community Reading: Your Community and the Human Experience." It is reprinted by permission of the authors.

Still's River of Earth

James Still's *River of Earth,* set in Kentucky in the early twentieth century, is the story of the Baldridge family and its survival through tough times. The Baldridges are torn between eking out a living on a farm or moving to a mining town in the hope that Father will obtain a steady income. Their situation is made more unstable by a series of parasitic relatives whom Father cannot turn away. But the love and the bonds of the family continue to be strong wherever the members move, and they carry a sense of home even to the unpleasant environment of the mining town.

Theme: Values and Community, The Good Society

The concept of the good society, one true to its principles, is explored in Plato's *Republic* and Jesse Stuart's *The Thread That Runs So True.* Although the two authors wrote in very different times about very different societies, both are concerned with questions that still trouble us today. Plato emphasizes justice as the value upon which the good society should be based. He thinks that an education system should help prepare a just person to function well in a just state. Stuart also looks to education as the means to a good society, if those who value education can gain political control of the schools. Stuart believes that education can enrich the lives of citizens of all ages.

Plato's Republic

Plato lived in the fifth and fourth centuries B.C., times somewhat like our own. While many people still held to traditional and moral values, many others had come to question those values. Plato watched the government of Athens, without good reason, put to death his friend and teacher Socrates. He came to feel that his native country had lost sight of justice, and that the people of Athens no longer knew the difference between right and wrong. Plato tried to correct this crisis of values by writing the *Republic,* in which he tries to show that there are true principles by which citizens can guide their government and their private lives. He does this through an imaginary dialogue with Socrates as the main speaker. Socrates and his friends try to discover what justice is, and where it can be found, both in government and in individuals.

Jesse Stuart's The Thread That Runs So True

Jesse Stuart's autobiography, *The Thread That Runs So True,* is an inspiring story of a dedicated teacher and writer in rural Kentucky in the early twentieth century. The story follows Stuart from his first teaching experience in a one-room schoolhouse to a position as superintendent of county schools for the State of Kentucky and beyond. His vision of education and its potential for developing the good society grow stronger through the books, but at the same time he becomes frustrated at the shortsightedness of local politicians. Stuart's dedication to teaching and learning shine through all his endeavors, and his

dreams of creating a better democracy through educating citizens seem closer
to becoming reality by virtue of his efforts and faith in human potential.

Theme: Individual vs. Community

Change, progress, growth: these words describe a society on the move. Change
may bring the benefits of a higher standard of living, new products, and new
advances in medicine, but it may also bring deterioration of the land, the air,
and a simpler way of life. Thus the process of change stirs conflict. Certain individuals living in a changing society may question whether progress is not actually destructive of the lives it touches. Because of their willingness to speak out
and express their concerns, such individuals may be criticized or even ostracized
by their fellow citizens. What happens to the person who dissents from the
community's views and values? Is there a possibility for individual growth and
expression in the community? These questions are addressed in Henrik Ibsen's
An Enemy of the People and Wilma Dykeman's *Return the Innocent Earth.*

Henrik Ibsen's An Enemy of the People
Set in Norway in 1898, Ibsen's *An Enemy of the People* is a play depicting a
doctor's conflict with his community. When he discovers that the town's primary source of revenue, its public baths, are dangerously polluted by a factory nearby, Dr. Stockmann announces his findings in the belief that the
townspeople will want to close and renovate the facilities as quickly as possible. He learns, however, that public opinion does not share his ideals. He is
viewed as a threat to the community and an enemy to the public welfare.
The drama is focused within the Stockmann family, for the doctor's brother
is the mayor of the town and the leading spokesman for the public opinion.

Wilma Dykeman's Return the Innocent Earth
Dykeman's *Return the Innocent Earth* is a novel about the impact of a large canning company and its policies on Southern Appalachia. Again, two family members are set against each other. Stull, the practical cousin, believes that testing
chemicals to improve production must continue even if a few individuals die as
a result. Jon, the idealistic cousin, sees how far the family company has strayed
from its original function as a support for the community, and he believes that
increased mechanization and reliance on chemicals have harmed the people and
their land. Can Jon return the company to its roots and still be able to maintain
the property of the company and the community that depends on it?

Theme: Community as Place

Many of the poets of the worker have closely associated themselves with the
land and the delights of rural life. The knowledge and experience drawn

from nature are found in work as varied as passages from the Old Testament and Thomas Jefferson's descriptions of the Virginia countryside. It is this feeling for the importance of place—of rural land, water, and sky—that link such diverse individuals as the Roman poet Virgil and the four Appalachian poets discussed below. Common themes to be examined are the importance of the land in definition of community, enduring qualities of communities, place, and the use of place to build community.

Virgil's Georgics and Eclogues

Virgil came to manhood during one of the most turbulent periods in Roman history, the time of the civil war which ended the Republic and brought in the Emperors. In this terrible time, he turned to writing about the enduring rhythmic world of farming. As one born on a farm, he writes with a special affection of growing grain, grapes, bees, and cattle. Through his verse and his images, he tries to show a stable world where hard work pays and where the forces which bend and twist people's lives have at least some order. *The Eclogues* are ten poems about shepherds and the life of the country. Virgil's shepherds compete with each other in song and in love. He gives us a sense that escape to the country is not so simple after all.

Appalachian Poets

Jim Wayne Miller's *The Mountains Have Come Closer* is a delightful compendium of poems that evoke the beauty of the Kentucky landscape. For Miller, a sense of place is rooted in the memory along with the experiences and values of his youth. To lose a sense of place, then, is to lose a proper sense of one's self.

Jeff Daniel Marion's *Out of the Country, Back Home* is a book of poems about East Tennessee—the land and its people. With precise description, he shows how much the land influences the character of its inhabitants, and helps us to rediscover the wonder of our natural surroundings.

Robert Morgan's *Groundwork* is a collection of poetry linking nature and culture. He conveys a special feeling for the mountains as they are experienced by the senses, kept alive in memory. Through recounting superstitions and legends, he shows how the land shapes the beliefs of the people of Southern Appalachia while it sustain their bodies.

Wendell Berry's *Farming: A Handbook* is a book of poems about pride in the land, working it, and appreciating its seasonal changes. Through evocative descriptions, Berry conveys the sights and sounds of Appalachia as a special place in which the reader also may dwell.

Theme: Family as Community

The family unit is the most immediate community we have. Individuals generally feel loyalty to their families before any larger community, and the reason is clear: our families nourish and support us until were are ready to enter the greater community of the world. Traditionally, Appalachian society has depended upon strong family ties for survival. Death of a family member can be a traumatic incident, but at the same time it can reaffirm the strength of the family as community. The reading selections, *Hamlet* by William Shakespeare and *A Death in the Family* by James Agee, treat this important theme.

Shakespeare's Hamlet
Set in Denmark, Shakespeare's play *Hamlet* presents a young man whose father has been murdered and who now must cope with grief and the desire for revenge. His torment is increased by his suspicions that his uncle, the King, now married to his mother, was responsible for the murder, so that any revenge must be carried out within the family. Even his mother must be partly culpable, for apparently she knows about the situation, has accepted it, and expects her son to do the same. *Hamlet,* then, is about a young man's dilemma when the community of the family has been destroyed for him. He must decide whether to continue the destruction involving the remaining family members.

James Agee's A Death in the Family
James Agee's *A Death in the Family* is a semi-autobiographical portrait of a family's grief over the sudden death of one of its members. The setting is Knoxville, in 1915, and the story centers around Rufus Follet, a young boy, and his family. Rufus's father, Jay Follet, goes to the country early one morning to check on his ailing father. He leaves without telling his children good-bye, because he expects to return by early evening. By that night, May Follet, Jay's wife, receives a phone call informing her that Jay has been killed in a car accident on his way back home. The novel shows the effect of the tragic accident on all those involved and their relationships with one another as they try to confront death and understand its meaning.

Theme: Loss of Community

Separation from community can have a variety of consequences for the individuals who leave. On the positive side, separation may provide the opportunity for personal growth. On the negative side, it may cause difficulties in adjusting to new environments. Henry James's *Daisy Miller* and Harriette Arnow's *The Dollmaker* focus on women who have been removed from their home community and the problems they face in relating to the new situations in which they find themselves.

Henry James's Daisy Miller
In *Daisy Miller*, James portrays young Americans traveling in the unfamiliar environment of Europe. Daisy, a young woman from New York, clings to the casual manners of her home community rather than conform to the rigid

social customs of Europe. Although she is innocent, her behavior is improper by European standards and leads to her exclusion from polite society. The meaning of her actions and the resulting problems are pondered by an expatriate American, who finally recognizes her true character.

Harriette Arnow's The Dollmaker

Gertie Nevels in *The Dollmaker* also finds herself transplanted to a new and strange locale. When her husband takes a factory job in Detroit, she and her children follow him from the hills of Kentucky to the large, northern industrial city. Gertie and the children have difficulty coping with the new environment—harsh winters, stifling summers, cramped living conditions, language barriers, and strange social customs and religions. The process of adjustment, and the sacrifices required, form the substance of this moving book about loss of community.

Chapter 2

Religion and Worship

Introduction

If there is a single feature that distinguishes the literature of Southern Appalachia from that of other regions, it is a religious sensibility, which may be regarded as a blessing or a curse. H. L. Mencken considered the South—the "Bible belt" in his words—to be intellectually retarded by its religious culture. Flannery O'Connor understood the South to be "Christ haunted" but, for that reason, full of spiritual struggle and artistic possibility. The fact that Southern Appalachia has not been able to embrace completely behavioral psychology, scientific positivism, the Gospel of Wealth, or any other panacea would seem to O'Connor as much a form of spiritual integrity as of intellectual stagnation.

As the selections in this chapter make clear, Southern Appalachia has been especially "Christ haunted" since the settlement period. The history of religion in the region reflects the collision of cultures, denominations, and ideas. This history includes: the early missionary phase, devoted to the conversion of Indians and new settlers; the Great Revival in the West (1787–1805); denominational strife prior to the Civil War; the confrontation with modernism, as seen in the Scopes Trial in 1925; and the postmodern period, in which contemporary poets and writers of the region struggle to come to terms with a long and powerful religious heritage. Through these various phases, religion has been both a serious concern and a source of considerable humor. From the earliest phase of its religious history to the contemporary period, however, Appalachia has been isolated only in terms of geography, for spiritual struggle inside the region has been representative of spiritual struggle everywhere.

Paul Curry Steele

Paul Curry Steele was born in Logan, West Virginia, in 1928. He studied at the University of Virginia, Harvard University, and the University of Iowa. He has had one book published, *Anse on Island Creek and Other Poems* (Charleston, W.Va.: Mountain State Press, 1981). He lives and writes in Charleston, West Virginia.

In Appalachia

As you near the town it stands beside the road
Like Isaiah before the walls of Jerusalem:
A signpost of molded concrete,
The message in depressed letters
On a flat conventional heart,
A gray fundamentalist lollipop
Sucked by storms without wearing away,
Announcing
As it has for over a century
JESUS / IS COMING / SOON

From *New Ground,* Southern Appalachian Writers' Co-operative and Mountain Review, 1977. Reprinted by permission of the author.

Walter Brownlow Posey

Walter Brownlow Posey, professor and scholar, has been one of the foremost documenters of the spread of Protestantism in the eastern United States. Born in Smyrna, Tennessee, in 1900, he studied at the University of Chicago and took his M.A. and Ph.D. at Vanderbilt University. He had a lengthy teaching career, retiring from the history faculty of Emory University in 1969, having accrued a long list of publications.

The following ecumenical narrative of Protestant denominations is taken from Posey's *Frontier Mission: A History of Religion West of the Southern Appalachians to 1861* (1966).

Into the Valley

The first Roman Catholics to settle in Kentucky were members of the Coomes family, who came from Charles County, Maryland, to Harrodsburg in the spring of 1775. Mrs. Coomes opened a school which was probably the first elementary school in Kentucky. The Coomes family later moved near Bardstown, secured several tracts of land, and in 1804 gave a farm of more than one hundred acres to the church. Unsatisfactory conditions in the East and news of attractive opportunities in the West led to the formation in Maryland of a Catholic colonization league, which influenced a group of Catholics to leave Maryland in 1785 and to settle in the Pottinger's Creek region a few miles from Bardstown. This band had traveled to Pittsburgh and then had come down the Ohio River to Kentucky. Other Catholic groups came to Kentucky overland by the way of the Cumberland Gap.[1]

French-born priests Stephen T. Badin and Michael Barriere, selected by John Carroll, Bishop of Baltimore, to go to Kentucky, arrived there in November 1793. After a few months Barriere departed, leaving Badin alone to serve the vast area. The twenty-five-year-old priest, the first to be ordained in the United States, was handicapped by a meager knowledge of the English language and was even less acquainted with the customs of Kentuckians. Between 1797 and 1799 three more priests arrived in Kentucky, two to find an early grave and one to withdraw because of temperament. By 1803 Badin again was alone. Within ten years the increase in the number of Catholic families made almost unbearable demands on the lone priest. The arrival of Father Charles Nerinckx in 1805 relieved Badin of some labors among his scattered flock.[2]

Catholic families did not migrate early to the region that became Tennessee. In 1790 a small party came from North Carolina, and in this group was Father Rohan, who stayed only part of a year. Nearly ten years later the number of Catholics in the new state did not exceed one hundred. In 1799 Governor John Sevier of Tennessee, in an effort to increase the state's population, sought to interest Badin in the possibility of settling one hundred families there and offered to sell parcels of land as inducements. Sevier defeated his purpose, however, by setting so dear a price on the land that the Catholic families were uninterested in the offer.[3]

Only in Kentucky did the Catholics secure a foothold, and this was accomplished amidst the Protestants' overwhelming advantages—lay workers and local preachers. Into the transmontane area adjacent to the Atlantic colonies, members of the Protestant denominations moved rapidly, established churches, and installed preachers of their own beliefs. The Methodist and Baptist congregations rarely had a preacher who had been ordained before he came to the West, but the Presbyterian and Episcopal churches used only regularly ordained ministers, a practice which greatly limited their expansion into the new lands.

From *Frontier Mission: A History of Religion West of the Southern Appalachians to 1861*, © 1966 by The University Press of Kentucky. Reproduced by permission of the publisher.

The Baptists in America had arisen as a denomination after the expulsion of Roger Williams from the Massachusetts Colony and the subsequent organization of a congregation at Providence, Rhode Island, in 1639. The Great Awakening of a century later stirred many controversies among the Congregational churches of New England and contributed a great deal to Baptist growth. The local Baptist congregations, scattered along the length of the Atlantic seaboard as far south as Georgia, were completely autonomous; no administrative office supervised the action of any congregation or dictated a program. The democratic form of Baptist church government matched the nature of its membership and appealed especially to a people of little property or culture. If a Baptist congregation needed a preacher, a man was chosen from its members and ordained. Baptists were generally regarded with disfavor by other denominations, particularly in Virginia, where they suffered severe treatment from the members of the Episcopal Church who deeply resented their inroads. Originally identified with the excesses of the Reformation and opposing themselves to long-established usages, the Baptists were not always comfortable companions. Their churches frequently were a member's only opportunity for self expression, and to him his voice sounded sweet and strong.

During the American Revolution the Baptists, like the Methodists and Presbyterians, sacrificed greatly on behalf of freedom from England. Their demands for non-interference from the state and equality for all religions before the law led them to support the Constitution strongly; indeed, any objections against the new government usually arose from the fear that it would not provide sufficient religious liberty.[4]

Despite wartime loss of church buildings, Baptists had gained in membership. Hard times and persecution, however, encouraged many of them to turn westward to lands across the mountains. A Baptist preacher, Thomas Tinsley, had preached in Harrodsburg, Kentucky, as early as 1776, but it was five years later, under the shade of a maple tree at Severns Valley, that eighteen people organized the first Baptist church west of the mountains. John Garrard served as pastor of this church until he was captured and murdered by the Indians. The Baptist ranks increased rapidly: by 1785 in Kentucky there were eighteen churches, nineteen preachers, and the Elkhorn and Salem associations. A third association was formed in 1787, at which time Baptists, both Regular and Separate, numbered more than three thousand in a total population of about seventy thousand. So great had been the Baptist migration westward that one-fourth of the Baptists in Virginia moved to Kentucky between 1791 and 1810.[5]

The Baptist migration into Tennessee paralleled the Kentucky movement. A permanent church was formed in 1780 at Buffalo Ridge on Boone's Creek by a group which had moved in a body from a congregation at Sandy Creek in North Carolina. Within six years there were enough congregations in East Tennessee to form the Holston Association. A church was organized in 1786 in Middle Tennessee, on a branch of the Red River, and within ten years the Mero Association was formed from the many churches in that section.[6]

ༀ

In 1740 John Craig, an Irishman educated at the University of Edinburgh, began a long pastorate near Staunton in the western part of Virginia. Two years after he was graduated from Princeton, Hugh McAden came into the back country of Virginia and the Carolinas and preached there in 1755. The Ebbing Spring and Sinking Spring churches, on the Holston River in Virginia near the boundary of Tennessee, secured in 1773 the services of Charles Cummings for a stipulated salary of ninety pounds a year. For more than three decades, this fearless native of Ireland preached in that section to various congregations, in which every man had his rifle at his side.

Samuel Doak, another graduate of Princeton, settled in Tennessee in 1778, and by doing so became the first minister of any denomination in this region. After preaching in Sullivan County for two years, Doak moved to Washington County and there combined preaching and teaching. His school, which eventually became Washington College, earned the distinction of being the first institution offering literary courses in the Mississippi Valley. Inured to the dangers of the West, Doak never quailed from fear or danger. Once in the midst of a sermon he heard the cry of "Indians! Indians!" Immediately he grabbed his gun and led the chase. Another alarm caused him to dismiss his school and hurry to the camp of Colonel John Sevier.

ༀ

Despite the dangers from Indian fighting, the land-hungry pioneer was willing to stake a claim for the virgin soil of Kentucky. Reports of bounteous yields coaxed people to the region; the population increased rapidly and so did the number of Presbyterians. By 1785 there were twelve Presbyterian congregations in central Kentucky and in the following year four ministers and five ruling elders formed the Transylvania Presbytery which covered all of Kentucky, the Cumberland region in Middle Tennessee, and settlements on the Big and Little Miami rivers in Ohio.

Before the end of the century the voice of Presbyterian preachers had been heard in Cincinnati and Kaskaskia, and among the Chickasaw Indians in Mississippi. In 1800 the Synod of the Carolinas sent James Hall on a missionary reconnaissance to Mississippi. Arriving in December, he remained in the territory until April and particularly enjoyed the hospitality of Natchez, which he thought "may vie with any part of the Union."[7] During this visit he found only one Episcopal, one Methodist, and two Baptist preachers—all illiterate except the Episcopalian.

The Presbyterian Church as a whole had emerged from the American Revolution in good condition and was exceeded in size only by the Congregational Church. Members and ministers had been active and prominent in supporting the revolutionary cause of the American colonies, in securing colonial liberties, and in forming a constitution for the new government. After the war the organization of the church was intact, its people were exultant over victory, and its determination to grow and expand was strong. Perhaps no other church gained so great a benefit from the successful prosecution of the war. Of all the churches in the South, only the Presbyterian denomination maintained a vigorous life during the Revolution.

The Presbyterian Church had been the first to send missionaries across the mountains with its migrating members. Presbyterians in the back country begged the Synod of New York and Philadelphia to send ministers. When a request came in 1779 from the Hanover Presbytery in Virginia, the synod stated that "it is greatly for the interest of the church to pay particular attention to the Southern and Western parts of this continent," for unless advantage is taken of the opportunity now theirs "in a few years [they] may be utterly lost by the prevalency and preoccupying of many ignorant and irreligious sectaries."[8]

Presbyterianism was not destined, however, to remain the leading religion of the frontier. The Methodists and the Baptists, far more democratic and less demanding than the Presbyterians, soon got control of the great masses of people. The basic belief in Calvinism left man alone in the presence of his God, and this was too helpless a state to suit many frontiersmen. The requirements for educated ministers limited the number available to the Presbyterians and handicapped the church in its competitive struggle with other churches that demanded little intellectual attainment from their preachers.

General worldliness and desecration of the Sabbath so disturbed the Presbyterian Church that the General Assembly of 1789 addressed a pastoral letter to the churches pointing out the "pain and fearful apprehension" which it experienced over the sad state of religion. The framers noted that "profligacy and corruption of the public morals have advanced with a progress proportioned to our declension in religion. Profaneness, pride, luxury, injustice, intemperance, lewdness, and every species of debauchery and loose indulgence greatly abound." Much of this accusation was, of course, directed to Presbyterians over the mountains.[9]

The Methodist movement, beginning in a small society of Anglican churchmen who desired a moving, personal religious experience, mushroomed in America. Its systems of leaders, classes, and circuits were peculiarly fitted to a widely scattered people. When the Bishop of London declined the request to send clergy to the American Methodists, John Wesley in 1784 ordained Thomas Coke, a presbyter of the Church of England, and sent him as superintendent to America with full power to ordain other preachers. Coke and Francis Asbury, a Methodist missionary who had been sent to America by Wesley in 1771, assumed a bishop's title and functions, organized a compact empire, cut the Methodist societies from the Anglican Church, and started the Methodist Episcopal Church on its independent way, free to create its own bishops, ordain its clergy, and adopt a discipline that would comport with the changing needs of America.

Despite the suspicion and prejudice under which the Methodists labored during the American Revolution, the church increased in membership and ministry. The people who identified themselves with the Methodist movement were aggressive and zealous, and because of their enthusiasms they were often unpopular with other folk in the communities. It was said that the Methodist preachers had only one sermon; without manuscripts they preached about an offended God, a perishing world, and a saving Christ. There must have been some power in repetition, for at the close of the war the Methodist Church had almost fifteen thousand members and nearly one hundred preachers in the American colonies.

In 1783 the Holston Circuit was formed in Tennessee and included settlements on the Watauga, Holston, and Nolichucky rivers. Jeremiah Lambert, a traveling preacher from Delaware, served this far-flung area. In 1786 Acuff's Chapel, the first Methodist church building in Tennessee, was erected near the present Blountville. The Cumberland settlements felt the power of Methodism through the preaching of Benjamin Ogden, who came from Kentucky in 1787. Two or three years later, a stone church was erected in the heart of the new town of Nashville, and James Robertson, a founder and a leading citizen of the town, and his wife joined the Methodist Church. Bishop Asbury crossed the mountains in 1788 to attend the first conference in the West held at Keywood's on the Holston River in Washington County, Virginia. The entire region was upset by the civil disturbances growing out of the abortive State of Franklin. The bishop did not allow the political trouble to disturb the conference, which included the few preachers in the Holston region and those in Kentucky. Although Asbury's *Journal* records a few instances of hostility displayed in the course of years by members and ministers of other denominations, particularly by the Baptists, he made numerous references to the demonstrations of good will. Some of the early Methodists felt that they had been persecuted or ridiculed by the Presbyterians, but the harsh relations had been modified at the opening of the Great Revival period. At the close of the century, 2,500 Methodists in Tennessee had been organized into six circuits.[10]

The spirit of Methodism spread into Kentucky at about the same time that its early preachers went to Tennessee. In 1783 a Methodist local preacher, Francis Clark, moved from Mercer County, Virginia, to Kentucky, where he immediately organized a class of Methodists and appointed John Durham as the class leader. Evidently Clark worked successfully wherever he lived, for by 1785 there were enough Methodists in the state for two preachers to be sent to the Kentucky Circuit. James Haw and Benjamin Ogden were assigned by Bishop Asbury to this initial organization of Methodists in Kentucky. In the spring of 1790, Asbury again crossed the mountains, the second of thirty-one trips, in order to attend the Kentucky Conference held at Masterson's Station five miles from Lexington. On his first visit to Kentucky, the bishop was disappointed in Methodist accomplishments, for he commented in his diary: "The Methodists do but little here—others lead the way."[11] And the bishop could have repeated his observation many times, for the Methodists did not increase in Kentucky as they did elsewhere. The area, however, served as a springboard for Methodist activities in other states; Methodist preachers moving from Kentucky spread the faith into Tennessee and Ohio and eventually into the Mississippi Territory. By 1796 a class had been formed in Milford, Ohio, and two years later Dayton and Cincinnati were stations included in the new Miami Circuit.

The chief impetus which sent the Methodist Church into Mississippi came from the South Carolina Conference. In January 1797, Tobias Gibson was chosen by Bishop Asbury to serve as a missionary to the Southwest. After a seven-hundred-mile trip by horseback and boat, Gibson reached Natchez; five hundred miles separated him from the nearest Methodist preacher, and four years passed before he saw one.

The circuit rider system which the Methodist preacher used in covering a vast area was effective. Many communities had too few Methodists to justify the use of a stationed preacher, and, where the membership was large enough to need a full-time preacher, they frequently were too poor to support one. The church responded to the situation by marking out a circuit, putting a rider on it, and bidding him cover it at least once a month, preaching at every possible opportunity. This system secured the greatest expansion at the least expense and triumphed in competition with the Presbyterian and Baptist method of having a preacher serve only one or two churches. Primarily a middle-class religious movement, Methodism made little effort toward a literate ministry. In face of the pressing need, the Methodist Church could not wait to train preachers. Experience was the basis of all Methodist training; men learned to exhort by exhorting, to preach by preaching, to teach by teaching.

Notes

1. Mary Ramona Mattingly, *The Catholic Church on the Kentucky Frontier, 1785–1812* (Washington, DC: Catholic U of America, 1936), chs. 1 and 2; Ben. J. Webb, *The Centenary of Catholicity in Kentucky* (Louisville, KY: Charles A. Rogers, 1884), passim.

2. Peter Guilday, *The Life and Times of John Carroll* (Westminster, MD: Newman P, 1954), chs. 12 and 19; Annabelle M. Melville, *John Carroll of Baltimore: Founder of the American Catholic Hierarchy* (New York: Scribner, 1955), chs. 8 and 16; J. Herman Schauinger, *Stephen T. Badin: Priest in the Wilderness* (Milwaukee: Bruce Publishing Co., 1956), passim; J. Herman Schauinger, *Cathedrals in the Wilderness* (Milwaukee: Bruce Publishing Co., 1952), 20–27; Victor F. O'Daniel, *The Light of the Church in Kentucky . . . the Very Rev. Samuel Thomas Wilson* (Washington, DC: Dominican Fathers House of Studies, 1932), 83–84; Ellis, *Documents*, 184–88.

3. George J. Flanigen, *Catholicity in Tennessee* (Nashville, TN: Tennessee Register, 1937), 10–13; Mary de Lourdes Gohmann, *Political Nativism in Tennessee to 1860* (Washington, DC: Catholic U of America, 1938), 34–35; Schauinger, *Badin*, 62.

4. See William W. Sweet, "The Status of the Baptists in America at the Close of the Revolution," *Religion on the American Frontier: The Baptists, 1783–1830*, ed. William W. Sweet (New York: Cooper Square Publishers, 1931), ch. 1.

5. Charles D. Kirk, "The Progress of Baptists and Baptist Principles," *Christian Repository* (Louisville, KY) I (1852): 160–61; John H. Spencer, *A History of Kentucky Baptists* (2 vols.; Cincinnati, 1885), vol. 1, passim; John L. Waller, *Historical Sketch of the Baptist Church* (N. p., n. d.), 108.

6. For the beginnings of the Baptist Church in the West, see Walter B. Posey, *The Baptist Church in the Lower Mississippi Valley, 1776–1845* (Lexington: UP of Kentucky, 1957), 1–7 and passim.

7. James Hall, "A Brief History of the Mississippi Territory," *Publications of the Mississippi Historical Society* 9 (1906): 560.

8. Sweet, ed., *Religion on the American Frontier*, 8.

9. *Minutes of the General Assembly of the Presbyterian Church {1789–1820}* (Philadelphia, ca. 1835), 153.

10. For a fuller discussion of Methodism in the West, see Walter B. Posey, *The Development of Methodism in the Old Southwest, 1783–1824* (Tuscaloosa, AL: Weatherford Printing Co., 1933), passim; William W. Sweet, ed., *Religion on the American Frontier: The Methodists, 1783–1840* (New York: Cooper Square Publishers, 1946), chs. 1–4.

11. Examine Walter B. Posey, "Kentucky, 1790–1815: As Seen by Bishop Francis Asbury," *Filson Club History Quarterly* 31 (1957): 333–48.

George Ella Lyon

George Ella Lyon is a writer and speaker popular in Southern Appalachia. Upon our request she provided the following biographical information:

"I was born and grew up in Harlan, Kentucky, a coal mining town in the mountains. My first occupational goal was to be a neon-sign maker, and I guess I am still trying to make words that glow. I studied creative writing with Ruth Stone at Indiana University, where I did my dissertation on Virginia Woolf. In 1972 I began sending out a manuscript of poetry, and in 1983 my chapbook, *Mountain,* won the Lamont Hall award from Andrew Mountain Press. Since then I have made my living as a freelance writer and teacher, publishing a number of children's picture books (including *Come a Tide* and *Who Came Down That Road?*) and two novels for young readers (*Borrowed Children* and *Red Rover, Red Rover*). I live with my musician-husband and two sons in Lexington, Kentucky."

The Foot Washing

"I wouldn't take the bread and wine
if I didn't wash feet."
Old Regular Baptist

From *Appalachian Journal* 9.4 (Summer 1982), © *Appalachian Journal*/Appalachian State University. Used with permission.

They kneel on the slanting floor
before feet white as roots,
humble as tree stumps.
Men before men
women before women
to soothe the sourness
bound in each other's journeys.
Corns, calluses, bone knobs
all received and rinsed
given back clean
to Sunday shoes and hightops.

This is how they prepare
for the Lord's Supper,
singing and carrying a towel
and a basin of water,
praying while kids put soot
in their socks—almost as good
as nailing someone in the outhouse.

Jesus started it: He washed feet
after Magdalen dried His ankles
with her hair. "If I wash thee not,
thou hast no part with Me."

All servants, they bathe
flesh warped to its balance.
God of the rootwad,
Lord of the bucket in the well.

Howard Dorgan

Howard Dorgan, professor of communication at Appalachian State University, Boone, North Carolina, has authored *Giving Glory to God in Appalachia: Worship Practices of Six Baptist Subdenominations* (1987); *The Old Regular Baptists of Central Appalachia: Brothers and Sisters in Hope* (1989); and *The Airwaves of Zion: Radio and Religion in Appalachia* (1993), all from the University of Tennessee Press. In addition, he has contributed to and served as a coeditor of two collections of original essays on southern rhetoric and public address, *The Oratory of Southern Demagogues* (1981) and *A New Diversity in Contemporary Southern Rhetoric* (1987), both from the Louisiana State University Press. Finally, he has published over thirty short works in academic journals, conference proceedings, or book-length collections of original essays. Dorgan is a past editor of the *Southern Communication Journal* and a former president of the Southern States Communication Association.

Footwashing

Footwashing is regularly practiced by all Primitive, Regular, Old Regular, and Union Baptists throughout the Southern Appalachian region. In addition, most of the Southern Highlands' Free Will Baptists and quite a number of the area's Missionary Baptist fellowships maintain the tradition.

The ceremony always takes place in conjunction with the annual communion, and because the observance is such a special one it is generally well attended—far better, it seems, than the average service. June, July, and August are the favorite months for the joint event; a few churches opt for late spring or early fall dates. Associations—of Old Regular churches especially—make some effort to control the scheduling of these local ceremonies, since church members often travel to the footwashing of other fellowships in the alliance. A mountain church community would not hold its annual communion and footwashing on a late fall or winter date simply because weather conditions might result in very low attendance. Summer months in the Southern Highlands bring very full church calendars, including not only communions and footwashings, but homecomings, memorial or decoration day services, union services (in Old Regular churches), revivals, and a great many baptisms.

The practice of footwashing derives from John's narrative of the closing moments of the Passover supper which Jesus had with his disciples just prior to events leading to his crucifixion (John 13:4–15). John's gospel is the only one of the four that reports this event. The King James version of the narrative goes like this:

> He [Jesus] riseth from supper, and laid aside his garments; and took a towel and girded himself.
>
> After that he poureth water into a basin, and began to wash the disciples' feet, and to wipe them with the towel wherewith he was girded.
>
> Then cometh he to Simon Peter: and Peter saith unto him, Lord dost thou wash my feet?
>
> Jesus answered and saith unto him, What I do thou knowest not now; but thou shalt know hereafter.

From *Giving Glory to God in Appalachia: Worship Practices of Six Baptist Subdenominations,* © 1987 by The University of Tennessee Press. Reprinted by permission of the publisher.

Peter saith unto him, Thou shalt never wash my feet. Jesus answered him, If I wash thee not, thou hast no part with me.

Simon Peter saith unto him, Lord, not my feet only, but also my hands and my head.

Jesus saith to him, He that is washed needeth not save to wash his feet but is clean every whit: and ye are clean, but not all.

For he knew who should betray him; therefore said he, Ye are not all clean.

So after he had washed their feet, and had taken his garments, and was set down again, he said unto them, Know ye what I have done to you?

Ye call me Master and Lord: and ye say well; for so I am.

If I then, your Lord and Master, have washed your feet; ye also ought to wash one another's feet.

For I have given you an example, that ye should do as I have done.

Most Southern Appalachian Baptist churches that practice footwashing consider the service an ordinance and believe that the ceremony must be preserved and that all church members should participate. "We believe that Baptism, The Lord's Supper, and feetwashing," declare the articles of faith of Mountain View Baptist Church, "are ordinances instituted by Jesus Christ, and should be practiced by all true believers."[1] John 13:14 does contain what appears to be a clear admonition, at least to the disciples, to continue the practice. Therefore, as far as these Baptist sects are concerned, since contemporary church members are considered to be current extensions of the original disciples, any argument as to the mandatory nature of this service has been settled.

The footwashing service, however, is one of those practices that constitute the boundary between small, independent "missionary" Baptist churches and more "mainline" Baptist fellowships that end up joining the Southern Baptist Convention. The pattern seems to be that, as a church moves toward becoming a full-fledged member of the local religious establishment, with its minister joining the area ministerial association, the traditional worship practice of footwashing, perhaps along with creek baptism, is dropped.

Note

1. "Articles of Faith," Mountain View (Missionary) Baptist Church, provided by Gaye Golds, film librarian, Belk Library, Appalachian State U, and a member of the Mountain View Fellowship.

George Ella Lyon

See volume 2, chapter 2, for biography.

Salvation

"What does the Lord want with Virgil's heart?
And what is Virgil going to do without one?"

O Lord, spare him the Call.
You're looking for bass
in a pond stocked with catfish.
Pass him by.
You got our best.
You took Mammy and the truck and the second hay.
What do you want with Virgil's heart?

Virgil, he comes in of a night
so wore out he can hardly chew
blacked with dust
that don't come off at the bathhouse.
He washes again
eats onions and beans with the rest of us
then gives the least one a shoulder ride to bed
slow and singing
Down in some lone valley
in some lonesome place
where the wild birds do whistle . . .

After that, he sags like a full feed sack
on a couch alongside the TV
and watches whatever news Your waves are giving.
His soul sifts out
like feed from a slit in that sack
and he's gone—
wore out and give out and plumb used up, Lord.
What do You want with his heart?

From *Appalachian Journal* 9.4 (Summer 1982), © *Appalachian Journal*/Appalachian State University. Used with permission.

Loyal Jones

Born in 1928 on a mountain farm in Western North Carolina, Loyal Jones graduated from Berea College and received his master's degree from the University of North Carolina at Chapel Hill. He is the author of several articles and books on Southern Appalachian culture and is especially noted for his scholarship in the fields of humor, music, and religion. For several years he has been director of the Appalachian Center at Berea College and a major force in Appalachian studies. With Richard Drake, also of Berea College, he was recipient in 1993 of the first Cratis Williams Award given by the Appalachian Studies Conference for outstanding contributions to the study of Appalachia.

Old-Time Baptists and Mainline Christianity

The late Reverend Buell Kazee, a native of Magoffin County, Kentucky, held to a rugged simplicity of faith. He found much in common with the Old Baptists on the problem of sin and the transformation of religion into entertainment, as he makes clear in the following:

> I take the position that we are in the day of the "light stuff": I don't think the *depth* of spiritual life in the churches today is very noticeable. . . . I could have played the banjo in church . . . , but I would have put myself in the position of mixing banjo-playing with . . . church work. Of course, that's what's happening right now. There's Johnny Cash on Billy Graham's program the other night, just whooping it up, you know, and telling all about what "the Lord meant to him" and playing in Las Vegas in the last six months. I just don't see how you can mix it . . . like that.
>
> The "Crusade" has taken people *away* from the church, away from the interest in church life. . . . They're drawing the money from the churches, the church members, to those "big" things. . . . There isn't a man or woman who can appear on Billy Graham's program who hasn't been a great "success" *in the world.* That is to say, his success in the world *qualifies* him to appear on the crusade program. He has to be a headliner in the world. . . . They had a fellow who was the world's champion yo-yo artist on this program in Lexington. . . . Now I've preached fifty-seven years, and my witness, beside his, wouldn't be worth two cents. . . . And this is, as I see it, pure sham, because most of the people who are dedicated to Christ in the real sense wouldn't have any time for any of that other stuff.[1]

From *An Appalachian Symposium,* ed. J. W. Williamson (Boone, NC: Appalachian Consortium Press, 1977), 120–30. Reprinted by permission of the author and publisher.

The Old Baptists and the liberal mainline Christians, then, are at logger-
heads over involvement with the world. The proponents of the social gospel,
as well as other Christians who feel that there is no separation between religion and the world, are critical of the fundamentalist Baptists for keeping
aloof from the world—for being otherworldly. But the Old Baptists are
equally critical of the more modern churches for getting too much involved
in the world, and not being able to see the difference between the world and
the life of the spirit. Had Saint Paul not said, "And be not conformed to this
world; but be ye transformed by the renewing of your mind, that ye may
prove what is that good, and acceptable, and perfect will of God" (Rom.
12:2). Had not Paul also asked how one may be justified under grace, "By
what law? By works?" and had answered, "Nay: but by the law of faith.
Therefore we conclude that a man is justified by faith without the deeds of
the law" (Rom. 3:27, 28).

The Old Baptists are opposed to getting involved in the world not just
because they see it as corrupt, but also because they see that it is easy to be
led away from the basic relationship with God. Neither do they doubt that
many "programs" are "good." Brother Kazee:

> Religion is popular now, it's good business and good entertainment,
> but it's shallow, nothing rugged about the Old Cross now. Well, it's got
> some good things in it and a lot of gospel. But, there's a lot of difference
> between "good" and that which is "from God." Keep that in mind. A
> Christian must never ask "Is it Good?" He must ask "Is it of God?" That's
> where the Christian's life is centered, and he must not become absorbed
> with the goodness of the world as if it were the godliness of the Lord. . . .
>
> But you understand, the Devil's not mean, he's not got a forked tail
> and horns; he's a god, he's a counterfeit god, he's going to be as much
> like God as he can without being God. . . . The Devil's got more religion
> going on than the Lord has, and it's "good" religion, it has humanitari-
> anism in it, it has morality in it, it's got all the marks that we are look-
> ing for as *good* in it. But godliness . . . that's something else. . . . You
> see, good, honest people are deceived by Satan: it isn't the fellow who's
> not honest. He's working on very religious people. . . . That's where he's
> working. But the deception lies in the Devil getting them to believe some-
> thing other than the word of God. You have to be guided by *that word.*[2]

Many of the Old Baptists are nevertheless involved in the world. It's just
that they are not involved *as the church.* They believe, if I may state it again
for emphasis, that the church is not of this world. It is not an institution
that can add new "programs." It is a fellowship of Christians, and it is a
preaching mission. To preserve this concept, they have kept their church
buildings simple; they have taken in and disbursed a minimum of money;
and they have not ensconced their ministers in an "office." As a church they
have tried to keep themselves "unspotted from the world." However, as

Christian individuals and non-church groups, they *have* been involved in the world. One could find numerous examples of community involvement—of comforting the bereaved, feeding the sick, caring for those in trouble, and the like. Some have gone further and done heroic battle in struggles about which their critics have accused them of not being concerned. It was Ollie Combs, a member of the Old Regular Baptist Church, who sat down in front of and stopped the bulldozers trying to strip her land, who was carried off to jail, and who later testified before the Kentucky legislature to bring in the first strong strip-mine regulations in Kentucky. This bill was called the "Widow Combs Bill." Dan Gibson, an Old Regular Baptist elder, stopped the strippers on his stepson's land, and he and Mrs. Combs were important members of the Appalachian Group to Save the Land and People.[3] The Reverend Otis King, a Missionary Baptist preacher from Harlan County, electrified viewers of the NET film, *Appalachia: Rich Land, Poor People*, with his evangelical denunciation of absentee ownership and the rape of Kentucky, and he lectured the state police with equal fervor during the Brookside strike in Harlan County for mistreating the women on the picket lines. Mr. King, who worked in the mines for forty-six years, stated with profound certitude, "I'm three things: I'm a Christian; I'm a Baptist; and I'm a union man." Recently, I heard the Rev. Tom Sutton, of the United Baptist Church at Vest, Kentucky, use the pulpit to announce a meeting of the Knott County Citizens for Social and Economic Justice. The sermon that followed was related strictly to God's kingdom, but that afternoon, in a public school building, Brother Sutton and other Knott Countians discussed ways of fighting an outside group seeking to take over the land of hundreds of Knott Countians on questionable colonial charters they claim to own.

I trust that my point is clear. The Old Baptist may get involved in whatever his conscience leads him to so long as it does not violate the doctrines of the church, but the church, as such, must not become involved in worldly pursuits.

There are ample Biblical passages, especially in Saint Paul's letters, that support the doctrines of these Baptist churches. The scriptures describe the baptism of the Holy Ghost and of the water (Matt. 3:11–17) in a way that is in keeping with Baptist belief. The act of foot washing is also described: "if I then, your Lord and Master, have washed your feet; ye also ought to wash one another's feet" (John 13:14). Saint Paul made it clear that "all have sinned, and come short of the glory of God," whether or not they have been saved and are trying to live right (Rom. 3:23). Indeed, "the scripture hath concluded all under sin, that the promise by faith of Jesus Christ might be given to them that believe" (Gal. 3:22). The devil and his influence in the world are discussed in Eph. 6:11, 12: "Put on the whole armour of God, that ye may be able to stand against the wiles of the devil. For we wrestle not against flesh and blood, but against principalities, against powers, against the rulers of the darkness of this world, against spiritual wickedness in high places." And the much debated point of predestination is dealt with in Ephesians 1: " . . . he hath chosen us in him before the foundation of the world, that we should be holy and without blame before him in love . . . in whom also we have obtained an inheritance, being predestinated according to the purpose of him who worketh all things after the counsel of his own will. . . . " Finally, the Second Coming and the Resurrection are described in 1 Thessalonians 4 and 5:

> For the Lord himself shall descend from heaven with a shout, with the voice of the archangel, and with the trumpet of God: and the dead in Christ shall rise first:
>
> Then we which are alive and remain shall be caught up together with them in the clouds, to meet the Lord in the air: and so shall we ever be with the Lord.

In passing, it seems important to acknowledge that Appalachian social values and mores have been greatly influenced by religion and by the scriptures. The familistic lifestyles, the leveling tendencies, the modesty, the love of tradition, the lack of a taste for confrontation are all part of the belief system. Here are some Bible verses which have influenced beliefs and behavior:

> Therefore, brethren, stand fast, and hold the traditions which ye have been taught, whether by word, or our epistle. (2 Thess. 2:5)

> Let not him that eateth despise him that eateth not; and let not him which eateth not judge him that eateth: for God has received him. (Rom. 14:2)

> For God hath not appointed us to wrath, but to obtain salvation by our Lord Jesus Christ. . . . See that none render evil for evil unto any man; but ever follow that which is good, both among yourselves, and to all men. (1 Thess. 5:9, 15)

I submit that the beliefs of the Old Baptists are out of kilter with modern religious thought, which is centered around missions, programs (within and outside the church), social action, and a belief that the Christian politician, educator, administrator, psychiatrist, T-group leader, etc., can change the world, can improve human nature, can perhaps create heaven here. That these Baptists have faults, as other Christians do, I acknowledge. But it seems to me that there is a quality of faith and of life among them that ought to be understood and appreciated. They operate in abstract and intellectual realms in discussing their faith, contrary to the claim by some that they lack an ability to think in the abstract. They have a clear sense of the spiritual, as opposed to the worldly. They are not led around by fads and styles. They believe in serving one another. In spiritual matters they place trust in no earthly beings but in the scriptures and in the Holy Spirit, and they have a respect for traditions. Perhaps they are too religious to suit our modern tastes.

Notes

1. "Loyal Jones and Buell Kazee," *Katallagete* 5 (Fall 1975): 6.
2. "Loyal Jones and Buell Kazee," 10.
3. Loyal Jones, "Mrs. Combs and the Bulldozers," *Katallagete* (Summer 1966): 18–24.

Robert Morgan

Born in Hendersonville, North Carolina, Robert Morgan graduated from the University of North Carolina at Chapel Hill and earned his M.F.A. in 1968 from the University of North Carolina at Greensboro. His awards and honors include four National Endowment for the Arts Fellowships, a Guggenheim Fellowship, and the 1991 James G. Hanes Poetry Award, presented by the Fellowship of Southern Writers. Morgan has worked as a farmer, a house painter, and a writer. Since 1971, he has taught at Cornell University, where he is currently Kappa Alpha Professor of English. Morgan's works include *Sigodlin* (1990), *Green River: New and Selected Poems* (1991), and *The Mountains Won't Remember Us and Other Stories* (1992)."The main issue of American poetry," Morgan has said, "has always been, What is self? What is America? I like the sense of discovery and spirituality in the risk of attempting definition." "The Hollow" may be considered an example of this effort.

"The main issue of American poetry," Morgan has said, "has always been, What is self? What is America? I like the sense of discovery and spirituality in the risk of attempting definition." "Bricking the Church" may be considered an example of this effort.

Bricking the Church

At the foot of Meetinghouse Hill
where once the white chapel
pointed among junipers and pulled
a wash of gravestones west,

they've buried the wooden snow that
answered sarvis in bloom
and early morning fogs, in brick,
a crust the same dull red

From *Groundwork,* Gnomon Press, 1979. Reprinted by permission of the publisher.

as clay in nearby gullies.
The little churchhouse now looks more
like a post office or school.
It's hard to find

among the brown winter slopes
or plowed fields of spring.
Brick was prestigious back when
they set their minds and savings to it.

They wanted to assert its form
and presence if not in stone
at least in hardened earth, urban weight,
as the white clapboards replaced

unpainted lumber which replaced
the logs of the original
where men brought their guns to preaching
and wolves answered the preacher.
The structure grows successive rings,
and as its doctrine softens
puts on a hard shell
for weathering this world.

Thomas G. Burton

Thomas Burton received his undergraduate degree at David Lipscomb College and his graduate degrees at Vanderbilt University. For many years a professor in the Department of English at East Tennessee State University, he is the author of articles and books on a wide variety of topics on Appalachian folklore and Victorian literature. He has also produced several films on the folklore of Southern Appalachia, including the award-winning film *They Shall Take Up Serpents*. These films form part of the extensive holdings in the Burton-Manning Collection of primary sources of folk material housed in the Archives of Appalachia at East Tennessee State University. He is the prime mover in the development of the Appalachian-Scottish studies, which involves an exchange between scholars and students in the Appalachian region and those at the University of Edinburgh. With Ambrose N. Manning, he was the recipient of the Laurel Leaves Award given annually by the Appalachian Consortium for outstanding service to the region.

Burton's latest book is *Serpent-Handling Believers,* from which the following essay is extracted.

Serpent-Handling Believers

Serpents have been associated with religion in some form since perhaps even prehistoric times. They were significant to the religions of the ancient world of the Fertile Crescent, from Egypt to India, and have continued to be prominent in religious rituals up to and including those in various places of the present age. Moreover, they have served as symbols of a wide spectrum of different aspects of both good and evil.

Serpent handling by Christians in modern times, however, has been evidenced for less than a hundred years, although contemporary adherents trace their belief to the words of Jesus to his disciples immediately prior to the Ascension, as recorded in Mark: "And these signs shall follow them that believe; In my name shall they cast out devils; they shall speak with new tongues; They shall take up serpents; and if they drink any deadly thing, it shall not hurt them; they shall lay hands on the sick, and they shall recover" (16:17–18). Because of the initial words of this text, serpent handlers are often referred to as "sign followers." They consider themselves simply Christians who are following the will of God.

Sign followers believe that at some point they are baptized by the Holy Ghost. They trace this baptism to the description of the Day of Pentecost found in the second book of the Acts of the Apostles, when the followers of Jesus "were all filled with the Holy Ghost, and began to speak with other tongues, as the Spirit gave them utterance" (Acts 2:4) and where "many wonders and signs were done by the apostles" (2:43).

Serpent handlers as a group are considered by church historians to be part of what is referred to as the Pentecostal movement in America. From a historical point of view, this movement may be said to have evolved around the turn of the twentieth century from the closely preceding Holiness movement, which itself was rooted in the much earlier (eighteenth-century) Wesleyan emphasis on experiencing Christian perfection after redemption. During the close of the nineteenth century and the early part of the twentieth, many individuals and groups separated themselves from established religious organizations in order to avoid what they perceived as liberalism, modernism, and worldliness. Initially "signs following" serpent handlers were members of several fundamentalist religious organizations, but later they formed independent Pentecostal holiness churches.

Apparently serpent handling sprang up during the first dozen years of the twentieth century in the South, perhaps in Tennessee, and certainly from this state it was widely disseminated. One might well ask why this ritual

---

From *Serpent-Handling Believers* (Knoxville: University of Tennessee Press, 1993). Reprinted by permission of the author and publisher.

got started in Tennessee, if in fact it did, instead of somewhere else? The necessary elements were certainly present, but what exactly those elements were and whether they were present in other places or not are difficult matters to explain, perhaps ultimately inexplicable. Certainly vital was the presence of a fervent fundamentalist religious community with a traditional approach to biblical interpretation and with traditional values that would evoke and reinforce the practice. Ministers in different areas were most certainly preaching on the key biblical text in some manner over and over as a part of Jesus's final words; and no doubt the situation in many places was as Pastor Henry Swiney describes it up on Newman's Ridge in Tennessee, where serpent handling had long been preached by those who didn't practice it. To sign-following believers, baptism by the Holy Ghost had been manifested by the speaking in tongues—taking up serpents was a phenomenon just waiting to happen.

Once the ritual started, that it spread quickly and widely indicates that the vital elements were present elsewhere, particularly in the Southern Appalachians and other parts of the South. One critical factor obviously necessary was the right person to take up a serpent first and to convince others to do the same. That person in East Tennessee was George Went Hensley.

Hensley may or may not have been the first person in the twentieth century to handle a deadly serpent in obedience to biblical text, but he did lay claim to being the first. George's account of his initial encounter with taking up a poisonous serpent circulates widely. The general outline of the incident is that he went up into White Oak Mountain near Ooltewah, Tennessee, at a spot called Rainbow Rock. There he prayed that a divine sign be given to direct him how he should respond to the verse in Mark relative to serpents. Then indeed before him was a rattlesnake which he picked up without being bitten.

As rewarding as it would be to know exactly where and when George first took up a serpent, as well as the subsequent events, the whole matter remains something of a mystery. A person writing a novel could choose any of several scenarios. As good as any might be the story that George, a relatively young married man of mountain stock who had not remained completely faithful to his strong religious background, hears during the late summer or early fall of 1908 another even younger man speak in strange tongues and preach about miraculous signs which would follow believers, such as taking up serpents without harm. He hears, believes, and answers the altar call. But he goes away puzzled though fascinated by the words of Jesus about handling serpents. He resolves that if it is meant for him to take up serpents, the Lord will somehow direct him. Time passes—perhaps that fall or the next summer or fall—and he goes up into the mountain to pray, still puzzled about the verse in Mark. He feels the power of God upon him, sees a rattlesnake, takes it up, and is not bitten. The Lord has spoken to him. Later he goes to the Grasshopper Church of God several miles down the road, which belongs to the same organization that the inspiring young preacher belonged to. There George testifies of his personal experience and manifests God's revelation to him by handling a serpent. Others believe, and some follow his example. Periodically during the summer months, serpents are handled. Then, in the summer of 1910, he is called to preach. He finds that he has no trouble drawing an audience even in brush arbors when he preaches, "They shall take up serpents." Crowds of hecklers and others come to see him prove his belief. In 1914, news finally gets to the headquarters of the Church of God in Cleveland, Tennessee, and the general overseer of that church—the father of the very same young man whose altar call he had answered only a few years earlier—invites George to come and preach. He goes. His reputation as a snakehandler precedes him. He is again tested by unbelievers and has "victory" over death. Even the overseer's own daughter takes up serpents. Others, who have already been filled with the Holy Ghost and spoken in tongues, see handling serpents as another sign of the Spirit confirming the word and the church. The papers hear about what is going on and have a field day with the story. The believers go forth, the signs following them. And it all started with George Hensley.

When these followers went forth handling serpents, they immediately came into conflict with those, both the rabble and the religious, who did not believe as they did. Later they confronted legal restrictions on the practice of their belief. George Hensley himself was faced with a city ordinance in Bartow, Florida, as early as 1936, forbidding the handling of venomous reptiles. This particular legal action was taken, as was to be the common circumstance, in response to a person's being injured by a serpent bite. In the Florida instance, the transaction was passed the day Alfred Weaver died after being bitten the previous evening in a revival service of a Pentecostal church. It was not many years after the Bartow ordinance that a number of southern states began to legislate against the practice. Kentucky was first in 1940; Georgia, Virginia, Tennessee, North Carolina, and Alabama were to follow. (Similar legislation failed to pass in West Virginia.) Individuals subsequently were arrested, tried, and convicted under these codes. The argument of the courts ran along this line:

A. Religious belief is guaranteed absolutely, but religious conduct can be prohibited constitutionally upon certain principles, e.g., maintaining a viable citizenry by protecting it from grave and imminent dangers.

B. The practice is inherently dangerous to the participants, and their precautions to avoid danger to others are inadequate.

C. The prohibition of religious serpent handling, therefore, is constitutional.

This argument at first seems conclusive, but in the context of contemporary constitutional interpretation it is necessary to show more than a rational relationship between the restrictions placed on religious conduct and the State's interest in those restrictions. The State's right to maintain a viable citizenry is not unconditional and must be viewed in respect to the individual's right in concrete circumstances where the balance can be evaluated. Also, interference with religious activity may be made only when the danger to the public interest is paramount, and the methods selected to restrict a religious activity may not be more than are necessary. Every possible leeway must be given to freedom of religious conduct.

The legal situation for serpent handlers, however, remains a classic conflict between church and state, even though some states (Georgia and Alabama) have rescinded their codes, and few prosecutions are executed.

Signs-following serpent handlers should not be viewed as simply people who go to church to pick up snakes. They are believers—believers in God, in God's power, in God's word the Bible, in God's direction through the Holy Ghost. Many of them have great faith, and they will often quote: "Now faith is the substance of things hoped for, the evidence of things not seen" (Heb. 11:1); but their faith in large part is based not on "things hoped for" and "not seen," but on personal experience. They believe in speaking in tongues, casting out demons, handling serpents, drinking deadly things, healing the sick because "it's Bible" and because they've "witnessed" these signs.

Contemporary serpent handlers explain that they are believers and that the signs follow them exactly as Jesus promised. The purpose, they say, is the same as for the disciples of the first century, that is, "confirming the word" (Mark 16:20) preached to unbelievers. Their experience in the signs, however, goes beyond the confirmation of the gospel to unbelievers; it confirms their own belief that the power of God is available to them. Furthermore, that power is unlimited; but it takes repentance, remission of sins, and a godly life for them to receive it fully. As serpent handler Perry Bettis forcefully expressed in one of his sermons:

> Jesus Christ come, brother, and he granted them a mission to go out.
> He sent them out, brother, two by two. And he give them power, hallelu,
> to cleanse the leprosy and raise the dead and give sight to the blind,
> heal the lame, heal every kind of disease there was. Jesus give them the
> power to do it. Why, there ain't no power like God's power.
>
> Have you got the Holy Ghost? Huh? Yeah. You got the greatest power
> in you that's in the whole world. Right inside that body is the greatest
> power that's ever been known to man and ever will be known to man,
> is God Himself. You that's got the Holy Ghost has got it in you. It's
> your fault for not usin' it. It's not God's fault. God give it to you to use,
> and if you don't want to get in shape to use it—hey listen, hold it, hold,
> let me tell your mind, listen to me. God give me the gift of ministry,
> the preachin' the word. I can't read, I know that; but, wait, when God
> moves on me, I can preach. God give me that gift. It's in me. I'll preach
> on the street corner, I'll preach on top of this building, I'll preach any-
> where that God—hallelujah, I'll preach it right in the Devil's face. I
> don't care. But God expects me, me, me, myself, to live the life to be
> proud of there to do that job.
>
> God expects you, brother, and you, sister, to live their life to where

God can work through ye. Why, God's not goin' to work through that den of Babylon. They is things that we do that God absolutely hates—six and sixteen, brother, Proverbs.

Tonight, children, we need to learn how to worship God worser than anything in the world. We learn how to repent a little bit, but some of us ain't learned how to fully repent. Repentance is to quit doin' anything and not go back to it. Change your walk of life, change your way of thinkin', change your way of talkin', change everything in you—Jesus can make a new creature in God out of you.

Serpent handlers believe, and that belief is a powerful force, both to them and to those who witness it. And there is much light associated with them: conviction, courage, affirmation, purpose, forthrightness, regeneration, humility, generosity, hope, joy, inner peace, love—"truth," as Faulkner says, "all things which touch the heart." There is also darkness: extremism, naiveté, illiberality, simplism, and foolhardiness.

The same ambivalence surrounds the practice. By biblical scholars it is almost universally repudiated. It endangers people, the mature as well as the impressionable. And even though it does not pose significantly a "grave and imminent danger" to society, it produces widows, orphans, and grieving relatives. On the other hand, for some individuals, taking up serpents provides meaning and insight into reality. It is an ultimate commitment that reinforces belief and shapes lives in a way that many other religious expressions do not. To serpent-handling believers, the ritual is an act of obedience to that which gives quality to living, and it is worth dying for. To the analyst, serpent handling provides insights into the efficacy of belief and perhaps even into the operative relationship between neurological and physiological responses.

Although handling serpents is strange from the viewpoint of mainstream Christianity, the practice from a traditional perspective is comprehensible: if you take people with their values and place them in their particular religious tradition, then even though you may reject the specific doctrine, you can understand why they believe it. That does not mean you understand everything else that may be involved: why these people turn ultimately to God; how religion or religious practice functions in their social circumstances; why they have particular psychological responses, religious or otherwise; or how their religious and cultural traditions have evolved. But if you are aware of their traditions personally or vicariously, you can understand their taking up serpents.

Serpent handling then is not simply a socially dangerous deviant civic practice of a relatively small group of people that should be ignored, pejoratively tolerated, viewed as spectacle, or legally terminated. It is a complex traditional religious belief of a group of American Christians that should be approached respectfully and sensitively—avoiding what Nathaniel Hawthorne saw as the unforgivable sin, the violation of "the sanctity of a human heart."

Lou Crabtree

Nationally recognized poet, playwright, and short story writer, Lou Crabtree was educated at Radford University, the University of Virginia, the American Academy of Dramatic Arts, and the Foreign School of Dramatic Arts. Known for her mystic writings, she has been adopted by the Cherokee Indians. Her book *Sweet Hollow* (1984) is in its fifth printing. From her home in Abingdon, Virginia, she is in high demand as a speaker, performer, and instructor in poetry workshops.

salvation

jesus jesus jesus i got something
    this old body aint so important
in this old body i feel holiness
    i got jesus flirtin with death

ever day in the coal mines flirtin with death
my daddy flirted and my brothers flirted
    and my uncles and cousins
and my daddy got his back broken
    flirtin with death

brother flirtin with death motor cycles, race cars
    not my way flirting with death
sister flirted i danced around her coffin
high in my hand same snake caused her death
laid her three weeks baby in her dead arms
sister got holiness flirtin with death

i feel holiness jesus i got something
washing feet laying on hands dancing the fire dance
    glory glory glory
prayin for the sign the wounded blood of jesus
    on the feet on the hands on the head
praying three years for the jesus sign
    glory hallelujah

in the church house old snake washed clean
i put him to my shoulders flirtin with death

Printed by permission of the author.

i touch him to my lips flirtin with death
flirtin with death i raise him to my breast
old velvet lips with his singing tail and lightning breath
i offer old velvet lips my snowy white breast

jesus jesus this old body aint so important
   i got holiness flirtin with death

Jim Wayne Miller

Jim Wayne Miller is a poet, essayist, professor of German, and student of the history and literature of his native Appalachian South. Born in Western North Carolina, he studied at Berea College and at Vanderbilt University, and has lived in Bowling Green, Kentucky, since 1963. He is a member of Western Kentucky University's Department of Modern Languages and Intercultural Studies. His books include *Dialogue with a Dead Man* (1974); *The Mountains Have Come Closer* (1980); *Vein of Words* (1984); *Nostalgia for 70* (1986); and *His First, Best Country* (1993). He has edited an anthology of Appalachian literature for secondary schools (*I Have a Place*, 1981), as well as Jesse Stuart's *Songs of a Mountain Plowman* (1986) and James Still's collected poems, *The Wolfpen Poems* (1986). Miller is a celebrated teacher of writing as well as a lecturer and workshop leader.

Brier Sermon—"You Must Be Born Again"

One Friday night the Brier felt called to preach. So Saturday morning, early, he appeared on a street corner in town and started preaching, walking up and down the sidewalk in front of a hardware and sporting goods store, back and forth in front of the shotguns and spin casting rods and Coleman camp stoves in the window, and looking across the street to the Greenstamp Redemption Store, where all the women brought their trading stamps. Cars and trucks were passing on the street, women were going in and out of the Redemption Store; and a few men and boys were standing around, in groups of three or four. The Brier knew they were listening even though they were not looking at him. He took as his text, "You Must Be Born Again," and started drawing the people closer, saying:

From *The Mountains Have Come Closer*, Appalachian Consortium Press, 1980. Reprinted by permission of the author and publisher.

You may say, Preacher, where is your black Bible?
Why ain't you preachin down sin?
You may say, Preacher, why ain't you talkin about hell?
What about lipstick and short dresses?
What about cigarettes and whiskey?
What about dope and long hair?

Well, I didn't bring my Bible for a purpose.
Because this morning I wanted to say to you
I've been through all the books and come out yonside.
I'm educated, but not like the Brown boys.
Let me tell you about the Brown boys.

Feller over close to where I live
wanted some little cedar trees dug up
and planted in a row beside his house.
Tried to hire the Johnson boys, his neighbors,
but they were too scared to do it, didn't believe
in digging up cedar trees; they'd always heard
you'd die whenever the trees got tall enough
for their shadow to cover your grave. Get somebody else,
they said. Get old Jim Brown and Tom Brown.
They're educated, don't believe in nothin.

Well, I'm educated, but not like the Brown boys.
There's something I believe in:
You must be born again.

*When he told about the Brown boys, the Brier heard some of the men laugh and say
things to one another. Across the street at the Redemption Store a woman had come out
and stopped, holding a little boy by the hand. The Brier figured the woman and the
little boy would like a story, too.*

You hear preachers talk about being lost.
What does it mean? What's it got to do
with being born again?—Feller I know,
he didn't go to church, but a church bus
always ran right by his house, and his boy,
about five or six years old, wanted to ride it.
So he let him go. Little boy got over there
in church and they were having a revival. Preacher
knelt down by the little boy, said, Son, are you lost?
Little boy said, Yes, for the bus had gone up several
creeks and hollers, picking up other people,

and carried the little boy so far from home
he didn't know where he was.

We're not so different from that little boy.
We can be lost, sitting right in the churchhouse.
Because we've been carried a long way around,
we've got so far away from home, we don't know where
we are, how we got where we are, how to get home again.
I know I wasn't so different from that little boy.

In my father's house, Jesus said.

Our foreparents left us a home here in the mountains.
But we try to live in somebody else's house.
We're ashamed to live in our father's house.
We think it's too old-fashioned.
Our foreparents left us a very fine inheritance,
but we don't believe it.
I just want to set you down, gather you together,
and read you the will!
You've wanted to run off and leave it, this inheritance.
You didn't want to see it,
ashamed to hear about it,
thought it wasn't pretty because it wasn't factory-made.
You put it back in the attic,
you've thrown it off in a corner of the barn,
thrown it down into a ditch.

In my father's house.

The house our foreparents left had a song, had a story.
We didn't care.
We said:
them old love songs
them old ballets
them old stories and like foolishness.

We were too busy anyway
giving our timber away
giving our coal away
to worry about love songs
to worry about ballets
to worry about old stories
and like foolishness.

But I know a man
he had a song from his foreparents.
It got carried off to New York City
and when he heard it played on tv one night
by three fellers who clowned and hip-swinged
he said he began to feel sick,
like he'd lost a loved one.
Tears came in his eyes
and he went out on the ridge and bawled
and said, "Lord, couldn't they leave me the good memories?"
Now that man wasn't lost
but he knew what he had lost.

You've done your best to disremember
what all you've lost.
You've spoiled the life that's yours
by right of inheritance.
You have to go around to the back door
of the life that belongs to somebody else.
You're neither here nor there.
You're out in the cold, buddy.

But you don't have to live in the past.
You can't, even if you try.
You don't have to talk old-fashioned,
dress old-fashioned.
You don't have to live the way your foreparents lived.
But if you don't know about them
if you don't love them
if you don't respect them
you're not going anywhere.
You don't have to think ridge-to-ridge,
the way they did.
You can think ocean-to-ocean.

You say, I'm not going to live in the past.
And all the time the past is living in you.
If you're lost, I say it's because
you're not living in your father's house.
It's the only house you've got
the only shelter you've got.
It may be just a mountain cabin,
but it's shelter and it's yours.

I left my father's house. Oh, I was moving.
But I noticed I wasn't getting anywhere.
I was living in somebody else's house.
I kept stepping out somebody else's door
and the roads I traveled kept winding, twisting,
had no beginning, had no end.

My own house, heired to me by my foreparents,
was right there all the time
yours is too
but I wasn't living in it. Well, I went home.
And when I stepped out of my own front door
when I knew where I was starting from
I knew then where I was going.
The only road I could go was the road
that started from my own front door.
—In my father's house, that's what the Bible says.

And it speaks of the sins of the fathers
sins of the fathers visited on the children
unto the fourth generation
says the sins of the fathers
will set the children's teeth on edge.
You were probably wondering why
I wasn't talking about sin. Well, I am.
But I say, Forget the sins of the fathers.
What about the sins of the sons and daughters?
We've got enough sins of our own to think about.
We're able to set our own teeth on edge.
Ours is the sin of forgetfulness
forgetfulness of the fathers
forgetfulness of a part of ourselves
makes us less than we ought to be
less than we could be.
Forgetfulness of the fathers makes us a people
who hardly cast a shadow against the ground.

You've heard it said you can't put new wine in old bottles.
Well, I don't know.
But don't be too sure you're new wine.
Maybe we're all old wine in new bottles.

Lee Smith

Born in Grundy, Virginia, Lee Smith received her B.A. at Hollins College. She is one of the most prolific and highly praised authors of the South. Noted for her humor and graphic description of character and place, Smith earns comparison with such southern writers as Flannery O'Connor and Eudora Welty. Her short stories have won a number of honors, including O. Henry awards, one of them for the story "Between the Lines." Her several novels include *Black Mountain Breakdown* (1982), *Oral History* (1983), *Family Linen* (1985), *Fair and Tender Ladies* (1988), and *The Devil's Dream* (1992).

Between the Lines

"Peace be with you from Mrs. Joline B. Newhouse" is how I sign my columns. Now I gave some thought to that. In the first place, I like a line that has a ring to it. In the second place, what I have always tried to do with my column is to uplift my readers if at all possible, which sometimes it is not. After careful thought, I threw out "Yours in Christ." I am a religious person and all my readers know it. If I put "Yours in Christ," it seems to me that they will think I am theirs because I am in Christ, or even that they and I are in Christ *together,* which is not always the case. I am in Christ but I know for a fact that a lot of them are not. There's no use acting like they are, but there's no use rubbing their faces in it, either. "Peace be with you," as I see it, is sufficiently religious without laying all the cards right out on the table in plain view. I like to keep an ace or two up my sleeve. I like to write between the lines.

This is what I call my column, in fact: "Between the Lines, by Mrs. Joline B. Newhouse." Nobody knows why. Many people have come right out and asked me, including my best friend, Sally Peck, and my husband, Glenn. "Come on, now, Joline," they say. "What's this 'Between the Lines' all about? What this 'Between the Lines' supposed to mean?" But I just smile a sweet mysterious smile and change the subject. I know what I know.

And my column means everything to folks around here. Salt Lick community is where we live, unincorporated. I guess there is not much that you would notice, passing through—the Post Office (real little), the American oil station, my husband Glenn's Cash 'N Carry Beverage Store. He sells more than beverages in there, though, believe me. He sells everything you can think of, from thermometers and rubbing alcohol to nails to frozen pizza. Anything else you want, you have to go out of the holler and get on the interstate and go to Greenville to get it. That's where my column appears, in the *Greenville Herald,* fortnightly. Now there's a word with a ring to it: fortnightly.

There are seventeen families here in Salt Lick—twenty, if you count those three down by the Five Mile Bridge. I put what they do in the paper. Anybody gets married, I write it. That goes for born, divorced, dies, celebrates a golden wedding anniversary, has a baby shower, visits relatives in Ohio, you name it. But these mere facts are not what's most important, to my mind.

I write, for instance: "Mrs. Alma Goodnight is enjoying a pleasant recuperation period in the lovely, modern Walker Mountain Community Hospital while she is sorely missed by her loved ones at home. Get well soon, Alma!" I do not write that Alma Goodnight is in the hospital because her husband hit her up the side with a rake and left a straight line of bloody little holes going from her waist to her armpit after she yelled at him, which Lord knows she did all the time, once too often. I don't write about how Eben Goodnight is all torn up now about what he did, missing work and worrying, or how Alma liked it so much in the hospital that nobody knows if they'll ever get her to go home or not. Because that is a *mystery*, and I am no detective by a long shot. I am what I am, I know what I know, and I know you've got to give folks something to hang on to, something to keep them going. That is what I have in mind when I say *uplift*, and that is what God had in mind when he gave us Jesus Christ.

My column would not be but a paragraph if the news was all I told. But it isn't. What I tell is what's important, like the bulbs coming up, the way the redbud comes out first on the hills in the spring and how pretty it looks, the way the cattails shoot up by the creek, how the mist winds down low on the ridge in the mornings, how my wash all hung out on the line of a Tuesday looks like a regular square dance with those pants legs just flapping and flapping in the wind! I tell how all the things you ever dreamed of, all changed and ghostly, will come crowding into your head on a winter night when you sit up late in front of your fire. I even made up these little characters to talk for me, Mr. and Mrs. Cardinal and Princess Pussycat, and often I have them voice my thoughts. Each week I give a little chapter in their lives. Or I might tell what was the message brought in church, or relate an inspirational word from a magazine, book, or TV. I look on the bright side of life.

I've had God's gift of writing from the time I was a child. That's what the B. stands for in Mrs. Joline B. Newhouse—Barker, my maiden name. My father was a patient strong God-fearing man despite his problems and it is in his honor that I maintain the B. There was a lot of us children around all the time—it was right up the road here where I grew up—and it would take me a day to tell you what all we got into! But after I learned how to write, that was that. My fingers just naturally curved to a pencil and I sat down to writing like a ball of fire. They skipped me up one, two grades in school. When I was not but eight, I wrote a poem named "God's Garden," which was published in the church bulletin of the little Methodist Church we went to then on Hunter's Ridge. Oh, Daddy was so proud! He gave me a quarter that Sunday, and then I turned around and gave it straight to God. Put it in the collection plate. Daddy almost cried he was so proud. I wrote another poem in school the next year, telling how life is like a maple tree, and it won a statewide prize.

That's me—I grew up smart as a whip, lively, and naturally good. Jesus came as easy as breathing did to me. Don't think I'm putting on airs, though: I'm not. I know what I know. I've done my share of sinning, too, of which more later.

Anyway, I was smart. It's no telling but what I might have gone on to school like my own children have and who knows what all else if Mama hadn't run off with a man. I don't remember Mama very well, to tell the truth. She was a weak woman, always laying in the bed having a headache. One day we all came home from school and she was gone, didn't even bother to make up the bed. Well, that was the end of Mama! None of us ever saw her again, but Daddy told us right before he died that one time he had gotten a postcard from her from Atlanta, Georgia, years and years after that. He showed it to us, all wrinkled and soft from him holding it.

Being the oldest, I took over and raised those little ones, three of them, and then I taught school and then I married Glenn and we had our own children, four of them, and I have raised them too and still have Marshall, of course, poor thing. He is the cross I have to bear, and he'll be just like he is now for the rest of his natural life.

I was writing my column for the week of March 17, 1976, when the following events occurred. It was a real coincidence because I had just finished doing the cutest little story named "A Red-Letter Day for Mr. and Mrs. Cardinal" when the phone rang. It rings all the time, of course. Everybody around here knows my number by heart. It was Mrs. Irene Chalmers. She was all torn up. She said that Mr. Biggers was over at Greenville at the hospital very bad off this time, and that he was asking for me and would I please try to get over there today as the doctors were not giving him but a 20 percent chance to make it through the night. Mr. Biggers has always been a fan of mine, and he especially liked Mr. and Mrs. Cardinal. "Well!" I said. "Of course I will! I'll get Glenn on the phone right this minute. And you calm down, Mrs. Chalmers. You go fix yourself a Coke." Mrs. Chalmers said she would, and hung up. I knew what was bothering her, of course. It was that, given the natural run of things, she would be the next to go. The next one to be over there dying. Without even putting down the receiver, I dialed the beverage store. Bert answered.

"Good morning," I said. I like to maintain a certain distance with the hired help although Glenn does not. He will talk to anybody, and any time you go in there, you can find half the old men in the county just sitting around that stove in the winter or outside on those wooden drink boxes in the summer, smoking and drinking drinks which I am sure they are getting free out of the cooler although Glenn swears it on the Bible they are not. Anyway, I said good morning.

"Can I speak to Glenn?" I said.

"Well now, Mrs. Newhouse," Bert said in his naturally insolent voice— he is just out of high school and too big for his britches—"he's not here right now. He had to go out for a while."

"Where did he go?" I asked.

"Well, I don't rightly know," Bert said. "He said he'd be back after lunch."

"Thank you very much, there will not be a message," I said sweetly, and hung up. I *knew* where Glenn was. Glenn was over on Caney Creek where his adopted half-sister Margie Kettles lived, having carnal knowledge of her in the trailer. They had been at it for thirty years and anybody would have thought they'd have worn it out by that time. Oh, I knew all about it.

The way it happened in the beginning was that Glenn's father had died of his lungs when Glenn was not but about ten years old, and his mother grieved so hard that she went off her head and began taking up with anybody who would go with her. One of the fellows she took up with was a foreign man out of a carnival, the James H. Drew Exposition, a man named Emilio something. He had this curly-headed dark-skinned little daughter. So Emilio stayed around longer than anybody would have expected, but finally it was clear to all that he never would find any work around here to suit him. The work around here is hard work, all of it, and they say he played a musical instrument. Anyway, in due course this Emilio just up and vanished, leaving that foreign child. Now that was Margie, of course, but her name wasn't Margie then. It was a long foreign name, which ended up as Margie, and that's how Margie ended up here, in these mountains, where she has been up to no good ever since. Glenn's mother did not last too long after Emilio left, and those children grew up wild. Most of them went to foster homes, and to this day Glenn does not know where two of his brothers are! The military was what finally saved Glenn. He stayed with the military for nine years, and when he came back to this area he found me over here teaching school and with something of a nest egg in hand, enabling him to start the beverage store. Glenn says he owes everything to me.

This is true. But I can tell you something else. Glenn is a good man, and he has been a good provider all these years. He has not ever spoken to me above a regular tone of voice nor raised his hand in anger. He has not been tight with the money. He used to hold the girls in his lap of an evening. Since I got him started, he has been a regular member of the church, and he has not fallen down on it yet. Glenn furthermore has that kind of disposition where he never knows a stranger. So I can count my blessings, too.

Of course I knew about Margie! Glenn's sister Lou-Ann told me about it before she died, that is how I found out about it originally. She thought I *should* know, she said. She said it went on for years, and she just wanted me to know before she died. Well! I had had the first two girls by then, and I thought I was so happy. I took to my bed and just cried and cried. I cried for four days and then by gum I got up and started my column, and I have been writing on it ever since. So I was not unprepared when Margie showed up again some years after that, all gap-toothed and wild-looking, but then before you knew it she was gone, off again to Knoxville, then back working as a waitress at that truck stop at the county line, then off again, like that. She led an irregular life. And as for Glenn, I will have to hand it to him, he never darkened her door again until after the birth of Marshall.

Now let me add that I would not have gone on and had Marshall if it was left up to me. I would have practiced more birth control. Because I was old by that time, thirty-seven, and that was too old for more children, I felt, even though I had started late of course. I had told Glenn many times, I said three normal girls is enough for anybody. But no, Glenn was like a lot of men, and I don't blame him for it—he just had to try one more time for a boy. So we went on with it, and I must say I had a feeling all along.

I was not a bit surprised at what we got, although after wrestling with it all for many hours in the dark night of the soul, as they say, I do not believe that Marshall is a judgment on me for my sin. I don't believe that. He is one of God's special children, is how I look at it. Of course he looks funny, but he has already lived ten years longer than they said he would. And has a job! He goes to Greenville every day on the Trailways bus, rain or shine, and cleans up the Plaza Mall. He gets to ride on the bus, and he gets to see people. Along about six o'clock he'll come back, walking up the holler and not looking to one side or the other, and then I give him his supper and then he'll watch something on TV like "The Brady Bunch" or "Family Affair," and then he'll go to bed. He would not hurt a flea. But oh, Glenn took it hard when Marshall came! I remember that night so well and the way he just turned his back on the doctor. This is what sent him back to Margie, I am convinced of it, what made him take up right where he had left off all those years before.

So since Glenn was up to his old tricks I called up Lavonne, my daughter, to see if she could take me to the hospital to see Mr. Biggers. Why yes she could, it turned out. As a matter of fact she was going to Greenville herself. As a matter of fact she had something she wanted to talk to me about anyway. Now Lavonne is our youngest girl and the only one that stayed around here. Lavonne is somewhat pop-eyed, and has a weak constitution. She is one of those people that never can make up their minds. That day on the phone, I heard a whine in her voice I didn't like the sound of. Something is up, I thought.

First I powdered my face, so I would be ready to go when Lavonne got there. Then I sat back down to write some more on my column, this paragraph I had been framing in my mind for weeks about how sweet potatoes are not what they used to be. They taste gritty and dry now, compared to how they were. I don't know the cause of it, whether it is man on the moon or pollution in the ecology or what, but it is true. They taste awful.

Then my door came bursting open in a way that Lavonne would never do it and I knew it was Sally Peck from next door. Sally is loud and excitable but she has a good heart. She would do anything for you. "Hold on to your hat, Joline!" she hollered. Sally is so loud because she's deaf. Sally was just huffing and puffing—she is a heavy woman—and she had rollers still up in her hair and her old housecoat on with the buttons off.

"Why, Sally!" I exclaimed. "You are all wrought up!"

Sally sat down in my rocker and spread out her legs and started fanning herself with my *Family Circle* magazine. "If you think I'm wrought up," she said finally, "it is nothing compared to what you are going to be. We have had us a suicide, right here in Salt Lick. Margie Kettles put her head inside her gas oven in the night."

"Margie?" I said. My heart was just pumping.

"Yes, and a little neighbor girl was the one who found her, they say. She went over to borrow some baking soda for her mama's biscuits at seven o'clock A.M." Sally looked real hard at me. "Now wasn't she related to you all?"

"Why," I said just as easily, "why yes, she was Glenn's adopted half-sister of course when they were nothing but a child. But we haven't had anything to do with her for years as you can well imagine."

"Well, they say Glenn is making the burial arrangements," Sally spoke up. She was getting her own back that day, I'll admit it. Usually I'm the one with all the news.

"I have to finish my column now and then Lavonne is taking me to Greenville to see old Mr. Biggers who is breathing his last," I said.

"Well," Sally said, hauling herself out of my chair, "I'll be going along then. I just didn't know if you knew it or not." Now Sally Peck is not a spiteful woman in all truth. I have known her since we were little girls sitting out in the yard looking at a magazine together. It is hard to imagine being as old as I am now, or knowing Sally Peck—who was Sally Bland then—so long.

Of course I couldn't get my mind back on sweet potatoes after she left. I just sat still and fiddled with the pigeonholes in my desk and the whole kitchen seemed like it was moving and rocking back and forth around me. Margie dead! Sooner or later I would have to write it up tastefully in my column. Well, I must say I had never thought of Margie dying. Before God, I never hoped for that in all my life. I didn't know what it would to do *me*, in fact, to me and Glenn and Marshall and the way we live because you know how the habits and the ways of people can build up over the years. It was too much for me to take in at one time. I couldn't see how anybody committing suicide could choose to stick their head in the oven anyway—you can imagine the position you would be found in.

Well, in came Lavonne at that point, sort of hanging back and stuttering like she always does, and that child of hers Bethy Rose hanging on to her skirt for dear life. I saw no reason at that time to tell Lavonne about the death of Margie Kettles. She would hear it sooner or later, anyway. Instead, I gave her some plant food that I had ordered two for the price of one from Montgomery Ward some days before.

"Are you all ready, Mama?" Lavonne asked in that quavery way she has, and I said indeed I was, as soon as I got my hat, which I did, and we went out and got in Lavonne's Buick Electra and set off on our trip. Bethy Rose sat in the back, coloring in her coloring book. She is a real good child. "How's Ron?" I said. Ron is Lavonne's husband, an electrician, as up and coming a boy as you would want to see. Glenn and I are as proud as punch of Ron, and actually I never have gotten over the shock of Lavonne marrying him in the first place. All through high school she never showed any signs of marrying anybody, and you could have knocked me over with a feather the day she told us she was secretly engaged. I'll tell you, our Lavonne was not the marrying sort! Or so I thought.

But that day in the car she told me, "Mama, I wanted to talk to you and tell you I am thinking of getting a d-i-v-o-r-c-e."

I shot a quick look into the back seat but Bethy Rose wasn't hearing a thing. She was coloring Wonder Woman in her book.

"Now, Lavonne," I said. "What in the world is it? Why, I'll bet you can work it out." Part of me was listening to Lavonne, as you can imagine, but part of me was still stuck in that oven with crazy Margie. I was not myself.

I told her that. "Lavonne," I said, "I am not myself today. But I'll tell you one thing. You give this some careful thought. You don't want to go off half-cocked. What is the problem, anyway?"

"It's a man where I work," Lavonne said. She works in the Welfare Department, part-time, typing. "He is just giving me a fit. I guess you can pray for me, Mama, because I don't know what I'll decide to do."

"Can we get an Icee?" asked Bethy Rose.

"Has anything happened between you?" I asked. You have to get all the facts.

"Why no!" Lavonne was shocked. "Why, I wouldn't do anything like that! Mama, for goodness' sakes! We just have coffee together so far."

That's Lavonne all over. She never has been very bright. "Honey," I said, "I would think twice before I threw up a perfectly good marriage and a new brick home for the sake of a cup of coffee. If you don't have enough to keep you busy, go take a course at the community college. Make yourself a new pantsuit. This is just a mood, believe me."

"Well," Lavonne said. Her voice was shaking and her eyes were swimming in tears that just stayed there and never rolled down her cheeks. "Well," she said again.

As for me, I was lost in thought. It was when I was a young married woman like Lavonne that I committed my own great sin. I had the girls, and things were fine with Glenn and all, and there was simply not any reason to ascribe to it. It was just something I did out of loving pure and simple, did because I wanted to do it. I knew and have always known the consequences, yet God is full of grace, I pray and believe, and his mercy is everlasting.

To make a long story short, we had a visiting evangelist from Louisville, Kentucky, for a two-week revival that year. John Marcel Wilkes. If I say it myself, John Marcel Wilkes was a real humdinger! He had the yellowest hair you ever saw, curly, and the finest singing voice available. Oh, he was something, and that very first night he brought two souls into Christ. The next day I went over to the church with a pan of brownies just to tell him how much I personally had received from his message. I thought, of course, that there would be other people around—the Reverend Mr. Clark, or the youth director, or somebody cleaning. But to my surprise that church was totally empty except for John Marcel Wilkes himself reading the Bible in the fellowship hall and making notes on a pad of paper. The sun came in a window on his head. It was early June, I remember, and I had on a blue dress with little white cap sleeves and open-toed sandals. John Marcel Wilkes looked up at me and his face gave off light like the sun.

"Why, Mrs. Newhouse," he said. "What an unexpected pleasure!" His voice echoed out in the empty fellowship hall. He had the most beautiful voice, too—strong and deep, like it had bells in it. Everything he said had a ring to it.

He stood up and came around the table to where I was. I put the brownies down on the table and stood there. We both just stood there, real close without touching each other, for the longest time, looking into each other's eyes. Then he took my hands and brought them up to his mouth and kissed them, which nobody ever did to me before or since, and then he kissed me on the mouth. I thought I would die. After some time of that, we went together out into the hot June day where the bees were all buzzing around the flowers there by the back gate and I couldn't think straight. "Come," said John Marcel Wilkes. We went out in the woods behind the church to the prettiest place, and when it was all over I could look up across his curly yellow head and over the trees and see the white church steeple stuck up against that blue, blue sky like it was pasted there. This was not all. Two more times we went out there during that revival. John Marcel Wilkes left after that and I have never heard a word of him since. I do not know where he is, or what has become of him in all these years. I do know that I never bake a pan of brownies, or hear the church bells ring, but what I think of him. So I have to pity Lavonne and her cup of coffee if you see what I mean, just like I have to spend the rest of my life to live my sinning down. But I'll tell you this: if I had it all to do over, I would do it all over again, and I would not trade it in for anything.

Lavonne drove off to look at fabric and get Bethy Rose an Icee, and I went in the hospital. I hate the way they smell. As soon as I entered Mr. Biggers' room, I could see he was breathing his last. He was so tiny in the bed you almost missed him, a poor little shriveled-up thing. His family sat all around.

"Aren't you sweet to come?" they said. "Looky here, honey, it's Mrs. Newhouse."

He didn't move a muscle, all hooked up to tubes. You could hear him breathing all over the room.

"It's Mrs. Newhouse," they said, louder. "Mrs. Newhouse is here. Last night he was asking for everybody," they said to me. "Now he won't open his eyes. You are real sweet to come," they said. "You certainly did brighten his days." Now I knew this was true because the family had remarked on it before.

"I'm so glad," I said. Then some more people came in the door and everybody was talking at once, and while they were doing that, I went over to the bed and got right up by his ear.

"Mr. Biggers!" I said. "Mr. Biggers, it's Joline Newhouse here."

He opened up one little old bleary eye.

"Mr. Biggers!" I said right into his ear. "Mr. Biggers, you know those cardinals in my column? Mr. and Mrs. Cardinal? Well, I made them up! I made them up, Mr. Biggers. They never were real at all." Mr. Biggers closed his eye and a nurse came in and I stood up.

"Thank you so much for coming, Mrs. Newhouse," his daughter said.

"He is one fine old gentleman," I told them all, and then I left.

Outside in the hall, I had to lean against the tile wall for support while I waited for the elevator to come. Imagine, me saying such a thing to a dying man! I was not myself that day.

Lavonne took me to the big Kroger's in north Greenville and we did our shopping, and on the way back in the car she told me she had been giving everything a lot of thought and she guessed I was right after all.

"You're not going to tell anybody, are you?" she asked me anxiously, popping her eyes. "You're not going to tell Daddy, are you?" she said.

"Why, Lord, no honey!" I told her. "It's the farthest thing from my mind."

Sitting in the back seat among all the grocery bags, Bethy Rose sang a little song she had learned at school. "Make new friends but keep the old, some are silver but the other gold," she sang.

"I don't know what I was thinking of," Lavonne said.

Glenn was not home yet when I got there—making his arrangements, I supposed. I took off my hat, made myself a cup of Sanka, and sat down and finished off my column on a high inspirational note, saving Margie and Mr. Biggers for the next week. I cooked up some ham and red-eye gravy, which Glenn just loves, and then I made some biscuits. The time seemed to pass so slow. The phone rang two times while I was fixing supper, but I just let it go. I thought I had received enough news for *that* day. I still couldn't get over Margie putting her head in the oven, or what I had said to poor Mr. Biggers, which was not at all like me you can be sure. I buzzed around that kitchen doing first one thing, then another. I couldn't keep my mind on anything I did.

After a while Marshall came home and ate, and went in the front room to watch TV. He cannot keep it in his head that watching TV in the dark will ruin your eyes, so I always have to go in there and turn on a light for him. This night, though, I didn't. I just let him sit there in the recliner in the dark, watching his show, and in the pale blue light from that TV set he looked just like anybody else.

I put on a sweater and went out on the front porch and sat in the swing to watch for Glenn. It was nice weather for that time of year, still a little cold but you could smell spring in the air already and I knew it wouldn't be long before the redbud would come out again on the hills. Out in the dark where I couldn't see them, around the front steps, my crocuses were already up. After a while of sitting out there I began to take on a chill, due more to my age no doubt than the weather, but just then some lights came around the bend, two headlights, and I knew it was Glenn coming home.

Glenn parked the truck and came up the steps. He was dog-tired, I could see that. He came over to the swing and put his hand on my shoulder. A little wind came up, and by then it was so dark you could see lights on all the ridges where the people live. "Well, Joline," he said.

"Dinner is waiting on you," I said. "You go on in and wash up and I'll be there directly. I was getting worried about you," I said.

Glenn went on and I sat there swaying on the breeze for a minute before I went after him. Now where will it all end? I ask you. All this pain and loving, mystery and loss. And it just goes on and on, from Glenn's mother taking up with dark-skinned gypsies to my own daddy and his postcard to that silly Lavonne and her cup of coffee to Margie with her head in the oven, to John Marcel Wilkes and myself, God help me, and all of it so long ago out in those holy woods.

George Scarbrough

George Scarbrough was born in Polk County, Tennessee, in 1915. He received degrees from Lincoln Memorial University (B.A.) and the University of Tennessee at Knoxville (M.A.). He worked as a newspaperman and farmer in East Tennessee from 1937 to 1943 and taught English for eighteen years in secondary schools and colleges. A southern writer, Scarbrough records locales and family traditions in a distinctive, articulate voice. Among his works are *Summer So-Called,* selected by the *New York Times* as one of the best books of 1956, and *Invitation to Kim,* which received a Pulitzer Prize nomination. His most recent publication is *A Summer Ago* (1986). Scarbrough's works also have appeared in over sixty-five magazines and periodicals, including *Atlantic Monthly* and the *New York Times.*

Grace

We groaned no thanks
At our ungroaning board.
What we had was ours,
Paid for with blister and cramp.

Our father said,
Gibing at misery,
"We'll eat what there is first
And save what there isn't for later."

From *Invitation to Kim,* Iris Press, 1989. Reprinted by permission of the author and publisher.

Winking at us,
His hungry seven
Strung on the long bench
Behind the oil-clothed table,

He swilled his cup
Of poor porridge,
Turning the vessel
Upside down at his place,

Signifying
It is finished.
I sipped along with my mother,
Amazed at the depth

Of a shallow share.
But I tallied with him.
If God passed by at the road,
I assured myself,

Tonguing the last drop,
Inverting my own cup,
Instead of gaping and groveling,
I'd spit in the sucker's eye.

Byron Herbert Reece

Born in 1917 in a log cabin in Union County, Georgia, on land long settled by ancestors on both sides, Byron Herbert Reece at an early age displayed a genius for poetry, as well as a distrust of all forms of modernity. Much in the tradition of Jesse Stuart, who promoted him, Reece was hailed as a plowboy poet and American Robert Burns. Fiercely independent and idealistic, Reece apparently possessed mystical insight that gave some of his poems characteristics of waking visions. One such poem, "Mountain Fiddler," meets Reece's own criteria for verse: "intelligible and vigorous."

Reece died in 1958. Three volumes of his poetry were published in 1985 (*Bow Down in Jericho*, *Season of Flesh*, and *Songs of Joy and Other Poems*). A film based on his life, listed in the bibliography of this anthology, has won a number of awards for excellence.

Mountain Fiddler

I took my fiddle
That sings and cries
To a hill in the middle
Of Paradise.

I sat at the base
Of a golden stone
In that holy place
To play alone.

I tuned the strings
And began to play,
And a crowd of wings
Were bent my way.

A voice said
Amid the stir:
"We that were dead,
O Fiddler,

"With purest gold
Are robed and shod,
And we behold
The face of God.

"Our halls can show
No thing so rude
As your horsehair bow,
Or your fiddlewood;

"And yet can they
So well entrance
If you but play
Then we must dance!"

Chapter 3

Folklore, Mythology, and Superstition

Introduction

Though they share certain features, folklore and religion differ substantially. Folklore springs from the common experience of people; religion, at least initially, from revelations of a chosen few through whom God speaks. Religion may be thought of as deriving from the voice of God (*vox Dei*); folklore from the voice of people (*vox populi*). Religion comes from "above," from a transcendent God or the Wholly Other; folklore from "below," from the collective conscious and unconscious of a group of people.

Both folklore and religion partake of myth, but they operate on different levels and with different aims. Myth offers spiritual instruction; folklore offers entertainment and instruction in more everyday, practical matters. The folk tale, for example, seems designed to instruct and admonish, especially the young, and to inculcate a healthy respect for mystery. There is often a pragmatic aspect to the songs, jokes, proverbs, rhymes, riddles, and superstitions that make up the body of Appalachian folklore (weather lore and the lore of gardening and farming are examples).

To be sure, folklore also reflects unconscious symbols as well as conscious thought based on experience. Stith Thompson's *Type and Motif Index* and the Baughman Index present ample evidence of the eternal cycle of symbols in the language of the folk. The vast body of Appalachian folklore reflects these symbols and presents localized and particularized versions of universal themes and experiences.

Fred Chappell

Fred Chappell was born in Canton, North Carolina, in 1936. From 1957 to 1960 he worked as general manager and then as credit manager for two Canton furniture stores. He earned his B.A. and M.A. degrees at Duke University. Chappell has taught English at the University of North Carolina at Greensboro since 1964. A nationally acclaimed poet and novelist, Chappell often draws on childhood memories to write about mountain experience. His first novel *It Is Time, Lord* (1963), published before completing his master's degree, is noted for its complex narrative structure. *The Inkling* (1965), *Dagon* (1968), and *The Gaudy Place* (1973) explore the theme of the destruction of the personality. Chappell's best-known work and winner of the Bollingen Prize is *Midquest,* a four-volume poetic autobiography that concerned the author's thirty-fifth birthday. As indicated in the title of one of his major works, *I Am One of You Forever* (1985), Chappell, like Faulkner and Welty, gives overwhelming evidence of the lasting bond with the people and place of his birth.

"My Grandmother's Dream of Plowing" shows both a knowledge and an appreciation of the hard life on the family farm and the compensating joys of work well done. Critics, with good reason, have remarked upon the parallel between Chappell's poetry and Virgil's *Georgics.*

My Grandmother's Dream of Plowing

I never saw him plowing, but Frank was well
And whole and plowing in the field behind
Jackson and Maude whose heads went up and down
Like they agreed on what they were talking over.
There was a light around him, light he was blind
To, light tolling steady like a bell.
The dirt peeled back from the share like meal, brown
Loam all water-smelling. What he'd uncover
With his plowing I felt I already knew:
He'd turn up that bell from the church the Klan
Burned down because of the Negro organist.
The bell they couldn't find had washed in the tide
Of earth and finally had come to rest
In our own bottom land that used to grow
Tobacco . . .

From *Epoch* 29, no. 1 (Fall 1979). Reprinted by permission of the publisher.

                     I was wrong; for when the sun
Gleamed on something in the furrow-side
I went to look, and it wasn't a bell at all.
It was a big and shining lump of gold.
It was a Mystery gold, and just the tip
Of it stuck out. With my bare hands I brushed
Away the crumbs and dug it out of the soil.
I got on my knees and tried to wrestle it up,
And after a while I did, aching, and rolled
It out and stood looking at it all hushed.
About as big as a twenty-five-pound sack
Of flour. And burning burning like the flame
Of Moses' bush. It lay there in the furrow
Like, like . . . Oh, I can't say what like.
I picked it up and cradled it to my breast,
Thinking how this was a Gold made out of a dream
And now we'd never fear about tomorrow
And give our frets and cares a well-earned rest.

"Is that your baby that was never mine?"
Behind me Frank had stopped the plow. His voice
Came up against me like another person,
Like a stranger maybe intending harm.
His voice was dressed in black and laid a curse on
All the fancies I'd thought up for us.
I turned around to tell him Hush, but then
I knew it *was* a baby in my arm,
The strangest baby. As fat and dimpled as
The Baby Jesus in the pictures of
The Upper Room. And this golden child was
Speaking to me, not just baby-talk,
But real words that I ought to understand.
Except I couldn't hear. Bent my head down
But couldn't hear, no more than you hear the dark.
"It's not my baby, and just never you mind,"
I said to Frank. "This baby I've found will bring
Us luck," I said, "because it turned from gold
To flesh. That means—it has to mean—something
To us, something to help us when we're old."
"We're old," Frank said, "we're old already, Anne.
And, see, the baby's changed to something else.
It's turned into an ugly little man."

I looked, and felt the beating of my pulse
Grow harder in my throat, knowing it was true.

I held to me an evil little goblin
With an evil smile. And, must be, astray in its mind.
The way its eyes were loose, and its head bobbling
Up and down like corn tassel in the wind.
All over I went water then and trembled
Like a flame of fire. I turned my face away
From Frank. I'd never felt so ashen-humbled.

What had I brought upon us? *Oh what, what?*
Something terrible the field had birthed,
And now I'd gathered it up, and who could say
It wouldn't haunt us forever from this day
Onward? I'd never thought such ugly thought
As standing there with what the plow unearthed
And wishing it would go away. Or die.
That's what I wished: *Please die, and let us be.*
Now here's the awfullest part. What I said
To do, it did. It rolled its eyes glass-white
Back in its head, and kicked and shivered like
A new-born calf, and murmured in white froth
A tiny whimper, and opened on its mouth
A glassy bubble and sucked it gagging back
Into its throat, and opened and closed its throat,
And sighed a sigh, and lay in my arms stone dead.

It was my fault. It turned into a stone,
And it was all my fault, wishing that way.
Whatever harm had the little goblin done?
And now I'd killed it. I began to cry,
And cried so hard I felt my eyes dissolve
To dust, to water, fire, and then to smoke.

"And then you woke," I said, "to the world you love."

"And now I know," she said, "I never woke."

Maggie Anderson

Maggie Anderson is the author of three collections of poems, including *A Space Filled with Moving* (1992) and *Cold Comfort* (1986). She wrote an introduction for, and edited, *Hill Daughter: New and Selected Poems,* by West Virginia poet Louise McNeill, and she coedited *A Gathering of Poets* (1992), a collection of poems read at the twentieth anniversary memorial for students killed or wounded at Kent State University in 1970. Maggie Anderson has received grants from the National Endowment for the Arts, the Pennsylvania Council on the Arts, and the MacDowell Colony. She teaches creative writing at Kent State University in Ohio.

Country Wisdoms

Rescue the drowning and tie your shoe-strings.
—Thoreau, *Walden*

Out here where the crows turn around
where the ground muds over and the snow fences bend
we've been bearing up. Although

a green winter means a green graveyard
and we've buried someone every month since autumn
warm weather pulls us into summer by the thumbnails.
They say these things.

When the April rains hurl ice chunks onto the banks
the river later rises to retrieve them.
They tell how the fierce wind from the South

blows branches down, power lines and houses
but always brings the trees to bud.
Fog in January, frost in May

threads of cloud, they say, rain needles.
My mother would urge, be careful what you want,
you will surely get it.

More ways than one to skin that cat.
Then they say, Boot straps.
Pull yourself up.

From *Cold Comfort* by Maggie Anderson, © 1986 by Maggie Anderson. Reprinted by permission of the University of Pittsburgh Press.

Verna Mae Slone

Born in Caney, Kentucky, in 1914, writer Verna Mae Slone did not begin her writing career until after the age of sixty. She attended Knott County High School for one and a half years before she married Willie S. Slone and had five sons. She operated a grocery store and service station for many years. Along with her writing, she continues to teach the mountain craft of quilting.

Slone began to write because she wanted to dispel the myths and misunderstandings surrounding Appalachia. Her many recollections and reflections on mountain life have been published under the titles *In Remembrance* (1974), *Common Folks* (1978), and *What My Heart Wants to Tell* (1979). Slone now lives in Pippa Passes, Kentucky.

Buggers and Spirits Pick Their Noses on Weekends

My father did not, nor would he let us, believe in ghosts. We called them "haunts" or "buggers," but many of our neighbors would "sware right down to ye" that they had "seed things." There were certain places where more than one person had encountered something that did not comply with the laws of nature, and heard voices or sounds when there was no reason (or so they said). We even still have a Bugger Branch on Caney and a Bugger Hollow just across the hill on Watts Fork. I wonder if any of our old folks really believed these stories. There were many great storytellers. We had few books, and listening to these stories were our only entertainment of this kind. Father would tell us it was all right to listen, but to never tell the person that we did not believe them. When we would hear some "bugger tale" from one of our schoolmates and come home and repeat it to him, he would make a fanning motion with his arms and a blowing with his lips and say, "Now, there, you see, I have blowed it all away. No more bugger."

When he heard or saw something strange, he never stopped until he found out what it really was. When he was a child, folks believed a cow could lose her cud. They had noticed how cattle would burp up their food and chew it the second time. They did not understand, and thought the cud was a special thing belonging to cows. If a cow lost this cud they thought it would die. They would make them another from an old dishrag and a salty meat skin, maybe adding something else. This would save the cow's life. One day Father was watching a small calf. His job was to see it did not get into the corn or garden patch. When the calf began to chew its cud, he held its mouth and made it spit it out, to see what it was.

Some of the folks also believed in witches. Some even said they were a witch themselves. To become one, you had to go up on a high hill on the first night of a full moon, spread a white sheet on the ground beneath an oak tree, kneel on this sheet, shoot a gun toward the sky, curse the Lord, and bless the Devil. Three drops of blood would fall on the sheet. Then you would have the powers of a witch. But when you died you would belong to the Devil.

Once there was this old woman who thought someone had bewitched her cow, causing her milk to "turn" and to taste awful. Father knew the reason was because she was not a very good housekeeper and did not sterilize her churn and milk bucket. So he told her to go to the north side of her spring where she got water, choose three small "gravels" or stones, wash her churn real clean, put the gravels in the bottom, then rinse it with boiling water. This would break the spell.

One story told and believed by some of my husband's folks was about the Devil. Some men had a habit of going to an old lonely shack every Saturday night to play cards, gamble, and drink moonshine whiskey. This one time, about midnight, a stranger rode up on a very fine black horse, hitched it up outside to the fencepost, and came in. He spoke to each one and called each by name, although none knew him. He asked if he could sit in on their poker game. No one refused. Very slowly, as the game went on for hours, he began to win all their money. One man dropped a card on the floor. When he stooped down to pick it up, he saw that the stranger had hooves where there should have been feet. This scared him so much that he jumped up, turning the table over, and ran out the door. All the other men ran after him, leaving all their cards, money, and jugs with the stranger. As they ran out of sight, they heard the stranger laughing, a strange high crackling sound, like the wind through a forest fire. The next day when it was daylight some of the men were a little braver and came back. The shack was burned to the ground. They looked in the ashes and found the silver money, melted and formed into the shape of a cross. None of these men ever played poker again.

One old lady gained a lot of fame because she had a "knocking spirit." Anyone who spent the night with her could hear it, ask it any question, and it would answer two knocks for a no, three for a yes. This was a great mystery, until someone found out that one of her sons had tied a thread spool to a string, and pulled it through a knothole near his bed.

There was another woman who heard a knocking in her loft, every night, three knocks—the second one not as loud as the first, the third one still fainter—only to begin again. She was a "wedder," living by herself. She asked my father to come and find out what this knocking sound was.

Now these old-fashioned lofts were much more than just a space beneath the roof. They were more like a second story to the house—not high enough for a bedstead, but feather beds or straw ticks were placed on the floor for the children or extra company. Some had a stairway that went up by the chimney inside, some, not so nice, had a ladder on the outside. In my father's house, this upstairs was very nice and comfortable, but I remember staying all night with some friends. We had to climb up an outside ladder. There was no shutter to the opening where we went in. The next morning we awoke to find a two-inch snow covering us, where we were warm between two big feather beds and many quilts. I would be scared to death for you, grandchildren, to sleep like that, but we thought it was a lot of fun. We put our clothes on under the covers and hurried, laughing, down to the fire and breakfast.

In these lofts we also kept our dried beans, cushaw, onions, and seed corn. Almost everyone had an old trunk or two full of dead folk's clothes, and anything else that needed storing away. So it was up in a loft like this that the old woman heard the strange knocking sound. As luck would have it, that night the moon was full, not a cloud in the sky. After supper and before dusk, my father went up the ladder and settled himself in a corner. It was very hard for him to keep from going to sleep. The light came in from a small opening where the wind had blown a board off. He thought, "Tomorrow I will nail that back on fer her." He tried counting the rows of boards, the strings of popcorn, the bunches of dried beans. He would first rub one eye, then the other—anything to keep himself awake. He could hear the squeak, squeak, of the old woman's rocking chair. At last there was something moving in the other corner. There was a board across a barrel, probably filled with dried apples. Next to this sat a large churn. Like a flash something ran across this board, made a dive from the end, and landed in the churn. Whack, whack, whack, three times went the other end of the board. He went over and looked into the churn. Mr. Rat gave a fast retreat. The churn had been full of cracklins, kept there until the "right time of moon" to be made into soap.

When one family went to stay all night with another (as they often did), after supper and the dishes were washed and put away, and all the other "work done up," everyone would get together. We'd gather around the fire, if it was winter, or on the porch, around a "gnat smoke" made by burning rags, if it was summer. The older folks would sit in chairs with the young children in their laps, or huddled around their feet. That's when we would hear all these scary bugger tales. By the time we were ready to go to sleep, it sure was nice to know the small ones would be stuck in at the foot of the grown-ups' bed, or so many of us in the same bed that we would have to sleep sideways so as to have room for us all.

These stories lose a lot in being written—the facial expressions, the movements of the hands, the bending forward of the body, the lowering and raising of the voice by the storyteller cannot be captured on paper. They added much to the enjoyment of listening to these bugger tales.

There was one story my father taught me that I have told my grandchildren so many times I know they will never forget it. It's kind of a poem, or maybe you would call it a chant. There is no end to it, and each line must be followed by a long, low moan:

> There was an old woman all skin and bone—mo-o-an
> She took a notion that she would not stay at home—mo-o-an
> She got up—she walked down—mo-o-an
> To the village churchyard ground—mo-o-an

She saw the dead a'laying around—mo-o-an
She saw the grave of her only son—mo-o-an
She thought of all the crimes he had done—mo-o-an

And on and on until you had your audience really listening. Then, very suddenly, maybe right in the middle of a word, you would jump and scream *boo*.
Even after telling it over and over again, and they knew the loud boo was
coming, I would still be able to scare them. Just think what it would do to
someone hearing it for the first time.

I think some of the parents used bugger tales to scare their children just to
make them be good. It seems as if every family had a "Hairy Mouth" or a
"Bloody Bones" that would come and get you if you were not good. My father
would not let us be told anything like this. We were taught to be good because
that was what Jesus wanted us to do. He told us there was a Devil, but not one you
could see with your natural eyes. And so have I taught my dear grandchildren.

Kitteneye knew a lot of fairy stories, some different and some very similar
to your versions today. Rumplestiltskin was named Tom Tit Tot, and the
girl with the glass slipper was Cinder Ellen. He knew hundreds of songs or
rhymes, all by heart. I can't recall all of them, but this story would not be
complete unless I gave you at least two: "The Fox Song" and "The Bird
Song," my favorite ones.

The Fox Song

It was a moon shining night
The stars shining bright
Two foxes went out for to prey.
They trotted along
With frolic and song
To cheer their lonely way.

Through the woods they went
Not a rabbit could they scent
Nor a lonely goose or stray.
Until at last they came
To some better game:
A farmer's yard by the way.

On the roost there sat
Some chickens as fat
As foxes could wish for a dinner
They hunted around
Until a hole they found
And both went in at the center.

They both went in
With a squeeze and a grin
And the chickens they soon were killed.
And one of them lunched
And hunched, and bunched
Until his stomach was fairly filled.

The other more wise
Looked around with both eyes
He would hardly eat at all.
For as he came in
With a squeeze and a grin
He noted the hole was quite small.

The night rolled on
And daylight dawn
Two men came out with a pole.
Both fox flew
And one went through
But the greedy one stuck in the hole.

The hole he stuck
So full of his pluck
Of the chickens he had been eating.
He could not get out
Or turn about
So he was killed by beating.

The Bird Song

I used to kill birds in my boyhood,
Black ones, robins, and wrens.
I hunted them up on the hillside,
I hunted them down in the glen.

I did not think it was sinful,
I did it only for fun.
I had such sport of royalty,
With the poor little birds and my gun.

One bright day in the springtime,
I saw a brown thrush in a tree.
She was singing so merrily and sweetly,
Just as sweet as a birdy could be.

I raised my gun in a twinkle,
I fired, the aim it was true.
For a moment the little bird fluttered,
Then off to the bushes it flew.

I followed it softly and closely,
And there to my sorrow I found,
Right close to a nest full of young ones,
The mother bird dead on the ground.

The young ones for food they were calling,
Yet how could they ever be fed?
For the dear darling mother who loved them,
Was laying there bleeding and dead.

I picked it up in my anger,
I stroked the motherly bird.
Not never again in my lifetime,
Would I kill a poor innocent bird.

Kitteneye was a good hand at making up his own rhymes or pieces. I am
sorry to say many were about his friends and neighbors, and he would picture their character so quaint and real that I would be afraid to repeat them.
He used his imagination in using swear words and expressions. Some of his
sayings he must have made up, because they seem to belong only to him:

If you don't stand for something, you will get knocked down by everything.
Cooked potatoes are easy to eat, but you have to do some gnawing to
get meat off the bone.
There are no "little white lies." They are all black, trying to hide from
the truth.
When you become discouraged, think of the hole a little ground squirrel
makes in the side of the hill. It does not bother him how large that mountain is.
Don't be concerned about something that don't concern you. It won't
make your bed any softer, or your meat fry any faster.
Two things I love to hear, but seldom do: truth and meat a'fryin'.

I think the one he used most was "Devil take it." He told about the one
time when he came in from picking blackberries without his shirt. His
mother asked him why he had no shirt and he answered, "Well, you see, I
kep' git'n caught in these blackberry briars. And ever'time I would say,
'Devil take it,' and I guess the Devil, he just come and took it."

Jim Wayne Miller

See volume 2, chapter 2, for biography.

Meeting

My shadow was my partner in the row.
He was working the slick-handled shadow of his hoe
when out of the patch toward noon there came the sound
of steel on steel two inches underground,
as if our hoes had hooked each other on that spot.
My shadow's hoe must be of steel, I thought.
And where my chopping hoe came down and struck,
memory rushed like water out of rock.
"When two strike hoes," I said, "it's always sign
they'll work the patch together again sometime.
An old man told me that the last time ever
we worked this patch and our hoes rang together."
Delving there with my hoe, I half-uncovered
a plowpoint, worn and rusted over.
"The man I hoed with last lies under earth,
his plowpoint and his saying of equal worth."
My shadow, standing by me in the row,
waited, and while I rested, raised his hoe.

From *Dialogue with a Dead Man,* University of Georgia Press, 1974. Reprinted by permission
   of the author and publisher.

Ambrose N. Manning

Ambrose N. Manning is a native of North Carolina and a graduate of Atlantic Christian College, Wilson, North Carolina, and of the University of
North Carolina at Chapel Hill. He holds the E.D.S. (specialist) degree from
Peabody College in folklore. The coeditor (with Robert J. Higgs) of *Voices
from the Hills* and several books of folklore with Thomas Burton, he also is
author of several articles on folklore and a well-known collector of songs
and lore. The Burton-Manning Archives at East Tennessee State University

are named in honor of him and Thomas Burton. He and Burton have received the Laurel Leaves Award for their contributions to the Southern Appalachian region. Manning, a past president of the Tennessee Folklore Society and the Appalachian Consortium, is professor emeritus at ETSU, which conferred upon him its Distinguished Professor Award.

The following story is a composite of variants of the theme of the "Vanishing Hitchhiker," as related by students over many years to Ambrose N. Manning and Thomas Burton in their courses on folklore and field research at East Tennessee State University. For a more detailed discussion of the "Vanishing Hitchhiker" theme, see Jan Harold Brunvaud, *The Vanishing Hitchhiker: American Urban Legends and Their Meanings* (1981) and see W. K. McNeil, *Ghost Stories of the American South* (1985), 190–91.

The Vanishing Hitchhiker

One cool, rainy evening in the spring, Josh Morton was driving along Gap Creek Road in upper East Tennessee. Gap Creek Road between Elizabethton and Upper Gap Creek contains several sharp curves; at one of them which is especially sharp there is a bridge over a small stream. As Josh was approaching the curve and the bridge, there appeared within the beam from his headlights a young woman standing beside the road. She was dressed in finery, but was wearing no coat; consequently, Josh noticed, she was becoming drenched.

He stopped the car and asked her if she wanted a ride. When she accepted, he offered her his coat, which was draped over the seat. During the drive she was very quiet except to give him directions to her home that was on a country road and up a lane off the main road.

Upon arriving at her home, Josh got out of the car and went around to the passenger side to help the young woman out of the car and into the house. But when he opened the door, she had disappeared. Assuming that she had silently slipped into the house while he was coming around the vehicle, he left and went on his way.

Suddenly it occurred to him that the young woman had kept his coat, so he returned to the farmhouse to retrieve it. When he rapped at the door, a woman came to answer his knock. After he told her his mission, she replied, "That sounds like my daughter; but it could not be, for she was killed in an accident at a curve on Gap Creek Road three years ago today. She and her girl friends in the community had worked for several weeks in preparation for their prom. Finally the evening arrived, and she left here with her boyfriend, all dressed up for the prom. She was killed in an accident on that curve. She is buried in the cemetery in the field at the edge of the yard. If you wish, I will show you her grave."

As they neared the spot where the young woman was buried, her mother directed the flashlight to the grave. There on the tombstone was Josh's coat.

Kathryn Stripling Byer

Kathryn Stripling Byer received her B.A. in English at Wesleyan College and completed her M.F.A. at the University of North Carolina–Greensboro. Her first collection of poetry, *Search Party* (1979), was followed by another, *Alma* (1983). *The Girl in the Midst of the Harvest* was published in the Associated Writing Program's award series for 1986. Byer has received a fellowship from the North Carolina Arts Council as well as from the National Endowment for the Arts. Her *Wildwood Flower: Poems* (1992) was chosen by the Academy of American Poets as the Lamont Poetry Selection for 1992. Her poems have also appeared in journals such as *Georgia Review, Southern Poetry Review,* and *Nimrod.* Byer is currently poet-in-residence at Western Carolina University in Cullowhee, North Carolina.

Ghost Story

She stalks these mountains
in high button shoes
and the silk skirt she wore
when she flirted with cowboys
and wild Irish miners
who came north to strike
it rich quick in the Black Hills
where winter was fiercer
than even the coldest ones here
in the tame Appalachians
she later called home.
On her deathbed she sighed
for the mountains of Brasstown,
Dahlonega, even the ridge
of the Balsams she'd seen
only once from a passing
car. Thirty years
she cursed the heat
of south Georgia, the flies,
and the infernal gossip
that branded her. Unsmiling
she walked the small streets.
Now she stalks these mountains

From *The Girl in the Midst of the Harvest,* Texas Tech University Press, 1986. Reprinted by permission of the author.

from Big Fork to Snowbird,
her shoe buttons gleaming,
her silk skirt a cloud
trailing after the full moon.

Henry D. Shapiro

Henry D. Shapiro was born in 1937 in New York, New York. He was educated at Columbia University (A.B.), Cornell University (M.A.), and Rutgers University (Ph.D.). After teaching at Ohio State University, he took a position at the University of Cincinnati, where he was professor of history. He became emeritus professor in 1989. He now lives in Cleveland Heights, Ohio. Among his works is *Confiscation of Confederate Property in the North* (1962), which won the Moses Coit Tyler Prize awarded by Cornell University. He is also the author of *Ethnic Diversity and Civic Identity: Patterns of Conflict and Cohesion in Cincinnati since 1820* (1992). His *Appalachia on Our Mind,* the 1978 recipient of the W. D. Weatherford Prize, studies the development of the idea of Appalachia and sheds light upon the larger issues of American cultural and intellectual history.

The Making of Mountain Folk

Sharp's demonstration of the "folk" character of Appalachian culture functioned not only to establish the peculiarities of mountain life as legitimate patterns in the present, rather than merely as patterns carried over from the past, but also to define the mountaineers themselves as a legitimately distinct people in the American present. As native-born, white, Anglo-Saxon, Protestant, American folk, their very status as "folk" defined their relationship to the rest of the American population even as the status of Italian-Americans or Afro-Americans as "hyphenates" or "immigrants" defined the relationship of these groups to, and in, America. As a distinct people, the mountaineers now appeared as one group among the many which made up the American population, just as Appalachia itself had come to seem one region among the many which made up the American nation. After 1917 the mountaineers lost their special status as one of the "exceptional populations" of the nation, whose deviances from more normal patterns of American life created a "need" for systematic benevolence and a threat to American unity and homogeneity, just as earlier Appalachia had

From *Appalachia on Our Mind: The Southern Mountains and Mountaineers in the American Consciousness, 1870–1920,* © 1978 by The University of North Carolina Press. Used by permission of the author and publisher.

lost its special status as an unknown land worthy of description for that reason. The publication of *English Folk Songs from the Southern Appalachians* thus involved the completion of that process of legitimation through explanation and definition which began in the 1880s, even as it effected the redefinition of Appalachian otherness as a reality to be accepted rather than as a problem to be solved.

Cecil Sharp's "discoveries" in the southern mountain region differed significantly, both in their nature and in their import, from those of earlier travelers in the region. The viability and public acceptance of his vision of the mountaineers as an American "folk," however, like the viability and public acceptance of the different visions of Appalachian otherness promulgated by local-color writers, home missionaries, advocates of southern industrial development, social scientists, social workers, or reformers of the Progressive period, depended on two factors only marginally connected with the merits of his argument or the accuracy of his vision: first, his reputation as an "expert," and, second, the appropriateness of his vision to contemporary conceptions of the nature of American civilization.

Sharp's reputation as an expert followed from his status as a leading authority on English folksong and folkdance, from the publicity which attended his theatrical ventures of 1915 and 1916 and his lecture tours, and from his connection with persons and institutions "prominent" in contemporary cultural affairs, including the Russell Sage Foundation. In addition, he was an outsider, hence presumably objective and free from self-interest, and he was an Englishman. During the war years especially, this fact alone gave his comments about the persistence of English folk culture in the United States special weight.

The work of earlier commentators on the mountain region had pointed to the distance which separated Appalachia and America, sought to explain this distance and its meaning and to design techniques for integrating Appalachia into American life, and thereby to resolve the dilemma posed by the fact of Appalachian otherness. All began with the assumption that America was, or ought to be, or was in the process of becoming, a unified and homogeneous national entity, and that the process of modern history itself inevitably yielded nationalism, political centralization, and social complexity. In this context, all saw that the existence of the strange land and peculiar people of Appalachia posed a problem, and directed their efforts at understanding the dimensions of the problem and at solving it, both abstractly and practically.

Sharp may or may not have known that the existence of Appalachia posed a problem for Americans when he came to the United States in 1914, and he may or may not have known that certain aspects of the dilemma of Appalachian otherness had been resolved in America by the designation of Appalachia as a discrete region of the nation. As an Englishman, and as a student of folksong and folkdance, however, he stood outside this tradition. As an Englishman, he accepted the normality of regional cultural differences. As a student of folksong and folkdance, he not only accepted the normality of cultural differences between urban and rural areas, but viewed such differences in terms which saw primitivism as simplicity and simplicity as a virtue, and which identified the historical primitivism of the past as a reduction to essentials of the civilization of the present. The otherness of Appalachia thus could not bother him either abstractly or practically. It was simply a fact, like Scottish otherness, and like Scottish otherness it was to be exploited for the consequences of that otherness, the persistence of a folk tradition which had died out elsewhere, or which perhaps had never existed in more traditionally urban areas of the Western world.

By accepting the otherness of Appalachia, and by providing Americans with a set of terms through which to understand both Appalachian otherness and the relationship of the mountaineers to the rest of the American population, Sharp not only established the peculiarities of mountain life as legitimate patterns in the present but also identified the mountaineers at once as a distinct people and as the conservators of the essential culture of America. And it was this, ultimately, which made his vision appropriate to contemporary conceptions of the nature of American civilization.

As a "folk," the mountaineers were for that reason a "people," with distinct cultural characteristics and perhaps with distinct genetic traits as well. Sharp was not the first to suggest that the mountaineers were a "people," but he was the first to suggest what kind of people they were: the American folk. Even so, in the nation of peoples which America seemed to be during and after World War I, the status of the mountaineers was not entirely clear. Were they simply one of the "ethnic" or "racial" groups of which the American population was composed, Appalachian-American hyphenates in a pluralist nation? Or did the traditional quality of mountain life and the identification of the mountaineers as American "folk" place them at the very center of American civilization and give them symbolic function in a culture fragmented by European adventures and the technological revolutions of modern life?[1]

The normalization of diversity which was the legacy of the war years made definition of the mountaineers as a people in a nation of people possible. They were "a subrace of the whites occupying the southern Allegheny mountains" according to the eugenicist Charles Davenport, for example, who found little else to say about them in his monumental survey of the American population classified by racial type, published in 1920. It is significant simply that the mountaineers are here included, however, as they were in other studies attempting to assess the strengths and weaknesses of the American population during the 1920s and 1930s, when examination of American society and the American economy, and of American civilization itself, seemed so compelling a task. As a people in a nation of peoples, moreover, it was only appropriate that their "racial" characteristics should be studied. In this effort Davenport himself made the first important beginning, although his conclusions appear as little more than transpositions of the conventional wisdom of the nineteenth century, unflattering replications of Will Wallace Harney's remarks a half-century earlier. "They are characterized by an exceptionally high proportion of mental defect and mental disease, by varicose veins, by numerous deformities of the extremities, and by underweight," Davenport said.[2] Later commentators would expand on these observations and debate the accuracy of some of them—especially concerning the mental abilities of the mountain people—but no one would challenge the fundamental assumption upon which they were made, that the mountaineers did form a "subrace" of the American population with measurably distinct characteristics.[3]

If the mountaineers were thus a people, they were also a special kind of people. Unlike the other "folk" whose peculiar culture and oral traditions engaged the attention not only of professional folklorists but also of American writers and American readers during the 1920s, the mountaineers were defined by ethnicity and history as an "American" folk. Unlike the lumberjacks and riverboatmen and cowboys, unlike the banjo-picking-spiritual-singing-tap-dancing blacks of the southern plantations and the northern ghettoes, unlike the Polish or Italian or Jewish children playing counting games on the sidewalks of New York or Chicago or Philadelphia, the mountaineers now appeared to be both in and of America. Their ethnic and historical characteristics connected them with the dominant white, Anglo-Saxon, native-born, Protestant civilization of the nation. As "our contemporary ancestors" in Frost's view or as the folksong-singing rural types of Sharp's vision, they now appeared as the conservators of the essential culture of America, the ur-culture from which all else, literature and life both, seemed to spring.

The story of the transformation by which Appalachia became a symbol of America, and of attempts during the 1920s and 1930s to reassess the meaning of mountain life as part of the search for an American folk tradition, cannot be fully told here. Its occurrence must at least be noted, however, for, in the twenties especially, the availability of that strange land and peculiar people of Appalachia as a source of information about the "real" America seemed to provide a necessary imaginative alternative to the necessities of contemporary reality. In a nation confused about the relationship of past and present, uncertain about its future, and desperately in search of a sense of self-identity, Appalachia seemed to provide a benchmark against which to measure how far the nation had come from its essential self. The persistence of Appalachia into the present seemed to hold out the possibility of returning to the nation's roots, of starting over, not in the past but in a simpler present, of refreshing the national spirit worn out by war and the peace, the possibility of going home. Although in the 1920s as at other times, going home was something one liked better to think about than to do, the possibility of "going home" which the existence of Appalachia seemed to offer had considerable attraction. The dramatist Percy MacKaye, in his characteristic 1920s distress at modern industrial civilization, said it as well as anyone.

> Over there in the mountains are men who do not live in cages; a million Americans, who do not chase the dollar, who do not time-serve machines, who do not learn their manners from the movies or their culture from the beauty parlors. Shall we not then, hasten to civilize them—convert their dirty log-cabins into clean cement cages? Or first shall we inquire whether they may have something to contribute to our own brand-new civilization—something which of old we cherished but now perhaps have forgotten?[4]

As an American "folk," and thus as a legitimately distinct people in a nation of peoples, the Americanness of the mountaineers was established. No longer could they be viewed as deviants from a monolithic American civilization. In the American postwar present, they were only deviants from a dominant *modern* civilization, and some said that was more a matter of choice than of necessity. No longer either could the alleged peculiarities of mountain life be viewed as a temporary condition, consequent to the isolation of the region or to the impact of a primitive social environment on social institutions. And if the mountaineers lacked an adequate sense of themselves as mountaineers, mountaineers they were nonetheless, Appalachian-Americans, or later simply Appalachians. Benevolent workers in the folk schools which sprang up during the 1920s and 1930s in the mountains, or workers in the settlement houses in cities to which the mountain people migrated during and after the world war, could easily provide the needed sense of self. So could they provide the survival skills essential to the construction of a viable rural life in Appalachia or to individual success in the life of urbanized, industrialized America.

The emergence around 1920 of the notion that the mountaineers composed a distinct element in the American population had one other important consequence which must be noted: it made possible, for the first time, the imaginative separation of the strange land and its peculiar people. For the local-color writers of the 1870s and 1880s, as we noted, the nexus between place and persona had been central. Mountaineers who left the mountains ceased being mountaineers. In the new pluralism of the 1920s, however, one was defined in terms of where one had come from.

It was in the apotheosis of Sergeant Alvin York as American hero around 1920 that the nexus between place and persona was first broken. York was a Tennessee mountain boy who entered the American Expeditionary Forces only with reluctance, it will be remembered. Once having accepted the draft, however, he "did his duty," as contemporary mythologizers put it, and his duty included capturing single-handedly a German machine-gun battalion after picking off 18 men with his rifle and 7 more with his pistol. Including stragglers whom York added to his group of prisoners on the way back to base headquarters, he captured a total of 132 German soldiers. For this derring-do, York received the Congressional Medal of Honor and the status of a folk-hero.

York took his Congressional Medal of Honor and returned with it to the Valley of Three Forks o' the Wolf, there to live out his life in relative solitude. It was as a mountaineer in France that he had made his fame, however, and this is significant, for, unlike other American folk heroes of the postwar years—Lucky Lindy, Babe Ruth, or Superman himself—York never was simply an American hero. He was first and last a mountaineer, and no less a mountaineer because his virtues were the virtues of the native American folk. Tall and lanky, stolid, loyal, simple, choosing duty over his Christian convictions and his pacifism, his sinewy muscles developed splitting logs on the hillside farm, his marksman's eye trained in squirrel hunting, Alvin York was the mythic mountaineer come to life, even before there was such a thing. He carried his skills and his persona as a mountaineer with him wherever he went, across the big ocean and back again.[5]

The separation of the mountaineers from the mountains made possible the emergence of a mythology about them, at the heart of which lay the notion that the mountaineers did in fact compose a distinct element in the American population. Thus they came to take their place alongside the shrewd Yankees, the sharp-dealing Jews, and the rhythmic blacks in the pantheon of American types. As feudists like the cartoon Hatfields and McCoys in *Song of the South,* Walt Disney's feature-length attempt to create a viable American folk tradition; as moonshiners and chicken thieves like Snuffy Smith in the funny papers; as representatives of an indigenous American folk tradition like the nameless country people in Doris Ullman's powerful photographs of the 1920s or like the weavers and dulcimer makers whose pictures appear in the crafts books of the 1930s and more recently in the *Foxfire* books; or as real-life American heroes like Daniel Boone, Corporal Fess Whitaker, or Sergeant Alvin York, the mythic mountaineer has represented a people. It was a circular process, for the emergence of a folklore about the mountaineers depended upon a vision of Appalachia as a legitimately discrete region and of the mountaineers as a legitimately distinct people, while the mythic representations of mountaineers in literature, art, and folklore have reinforced the view of reality from which they sprang; but it was a process of enormous significance, and it began in the twenties.

Since the 1920s, as a result, no one has been able to ask whether the mountaineers do in fact compose a distinct group in the American population with distinct cultural and genetic traits, anymore than anyone has been able to ask whether Appalachia—originally the mountainous portions of eight southern states—does in fact compose a discrete region of the nation. Indeed, those assumptions lie at the heart of the myth of Appalachia. More precise statement about the region or the people has been peripheral to this central fact. Even the debunkers, within and without the universities, who have risen to the occasion and challenged the accuracy of particular generalizations about the mountaineers in order to paint them in more "realistic" light, have refused to ask the central question of their craft, about the reality of the phenomenon they seek to explicate. Instead, they have begun with the assumption that the mountaineers do in fact compose a distinct people with distinct and describable characteristics. They have argued from within a mythic system about the accuracy of mythology, and attacked the generalizations of folklore which are at once so vague and so potent as to defy examination or correction.

Notes

1. In the context of the "cultural crisis" of the 1920s, the meaning of Appalachian folk culture became transformed, as in [unsigned], "Fireside Industries," *Survey* 47 (24 Dec. 1921): 454: "Finally, America has some native art worth perpetuating. Weaving and basket making as found in many of the highland homes constitute a highly developed art that is thoroughly American and well worth encouraging." Helpful guides to the "cultural crisis" of the 1920s and its consequences are Alan Trachtenberg, ed., *Critics of Culture: Literature and Society in the Early Twentieth Century* (New York: John

Wiley and Sons, 1976), and Warren Susman, ed., *Culture and Commitment, 1929–1945* (New York: George Braziller, 1973)

2. Albert G. Love and Charles B. Davenport, *Defects Found in Drafted Men: Statistical Information Compiled from the Draft Boards* (Washington, DC: U.S. Govt. Printing Office, 1920), 290–91; also 238, 255, 270, 292–93. An important index of the "peopleness" of the mountaineers in the American consciousness was their inclusion in studies which viewed literature as a source of information about social systems, as, for example, Harry Aubrey Toulmin, Jr., *Social Historians* (Boston: Richard G. Badger, Gorham Press, 1911); Marion Clifford Harrison, "Social Types in Southern Prose Fiction" (Ph.D. thesis, U of Virginia, 1921; Ann Arbor: Edmund Brothers, 1921).

3. Of particular interest in this connection is the long debate between hereditarian and environmentalists concerning the intelligence of "the" mountaineer, which flourished during the 1920s and 1930s; see, e.g., N. D. M. Hirsch, "A Summary of Some of the Results from an Experimental Study of the East Kentucky Mountaineers," National Academy of Sciences, *Proceedings* 13, no. 1 (15 Jan. 1927): 18–21; N. D. M. Hirsch, *An Experimental Study of the East Kentucky Mountaineers: A Study in Heredity and Environment,* Genetic Psychology Monographs, vol. 3, no. 3 (Mar. 1928), abstracted in *Science* 67: supplement, xii–xiv (6 Apr. 1928); Mandel Sherman, "Environment and Mental Development: A Study of an Isolated Community," *Journal of the American Association of University Women* 23, no. 3 (Apr. 1930): 137–40; Lester R. Wheeler, "The Intelligence of East Tennessee Mountain Children," *Journal of Educational Psychology* 23 (May 1932): 351–70; Mandel Sherman and Cora B. Key, "The Intelligence of Isolated Mountain Children," *Child Development* 2 (Dec. 1932): 279–90; Mandel Sherman and Thomas R. Henry, *Hollow Folk: A Study in the Blue Ridge* (New York: Thomas Y. Crowell Co., 1933); Lester R. Wheeler and Viola D. Wheeler, "The Musical Ability of Mountain Children as Measured by the Seasore Test of Musical Talent," *Journal of Genetic Psychology* 43 (Dec. 1933): 352–75; E. J. Asher, "The Inadequacy of Current Intelligence Tests for Testing Kentucky Mountain Children," *Journal of Genetic Psychology* 46 (June 1935): 480–86; Jack Manne, "Mental Deficiency in a Closely Inbred Mountain Clan," *Mental Hygiene* 20 (Apr. 1936): 269–79; Lester R. Wheeler, "A Comparative Study of the Intelligence of East Tennessee Mountain Children," *Journal of Educational Psychology* 33 (May 1942): 321–34.

4. Percy MacKaye, "Untamed America: Comment on a Sojourn in the Kentucky Mountains," *Survey* 51 (Jan. 1924): 327. On MacKaye's love affair with the southern mountains, see his preface to *This Fine-Pretty World: A Comedy of the Kentucky Mountains* (New York: Macmillan Co., 1924) and his several ventures at using mountain materials as the basis for dramatic literature, esp. *Tall Tales of the Kentucky Mountains,* first printed in the *Century* 108 (July–Nov. 1924): 357–63, 442–48, 657–65, 819–27, as "A Mountain Munchausen," and *Kentucky Mountain Fantasies: Three Short Plays for an Appalachian Theatre* (New York: Longmans, Green & Co., 1928).

5. Sam K. Cowan, *Sergeant York and His People* (New York: Funk and Wagnalls Co., 1922); also [unsigned], "Sgt. York, War Hero, Dies," *New York Times,* 3 Sept. 1964, pp. 1, 26, and editorial note, 28; William Bradford Huie, "Last Humble Wish Fulfilled, Sgt. York is Buried in the Land He Loved," *New York Herald Tribune,* 6 Sept. 1964, 1: 8.

"Darlin' Cory" (Sharp 152)

Whether or not Henry Shapiro's thesis of the importance of Cecil Sharp as a creator of the "otherness" of mountain people is accurate, there is no denying a plethora of stereotypes in the Sharp collection. In "Darlin' Cory," for example, the following are evident: moonshining, eluding revenuers, pistol packing, banjo picking, bad whiskey, bad women, highway robbery, church going, dancing, and dying in the cold, cold ground.

Wake up, wake up, Darlin' Cory.
What makes you sleep so sound
When the revenue officers are comin'
And tearin' your still-house down?

First time I saw Darlin' Cory,
She was standin' by the sea
With a forty-five buckled around her
And a banjo on her knee.

Go away, go away, Darlin' Cory,
Quit hangin' around my neck;
Bad whiskey surroundin' my body,
Pretty women all muddle my head.

Wake up, wake up, Darlin' Cory.
What makes you sleep so sound
When the highway robbers is a-comin',
This old town is a-burnin' down?

I went to church the t'other Sunday,
Darlin' Cory she was there;
Only change I could tell in Cory
Was the way she fixed her hair.

Do around, do around, Darlin' Cory,
Go do the best you can;
I got me another woman,
You can hunt you another man.

From *Folksongs II*, ed. Thomas Burton and Ambrose N. Manning (Research Advisory Council of East Tennessee State University, 1969). Used by permission of the editors.

Wake up, wake up, Darlin' Cory.
What makes you sleep so sound
When the revenue officers are comin'
And tearin' your playhouse down?

Last night I laid on the pillow,
Last night I laid on the bed;
Last night I laid on the pillow,
And I dreamed that Darlin' Cory was dead.

Go dig me a hole in the meadow,
Dig a hole in the cold, cold ground;
Dig a hole out in the meadow,
Let me lay Darlin' Cory down.

Bill C. Malone

Bill C. Malone is a professor of history at Tulane University in New Orleans, Louisiana. His teaching and research specialties are southern music and southern folk culture. His publications include *Country Music, USA* (1968; rev. ed., 1985); *Southern Music/American Music* (1979); *Stars of Country Music* (coedited with Judith McCulloh in 1976); and *Singing Cowboys and Musical Mountaineers* (1993). Malone also organized and annotated the *Smithsonian Collection of Classic Country Music* in 1981 (a boxed collection of over one hundred recordings), and was music editor for the *Encyclopedia of Southern Culture*. Malone sings, plays the guitar, and does lecture concerts with his wife Bobbie, who plays the mandolin.

Appalachian Music and American Popular Culture: The Romance That Will Not Die

A recent ad for a popular New Orleans–based rock band, the Subdudes, noted that, in addition to their contemporary qualities of musicianship, the group also projected an "Appalachian flavor." Though unexplained, the phrase was merely the most recent example of an uncountable number of scattered references to "Appalachian" or "mountain" that have crept into descriptions of musicians, songs, styles, or quality of life over the last century or so.

From special issue of *Appalachian Heritage* in honor of Loyal Jones, 1994, © *Appalachian Heritage*/Berea College. Reprinted by permission of author and *Appalachian Heritage*.

Such usage is often merely lazy—a short-hand term to describe a quality that the writer, critic, musician, or fan cannot explain or comprehend. But it also reflects an impulse often encountered in attempts to define American folk music styles—the investing of music with descriptions or labels that connote or conjure up certain qualities of life that are appealing to listeners (as in Downhome Blues, Western Swing, Plantation Melodies).

The linking of "Appalachian" and "music" began approximately one hundred years ago, as did the perception that such music was not only *different* from other forms of music but also *better* in certain respects. These perceptions first took shape, in the period running roughly from the turn of the century up to the beginning of World War I, in the minds of a small cluster of academicians and professional musicians who had discovered that people were still singing very old British songs in some of the mountain counties of the South. The discovery of Appalachian balladry was both cause and effect of the larger discovery of the Southern Appalachians and the conception that they constituted a special place.[1]

Appalachian music's reception as a unique and presumably homogeneous form of cultural expression was shaped by a variety of contradictory perceptions. While the music was presumed to be very old, and even of Elizabethan British origins, it could also be described, in Emma Bell Miles's suggestive phrase, as "real American music."[2] It was attractive to those who wanted to believe that a subculture still survived in the United States that was different from the racially heterogeneous and crassly materialistic society that prevailed elsewhere in America at the turn of the century. Although dramatically different from mainstream America, Appalachian society nevertheless had preserved a body of music and folklore that was reminiscent of the nation's cultural roots. Appalachia was, in short, both a museum of early British music and a source of American music. Appalachian music and dances, it was argued, were relatively uncontaminated by modern or commercial influences—Cecil Sharp, for example, described the "Kentucky Running Set" as a dance that predated those collected by John Playford in 1651.[3]

The early assumptions that Appalachian music was very old, relatively pure, and simultaneously British and American have never really died, nor has the corollary view that such music was inherently decent and moral. Although the songs spoke often of such topics as murder, violence, feuds, seduction, illicit love, and moonshining, the music nevertheless seemed to convey the image of a simple but decent people who lived in primal and direct relationship with the earth and nature.[4] Mountain music stood in strong contrast, it seemed, to such urban-born styles as ragtime and jazz, which, like the city itself, exuded a tone of sinfulness and immorality.

Until the 1920s, little awareness of Appalachian music existed outside the circles of academicians or concert audiences who read Cecil Sharp's books, or who perused the small body of available songbooks, or who had access to the recitals given by such professional musicians as Howard Brockway and Elaine Wyman. While some songs of presumed Appalachian provenance had become available, almost nothing was known about the singers from whom the music was collected, and even less about the styles of performance indigenous to Appalachia. In the decades since the 1920s, however, two conceptions of "mountain music" have contested for legitimacy in American life, each supported basically by two very different audiences. Scholars; concert recitalists; folk festival promoters like Jean Thomas, John Powell, and Annabel Morris Buchanan; and the record labels that catered to a specialized, academic audience promoted one approach; while the other was popularized by the hillbilly musicians of radio and recording.

Hillbilly music provided a forum for the commercial dissemination of mountain songs and styles, and for the national exposure of mountain singers themselves. The music also provided a format through which new songs and styles could *continue* to enter the repertories of mountain people. The hillbilly business, of course, presented conflicting images of mountain life, images which reflected a similar confusion of attitudes held by both the American public and the mountain people. Li'l Abner types appeared early and often (and may even have influenced Al Capp's creation of the comic strip).[5] The remarkably popular "Hee Haw" television show is only the most recent example of media exploitation of mountain stereotypes that extends back to the beginnings of commercial country music, when some entertainers performed under such names as "Moonshine Kate" or "the Beverly Hillbillies," sang cliché-ridden songs like "The Martins and the Coys," or recorded "rural dramas" that portrayed feuding and moonshining.

More positive, though romantic, images also clung to the music at the moment of its commercial birth. It is difficult to know which of the images—negative or positive—was most influential in popularizing mountain music among potential listeners. If my own introduction to "mountain music" is in any sense representative, contending visions of laconic, hard-drinking, feuding, and yet gentle Christian ballad singers were easily absorbed and reconciled. From the time the little Philco battery radio entered our East Texas farm home in 1939, an overall perception of mountain life—an amalgam of John Fox, Jr., Sergeant York, Roy Acuff, and, yes, Li'l Abner—began to fill my mind. I gravitated especially toward the feelings projected in such songs as "Blue Ridge Mountain Blues" and Roy Acuff's sometime theme song, "Carry Me Back to the Mountains." Like the message found in these songs, the Appalachian metaphor has always been used to describe or suggest those musicians, styles, or songs that call us back to a symbolic "home"—to presumably purer styles, values, or lifestyles that are either real or imagined.

While the term "mountain music" was used often to describe certain styles of country music, the promotional material surrounding Bradley Kincaid offered the most explicit early assertion of the mountain image. When Kincaid began presenting his repertoire of old-time songs on the broadcasts of WLS in Chicago, neither he nor his program directors could have been unaware of or uninfluenced by the public perception that the Southern Appalachians were the repository of traditional people and traditional songs. Kincaid was from Kentucky and, to many people, Kentucky meant mountains. Kincaid, on the other hand, carried to Chicago a cluster of perceptions concerning mountain balladry shaped by his education at Berea College. He sincerely believed that mountain music was not simply old; it was also deeply moral, just as its creators and preservers were. Performing as "The Kentucky Mountain Boy" on a variety of radio stations in the Midwest and Northeast, Kincaid contributed powerfully to the idea that mountain songs came from an undefiled Anglo-Saxon past, and that, unlike most commercial hillbilly songs, they were decent and moral.[6] In Kincaid's way of thinking, his music fulfilled the formulaic criteria associated with mountain music: it was old, pure, honest, and moral. In short, Kincaid tried to stake out within commercial country music the kind of moral high ground that the academic folklorists, concert recitalists, and mountain settlement schools had already occupied in their treatment of Appalachian music.

Kincaid's employment of mountain metaphors can be easily understood, but it must be admitted in all candor that neither he nor his music really fell under the "mountain" rubric. He was not a mountain boy. His songs, while usually old—and probably moral—were not exclusive to the mountains, although they were undoubtedly loved by mountain people as they were by rural and working-class people everywhere. Kincaid succeeded in linking a basically Victorian, though rural, parlor style to the performance of a presumably mountain-derived repertoire. Most important, he succeeded—perhaps unintentionally—in convincing much of the American public that such performance was authentically "Appalachian" in style and content.

Although the idea of a distinctly recognizable entity known as "Appalachian music" exerts a strong appeal, we should recognize by now that Appalachian people always have made music in a wide variety of styles. Variety was present, though ignored, when Cecil Sharp made his first forays into the mountains in 1916.[8] It was also there when Ralph Peer brought his recording crew to Bristol, Tennessee, in 1927, and when Jean Ritchie was growing up and singing her family's songs in Viper, Kentucky. Variety remains a defining trait of Appalachian music today, even as festivals and workshops strive to preserve the older styles.

The myth of Anglo-Saxonism has been, for the most part, discarded, even though a preoccupation with Celticism still creeps into discussions of Appalachian music. Scholars such as David Whisnant, William Tallmadge, and Robert Winans[9] have noted increasingly the African-American presence in and contributions to Appalachian culture. Abundant evidence suggests that songs of popular, gospel, and commercial origin successfully competed with the older British ballads and love songs long before the hillbilly music business began disseminating its products in the southern hills. Songs and song lists collected from students at Berea College before World War I, for example, display a large percentage of Tin Pan Alley songs.[10] Published folksong collections exhibit similar choices, as do the early commercial recordings of mountain musicians such as Ernest Stoneman, Frank Hutchison, Fiddlin' John Carson, and Bradley Kincaid. Songs like "The Fatal Wedding," "Maple on the Hill," "I'll Remember You, Love, in My Prayers," and "I'll Be All Smiles Tonight" were not foisted upon an unwilling public by the hillbilly musicians. Such songs were already present in the mountain consciousness well before the first hillbilly records were made. Among the many contributions made by Jean Ritchie in her delightful reminiscence, *Singing Family of the Cumberlands*, is the evidence she presents of the early penetration of the Kentucky hills by outside commercial influence. The songs included in her dad's songbook, produced on his own printing press, provide vivid evidence of the mountain folk's easy absorption of new material. "Sweet Kitty Wells," of blackface minstrel origin, lies in comfortable companionship with old ballads and spirituals. Even more revealing is the information about the talking machine and its supply of such records as the vaudeville coon song, "Whistling Rufus," which entered the Ritchie household in 1905.[11]

Despite the growing recognition of ethnic and cultural diversity in Appalachia, as well as the knowledge that many types of songs, both British and American, have long competed for the affections of mountain folk, the "idea" of a special entity known as "Appalachian music," with certain enduring but hard-to-define traits, has clearly preserved its force in American culture. One often encounters, for example, the assertion that country music began in the southern hills, and that its purest and perhaps most moral expressions still reside in those hills or in those performers (like Ricky Skaggs) whose styles seem closest to the Appalachian source.

Still another oft-encountered assumption is the belief that musical purity and tradition can most easily be found off the commercial beaten track and within the Appalachians themselves. The Appalachians as a geographical entity, as well as "Appalachian music," have continued to be retreats for musicians and others who seek alternatives to mainstream culture or a return to the roots of American culture. Most Americans have found such retreat only in the lyrics or rhythms of a song (such as "Rocky Top, Tennessee" or "Country Roads"), in attendance at a mountain folk festival, or in the occasional visit to a folk museum or theme park. John Lair, though, demonstrated almost sixty years ago that fantasy can become reality. While working for WLS in Chicago, this homesick Kentuckian wrote a song called "Take Me Back to Renfro Valley" which expressed his nostalgic recollections of a community that had never really existed. He later built a big barn near his old Kentucky home place, christened it the Renfro Valley Barn Dance, and eventually saw a real community and post office emerge around the very popular radio show.

No one has duplicated John Lair's feat, but, beginning with Bascom Lamar Lunsford's establishment of the Asheville Folk Festival in 1928 and extending through the consummation of John Rice Irwin's personal vision, the Appalachian Museum near Knoxville, and Dolly Parton's theme park, Dollywood near Sevierville, Tennessee, several enterprising individuals have presented us with alternative ways of viewing and appreciating Appalachian culture at least for a day. The Folk Music Revival of the 1960s drew much of its inspiration from the idealization of Appalachian culture, or from the borrowings made from musicians of that culture. The folk boom began, of course, with the Kingston Trio's immensely popular 1959 recording of the North Carolina murder ballad, "Tom Dooley." Many young musicians, however, were not content to perform in such a watered-down style, and they sought sustenance in other presumed Appalachian forms, drawing songs and styles from such earlier protest singers as Aunt Molly Jackson and Jim Garland, or from the traditional balladry of Jean Ritchie or Texas Gladden, or from the hillbilly recordings of people like the Carter Family or Clarence Ashley. Led by the New Lost City Ramblers, a growing number of mostly northern-born musicians began experimenting with old-time string band styles or with bluegrass music, a newer style that was presumed to be a modern adaptation of mountain music.

The Folk Revival enjoyed its brief moment of glory in mainstream American popular culture and then faded from the limelight. Before it departed, however, the revival provided a forum for the rediscovery of such pioneer hillbilly musicians, and genuine mountaineers, as Dock Boggs, Buell Kazee, and Clarence Ashley, and it introduced new musicians like Doc Watson to the American public. The revival also left behind a thriving culture composed of string bands, ballad singers, clog dancers, annual workshops (like the one at Augusta, West Virginia), and dedicated journals such as Alice Gerrard's *Old Time Herald.*

Meanwhile, bluegrass music left its base in the Upper South and reached out to an increasingly larger audience that now extends around the world. While superb musicianship clearly marks the driving force behind bluegrass's worldwide expansion, the music's identification with the Folk Revival was also a major factor in its winning a youthful audience outside the South. It would be impossible to determine the extent to which visions of Appalachian purity, tradition, and virtue contributed to bluegrass music's acceptance, but early accounts of its expansion routinely linked the music to mountain beginnings. The first recorded anthology of the music was titled *Mountain Music: Bluegrass Style.*[12] And Robert Cantwell, in his provocative study of the form, *Bluegrass Breakdown: The Making of the Old Southern Sound,* spoke for many fans and commentators when he described bluegrass as *"the* music of the Appalachian people."[13] Bluegrass music *is* popular among many Appalachian people, both within the region and in such cities as Detroit, Dayton, Cincinnati, and Washington, D.C., where southern hill people have thronged. Many pioneer bluegrass musicians were born in the Appalachians, and many younger musicians still come from the region. The founding "father" of bluegrass, however, Bill Monroe, whose "high, lonesome" style of singing originally set the standard by which singers were judged, came instead from western Kentucky and looked toward singers like Jimmie Rodgers, the Mississippi Blues Yodeler, as his personal mentors. Indeed, no Appalachian musicians played in the seminal Monroe band, the Blue Grass Boys, which made the first bluegrass records in the period from 1945 to 1948. Earl Scruggs, the popularizer of the sensational three-finger style of banjo playing, came from the southern Piedmont region (near Shelby, North Carolina), as did Don Reno (from Spartanburg, South Carolina), whose banjo style was even more eclectic than that of Scruggs. These musicians' styles represented not the purity nor archaicism of Appalachia, but instead the dynamic fusion of folk and commercial pop styles born in a cotton-mill region inhabited by rural people.

The linking of bluegrass music to mountain images again represents the powerful persistence of the Appalachian idea in American popular culture—the preference for imagination over reality. Bluegrass means many things to many people, but it has also been a refuge for those who would preserve older country styles, and for those who resent the seaminess and tawdriness of mainstream country music. Similar quests for tradition, purity, and basic morality had helped to inspire the search for the "lonesome tunes" of Appalachia early in the twentieth century; they had accompanied Bradley Kincaid's career as a "mountain singer" in the 1920s and 1930s; and their association with Roy Acuff's style during the World War II era makes that entertainer's great success more understandable. Revisionist academicians might wish for greater clarity in the conception of "Appalachian music" and for more precise historical understanding of the ways in which the concept developed, but no one should really despair over the consequences of the romantic preoccupation with mountain songs and styles. If the Appalachian idea has inspired a search for and preservation of old songs and styles, as it clearly has, then that idea has wrought beneficial consequences for a society that is too much wedded to progress and change. Numerous "outsiders" who have made Appalachia their special musical province—from Olive Dame Campbell and Cecil Sharp to Mike Seeger, Ralph Rinzler, Si Kahn, John McCutcheon, and Jeff Titon—have worked mightily to make the world aware of the region's musical wealth. Their contributions are in no way diminished by the reminder that our main emphasis should be on the music of the Appalachian people themselves. When we assay the music of the region today, in the Old Regular Baptist and Pentecostal churches, in the honky-tonks of any city, on radio stations throughout the region, at VFW jam sessions, and at fiddle contests, folk festivals, or rock concerts, we find that music is as important in the lives of Appalachian people today as it was when Cecil Sharp collected his songs almost eighty years ago. But when we make our investigation, we will find that the music's strength and vitality comes from its diversity. Above all, I believe that we will find that the *reality* of Appalachian music is even more fascinating than any fantasy that yet lingers.

Notes

1. Henry D. Shapiro, "The Folksong Revival," in Shapiro, *Appalachia On Our Mind: The Southern Mountains and Mountaineers in the American Consciousness, 1870–1920* (Chapel Hill: U of North Carolina P, 1978), ch. 10, pp. 244–65.

2. Emma Bell Miles, "Some Real American Music," in Miles, *The Spirit of the Mountains* (1905; Knoxville: U of Tennessee P, 1975), 146–71.

3. Cecil Sharp and Olive Dame Campbell, *English Folk Songs from the Southern Appalachians* (New York: Putnam's, 1917).

4. Howard Brockway spoke of the "poise and innate dignity" of mountain people in "The Quest of the Lonesome Tunes," *Music On the Air,* ed. Hazel Gertrude Kinscella (Garden City, NY: Garden City Publishing, 1934), 162.

5. See Edwin T. Arnold, "Al, Abner, and Appalachia." *Appalachian Journal* 17 (Spring 1990): 266.

6. Bradley Kincaid, *My Favorite Mountain Ballads and Old-Time Songs* (Chicago: WLS, 1928) and *Favorite Old-Time Songs and Mountain Ballads* (Chicago: WLS, 1930), and

Kincaid to H. E. Taylor, Berea College, 24 Nov. 1932 (Berea Archives, Berea College, Berea, KY).

7. Folklorist Archie Green notes that Anglo-Saxon attributions "were used by Harvard rhetoricians as well as by Kentucky mountain settlement school teachers to give American folksong a blue ribbon pedigree" and that "patriotism and purity formed a banner which waved over folksong, and eventually over country music." Quoted in Loyal Jones, *Radio's Kentucky Mountain Boy Bradley Kincaid* (Berea, KY: Appalachian Center, Berea College, rev. ed. 1988), 4.

8. Sharp came to the mountains imbued with the conviction that people were actually singing the ballads collected by Francis James Child. He therefore searched for no other kind of musical material.

9. See David Whisnant, *All That Is Native and Fine: The Politics of Culture in an American Region* (Chapel Hill: U of North Carolina P, 1983); William Tallmadge, "The Folk Banjo and Claw-Hammer Performance Practice in the Upper South: A Study of Origins," *The Appalachian Experience: Proceedings of the Sixth Annual Appalachian Studies Conference,* ed. Barry M. Buxton (Boone, NC: Appalachian Consortium P, 1983); Robert B. Winans, "The Folk, the Stage, and the Five-String Banjo in the Nineteenth Century," *Journal of American Folklore* 89 (Oct.-Dec. 1976): 406–37.

10. The catholic receptivity of mountain singers to nontraditional material, as well as their ability to adapt such material to older melodic forms, was brought home to me dramatically and delightfully when I heard the great North Carolina ballad singer, Doug Wallin, sing "After the Ball" in a modal style at a conference on traditional music in Chapel Hill, NC, in April 1989.

11. The name of the Ritchie songbook suggests the range of songs that were included: *Lover's Melodies, A Choice Collection of Old Sentimental Songs Our Grandmother Sang, and Other Popular Airs.* Jean Ritchie, *Singing Family of the Cumberlands* (1955; New York: Geordie Music Publishing, 1980), 73–76.

12. *Mountain Music: Bluegrass Style,* Folkways FA2318, was produced and edited in 1959 by Mike Seeger.

13. Robert Cantwell, *Bluegrass Breakdown: The Making of the Old Southern Sound* (Urbana: U of Illinois P, 1984), 143.

Judy Odom

Judy Odom grew up in Birmingham, Alabama. She is a Phi Beta Kappa graduate of Birmingham-Southern College and holds a master's degree in English from Emory University. In 1985 she received a Stokely Fellowship at the University of Tennessee

Her short stories and poems have appeared in numerous journals and anthologies such as *Now and Then, Crescent Review, Homewords: A Book of Tennessee Writers,* and *Readings in Southern Appalachian Literature.* In 1986 and

1987 her stories won Sherwood Anderson Awards. A collection of her poems, *Blossom, Stalk, and Vine*, was published in September 1990 by Iris Press.

The Diviner Choosing A Well Site

Limestone, Tennessee, 1986

"I mostly use
a cherry limb,"
she said.
"Young cherry.
A new limb
forked
by growing
to a natural Y.
It seeks
the water
for its own
green pleasure.
I can feel
its hunger
singing
in my hands.
The rod
dips down
into a stillness.
Then the water
answers,
true and cold
as children's
voices calling
on a winter night.
Some people
name me witch
and shun
my power,
but it's just
a kind of listening
with your fingers.
I set the music free.
I don't create
the song."

From *Blossom Stalk and Vine* (Iris Press, 1990). Reprinted by permission of the author and publisher.

Thomas G. Burton
and Ambrose N. Manning

See volume 2, chapter 2, for biography of Burton; volume 2, chapter 3, for biography of Manning.

Superstitions and Riddles

The term *superstition* is a word of uncertain origin, and means many things to many people. For purposes of this study, however, *superstition* is considered to be an irrational fear of, or belief in, what is unknown, mysterious, or supernatural.

The early history of man produced a huge mass of superstitions. Today, many of the most highly educated men and women have some of these same or similar superstitions that were born of ignorance and fear. Many of these appear to be survivals of childhood practices, while others are retained as amusing, playful pastimes.

These superstitions and riddles were collected by students from Hawkins and Carter counties, Tennessee, in the 1960s.

Weather Superstitions

If it rains while the sun is shining, it will rain at the same time the next day.
If it rains on Monday, it will rain three days that week.
If it rains on Sunday, it will rain three Sundays in succession.
If a train is especially noisy, it will rain.
Aching joints indicate rain.
If your bunions hurt, it will rain.
If an owl hoots on the mountain, the weather will be fair; if it moves to lower lands, foul weather is approaching.
If a peafowl struts before six o'clock, it will rain that day.
When a herd of sheep gather around each other, it is going to rain.
Killing and hanging a black snake on a fence with its belly turned toward the sun will bring rain before the next setting sun.
When a bobwhite starts calling, he is praying for rain.
When a "rain" crow begins to crow, rain is coming.

From *A Collection of Folklore by Undergraduate Students of East Tennessee State University,* ed. Thomas Burton and Ambrose N. Manning (Research Advisory Council of East Tennessee State University, 1966). Used by permission of the editors.

"Dry weather" lightning (jagged lightning at a far distance) indicates rain.
Thick and tight shucks on corn indicates bad weather.
Red sky at night, sailor's delight; red sky in morning, sailor take warning.

Good and Bad Luck Superstitions

You will have good luck if you
> find a four-leaf clover
> find a four-hole button
> find a pin and pick it up
> find a horseshoe and hang it up
> carry a rabbit's foot
> believe in good luck charms
> knock on wood (will keep away bad luck)
> always put your right sock and shoe on first in the morning
> see a bluebird
> get up and put on your dress inside-out and wear it all day

You will have bad luck if you
> count the stars
> count saw teeth
> go out a window
> hit someone with a broom
> stub your toe
> wear clothes inside-out
> meet a funeral procession
> turn a chair around on one leg
> sit on a table
> open an umbrella indoors
> bring an implement (such as a hoe) into the house
> rock a chair with no one in it
> find a pin with the point turned towards you
> wear a peacock feather
> start a journey and come back
> kill a cricket
> postpone a wedding
> see a falling tree
> cut a baby's fingernails with the scissors
> find a frog on your window
> spill salt
> wear black to a wedding
> stir batter in a direction opposite to that in which you began
> sweep dirt out of the house after dark
> burn sassafras wood
> take ashes out on Friday

borrow salt and pay it back
mention funeral on a wedding day
sweep under a bed with someone sick in it
hear a hen crow
enter a house for the first time and go out the same door
cross the path of a black cat that walks in front of you

Remedies or Superstitions Concerning Medicine

To cure the earache:
    blow smoke in your ear
    put urine in your ear
To remove a wart:
    get "stump" water early in the morning and put it on the wart
    steal a dishrag and rub over wart, put the dishrag under a rock, and by the
    time the dishrag rots the wart will be gone
To cure headache, put a cornmeal plaster on the forehead.
To remove the pain of a sting, put snuff on it.
To take "fire" from burns, put toothpaste or soda on it.
To help rheumatism pains, carry an Irish potato in your pocket.
To prevent rheumatism, wear copper bands around your wrists or ankles.
To keep from getting "car sick," carry an Irish potato in the car.
To stop the flow of blood, put soot on the wound.
To stop the flow of blood, put cobwebs on the wound.
To cure "hiccups," take nine sips of water without breathing.
For diseases of the brain, eat walnuts.
To prevent an amputated limb from hurting, bury it immediately.
To ward off diseases, tie an "asafetida" bag around a child's neck.
For the bold hives, "scarify": take a sharp knife and stick in the baby's back, get
    one teaspoon of blood and give to the baby in its mouth.
To make the hives "come out" on a baby, get three "roly-poly" bugs, put them
    in a bag and tie it around the baby's neck and leave them until they dry
    up; if you don't do this, the baby will die.
To cure the "thrash," a midwife blows in the child's mouth.

Miscellaneous Superstitions

If you walk under a grapevine backwards, you won't grow any more.
If your ears burn, someone is talking about you; throw salt in the fire and they
    will have a toothache.
If you set your shoes together straight, you will prevent bad dreams.
If you sweep under a person's feet, he will never get married.
If you dream of death, there will be a wedding in the family.

If four people cross one another's hands when they shake hands, there will be a wedding.

Rain on your wedding day indicates the tears you will shed.

If a girl splashes dishwater on herself, she will marry a drunk.

If you cut your toenails on the "old" of the moon, you'll cause ingrown toenails.

If you believe in Christ, you can take off warts.

If you have moles on your head, you have a lot of money.

Cold shivers indicate that someone is walking over the place that will be your grave.

If you find a five-leaf clover, pull it and make a wish and it will come true; if you do not pull it, you will have bad luck.

If you dream of death, there will be a birth in the family.

A blister on the tongue means one has told a lie.

Every stitch you take on a garment while wearing it indicates the number of lies that will be told on you.

The gift of a knife cuts friendship.

If you let a baby look in a mirror before it is six months old, it will die before it is one year old.

If your back itches, you will get a "whipping."

If the hem of your dress is turned up, kiss it and you will get a new one.

If you find a bobby pin, make a wish and with your right hand, throw it over the left shoulder, and the wish will come true.

If you make a wish on the first star you see at night, your wish will come true.

A wish made on a falling star will come true.

When you see a robin sitting still, make a wish and count to one hundred; if he hasn't flown, your wish will come true.

If you drop a dishrag and it spreads out, a woman is coming, and if it wads up, a man is coming.

If a rooster crows in the front yard, someone is coming.

If you throw silverware out a window, someone will come.

If you spill salt, you will have a quarrel.

If you kill a toad frog, the cow's milk will turn bloody.

If your right hand itches, you will shake hands with a stranger.

If your left hand itches, you will receive money.

If your right eye itches, you are going to cry.

If your left eye itches, you will be pleased.

If you sing before breakfast, you will cry before night.

When someone in the family dies, go tell the bees; if you don't, they will sting you when you go to rob their hives.

When someone in the family dies, turn the mirror to the wall.

Don't comb your hair on New Year's Day; if you do, the well will dry up.

To keep the witches away on Washington's Birthday, cook dried pumpkin for dinner and serve sassafras tea.

To keep the witches away, put a broom under the doorstep.

To keep the devil away, throw a pinch of salt over your left shoulder.

Sources

The preceding superstitions were gathered by Madalyn Stair from the following people in Hawkins County, Tennessee: Mr. John Hughes (formerly of West Virginia), Mr. Charlie Carter, Mrs. Roy Morgan, Mrs. Mary Bowman, Mr. Lawrence Bailey (formerly of Kentucky), Mr. Charles Hinshaw (formerly of North Dakota), Mr. Rufus Stines, Miss Mary Edith Ward, Mrs. Beulah Robinette, Mrs. Eva Long.

A Collection of Riddles

Riddles, like fables and folk stories, belong to all races and ages. The riddle is a form of puzzling or clever question, the answer of which is to be guessed. Sometimes it is a statement which has a hidden meaning to be discovered or guessed. The earliest ones were presented by ancient oracles and bards and were of serious character. Later, as a game, high prizes or heavy forfeits were paid. Today they are a form of social amusement. (These riddles were collected by Patsy Buck from English students at Elizabethton High School, Elizabethton, Tennessee. Thanks go to the English students of Mrs. Louie Kinch and Miss Hildred Wagner at Elizabethton High School, Elizabethton, Tennessee, for their assistance in collecting these riddles.)

R. I rode across the bridge on Sunday, stayed three days, rode back on Sunday, but Yet walked.
A. Horse is named Sunday, dog named Yet.

R. Between earth and heaven, knot on a tree; I told you, now you tell me.
A. Knot on a tree.

R. As I went across the London Bridge, I met a man. He tipped his hat and drew his cane. In this riddle, I've told you his name.
A. Andrew.

R. Big at the bottom, little at the top,
   Little thing in the middle, goes flippity flop.
A. A churn.

R. Twelve men came riding by,
   Twelve pears were hanging high,
   Each took a pear and left eleven hanging there.
A. Each was the man's name who took the pear.

R. What has legs but can't walk?
A. A table or a bed.

R. What is black and white and read all over?
A. A newspaper.

R. What has an eye but can't see?
A. A needle or a potato or a stove.

R. What has a tongue but can't talk?
A. A shoe.

R. What goes around the house and makes only one track?
A. A wheelbarrow.

R. Little Mary Ettiecoat
    In her white petticoat,
    The longer she stands,
    The shorter she grows.
    What is she?
A. A candle.

R. Legs I have but never walk;
    I backbite all, but never talk.
A. A flea.

R. What has eighteen legs and catches flies?
A. A baseball team.

R. What has four wheels and flies?
A. A garbage truck.

R. When is a car not a car?
A. When it turns into a driveway.

R. Why are fish so smart?
A. They travel in schools.

R. If you have a cow and a duck in a cage, what would you have?
A. Quackers and milk.

R. What is it that gets larger the more you take away?
A. A hole.

R. Which month has twenty-eight days?
A. They all have.

R. What is the correct height for people to stand?
A. Over two feet.

R. Why is snow like an apple tree?
A. It leaves in the spring.

R. When was meat the highest?
A. When the cow jumped over the moon.

R. What has a bed, but does not sleep?
    What has a mouth, but does not speak?
    It always runs and never walks.
    What is it?
A. A river.

R. What has teeth but no mouth?
A. A comb.

R. What has ears but cannot hear?
A. Corn.

R. A house full, a hole full, you can't catch a bowl full.
A. Smoke.

R. Two lookers, two crookers, four stiff standers, and one switch about.
A. Cow.

R. All over the hills and hollows and sits under bed at night.
A. Shoes.

R. What is it that never was and never will be?
A. A mouse's nest in a cat's ear.

R. What goes to bed with shoes on?
A. A horse.

R. What animal goes on four legs in the morning, on two legs at noon and on
    three legs in the evening?
A. Man, who crawls when a baby, stands erect on two legs, and in old age walks
    with a cane.

R. What has arms but can't move?
A. Chair.

R. When is a door not a door?
A. When it's ajar.

R. What flies forever, and rests never?
A. Wind.

R. Four legs and can't walk,
    Got a tongue but can't talk.
A. A wagon.

R. Round as a biscuit, busy as a bee;
    The prettiest little thing you ever did see.
A. Watch.

R. Goes all over the house and doesn't make a track.
A. A broom.

R. Black without, red within,
Has double lips and no chin.
A. Blacksnake.

R. Why does a sick person not feel a sense of touch?
A. They don't feel too good.

R. A duck before two ducks;
A duck behind two ducks;
A duck between two ducks.
How many ducks?
A. Three.

R. If six birds were sittin' on a limb, and two took a notion to fly off, how many would be left?
A. Six, they just took a notion.

R. What is the difference between an old dime and a new penny?
A. Nine cents.

R. How did the firefly feel when he backed into the fan?
A. He was de-lighted.

R. When is a cow not a cow?
A. When it is turned into pasture.

R. Which is bigger, Mr. Bigger or Mr. Bigger's baby?
A. Mr. Bigger's baby because it is a little Bigger.

R. What goes up and down and over hills, but stays in one place?
A. A road.

R. What do they call a sailor who crosses the ocean twice without bathing?
A. A dirty double-crosser.

R. What day of the year is in command?
A. March 4th!

R. What is nothing but holes tied to holes and yet as strong as steel?
A. A chain.

R. How far can you walk in the forest?
A. You walk half way in, because you come out the other half.

R. I'm a humble little thing,
always coming in the spring.
In the meadow green I'm found,
peeping just above the ground.
And my stalk is covered flat,
with a white and yellow hat.
A. Daisy.

R. Why is a schoolboy like a postage stamp?
A. They both get licked and stuck in the corner.

R. If April showers bring May flowers, what do May flowers bring?
A. Pilgrims.

R. Why is a baseball game like a biscuit?
A. It depends on the success of the batter.

R. Name two coins that will make fifteen cents, but one of them is not a nickel.
A. A dime and nickel. Only one of them was not a nickel; the other could be.

R. How can you tell when a train is gone?
A. It leaves its tracks behind.

R. What is it?
    Old Mother Twichett
    Has but one eye
    And a long tail
    Which she can let fly;
    And every time
    She goes over a gap,
    She leaves a bit
    Of her tail in the trap.
A. A needle and thread.

R. What is it?
    Thirty white horses upon a red hill;
    Now they tramp; now they chomp;
    Now they stand still.
A. Teeth.

R. In marble halls as white as milk
    Lined with a skin as soft as silk,
    Within a fountain crystal-clear,
    A golden apple doth appear.
    No doors there are to this stronghold,
    Yet thieves break in and steal the gold.
A. An egg.

R. Why was the Mother Flea so sad?
A. Because all her babies were going to the dogs.

R. What's the first thing you lose when you stand up?
A. Your lap.

R. There is a green house. Inside the green house is a white house. Inside the white house is a red house. Inside the red house live little black men. What is it?
A. A watermelon.

R. What is the worst weather for rats and mice?
A. When it's raining cats and dogs.

R. What animal took the most luggage into the ark?
A. The elephant. He took his trunk.

R. What animals took the least luggage into the ark?
A. The fox and rooster. They took only a comb and a brush between them.

R. What did the little porcupine say when he backed into the barbed wire fence?
A. "Is that you, Mother?"

R. What has a face and hands but can't wash them?
A. A clock.

R. Why did the hummingbird hum?
A. He didn't know the words.

R. Use me well and I'm everybody,
   Scratch my back and I'm nobody.
   Who am I?
A. A mirror.

R. Goes up and down, up and down,
   Touches neither sky nor ground.
A. A pump handle.

R. Can you spell hard water with three letters?
A. I-C-E.

R. Which travels faster, heat or cold?
A. Heat. You can catch a cold.

R. Where can happiness always be found?
A. In the dictionary.

R. What occurs twice in a moment but not once in a thousand years?
A. The letter "M."

R. What can you keep even after giving it to everyone else?
A. Your word.

R. Which is the wiser, the stork or the owl?
A. The stork. The owl says "Who? Who?" The stork knows who.

R. What is it that, the more it dries, the wetter it gets?
A. A towel.

Robert Morgan

See volume 2, chapter 2, for biography.

Death Crown

In the old days back when
one especially worthy lay dying
for months, they
say the feathers in the pillow would
knit themselves into a crown
that those attending felt in perfect
fit around the honored head.
The feather band they took to be
certain sign of another crown,
the saints and elders of the church,
the Deep Water Baptists said.
I've seen one unwrapped from its
cloth in the attic, the down
woven perfect and tight for
over a century, shiny but
soft and light almost as light.

From *Groundwork,* Gnomon Press, 1979. Reprinted by permission of the publisher.

Ron Giles

A native of Alabama, Ron Giles received his Ph.D. in English from Auburn University and now teaches at East Tennessee State University, where he is professor of English. His criticism has appeared in *College Literature, South Atlantic Review,* and *Poesis.*

"Moon over Phu Bai" is from a series of poems reflecting Ron Giles' experience as a veteran of the Vietnam War.

Moon over Phu Bai

Top swapped the seabees
two bottles of scotch
for lumber
and built a porch
on his hootch.
We sat there with Dave Hall
and watched the moon
the first time they walked on it.
I said the scriptures prophesied
it would turn to blood,
and Top (whose name I swear was Tommy Tell)
said the Mets would win the pennant too.
Top and Dave Hall laughed,
and Top held his knuckles out
and said,
feel that moon drip.

From *Now and Then* 4.3 (Fall 1987). Reprinted by permission of the author and *Now and Then.*

Chapter 4

Dialect and Language

Introduction

Southern Appalachian speech is typically considered a dialect of the English language. Every region, of course, has its own dialect, and the English language is but the sum of its dialects. But Southern Appalachian speech is often considered so distinct a form of expression from that of other English speakers as to be archaic, quaint, backward, and/or amusing. Indeed, the dialect of the region is amusing, not because it is backward or inferior but because it often employs humorous metaphor and colorful expression.

Appalachian speech reflects the tendency of language to vary, over space and through time. Degree and rate of variation in Appalachian speech, which offers evidence of both the force of tradition and the love of improvisation, is a matter of debate. On the one hand, Appalachian English is thought to be the oldest living English dialect; on the other, present British dialects are thought to be closer to those of the seventeenth and eighteenth centuries than any dialect of American English, including Appalachian English, which has undergone significant change over the last hundred years.

Appalachian speech also gives rise to a debate about correctness, effectiveness in communication, and the relationship of the Appalachian dialect to "standard" English. It can be safely said that merely correct language is not always effective, while technically incorrect language is not always ineffective, and may be delightfully charming and memorable.

Jim Wayne Miller

See volume 2, chapter 2, for biography.

Land and Language

People put on new clothes, live in a new
house by the big road, move to town.
But that country of coves and ridges lives in their language.

Their talk becomes a landscape where words glint
like tin-topped barns on September afternoons,
loom dark and thick as a laurel hell,
or clear as a mountain spring, let you see
below the surface ripple, magnifying
clean sand and pebbles in a standing depth.

Still at home in their talk, they light a shuck
when hurrying somewhere, take two rows at a time,
hoping to make it home by the edge of dark.
Thunder is still a wagon crossing a bridge.
Their latch string's always out. And if you come
early, it must be to borrow fire.
But light down. If there's not room, they'll hang
you on a nail. If George's wife is going to
have a baby, his bees are about to swarm.

But nobody ever knows a countryside
until he knows it at night—in the dark
of forgetfulness. (What was it Papa called
the little perch we caught in the creek
when we were growing up down in Pick Britches?)

And in a swirling storm of new sensations
words melt—firedog, milkgap, singletree, sundad—

like snowflakes on the tips of children's tongues.

From *Brier, His Book*, Gnomon Press, 1988, © 1988 by Jim Wayne Miller. Reprinted by
permission of the author and publisher.

Elizabeth Hunter

A native of Boston, Elizabeth Hunter, after spending part of her youth in New Hampshire, entered Radcliffe College, where she graduated in 1967. Heading south, she earned a master's degree in teaching at East Tennessee State University, but she never taught. "I couldn't get a job teaching," she jokes, "because I wasn't related to anybody." After working for a number of newspapers in the mountains, Hunter in 1981 became a freelance writer. In addition to writing for magazines, she contributes to several local papers, but on her own time and on subjects she chooses. Among her credits are *The State, Blue Ridge Country,* and *North Carolina Homes and Gardens.* In her house overlooking the Toe River, she sometimes hears at night her three favorite sounds: rain on a roof, a train passing, and a cat purring. Then she knows she is "ideally situated."

The following article, written in 1978, serves to introduce the phenomenon of Ray Hicks.

Ray Hicks: A Teller of Tales

Ray Hicks says there are good spirits and evil spirits. He's seen both kinds. Driving home in the rain after talking to him, I wondered whether it was a good—though unseen—spirit that led me to his door.

I stopped at what turned out to be Ray Hicks's house Tuesday afternoon for the simple reason it was the first inhabited building I'd seen in miles and miles and miles. I'd gotten lost on a vague "going home again" trip over the southeastern face of Beech Mountain, looking for a half-built cabin friends of mine and I had camped out in ten years earlier.

The road I took—it was the wrong one—had gotten progressively narrower and more rutted and rocky the further up and over the mountain it climbed, until at the top I had the crazy sensation I was somewhere near the ocean. Fenceposts and barns and ancient fallen trees bleached silver-gray and that limitless, cloud-filled gray-blue sky surrounded me until I was half-convinced that over the next lip of mountain I would come upon the equally limitless sea.

As it was, I came upon Ray Hicks's house—a rambling two-story farmhouse weathered a darker grayish brown, rusty-roofed—laid out below me like the quintessential mountain farm, with the quintessential bib-overall-clad mountain man seated on the front porch.

I waved, and he threw up a languid arm in return. I decided to drive as

From Johnson City, Tennessee, *Press-Chronicle,* June 3, 1978. Reprinted by permission of the author.

close as I could and go down and ask where on God's gray-green earth I had come to rest.

During the next hour or so, I came to learn why Ray Hicks is offered $250 a day to come spin tales—he's known far and wide for his telling of Jack tales—at storytelling festivals. Though he told me no Jack tales as we sat there on the front porch of the house in which he was born, below the brown and white hex signs ("to keep the ghosts away") that his father had painted on the porch ceiling fifty years earlier, he did tell me what it was like to be (and have been) Ray Hicks, living out a life on Laurel Creek.

"I was born right there in that room," Hicks said, pointing with his walking stick to the room to his right. "They had a lot of midwives in those days, but I was delivered by a doctor, who came riding up the mountain on a horse, with his black doctor bag beside him."

Ray Hicks said the last two winters have been hard, but he and his wife and boys could get in and out without any trouble to speak of. "But back in those days when this country was settled," he said,

> when you settled here, you stayed. You planted a little patch [of] corn and taters, if they'd grow, and cornfield beans and a few pumpkins, and that's what you got by on.
>
> There wasn't much of a way to make money then, in this country. Except selling tanning bark. They'd peel the bark off the chestnut, oak and hemlock, in the summer when the juice was in it, and let it dry until winter, when they'd cord it up and load the wagon drawn by oxen in a double harness, and wagon it down to [the road] that ran from there up past Elizabethton, Tennessee—sending it to the tanneries in Bristol, Virginia. They did that for $25 a wagonload. That's how they made money.

Hicks went to school three miles down the mountain, walking back and forth each day. School let out at Christmas time ("The teachers would always give us a present, usually a few peanuts," he said.) and resumed in the spring. "I remember one time, it was the sixteenth of March, I was eleven years old, when we were in school and along about two o'clock it started snowing flakes as big as this." Hicks pointed to the first joint on his middle finger.

> I was in school and I remember thinking I wished they'd let us out, because I wanted to get started home. But they didn't until about three. My cousin, she was a year or so older than me, and I started walking back home, and the wind was blowing so hard she was smothering, couldn't get her breath.
>
> Pretty soon I was smothering too. I thought right quick and stuck my head in a snowbank to get my breath. She did too. Then we'd go on a little way. Then we'd do it again. That's how we got home that day.

Back when Hicks was growing up, he said, children believed in Santa

Claus a lot more—and for a lot longer—than they do today. "I didn't find out about Santa Claus until I was almost grown," he said.

> Mama told us if we didn't hang up our stockings, Santa Claus wouldn't come. One Christmas, though, we hung up our stockings and when we looked in them the next morning, there wasn't anything in them. Oh, we never got much—a few sticks of hard candy, sometimes an orange, some peanuts, never a toy, except once or twice a yoyo. The year we didn't get anything, though, Mama told us that Santa had started out from the North Pole and got froze in. I cried. I saw Santa lying dead on the snow—Santa and all his reindeer. It wasn't till years later I found out that the hard winter that had set in early that year had kept Daddy from hauling in his tanbark. I never dreamed Daddy was standing in for Santa.

As Hicks told his stories, he poked endlessly at the dirt in front of him with his stick, stopping only long enough to point with it up the mountain or toward the horizon to his left, where an increasingly dark gray sky set off the creamy white blossoms on a magnolia or to his right, where the family graveyard where his mother and two little brothers are buried below statues of the Virgin Mary was outlined against a less-threatening sky. I'd asked where I was—Ray Hicks told me.

I told him I'd heard him tell Jack tales at a festival at East Tennessee State University years earlier. He said he remembered my face, though that hardly seems possible, and asked after his friends there—Thomas Burton, Ambrose Manning, Jack Schrader, and a few others I didn't know. Though he's long been a fixture at folk and storytelling festivals in Tennessee, Ray Hicks hasn't been able to attend many the last couple of years. He's been sick, too weak to stand for long, had operations he just can't seem to get all the way well after.

He asked me, had I heard him play his harp when he was at the university. When I told him no, he offered to step inside and get some of his harps and play me a few songs.

Hicks stood up to go inside and it was like a carpenter's rule unfolding. Sitting there on the porch, folded up, so to speak, you get no hint of his startling height. He had to duck in his front door.

He returned with the harps and played a half-dozen numbers, including "one called 'Tweetsie,'" a fine imitation of the sad wail and businesslike puff-puff-puff of a steam engine. And after playing one song, he sang it—a story of short life, hard times, lost love, and broken promises "you made standing in your mama's door."

Sitting below the hex signs in front of his father's door, we watched the storm gather to the south, and the talk turned to spirits.

Hicks has seen one evil spirit. It came in the form of a black dog—a big black dog standing before him with light-shining eyes. "You think maybe it's a real dog," he said, "and you take a step backward. But he comes right up on you and over you and disappears over your head." Others have seen the evil spirit in other forms. He's seen lots of good spirits, he said, though he only told me about one:

> It was back when I was young and single. I'd walk across the mountain and down, to go to revivals. They was different then—the preachers really poured it on. People'd shout, and get happy, singing the praises of the Lord.
>
> One night I was walking back. It wasn't really dark yet, though I was walking through a woods of uncut hemlock, where it was dark most of the time, even during daylight. Ahead of me was a clearing. I sort of stumbled with my left foot—I hadn't had any lunch or dinner and I was hungry—and when I looked up I saw an old woman stooped over, wearing an old bonnet and a dress that swept the ground, gathering apples in her apron. I'd heard about the old woman spirit before, that her cabin had been there. But she was so clear I thought it was somebody playing a trick on me.
>
> I stood and watched. When she had an apronful, she started walking away from me, through the clearing. I thought, 'she's not making any noise walking through that stubble' where the field had been cut and the stalks had dried. And then I noticed she was walking along with her feet about six to eight inches off the ground. I watched, and suddenly she vanished in the air.

As Hicks finished the story, the first drops of rain hit the roof, playing loudly on the tin. My car windows were open. The rainstorm appeared to be bringing night with it. I wanted to get off the mountain before darkness descended.

I dashed for the car and began the long drive down the mountain as the rain darkened the road and plowed fields and drove the petals of apple blossoms from the trees. Almost instantaneously, mist rose from the valley, and as I drove on I wondered whether I would catch a glimpse of the old woman gathering apples in the gathering dark.

Ray Hicks

The text used here is a combination of the slightly differing versions of the narrations by Ray Hicks found in "Fixin' to Tell About Jack," Appalshop, 1974; and in "Whickity-Whack: Get into My Sack," the Burton-Manning Collection, Archives, East Tennessee State University; both used with permission. The Appalshop film, directed by Elizabeth Barret, shows Hicks at home and at work on his mountain farm.

For a dramatic (and humorous) treatment of this Jack Tale, see the film *Soldier Jack,* directed by Tim Davenport. (See "Films" in the Selected Bibliography at the end of this book).

This tale is also known as "Soldier Jack and the Magic Sack." For a text of that version, see Charles L. Perdue, Jr., *Outwitting the Devil: Jack Tales from Wise County, Virginia* (1987), 72–75.

Whickity-Whack: Death in a Sack

This here's one about Jack where he tied death up in a sack. He went to the army and spent thirty years. Back at that time, all you got was a suit of clothes and two loaves of light bread. And so he stayed his thirty year and they discharged him and give him his two loaves of light bread. And he started home and got to a little ole town and he met a beggar. And this beggar was a-beggin' him for something to eat and he retch him one of them loaves of light bread which he spent fifteen years fer. So, he give him one. And so he got on out to the other edge of the little town, and he met another 'un. So, he begin to beg. And Jack cut that loaf in half, in the middle, and he give 'em half of it. And he got on a little ways from him and got to studyin' that he cheated that last one! That he give the first one a whole loaf and give that one a half. And so, he run back and overtook that beggar. And when he went and overtook him, he said, "Here," says, "I cheated you." That beggar says, "How?"

He said, "Well, I had two loaves and I met a beggar 'fore I did you," and says, "I give him a whole loaf and I jist give you a half." Said, "I ran back to give you this other half, to make it fair to you." He said, "Well, being you was wantin' to be that fair with people and honest," he said, "I'll just give you something." He said, "Here, now, is a sack." Said, "You can carry it with you and if you get in any trouble or anything a-botherin' you," said, "just say, 'Whickity-whack, into my sack!'" He said, "It'll go down in there." He said, "Here's a drinkin' glass." He said, "If anybody's gonna die, get it half or a third full water. And the blubbers will stay to the top if they're goin' live and if they're gonna die they be to the bottom." An' so Jack thanked him and went on.

So, when he come to a little, uh, patch of woods directly and he wanted to try that sack out and he heared some wild turkeys a-hollerin'. And so he looked and they was twelve of 'em. It struck his mind, he say, "I, bedad!" He say, "I believe right here is, uh . . . a good place to try this sack out." He kept easing out in the woods and he got pretty close to 'em, and he . . . he squatted down and he got the sack between his legs an' looked up at the turkeys and he said, "Whickity-whack." He said, "Turkeys come down in this sack." He said, "Bedad, it was a sight to watch, twelve big 'uns stuffed down in there." And he drawed the sack shut and he slung it across his back and he went on.

From "Fixin' to Tell about Jack" (color 16-mm film, APPALSHOP, Inc., 1974), and "Whickity-Whack: Get into My Sack," the Burton-Manning Collection, East Tennessee State University Archives. Both are used by permission.

He come to another little ole town an' it got to gettin' dark. Gettin' down to nighttime, and him no supper, no money. He hunted around it and he found a little restaurant. He went in to see the waiter and he said, "Now . . . I want a place to stay." An' he said, "I ain't got no money, but I got twelve wild turkeys out here on the porch in a sack." And the waiter said "Turkeys! Twelve wild turkeys!!" He says, "That was awful! Twelve wild turkeys, hard as they was." Said, "You mean you got twelve wild turkeys?" He said, "Yeah, bedad, twelve wild turkeys out there in a sack." So the waiter went out and looked at 'em and sure 'nuff, they was in there. Twelve big 'uns! An' he took 'em in the buildin', got 'em out, an' the waiter said, "Well, we'll keep ya the night, give ya eats, your bed, and your breakfast in the morning for the turkeys, and give ya fifteen cents to boot."

And so the next morning he got his sack and left on out then with his sack and drinkin' glass, and he finally got on in home. Well, the time he'd been thirty years in the army, a lot of his people had deceased and he got around to seein' all the people that was livin' yet that he remembered, and some he'd forgot, he could get to remembering them and knowin' them again.

Well, while he was around like that, going around, there's a feller, another man, had two tracts, owned two tracts of land, and something had got, uh, a enchantment, ghosts, up on the upper place and killed a man dead. He buried men 'til it looked like he was wore out. Every man he put up there would be dead next morning. Nobody to tell the tale. And he put out an advertisement of any man, anywhere, could come and find out what was up there, he'd make 'em a clear title, or clear deed, to that tract of land up there, because it was botherin' him down on his other place, about to run him off.

An' so Jack heared it, and got out inquiring and askin' what few he'd meet and they'd give him, put him on the direction. And finally, he met one said, "Just over in the other holler," said, "is where he stays." And got over there and found him and asked him if that was right. And he said, "Yes, sir, that's right." Said, "I advertised that." So the man took 'im up, to stay there that night.

Well, the feller, he went back to the house and got Jack a fryin' pan and some vittles for his supper. And so Jack fried some meat he brought and fixed him some supper to eat and laid down on the floor to the fireplace to let his supper set. He hadn't laid there very long 'til he was takin' a kind of doze, a little nap had started on him. About that time it woke him back up out of it. He said he thought he heared somethin' upstairs and he kept listenin' and directly it come down the stairs and when it come out, it was six little black devils, had a sword apiece and a bag of money, and a deck a playin' cards. And so they bantered Jack for a game of poker and he had that dime and a nickel. There's no stores much yet; he hadn't spent it. And so they run the first game out and bet 'em a nickel apiece. And they got Jack's nickel an' that left him two. A dime. And so the second time, they beat his nickel and got it an' that left him one. And he said, "Bedad." He said, "They must be a-seeing my hole card." He said, "I got to watch close; don't, I'm gone." So, he watched close and winned that time. And got their nickel. And so the second time he winned again.

And he kept in playing, in and out, 'til finally he broke all six of 'em up and their bags was empty. Jack had it all. And they flew mad. They flew mad and begin to make at 'im with a sword apiece. And so Jack had forgot the sack laying over there in the corner and they was a pressin' on him too, all six on to one with a sword apiece. And Jack was just whippity-cut and dodging all that six, an' didn't look like he was gonna make it. And finally he got dodged a little over in the corner and it hit his mind about that sack. He just grabbed it, snatched it quick as he could, and said, "Whickity-whack into this sack," and they stuffed right down in it. Said, "It was a sight to see them six devils go down in there. It sucked 'em in." And he shet it up. He shet it up and throwed it over in the corner and went to sleep, and slept good.

An' the man come up the next mornin', 'specting to see him dead and bury him. He done buried everyone that tried to stay there, had to dig a grave and bury 'em. And so he went on up there, and Jack was a-singin' in there, and tole him then, he said it was six little black devils come out on him. He said, "Over here, they is in the sack." An' he said, "I'll swear," he said, "that's hard to believe!" And he peeked in at 'em and he said, "Well," he said, "them scandals!" He said, "With all the trouble they give me, I won't be satisfied 'til I see them beat up on a anvil!"

And they run a blacksmith shop back at that time. It was way down in the holler and they carried the sack down there and told the blacksmith man that they wanted him to beat them up. And they said when he 'gin to beat them on the anvil, they's so many sparks flew out of it, it set the blacksmith shop afire and burned it down!

Well, he made Jack a clear title, a clear deed for the place, and Jack began to work there, seeing to the place, and raising crops, tending sheep, cattle. And finally, the king in that country's daughter had got sick. And was near dead. The doctors had come an' to doctor her, and they couldn't cure 'er. And he had every doctor beheaded 'cause he couldn't cure his daughter. And so he put an advertisement, "If it was any man in the community, anywhere that could cure his daughter, the money wasn't a-lackin'. Gold and silver."

And so Jack got to studyin', and he got that sack . . . and he took the drinkin' glass, and he kept inquirin', and he got to the king's palace and, "Gosh!" he said, "Ah, them gold gates a-hangin' there." He said, "Bedad, that was something to look at! That he even had entered the king's palace!" And so he hollered, hollered the king out, and the king come out, spoke to 'im and said, "What are you here for?" And he said, "I've come here with your advertisement, come to give life, feelings, or what I can do to cure your daughter." "Well," he said, "now you un," he said, "you don't look like maybe probably you could do a job like that." But he said, "Do you know my orders?" "Well," he said, "You know the deal?" He said, "If you fail," said, "your head comes off the same as the doctors'." "Well" he says, "that don't bother me." He said, "I'm gonna try."

So he took 'im on in. He went in the room where she's in the bed and he told one of the other kids to go get that drinkin' glass about half or third full of water. And they went and got it, come back, and the blubbers shot right to the top and then went back down; death was on. She's a-dying, day and night, done gone. And he grabbed the sack right quick, and shuffled up agin the bed and said, "Ooooh pray death, whickity-whack. Death come down in this sack!" And death went right down in it, and he shet *it* up, and the girl she jumped, come up out of that bed just jumping all over the floor, well as she could be.

So they all come in a-praisin' him, the king tried to pay 'im all that gold, and he wouldn't take nothin'! So he went back to his farm and there was a big poplar tree, was a-growin' in the yard, and he clumb that tree and tied that sack plumb to the top of it, high as he could climb. The sack with death in it. An' so, he got to workin' there and stayed around, paying attention. Finally last, that sack with death in it had lost his mind, had left his memory. And it went on an went on, years went on. And he didn't know how, and the other people didn't know how long they'd lived. Hit had been a million years, and nobody could die.

And so finally one day, Jack decided he'd walk around the public road. Been there working, decided he'd take a walk. And so he hadn't went around the road too fer 'til he heard somethin' a-comin' round that road. "Rickety-rack, bumpety-bump. Rickety-rack, blumpety-bump." And so he got on around they's an old lady all drawed over that's just went to bones and hide. And her knee joints were just screekin' and her nose was a-bumpin' her knees. "Rickety-rack, bumpety-bump. Rickety-rack, blumpety-bump."

And he said, uh, he said, uh, "Hallo there, ma'am." She said, "Hallo there." Said, "I've heared that some blame rascal got death, death, tied up in a sack somewhere round." An' said, "I've been wantin' to die seem like fer a million years." Says, "I can't die." Say, "Looky here," say, "I just went to bones and hide. That's all that's left to it."

Well, that made Jack's memory come back. He went back and got some boys, he's, he's a-bumpin' pretty bad too. But he wasn't quite as bad as the old lady was, but he was a-bumpin' pretty bad and he couldn't climb that tree. Had to go get some younger boys of another generation to climb it. They clumb up there, got that sack, and so they brought it down and reached it to Jack. And they said that when he untied it, Jack was the first that fell dead. And in that tale is the end of Jack. "Whickity-Whack, Into My Sack."

James Robert Reese

Born in St. Louis, Missouri, James Robert (Jay) Reese attended the University of Missouri at Columbia, where he received a B.A. degree in English. He holds an M.A. in Spanish from the University of Illinois and a Ph.D. in English from the University of Tennessee at Knoxville. He completed his dissertation on dialectology under the direction of Harold Orton, director of the Survey of English Dialects, which was conducted at Leeds, England; and Nathalia Wright, Melville scholar and student of American and English dialects. At East Tennessee State University he continues his work in the study of dialect and the relationship between dialect and the folk tale.

Ray Hicks and the Oral Rhetorical Traditions of Southern Appalachia

The belief that a distinct Southern Appalachian culture exists is now so accepted that those who question it must defend their position. Not too many years ago, however, the burden of proof was on those scholars who audaciously proposed such an idea. Even when the proposition was obvious to many, it was not easy to confirm scientifically. The process of amassing credible scientific evidence to support the existence of a distinct subculture is often long and complicated. Researchers must identify a series of major behavioral patterns or beliefs either unique to the people of an area or which form a distinctive pattern. To gain such evidence, social mores, patterns of social interaction, cultural myths, organizational structures, family relations, and even physical characteristics are studied. Frequently, one of the early clues that a subculture exists is a perceived difference in language use. In fact, it is often a group's use of language which sparks the initial suggestion that its members are dissimilar from those around them. This was true in the initial identification of the Southern Appalachian culture; the first suggestions that there might be such a culture were intimately intertwined with the belief that the people who lived in the area used a type of English, *Appalachian English,* which was distinct from that of the rest of America.

The term *Appalachian English* is ambiguous. Currently, it most often refers to phonological, morphological, and syntactic differences among the dialects of Appalachia in contrast with those of non-Appalachian regions, but earlier it and *Appalachian dialect* more frequently referred to parts of a very complex cultural entity which is better identified as *Appalachian Oral Rhetoric.* When early cultural observers initially encountered the Appalachian, they were amazed by what they thought to be a unique and strange phenomenon, a group of wondrously articulate illiterate or semiliterate mountain people. In their search for an explanation of the verbal abilities of the *Appalachian mountaineer,* writers such as Chapman, Combs, Kephart, Williams, and Wilson mistakenly identified the dialect itself as the source of the speakers' rhetorical abilities. To them the Appalachian's power of expression was inherent in the particular dialect spoken, a dialect they thought to be uniquely capable of reflecting the area's peculiar cultural perspective. It was considered the binding strand linking the various elements of the mountaineer's verbal abil-

---

Printed by permission of the author.

ity and his culture. In this view, as the dialect of the older generation of mountaineers died, so would the culture's rhetorical ability.

Such observations are from a time before our modern understanding of language and dialect. The dialects of Appalachia follow the same general rules of all dialects. They do not shape the thoughts of the individuals who use them, nor do their grammatical structures alter to conform to the peculiar cultural beliefs of a people. No dialect is more or less creative or expressive than another, and though the dialects of Appalachia play a minor role in Appalachian oral rhetoric, it is not the one suggested above.

Nevertheless, anyone who has ever listened to Appalachian tale tellers like Ray Hicks and experienced the subtle spell of wonder accompanying the encounter has felt the same need as the early researchers to comprehend it. A 1974 Appalshop film on Ray Hicks, "Fixin' to Tell About Jack," contains clues as to why non-Appalachians respond so favorably. Viewing the film, we are lost in a world of our imagination. We sit and watch Ray Hicks on the screen as he weaves the world of Jack into reality for the children around him. We follow him as he gathers herbs from his North Carolina mountains, his tall, lank body moving with the natural grace of a man at home in his surroundings. We listen to him talk of galax, of how the same galax he gathers always was and always will be, and suddenly we realize he is not talking just about gathering herbs—he is talking about the nature of man, the nature of the universe, the nature of God, and the way these are intertwined.

If we continue to watch Ray Hicks, we decide we would like to know him better. He is interesting—more than interesting, for we are fascinated by him. Here is a man, unlettered for the most part, a man poor by the monetary standards with which we measure our lives, a man who gathers mountain herbs for a living, a man who tells tales to children, who smiles readily, but one, we believe, who possesses a natural wisdom we know did not come from books. If we sit and ponder Ray Hicks long enough, we will ultimately ask ourselves three questions: Why do we feel we know him better than we should? Why are we so attracted to him? What are the traditions that have formed him?

The answer to the first two questions is found in non-Appalachians' response to people like Ray Hicks. They see these mountaineers not as actual people who reside in the same world as they do, but as mythic personages who represent a way of life incompatible with the essential, rational, everyday mode of behavior within their culture—a way of life which, nevertheless, they find attractive.

We can identify Ray Hicks as one pole of a mythic structure of opposing conceptions of the nature of man well established before the American Revolution. This identification transforms our response from one of man to one of myth. It is, therefore, not surprising that he seems familiar to us. He has appeared in many guises—Daniel Boone, Davy Crockett, Rip Van Winkle, Natty Bumppo, and Grandpa Walton—all of whom are slightly varied forms of the same natural man. He is the man who developed in accord with God's true natural plan, grew up surrounded by natural beauty, and altered his senses to the lessons it taught. His life is intertwined with the natural flow of the seasons, and he is one who knows the land not just as a farmer but who understands it in its original state—its plains and forests. He knows its secrets, its herbs and their cures, and the way of the beasts. He appreciates this natural beauty and sees man as its protector. He is a keeper, not just a user, of God's world. This natural world fosters a life and a sense of values within the reach of all, because it is independent of social advantage, formal education, or urban opportunity.

A consideration of American mythic stereotypes explains why non-Appalachians respond favorably to tale-tellers like Ray Hicks, but it is not the source of his verbal bounty. The answer to this is found in the common oral rhetorical traditions embedded in the Appalachian culture. Oral rhetoric, the art of speaking interestingly with beauty and persuasion, is a conscious manipulation of language within preexisting forms used to create an effect on the listener apart from that of the message. An oral rhetorical tradition is a series of verbal and cultural forms passed from generation to generation which enables a speaker to talk about personal and cultural experiences in a way that distinguishes the narration from normal conversation. It allows a speaker to tell a complex and interesting story seemingly extemporaneously. It is similar to other popular art forms in that it has form and structure and is informally learned; however, instead of producing music or painting, a rhetorical tradition produces tale tellers with the ability to verbalize the cultural traditions, values, and shared experiences. Such traditions are expressions of cultures rather than individuals and as such are more similar to other shared, collective traditions than to personal experiences.

All oral rhetorical traditions contain a series of verbal constructs (metaphors, similes, set images, standard ways of expressing certain ideas, set vocabulary) which are learned by the teller and later woven into a narration. The number of verbal constructs must be sufficient to allow the teller to improvise with creativity and to adapt the same or similar narration to different audiences and themes. Such traditions reflect particular accepted cultural mores or values and provide insights into the structure of the culture. No oral rhetorical tradition is exclusively the domain of cultural preservation and transmission; it must also serve a function in the day-to-day activities of the culture.

There are specific cultural traits necessary for oral rhetorical traditions to survive and flourish. First, such traditions can only exist in a culture that places a high positive value on human interaction and more value on people than on objects. Second, the culture must prize verbal ability and encourage its artistic use. The ability to talk in such a way that the audience wants to listen, no matter how common the subject, is prized throughout Appalachia. To a large segment of its population, how something is said is as important as what is said, and the ability to weave common, natural events into a tale worth repeating again and again is respected. Third, it must have a designated forum for the practice of the tradition and provide positive reinforcement to those who participate in it. Fourth, the tradition must not be in opposition to other major elements of the culture, that is, it must increase the narrator's ability to succeed in other ways in the culture. Fifth, the tradition itself must be an unconscious part of the culture and learned through living participation rather than formal study.

In the Appalachian mountains there are two rhetorical traditions, the Set and the Everyday Tale. In Set Rhetorical Traditions, the teller inherits a form in which the artistic work must be developed. The most famous Appalachian set rhetorical genre, the only one that has become of interest to the general American public, is the Jack Tale, a series of stories told for generations in the Southern Appalachian Mountains about the adventures of a persona named Jack. Such tales are cousins of the "Jack and the Beanstalk" tale we are all familiar with, a tale which appears in the mountains sometimes as "Jack and the Bean Tree." The Jack Tales we are aware of are not original to the teller but belong to a Set Rhetorical Tradition in which the speaker learns the tale from another member of the community, usually an older person. Although a teller may alter a tale in the telling, the changes are minor. They, the tales, are recognizable from teller to teller, from age to age. Some of the more familiar Jack Tales are "Whickity-Whack, Into My Sack," "Unlucky Jack and Lucky Jack," "Cat 'n the Mouse," and "Sop Doll."

Though the original form of the Jack Tales was carried across the ocean hundreds of years ago in immigrants' minds, once these immigrants sat on American soil and told the tales to children born in the Southern Appalachian Mountains, they did more than simply repeat tales from their childhood; they transplanted a Set Rhetorical Tradition. It is this tradition, not the tales themselves, that is of primary significance. One must see a rhetorical tradition as separate from any particular manifestations of it. Even if the Jack Tales were to disappear completely, that would not mean that the Appalachian Set Rhetorical Tradition would also become extinct. Rhetorical traditions are more enduring than any of their particular manifestation and may take on forms unthought of by previous generations.

Though they are passed from generation to generation, Set Rhetorical tales, like the Jack Tales, do not exist isolated from the culture that preserves them. In time, like all transplants, they absorb the peculiar qualities of the new earth and slowly, almost imperceptibly, change. Thus, the Jack Tales found in the Southern Appalachian Mountains are not the same as those that remained to grow in English soil. All art reflects the culture that creates it, and the Jack Tales which Ray Hicks tells are peculiarly American. The protagonist of the tales, Jack, does not have the same personal characteristics in the Southern Appalachian Mountains as he does in England. Because they are intended for the young, the tales reflect the values and modes of behavior the culture wishes its children to learn. They are, in a sense, an indirect method of teaching children how to behave in certain situations, how to know what is right or wrong, what is valuable or worthless, and whom to trust. If one examines the Jack Tales in this light, many interesting aspects, at first not obvious, emerge.

Ray Hicks often narrates the Jack Tale "Whickity Whack: Death in a Sack." Asking what cultural values children would learn by listening to such a tale is revealing. They not only learn that generosity is a good quality, but that Jack is not rewarded for just being generous. He gives bread to the first beggar and receives no reward. He then gives the second beggar half a loaf and still receives no reward. He is rewarded only after he decides he has been unfair and runs after the second beggar to give him the other half of the loaf. A suggestion must be planted in a child's mind that giving to the poor is not something for which one should expect recompense; it is one's natural, Christian duty. Fairness, however, is a virtue for which one is rewarded. Because Jack believed if he gave the first beggar a loaf he should also give the second a full loaf, he received the magic sack and glass. A child, therefore, is shown that the virtue of fairness is the starting place of good returns.

There are numerous other values implicit in the tale revealed by such incidents as Jack's freely helping the king's daughter, his self-confidence in the face of even supernatural danger, his quick thinking in outwitting the devils and in catching death in a sack, and his not using his magic sack to make himself rich. To a child, the tale suggests that a person can beat even devils if he keeps his courage and uses his wits. Unlike other heroes in many old-country fairy tales, Jack does not marry the king's daughter, an attitude which must surely tell the child something about one's place in the social order. It is possible to change one's social station, but there is nothing wrong in being where one is. We also notice that although Jack accepts a tract of land as payment for ridding the man's house of devils, he then settles down to work it.

Courage and shrewdness (as well as his magical sack) help Jack get his start in life, and, once he has it, he leads the normal life of any Appalachian farmer, clearing his land and raising his crops. Later, however, when the king's daughter is deathly ill, he cures her and refuses payment. Ridding the man's house of devils was a business transaction and, therefore, pay is to be expected; however, curing the sick is something a person must do if he can. To take money for curing would not be neighborly. Hearing the tale, a child could easily learn something about the value of death—how, without it, life becomes a burden.

Ray Hicks and other masters of the Appalachian Set Rhetorical Tradition are natural, amateur storytellers only in that they did not learn their craft to make a living. In every other sense, they are professional storytellers. To understand their basic storytelling abilities, however, we must be aware of another Appalachian oral rhetorical tradition. Even though Set Tales, such as the Jack Tales, are the best known examples of Appalachian oral rhetoric, they are certainly not the most pervasive ones. In fact, the Set Rhetorical Tradition could not exist were it not for a broader, often unnoticed one—the Everyday Rhetorical Tradition. It is the foundation of the more formal one and provides the basis for understanding not only how tale tellers such as Ray Hicks learn their tales but also how they perfect their delivery. The Jack Tales are but the apex of a much deeper tradition that underlies the Appalachian culture. It is this second rhetorical tradition which produces an extraordinary number of persons who can transform a common, mundane daily event into a fascinating experience. It is the Everyday Rhetorical Tradition which prepares persons to relate common happenings clearly, interestingly, and humorously.

The Everyday Rhetorical Tradition shares certain characteristics with its more formal cousin, in that the teller learns a number of rhetorical devices and uses them within the defined parameters of a rhetorical form. The tradition supplies each teller with a hoard of set rhetorical expressions. These, which often seem unique to the speaker, are part of the word hoard the teller draws on to increase the effect of his tale. These similes, images, metaphors, figures, and special words, inserted throughout the fabric of the story, provide the tale with a vividness and a creativity that separate the tale teller from just a talker.

The Everyday Tale can be defined as an isolated, non-interactive verbal construct that arises during normal oral situations, most often when three or more persons are present, which transforms the common, daily events of life into a colorful story, a story that often serves to provide information not only about the subject but about other aspects of community life. The presence of at least a third person who serves as the audience is important, if not obligatory. An Everyday Tale can, of course, be elicited by a field worker requesting information from an informant, but it normally occurs as persons transact the routine affairs of living within a community. Although Everyday Tales can be told anywhere, most frequently they are told where men and women gather to converse while performing other functions—such as in small stores or before and after church. They usually conform to the traditional pattern of rhetorical intercourse among Appalachians, in that men more frequently tell tales to men and women to women; however, an elderly person may tell a tale to any younger person regardless of gender. This gender separation is not the result of the subject of the tale, for seldom is there anything in a tale which could not be mentioned in mixed company. It is more a matter of tradition.

The Everyday Tale differs from the Set Tale in both the nature of its basic form and its purpose. The Everyday Tale serves both as a way to transmit the values and history of the community from one member to another, from one generation to another, and to transmit information indirectly throughout the community network—including circuitously insulting a neighbor or letting a listener know that the speaker does not agree with certain actions or attitudes.

Appalachian Everyday Tales originally were created by individuals in response to conversational stimuli, but once constructed they can be modified and retold by others as their personal experiences. If we examine the Everyday Tales of several Appalachian communities closely, we find that different people tell the same tale with adaptive variation. While there is not one set phrase used to begin each tale, there are verbal signs that clue the listeners to the fact that a tale has begun and that the rules governing normal conversation have been suspended. During the telling of an Everyday Tale, the speaker will not be interrupted by questions or comments from the listeners.

There is considerable freedom in form and content of the Everyday Tale, but many of these tales have common characteristics. For instance, the topic is usually familiar. Everyday Tales are concerned with those events that explain the relations of members of the family or community and those events that reveal the nature of their lives. Even though any happening can be the subject of an Everyday Tale, certain happenings seem more common than others. Many tales concern the manner in which people approach their jobs. Other topics reveal how members of the family face the common dangers, how persons of different generations interact, how children are disciplined and taught, and how fusses altered relationships. We find tales about the qualities of ministers, the behavior of animals and machines, the building of new houses, breaking new ground, special trips up the mountain to find lost animals, socializing at church, the hiding of home-made wine from unwelcome guests, collecting tan bark, the special characteristics of family or neighbors, and a host of miscellaneous events of daily living. Serious feuding and personal religious experiences are seldom topics of Everyday Tales, and two topics which are almost always treated humorously are preacher tales and fuss tales.

Each tale will appear to be spontaneously generated by a particular conversation; however, a careful observer can see how the conversation is manipulated to the point where a tale can be told. In the Everyday Tradition, a teller is free to alter a previous tale to fit a present situation; he or she often combines, adds, subtracts, and varies parts of other tales to meet the demands of the new rhetorical event.

Another common characteristic of the Everyday Tradition is the use of humor. Many Appalachian Everyday Tales are humorous; however, the humor often is not inherent in the situation or event itself but is derived from either the attitude of one of the participants toward the situation or the perspective of the teller. The humor involves exaggeration, one-upsmanship, subtle understatement, and misdirection. Another essential element of the style of the Everyday Tale is the establishment of the authenticity of the event, which is accomplished in several ways. The speaker often prefaces the tale with a testimonial to his or her own honesty, reveals a dislike of liars, and avows a hatred of them worse than yellow dogs. Once into the tale, the narrator introduces other elements of verification, such as the witnessing of the event by another member of the community who will (if still alive) support the truth of the narration. The more implausible the proclaimed facts, the greater the testimonial to their authenticity. At times the teller even becomes a persona who denies the possibility of the events about to be narrated: "You'uns know I don't believe in no haints or sich as that, but oncet when. . . ."

Two other qualities ordinarily present in Everyday Tales are accurate dialogue and abundance of details. Both contribute to the verisimilitude of the tales and increase the richness of the fabric and sense of immediacy so prevalent in this rhetorical tradition. Dialogue can occur throughout the tale; it almost always present at the transition between the second and third sections of the tales and absent at the end.

In form, the Everyday Tale is similar to an extremely brief short story with a three-part structure. The first part of the tale is a very brief preface which funnels a generalized conversation into a specific notional area that is in accord with the tale; the topic of the preface is not directly related to the events of the tale. The second and third parts are roughly of equal length, with the suspense of the tale being dispelled at the end of the second part. The third part builds upon the topic of the second but appears to be expanding to another main point as the tale suddenly ends. This abrupt ending is often mistaken by non-Appalachians who, not recognizing the tale as a self-contained verbal entity, ask for more information about the event and are often slightly disturbed to find that no number of questions can return the speaker to the topic. Non-Appalachians sometimes do not realize that what they heard was a tale and not a revelation of personal experiences; therefore, it cannot be added to or developed further.

An example of an Everyday Tale that contains several, though not all, of the above characteristics was recorded from an unlettered elderly woman of Greene County, Tennessee:

> And you know, honey, used to, whenever I were growin' up, wasn't no sich things as undertaker's place. A person died at home. They'd a-doctor 'em at home and they'd die at home. Get some board and put 'em betwixt two chair—and lay 'em out on that. Put a nickel on each eye and tie a string 'round their neck to keep their jaw from a-fallin' down. Then the neighbor wimen, if hit were a woman what died, come in and wash that lady and comb her hair and dress her up right pretty. Then the men-folks they put her in the casket.
>
> Back in them times, people makes their own caskets. My daddy, he has made a many of a casket. He were in the goods business—had hisself this country store, you know—and carried little boxes and pretty little silver screws and handles that went along the side. He carried them jist laik he done salt, sody, and sugar and stuffs like that.
>
> They'd get the lumber down what they saved special and go-white material and cotton and padded it on the insides. And put a white edging of lace 'round the top. They had the outside all lined with black, black cambric, I think they calls it.
>
> They's a little baby what died oncet and Daddy makes its casket. Hits daddy carried it over to our store in his arms. They fitted it in this little casket and hit were too shallow and they had to lay that little baby—hit were so small—out. Daddy, he took a spread and they laid that baby on top of some overhalls. And they worked on that casket jist a-talkin' hushed you know—til they got hit just right, and put hit down in it; real respectful, I remember.
>
> It were so sad to see that little'un there so still and he being jist so

young. I were jist little myself and I watched so clost. That night atter my mother was abed, that little dead baby worried me so—I got up and sat by the far [fire] with my daddy.

He said, "Mule"—they called me Mule—"Mule, what's the matter?" I tol' him and he didn't say nothin' fer what was the everest longest time. Then he tol' me to retch my eyes out and catch a spark as hit flew up from the far. And I did. Then he asked me ifen it were gone. And hit were. Then he asked me what I could call of it. I said it were pretty and warm and bright and hit made me feel good to see it.

He helt me ever so clost and said that's what we has to fix our hearts to when someone we loves dies. We have to be warm and give off life before we spark off to heaven. He said we all jist sparks—jist God's sparks and some day we fly up to Him jist as natural as them that's in that far.

And you know what—I can call that so clear even after all these years. And I remembered that when we was a-burying him when he passed. We's all jist sparks—God's sparks and we give our warmth while we are there and then we sparks up to heaven. Jist sparks.

A good Everyday Tale teller can walk to the local store, buy a sack of six-penny nails, talk to a few persons along the way, return home, and make the rest of the family envious of his or her wondrous adventure. But the reality of an oral rhetorical tale cannot be caught in print. Although the Everyday Tale above has been transcribed from a tape-recorded interview, it is not the tale itself. Sentence divisions and paragraphing were added, and arbitrary decisions on which words to represent with dialectal spelling were made. Most importantly, the effects the speaker had on the audience through gestures, length of pauses, and intonation patterns were lost. In writing, we get only the words of the tale but not the rhetorical experience. It is in participating in the experience, watching the mastery of artistic delivery, that oral rhetoric comes alive.

One of the major aspects of any tale teller's style is the absence of sharp differentiation between his or her voice and mannerism when talking to an interviewer and when telling a Set or Everyday Tale. The teller's stage personality is not a suit of clothes slipped into for a performance, but a role worn whenever he or she is talking. It is the rhetorical tradition which allows the teller to be natural, compelling, and vivid when talking. The effective teller of tales never manifests signs of verbal self-consciousness, never even hints at the possibility that the audience—whether a group of friends or children gathered around—could be less than fascinated by the story. There is an intensity and directness in the narration that compel us to listen and become actively involved in the topic, whether it be the gathering of galax or the adventures of Jack. The speaker strengthens the enchantment by pausing at the right moment, inflecting the voice to indicate surprise or disappointment, matching the rhythms of speech to the action of the tale, gesticulating with the hands, and using facial expressions to give emphasis.

While a storyteller must have the ability to read an audience and interact with it, at the same time he or she must convey the impression of being unaware of that audience. The storyteller occupies two realms at once, the temporal and the transcendent. It is impossible to capture in words the subtle yet intense interaction between Ray Hicks or the woman in Greene County and their audience, yet a hint of it is reflected in the rapt faces of listeners. So intense an interaction occurs only when the storyteller has the ability to transform words into artistic reality. This skill defines the master of an oral rhetorical tradition. Without this shared magic, such persons would be as boring as the rest of us.

The rhetorical traditions of the Appalachian Mountains that produce both Set and Everyday Tales remain important to the culture. Their enduring strength lies in the fact that they are not entirely founded on folk traditions, but are rooted in the very lifestyles of the people. Because of this social rooting, it will take more change than has taken place to destroy the tales and the way they are told. Ray Hicks, the woman of Greene County, and the speakers Malone Young has written of in *Latchpins of the Lost Cove* attest to the vitality of both of the Southern Appalachian rhetorical traditions. By recognizing the rhetorical traditions of Southern Appalachia as living entities, we can best explain an aspect of Southern Appalachian culture that has fascinated Americans for over a hundred years.

There are, however, three other aspects of the tradition that need to be explored briefly. How do the traditions perpetuate themselves? In what ways are the traditions related to the dialects of Appalachia? Is there a connection between the oral rhetorical traditions of Appalachia and the flourishing of Appalachian literature after World War II?

Of these three, the easiest to come to terms with is the first: How do the traditions perpetuate themselves? No oral rhetorical tradition can survive unless it is compatible with the basic nature of the culture. In Appalachia, two of the most significant elements that undergird the continuous existence of the traditions are the culture's rural focus and its emphasis on personal interaction. Even in those areas of Appalachia where the population and industrial base suggest that a transformation from rural to urban environment has taken place, the people still conceive of themselves as rural. It may be a cultural self-deception, but it permeates the area. In Appalachia, few things are worse than being perceived of as having become urbanized. Perhaps because of this, most people have retained one of the more distinguishing characteristics of the culture—person-to-person relationships. Appalachians personalize almost all social and business interactions. They do not buy and sell independently of the person they are buying from or selling to. Often they will not sell or buy an object at any price from someone they do not like, and they will respond enthusiastically to a face-to-face request from an acquaintance they would ignore were it written. Because an emphasis on personal interactions permeates the culture, Appalachians tend to preface and append business transactions with a certain amount of verbal interplay which establishes the fact that any transaction is not merely business. The rhetorical traditions indirectly reinforce this emphasis on personal interaction by providing necessary information about people in the community and by allowing a speaker to convey indirectly the parameters of acceptable behavior to someone being spoken to.

There are two primary opportunities to learn the rhetorical traditions of Appalachia. The first is in the family itself. Usually, at least one child in every family will become a tale teller by associating with an older member of the extended family who has perfected the tradition. Later, this person will practice the skill in those places where other tale tellers gather. Traditionally, this has been the small country store. The tales told in this location are different from those that men or women tell within the family; they are more community oriented and are more subtle and oratorically refined. In such locations, the telling of Everyday Tales becomes an artful contest between audience and teller or between two tellers, each trying to produce a tale which will test, but not exceed, the limits of credibility. It is in these situations that the tale teller perfects his delivery. Here he learns to pause at exactly the right moment, to inflect his voice to indicate surprise or disappointment, to match the rhythms of his speech to the action of the tale, and to control the gesticulations of hand and face which give the proper emphasis to subtle points.

We have stated that the essence of the Appalachians' use of language is rhetorical rather than dialectal, but that does not mean that dialect is irrelevant to rhetorical patterns. One must remember that, for the most part, within the Appalachian area the dialect of the teller and of his or her audience is either the same or very closely related. Since dialectal features (like language itself) are unconscious, they cannot be used for rhetorical effect within the community. Thus, many features of Appalachian dialects that strike non-Appalachians as unusual and colorful would be unnoticed by an Appalachian audience. To establish that a particular dialect feature is being used for rhetorical effect, one must first show that the audience perceives it as something other than normal speech. For example, vocabulary items such as "reached it to" someone (passed it), "plumb" (entirely), "pert" (almost), "right smart" (plentiful) or pronunciations indicated by such occasional-spellings as "laik" (like), "ol" (oil) or "jist" (just) seem unusual only to those whose dialects do not contain them. They would go unnoticed by most Appalachians. On the other hand, since all dialects contain items associated with older persons or earlier times, a tale teller can evoke a certain rhetorical atmosphere by using them. Pronunciations such as "scandals" (scoundrels), "hit" (it), "oncet" (once), "atter" (after), "blubbers," (bubbles), and words such as "vittles" and "nigh" can be used to establish a distance between the time of the tale and the real time of the telling, adding to the rhetorical effect because these terms are no longer common in the area. Additionally, all dialects have various registers or styles, ranging from the informal to formal which can be also be used to identify characters or set tones.

Oral rhetorical tales can never adequately be represented in writing. Writing and speaking are such different linguistic systems that it is as difficult to translate a short story into a poem as it is to translate an oral tale in some type of written counterpart. Nevertheless, oral rhetorical forms can co-exist in literary cultures and often serve as a foundation for certain developmental stages in regional and national literatures.

The tales themselves can be the basis for literary productions, whether they be in the form of poems, short stories, or sections within novels. By using oral rhetoric, regional authors frequently are able to begin with a prepackaged artistic base for their literary creations. This practice does not detract from the creative ability of the author; for the tales, expressions, and forms must be changed if they are going to succeed as literature.

There are various ways that the oral rhetorical traditions may influence Appalachian literature. They serve as the foundation for a type of dramatic literature, such as the portrait pieces of Jo Carson which resemble oral tales in that they need to be delivered orally and heard rather than read. At other times, the traditions serve as the basis for the dialogue found within stories and poems, as is sometimes the case in works by Jeff Daniel Marion, Rita Quillen, and Jim Wayne Miller. Sometimes the underlying structure and intonational patterns of the dialect have been worked into the fabric of the poems and stories of regional writers. One can even suggest that various regional writers were first trained in the oral traditions and then welded a literary one onto them, giving them a greater power to create beauty and effect. Whether the Appalachian oral rhetorical traditions serve as yeast or even grist for literature, there is one element that is distinct. The Appalachian writer, unlike the oral tale teller, is no longer addressing only Appalachians; therefore, he or she has greater freedom in using Appalachian dialect and content than the oral artist has. For instance, elements of language mentioned above which would be unnoticed by an Appalachian listening to an oral tale can, when transferred to literature, become ways of establishing the Appalachianness of setting and character.

Suggested Readings

Chapman, Mariston. "American Speech as Practiced in the Southern Highlands." *Century* 117 (Mar. 1929): 617–23.

Combs, Josiah H. "The Language of the Southern Highlander." *PMLA* 46 (Dec. 1931): 1302–22.

Fixin' to Tell About Jack. Whitesburg, KY: Appalshop, 1974.

Williams, Cratis. "The Content of Mountain Speech." *Mountain Life and Work* 37, no. 4 (1961): 13–17.

Wilson, Gordon. "Some Mammoth Cave Sayings, I: Sayings with Farm Flavor." *Kentucky Folklore Record* 15, no. 1 (Jan.-Mar. 1969): 12–21.

Young, Malone. *Latchpins of the Lost Cove.* Johnson City, TN: Latchpins Press, 1991.

Malone Young

Malone Young was born July 1, 1920, at Cove Creek, Tennessee, five miles from Roan Mountain, Tennessee. He lived in this community until 1938, when he left to attend East Tennessee State University; but he later returned to teach at the Cove Creek school before serving four years in the Army Air Force in World War II. He also attended Milligan College, the University of Tennessee, and the Instituto Technológico at Monterrey, Mexico. A professor of geography at East Tennessee State University for twenty-nine years, he has traveled over much of the world; but his main focus of interest has remained Appalachian folklore, geography, and language.

Latchpins of the Lost Cove, from which the following is extracted, is based on Young's memories of Lost Cove and on six years of interviews with more than fifty of the older residents of the area. "Fish Tales" exhibits the social interaction and reported characteristics of the Everyday Tale described by James Robert Reese.

Fish Tales

A soft May shower had mellowed the creek just enough for the fish to lay their lives on the line. A dozen or so of the loafers were sitting under the wahoo tree aside the store telling fish stories. Even the trout in the nearby creek were getting the jitters as the tales grew bigger. Fonzer Hicks was listening while he whittled away on a do-gadget. He was still pondering about a big two-pound trout that he had caught and left tied to a willow root the week before. It so chanced that Nath Young had found the fish and replaced it with a little one no bigger than a horneyhead. When Fonzer returned after fishing farther down the creek, and pulled his fish out of the water, he couldn't believe his own eyes. "Damnation!" he exclaimed. "This here fish has done puffed in 'til it ain't worth taking home."

Morefield Hopson cootered [*to cooter* = to desire or sneak] over to where Fonzer was meditating. "I reckon that this here mizzle [drizzle or light rain] will get all the fish to stirring," he offered as a way to start a noration [*to norate* = to tell or converse] with his old friend.

Fonzer stopped whittling a moment before speaking. "You can't ever tell about fish any more," he offered. "They seem to have a mind of their own. 'Tuther day I caught a big rainbow peart nigh long as your arm. It wrestled me so hard that it wore itself down 'til it wasn't much bigger than a horneyhead. These fish around here seem to be acting up here of late, and I think I know the reason."

From *Latchpins of the Lost Cove,* Latchpins Press, 1987. Reprinted by permission of the author and publisher.

"How in the thunder are they acting?" Morefield asked.

"Real crazy, Morefield. Some of them try to swim sideways and others swim backards. One old red hoss I seen yesterday was trying to swim two ways at the same time."

"I do declare!" Morefield responded. "I wonder what has got into them."

"Them fish were drunk, Morefield, just as sure as I sit here. When the High Sheriff come up 'tuther day and tore up Bear John's still, he dumped all the mash in the creek. It can't be anything else."

"You make sense," Morefield murmured. "Bear John's likker has got the kick of a mule. I recollect the time I ate a dying bait [full meal] of fish that foundered on corn meal mash. My head swimmed for two days and my breath smelled so bad that I had to miss a good preaching at the Meeting House."

While the two oldtimers were meditating, Ceart Hughes sauntered by with a big string of horneyheads. Morefield eyed the fish. "Ceart, you ain't been gone more than twenty minutes. How in the Sam Hill did you hook all them there fish?"

"I didn't hook nary a none," Ceart replied.

"Don't tell me you seined them and the water this high," Morefield offered.

"Nothing of the kind," Ceart quipped. "I out-thunk them."

"What you mean?" Fonzer piped in.

"There wasn't much to it," Ceart declared. "All I did was sprinkle a can of Bruton snuff in the creek and before you know it, them there fish started coming upon the bank to get them a birch toothbrush to use with the snuff. All I had to do was just grab them up before they had time to get back in the water. Fish, you know, especially these around here, ain't got much sense."

"That's what I've just been trying to tell Morefield," Fonzer declared. "Now I reckon that he will believe me."

While the oldtimers were meditating on the eccentric behavior of the fish, Mitch Putman arrived at the store. Old Mitch was one of the three confessed Democrats on the Creek and lived off to himself way up aside Fishing Pole Ridge. He was a good man who minded his own business and never harmed a soul. Big Will, and all the self-righteous Republicans, thought right well of him despite his shortcoming. He couldn't help it 'cause his pappy had fought with the Rebels and caused him to be born a Democrat. One thing about Mitch had always puzzled his neighbors. Why was it that he forever and a day had plenty of spending money?

Mitch tied his flea-bitten gray horse to the rail fence and crow-hopped over to the bench where the loafers were meditating.

"How are things going up on the ridge?" Morefield offered as Mitch squared around and sat down.

"Just fair-to-middlin, I reckon," Mitch replied. "I can't complain much 'cept for not getting much sleep."

"What seems to be the matter?" Big Will, who was listening, queried.

"Ah Lord! I reckon hit's that there blasted painter again," Mitch replied with a somber tone. "Hit screams and carried on something awful night after night. I ain't had ten good winks of sleep in goodness knows when."

"I bet it's the same one that tore after Aaron Wright 'twile back up there 'neath the Licklog Gap," Fonzer declared.

"I've thought of getting me a good hound to guard the house," Mitch murmured, "but they say a mortal dog don't stand a chance agin a black painter. What do you think?"

"You're right, Mitch. The dog that can stand up to a big painter ain't been born yet," Big Will offered. "A painter would lay hold of him with his front claws and tear his insides out with his hind ones. I seen what them wildcats done to Conner's dogs 'twile back. The ones that Johnny Stockton killed was nigh on to five feet long. Its tail wasn't any longer than your fingers, but it had claw-nails bigger than rooster spurs."

The fish and everything else were forgotten now that the problem of the painter was being norated. Joe Lum Benfield had been listening to the others and was giving the problems some hard thought.

"I would bet my bottom dollar that the painter up there on Fishing Pole Ridge is the same one that might nigh scared the britches off of old Doff 'twile back," he declared. "I didn't put much truck in what he told me at the time, but now I reckon he was telling the truth. A painter on the prowl is might bad business."

Before the sun neared the Hughes Gap, word had spread that a big black painter was prowling about the Cove. By good dark, the news had reached Ripshin and Big Rock Creek. Bear John Smith was in a dither because he was all set to run off the mash at his still above the Simerly Clearing. Conner heard the word and decided to put off any groundhogging for the time being. Everyone put oil in their lanterns and cleaned the globes. The Lost Cove was a dangerous place. One thing was for sure, neither Deputy Johnny Miller or anyone else would be going near the Licklog Gap or Fishing Pole Ridge.

After consorting with the loafers a while, Mitch had Wess fill a tow sack with vittles before climbing on his flea-bitten gray and riding up the Big Road. Tonight, the Good Lord willing, he would try out his new copper still on the side of Fishing Pole Ridge.

Clate Miller, when he had a dime to spare, allowed himself to buy a tin of sardines long about noon rather than hoof it all the way home to put a little food in his stomach. Wess, being sort of big-hearted, always threw in a few crackers free of charge. Clate loved sardines the way that Doff relished goobers. He would devour the little fishes with pleasure and exaltation, savoring every morsel 'til he came to the last one, which he always tossed out the open window of the store.

Big Clyde had observed Clate's eccentric behavior all summer as his curiosity increased. Why in tarnation would anyone in their right mind do such a strange thing? It didn't make a lick of sense.

One day while Clate was eating his sardines, Big Clyde up and eased around to the back of the store to find out what was going on. Sitting there under the window was R. J. Boozi, Clate's old dog, with his mouth ajar and his eyes glued to the window. A few seconds later a sardine came out, and R. J. hardly moved his head to catch it.

Big Clyde mulled the matter over a minute and finally a thought struck him. Thinking so hard would give him a headache for sure and cost him a whole dime, but it would be worth it for being bumfuzzled by Clate's antic.

He went in the store and opened a tin of fishes, and with the point of his knife he proceeded to carefully flip each one out the open window until he came to the last one, which he ate.

By the time he had finished, all the loafers, especially Clate, were giving him their undivided attention. Big Clyde nonchalantly wiped his knife blade on the leg of his trousers and left the store. Now he reckoned that he would let his friends do a little pondering on their own.

Old Doff was so busy eating goobers that he didn't pay any mind to Big Clyde's doing. In a little while he propped his chair back on two legs and dozed off. Nath and Babydoll, who had eased into the store and took count of Doff, knew the opportunity they had been waiting for all summer had arrived. They took some twine and carefully tied Doff's suspenders to the back of the chair. Nath then set fire to a paper poke. As the smoke curled upward, he yelled at the top of his voice. "Fire!" Someone banged on a washtub as the two no-count boys dashed out the door with several in mock pursuit.

Doff awoke with a snort and lit out after them. The chair caught against the door frame while his gaunt body continued forward. His suspenders finally snapped while his earthly body sailed half way to the Big Road. It was a wonder that he wasn't killed dead. The two culprits were long gone by the time Doff revived himself and reckoned he was the victim of his own bad dream.

In a little while things settled back to normal and the loafers resumed their colloquy concerning the evils of the modern world.

Michael Ellis

A native of East Tennessee, Michael Ellis attended East Tennessee State University, where he received his bachelor's and master's degrees. After obtaining the Ph.D. in English from the University of Kentucky, he joined the English faculty at Southwestern Missouri State University. For Ellis, the body of nineteenth-century Southern Appalachian literature is a rich reservoir of linguistic information which may be used, among other things, to measure change, and even the rate of change, of dialectal features.

Albion's Seed in Appalachia:
The Use of Dialect as Evidence

Of the various ethnic groups present among the early settlers to the Southern Appalachians, the Scotch-Irish most frequently have been given credit
for establishing the predominant cultural patterns in the region and for in-
fluencing the varieties of English spoken there. As early as 1928, Hans
Kurath, future director of the *Linguistic Atlas of the United States and Canada,*
was arguing that the Scotch-Irish predominated in the "mountain country"
of the eastern United States and went so far as to maintain that the speech of
the region was "strongly Scotch."[1] Since there was little in the way of linguistic evidence at that time which might support this assertion, Kurath's
argument was probably influenced by popular historical assumptions which
claimed a Scotch-Irish hegemony on the Appalachian frontier.[2] Recently, the
notion of a demonstrable Scotch-Irish connection in Appalachian English has
come full circle in *Albion's Seed* by historian David Hackett Fischer, who uses
dialect as evidence to support his theory that four distinctive regional cultures in America can be traced to distinctive regional cultures in Britain.[3] In
a section titled "Borderlands to the Backcountry," Fischer uses folk speech as
one of several folkways which illustrate both the distinctiveness of a regional
culture with the Southern Appalachians at its heart and the similarity of this
culture with the regional culture of North Britain, including the border
counties of northern England, the lowlands of Scotland, and the Scotch-Irish
sections of Ulster.[4] However, until recently, linguists have made little attempt at a systematic investigation of the relationship between Appalachian
English and British regional dialects.[5] As a result, *Albion's Seed* tends to accept and promote existing assumptions about the ancestry of Appalachian
English without offering convincing evidence that there is a valid empirical
basis for connection between Appalachian English and Scotch-Irish or northern British dialects.

Since the actual numbers of various ethnic groups in colonial America can
only be estimated, and since it is difficult to determine the exact proportion
of settlers of various British origins who made up the original population of
the eastern United States, Kurath and other American dialectologists hoped
that a comparison of British and American regional dialects might be used
to trace variant features in American English to specific British sources. According to Kurath, isolating those features in present-day American dialects
which deviate from the standard language, and then comparing these American regional variants with present-day British regional variants, might provide evidence to help reconstruct the early settlement history of the United
States.[6] There are, however, a number of complications inherent in attempting a comparative investigation:

From *Appalachian Journal* 19 (1992): 278–97. Reprinted by permission of the author and
publisher.

1. Our knowledge of seventeenth- and eighteenth-century English is limited, and since the English language has continued to change, both in Britain and in America, it is impossible to be absolutely certain about the frequency and distribution of seventeenth- or eighteenth-century dialectal features based on contemporary evidence. Despite the common characterization of Appalachian English as an especially archaic form of the language, there is no logical basis for the notion that Appalachian English is the "oldest living English dialect,"[7] or that British dialects have somehow become modern while Appalachian English has remained in the sixteenth century.

2. The essentially innovative nature of colonial or "extraterritorial" Englishes as a consequence of migration and dialect contact suggests that many present-day British regional varieties are closer to the dialects of seventeenth- and eighteenth-century immigrants than any present-day dialect of American English.[8]

3. Each of the three basic categories of linguistic features, i.e., vocabulary, pronunciation, and grammar, presents special challenges for a comparative approach, and a trans-Atlantic connection based on one category cannot necessarily be extended to include the others.

4. Differences between various linguistic surveys, including differences in questionnaire design, differences in methods of collection and transcription, and differences in emphasis, create challenges for a comparative approach.

5. An objective comparison must consider all categories of linguistic features, must consider the relationship between Appalachian English and other regional American dialects, and must extend to include all British regional dialects.

Comparison of Linguistic Features

While folk vocabulary traditionally has received a great deal of attention from dialectologists and linguistic geographers, it is perhaps the most difficult to use for establishing connections between British and American varieties. Although linguists have been relatively successful in using vocabulary to establish regional characteristics in present-day English, American surveys were designed to determine American dialect areas, and British surveys were designed to determine British dialect areas. Even lengthy questionnaires will cover only a fraction of the total vocabulary, a limitation which results in a relatively small amount of British and American regional vocabulary which can be directly compared. Dialect dictionaries contain much larger collections of folk vocabulary and are therefore valuable sources of information, although they rarely contain detailed information on frequency and distribution of vocabulary items. Finally, folk vocabulary is relatively unstable and is subject to borrowing between dialects, especially during periods of dialect contact resulting from immigration and colonization.

One of the few studies to attempt to directly compare British and American regional vocabularies is Alan Crozier's "The Scotch-Irish Influence in

American English," in which the author lists thirty-two American words or expressions which he attributes to a possible Scotch-Irish origin.[9] However, the majority of these are found or are known to have occurred in other British regional varieties, leaving a smaller list of nine words or expressions of probable Scotch-Irish origin: *diamond* (town square), *dornick* (a rock for throwing), *drooth* (drought), *fireboard* (mantel), *flannel cake* (a thin wheat cake), *hap* (quilt), *muley* (hornless cow), *nicker* (whinny), and *wattle* (a stick for driving cattle). Of these words, only *fireboard* and *nicker* appear to be restricted to the region (Kurath's "South Midland") which includes the Southern Appalachians.[10] While Crozier's work is an important step in exploring the Scotch-Irish words that exist in American vocabulary, it only tells us that Scotch-Irish words exist in American English, and we cannot infer from this evidence that the Scotch-Irish or Northern British influence was greater than the influence from other British varieties without investigating the occurrence of American regional vocabulary items in all varieties of British regional English. An investigation of the possible British ancestry of Appalachian folk vocabulary must include a comparison with all regional forms of British English before any possible regional influence can be assessed. Unfortunately, differences in American and British questionnaires result in a frustratingly small number of words which can be directly compared. A comparison of twenty words collected in two separate East Tennessee studies with data collected by the *Survey of English Dialects* and the *Linguistic Atlas of Scotland* indicates a mixture of British influences, with a somewhat stronger influence from British West Midland and Northern dialects (including those of Scotland and Northern Ireland).[11]

While it is possible to find points of comparison between Appalachian and Northern British vocabulary, the patterns of regional pronunciation found in Appalachia are so different from those found in Scotland and the Scotch-Irish sections of Ulster that the two do not appear to be even remotely related. Moreover, systematic investigation of pronunciation in the Southern Appalachians[12] indicates that there is considerable phonological variation within the Southern Appalachian region, and that the pronunciation of the region is much less uniform than many popular representations of Appalachian dialects, which often rely on impressionistic observations and on literary stereotypes, suggest. It is also important to recognize the many pronunciations which Appalachian English shares with other varieties of American English, for, as Kurath and McDavid point out, the South Midland region "has hardly a single feature that does not occur either in the North Midland or the South."[13] For example, pronunciations represented by *critter, chaw, deef, pizen,* and *shet* are too widely distributed among American varieties to be characterized as distinctive Appalachian pronunciations.[14] Among other stereotypical examples, *whar, thar,* and *sartin* resemble a common pattern which is used in nineteenth-century literary representations of dialect but which cannot be characterized as typical of present-day Appalachian English.[15] Indeed, while Appalachian English may differ *phonetically* from other varieties of American English, its overall phonological system more closely resembles

American English in general than it does any form of British English. In other words, while phonetic features like that suggested by the spelling *he-it* for the verb "hit" may set Appalachian English apart from other American varieties, the underlying sound (phoneme), as well as the overall distribution of sounds within the system, conforms in most ways to other forms of American English. Systematic differences make it extremely difficult to make direct comparisons between Appalachian English and British regional dialects; however, anyone examining Ulster Scots pronunciation will soon notice the extreme systematic differences between American English and the Ulster Scots dialect.[16] To an American, the Ulster Scots pronunciations of *live, shed, head, dog, beak, father, broad, do, die, cow,* and *bone* would probably sound more like *leave, shade, heed, Doug, bake, feather, braid, day, dee, coo,* and *bane.*[17] The Ulster Scots system of vowel sounds in the words *eye, mine* (noun), *mine* (pronoun), *climb, either* is particularly complex. Where most American varieties have a single vowel sound for all of these words (although the vowel differs from dialect to dialect), Ulster Scots may have as many as five.[18]

The lack of similarity between present-day Ulster Scots English and American English does not mean that the eighteenth-century Scotch-Irish or Northern British English had no influence on the development of American dialect pronunciations. There are, however, few apparent Appalachian–Northern British correspondences, and, based on regional pronunciations mapped in the *Linguistic Atlas of England,* where a variant form in Appalachian English resembles a British form (e.g., the pronunciations suggested by the spelling *pizen, nekkid, narrer, winder,* and *widder*), it is more likely to resemble a form found in the West Midlands or South of England. The presence of post-vocalic *r* (*r* pronounced after vowels in words like *farm* and *door*) in Appalachian English has frequently been attributed to the influence of Scotch-Irish immigrants in colonial America, but post-vocalic *r* was also a feature in standard British English until the end of the eighteenth century and is common to several present-day British regional dialects, not only in the North but also in the West Midlands and South.[19]

Of the three major categories of linguistic features, grammar traditionally has received less attention than vocabulary and pronunciation, although, as Michael Montgomery very effectively argues in his investigation of the Scotch-Irish/Appalachian connection, since grammar is perhaps the category most resistant in change, it represents the area of investigation most likely to yield useful insight into the ancestry of Appalachian English.[20] Although there are a number of excellent studies which deal specifically with Appalachian grammatical systems, most popular descriptions of Appalachian English rely on nonstandard grammatical forms which have stereotypically become associated with Appalachian English, but which often are common in other varieties of American English. For example, E. B. Atwood's *Survey of Verb Forms in the Eastern United States* reports that *come* and *growed* as past tense forms, *was* as the past tense of *be* regardless of person or number (e.g., *you was, they was*), *a*-prefixing (e.g., *a-goin*), and the negative form *he don't* all are widely distributed in the eastern United States.[21]

An examination of British sources, particularly the *Linguistic Atlas of England*, indicates that many nonstandard grammatical features commonly associated with Appalachian varieties have too wide a distribution in Britain to identify with a particular region (e.g., *come, seed,* and *catched* as past tense forms, *ax* for *ask,* and *them* as a demonstrative pronoun in constructions like *them boys*). Several other grammatical forms commonly found, but not exclusive to, Appalachian English are typical of British Midland and Southern dialects (e.g., *growed* and *knowed*; the past tense form *seen*; *ain't*; the negative form *he don't*; the possessive pronouns *hisn, hern, yourn,* and *theirn*; and the reflexive pronoun *hisself.* According to the *English Dialect Dictionary* and other British sources, *a*-prefixing is British Southern and is infrequent in the northern counties of England, in Scotland, and in Ireland.

While the available evidence suggests that many of the nonstandard grammatical forms commonly associated with Appalachian English are too scattered in British regional dialects to infer a specific British connection, Montgomery has been able to identify a number of other Appalachian grammatical forms which derive ultimately from Scottish English. One of these is the system of subject-verb concord which adds -*s* to plural verbs (e.g., *Me and my sister gets in fights sometimes*). Some other grammatical features occurring in Appalachian English identified by Montgomery as having a probable Scotch-Irish origin include: multiple modal verbs (*might could, might should*); perfective *done* (*They have done landed in jail again*); *used to + would, could (I used to could*); *need* + past participle (*That boy needs taught a lesson*); *you all/y'all* (and other combinations with -*all*); existential *they = there* (*They's about five people in that house*); *fornent* (= next to); *wait on* (= wait for); *whenever* (= at the time that or as soon as); and *till* (= so that).[22]

Montgomery's research is particularly important because it allows a distinction between two groups of nonstandard grammatical features which are used in Appalachian English and which have regional distribution in Britain. One group includes forms which are derived from Southern British English and found in a variety of American dialects. The other group includes forms which are derived from Scottish English (or from Scottish English through Ulster dialects), and which linguists have more specifically identified with Appalachian English, although some of these also appear in other dialects in the American South.

Dialect Contact and New Dialect Formation

This preliminary investigation indicates that the common notion that Appalachian English was strongly influenced by the Scotch-Irish dialect is not supported by the available evidence. This evidence points to a more complex situation, with different British regional dialects having a varying influence on separate categories of linguistic features. British Northern and West Midland dialects may have had a stronger influence on Appalachian vocabulary; British Southern (or perhaps Southern and West Midland) dialects had a stronger influence on Appalachian pronunciation; British Northern and South-ern dialects both had an influence on Appalachian grammar. Since there is evi-dence that Scotch-Irish immigrants or their descendants were at least nu-merous, if not predominant, on the Appalachian frontier, we are left with the problem of accounting for the apparent loss of many of the more distinc-tive or stereotypical features of their dialect. Approaches which are overly dependent on *colonial lag*, a concept which is concerned with conservative aspects of American English, have tended to focus more on archaic elements in American regional dialects and on the direct one-to-one comparison of individual features, without sufficiently considering the innovative nature of American dialects or the importance of comparing linguistic systems. It is the unique combination of linguistic features which sets Appalachian English apart from other varieties of American English and which complicates attempts to establish direct connections with a specific British regional variety.

British linguist Peter Trudgill gives perhaps the fullest treatment of the phenomenon of dialect contact, and in particular the development of new dialects through the mixture of various regional forms as a consequence of immigration.[23] According to Trudgill, in a situation where two or more mu-tually intelligible dialects are mixed, there will be an initial period of *accom-modation* between these dialects, in which a speaker of one dialect may con-sciously or unconsciously attempt to approximate the features of another dialect. This contact between dialects results in an overall increase in the number of variant features, including intermediate forms resulting from ac-commodation, as well as variants from the source dialects. Eventually, through *focusing,* the number of variants is reduced, resulting in a new dialect within three generations.[24]

A number of factors, both social and linguistic, will determine which variants will be eliminated and which will be preserved in the new dialect. Social factors include the relative proportions of speakers of different dialects in the mixture, as well as the relative degree of prestige or stigma associated with individual dialects, factors which could have contributed to the reduc-tion of Scotch-Irish features. In colonial America, even in the colonies where they were most numerous, it is possible that the newly arrived Ulster Scots were a linguistic minority. Since immigration from Ulster took place over an extended period of time (1717–75, with five peak periods),[25] the descen-dants of the earliest immigrants may have undergone a significant degree of cultural and linguistic assimilation by the time the last ones arrived. More-over, it is important to recognize that eighteenth-century immigrants from Ulster were not limited to Ulster Scots, but also included a substantial num-ber of Ulster Anglo-Irish, whose ancestors were transplanted from the En-glish West Midlands and South, and whose dialect reflects the influence of those parts of England. The dialect of these English emigrants to Ireland is known as Mid Ulster English, and it still remains distinct from the Ulster Scots dialect, although each of these dialects has had an effect on the other as a result of dialect contact.[26] Therefore, not only did many of the eighteenth-century immigrants from Ireland arrive in America speaking Mid Ulster English, a dialect with a close affinity to British West Midland and Southern dialects, but also the processes of dialect contact and new dialect formation had already started before the first ships left Ireland for America. If the Ulster Scots were less numerous than is commonly assumed, then this group might have experienced some social pressure to conform to the dialect of the majority. Although Scotch-Irish solidarity was maintained in some of the colonies, particularly in Pennsylvania, this ethnic solidarity and identification with Ulster began to break down as immigrants began moving southward and westward into the Appalachians, and ancestry came to be identified with a particular American rather than British origin.[27] Since Southern Appalachian settlement continued well into the nineteenth century, there would be a gradual decline in direct influence from major Scotch-Irish population reservoirs during the later stages of westward migration.[28]

Perhaps more important than social influences are those purely linguistic factors which determine what variants will be eliminated and which will be preserved in the new dialect. According to Trudgill, reduction of variant features is primarily accomplished through the dual mechanisms of leveling and structural simplification, a process known as *koinéization*. Through leveling, features which a majority of the source dialects have in common are most likely to be preserved, while socially or regionally identifiable variants are most likely to be eliminated.[29] Preservation of post-vocalic *r* was assured since it was a common feature of most British regional dialects, as well as the eighteenth-century British standard. Although there would have been loss of some features from all of the British dialects present in colonial America, since those from the British Midlands and South would have had the most features in common with each other and with the standard language, one might expect these varieties to have lost the fewest features through leveling. Northern British dialects, on the other hand, would have been the most geographically and linguistically distant from the British standard and would have contained the highest number of marked or minority forms.

Conclusions

While this preliminary comparison of Appalachian English and British regional English does not prove or disprove the idea that the Scotch-Irish were the predominant ethnic group on the Appalachian frontier, the mixture of British regional influences in Appalachian English suggests that the Southern British element must be taken into account. Moreover, consideration of eighteenth-century immigration from Ulster and the possible effect this immigration had on the ethnic background of the Southern Appalachians and on Appalachian English should be extended to include not only the Ulster Scots, but also the Mid Ulster Anglo-Irish. The mixed British influences in Appalachian English are not particularly surprising, but the way in which these British influences are combined is of great importance for linguists investigating the processes of dialect contact and new dialect formation, since it is appears that not all categories of linguistic features in Appalachian English were affected the same way or by the same British regional varieties. Obviously, there is a need for continued research on both sides of the Atlantic before we can describe with any confidence how Appalachian English came to be. However, any attempt aimed at establishing connections between Appalachian English and British regional English should proceed with caution, taking into account the overall structure of the dialect or dialects under investigation and avoiding broad generalizations based on a limited number of features. While dialect studies need not ignore what is known about migration routes and settlement patterns, these historical considerations should not control or limit the scope of a linguistic investigation.

On the other hand, we can conclude with confidence that statements such as those made in *Albion's Seed* that "the earliest recorded examples of this 'Scotch-Irish' speech were strikingly similar to the language that is spoken today in the southern highlands" and that "this American speech way is at least two centuries old" are either inaccurate or misleading, since it is clear that Appalachian English has undergone significant change over the last hundred years. In the 1930s, when Joseph Hall was investigating dialect in the Smoky Mountains, he was often given examples of pronunciations which his elderly informants considered old-fashioned, an indication that, even in relatively remote areas of the Southern Appalachians, the language has continued to evolve. Evidence that the processes of dialect formation were still at work throughout the nineteenth century has important implications for the notion that the Southern Appalachians underwent an extended period of physical and cultural isolation. Ultimately, the search for the British ancestry of Appalachian English will reveal a complex combination of influences which resulted in a dynamic process of innovation and change, and which produced a distinctively American form of English spoken in the Southern Appalachians.

Notes

1. Hans Kurath, "Dialectal Differences in Spoken American English," *Modern Philology* 25 (1928): 385–95.

2. In his 1928 article, Kurath lists as sources Henry J. Ford, *The Scotch-Irish in America* (Princeton: Princeton UP, 1915) and Frederick Jackson Turner, *The Frontier in American History* (New York: Holt, 1920), both of which promote the assumption of Scotch-Irish predominance on the frontier, although Turner also includes German immigrants among the "dominant element" (22).

3. David Hackett Fischer, *Albion's Seed* (New York: Oxford UP, 1989).

4. Fischer, *Albion's Seed*, 652–55.

5. See esp. Michael Montgomery, "Exploring the Roots of Appalachian English," *English World-Wide* 10, no. 2 (1989): 227–78; and Montgomery, "The Roots of Appalachian

English: Scotch-Irish or British Southern?" *Southern Appalachia and the South: A Region within a Region,* ed. John Inscoe, *Journal of the Appalachian Studies Association* 3 (1991): 177–91 (Johnson City, TN: Center for Appalachian Studies and Services, East Tennessee State University). Special thanks to Montgomery for his advice and for providing copies of published and unpublished manuscripts.

6. Kurath, *World Geography of the Eastern United States* [hereafter *WGEUS}* (Ann Arbor: U of Michigan P, 1949), 8, 10. Despite his interest in trans-Atlantic connections, Kurath did not consider American regional dialects to be reflexes of specific British regional dialects, but argued that each regional dialect in America was basically a "unique blend of British types of speech" (*WGEUS* 1).

7. Cratis Williams, "Appalachian Speech," *North Carolina Historical Review* 55 (1978): 174–79.

8. On innovation in Appalachian English, see Walt Wolfram and Donna Christian, *Appalachian Speech* (Arlington, VA: Center for Applied Linguistics, 1976), 161.

9. Alan Crozier, "The Scotch-Irish Influence on American English," *American Speech* 59, no. 4 (1984): 310–31.

10. *Redd* (to clear/clean up) and *clabber/bonny clabber/clabbered milk* also occur in lists of South Midland words, but although these terms are often identified with a Scotch-Irish origin, the *English Dialect Dictionary* also lists *redd* as occurring in the English Midlands, and Crozier, "Scotch-Irish Influence," notes the use of *clabber* in variety of English dialects. *WGEUS* fig. 21 shows *flannel cake* extending only as far south as the Valley of Virginia. *Doodle* (haycock), another word also given a Scotch-Irish origin, occurs only in western Pennsylvania and in western West Virginia (*WGEUS* fig. 25). *WGEUS* fig. 28 suggests *hickory* rather than *wattle* as the common Appalachian term for "ox goad."

11. The two East Tennessee studies are Tracy R. Miller, "An Investigation of the Regional English of Unicoi County, Tennessee," diss., U of Tennessee, 1973; and James R. Reese, "Variation in Appalachian English: A Study of Elderly, Rural Natives of East Tennessee," diss., U of Tennessee, 1977. British sources include Harold Orton and Wilfred Halliday, eds., *The Survey of English Dialects—Basic Materials* [hereafter *SED*], 4 vols. (Leeds: Arnold, 1962–71); Harold Orton, Stewart Sanderson, and John Widdowson, *The Linguistic Atlas of England* (London: Croom Helm, 1978); J. Mather and H. Speitel, eds., *The Linguistic Atlas of Scotland, Scots Section,* vols. 1 and 2 (Hamden, CT: Archon, 1975–77). The two East Tennessee studies were carried out under the direction of *SED* director Harold Orton while he was a visiting professor at the University of Tennessee at Knoxville.

12. Hans Kurath and Raven McDavid, *Pronunciation of English in the Atlantic States* [hereafter *PEAS*] (Ann Arbor: U of Michigan P, 1961); Lee Pederson, *East Tennessee Folk Speech: A Synopsis* (Frankfurt, Germany: Lang, 1983); Joseph S. Hall, *The Phonetics of Great Smoky Mountain Speech* (New York: King's Crown P, 1942).

13. *PEAS* 18–19.

14. *The Dictionary of American Regional English* suggests a wide distribution for *critter* and *chaw*; E. B. Atwood's *Survey of Verb Forms in the Eastern United States* (Ann Arbor: U of Michigan P, 1953) suggests a wide distribution for *a*-prefixing in the eastern states (34–35); *PEAS* maps 62, 90, and 143–44 suggest a wide distribution for the variant vowels sounds in *deaf, shut,* and *poison.*

15. Pronunciations represented by *whar, thar,* and *sartin* were common in late Middle and early Modern English. For treatments of the *ar* sound in these words, see E. J. Dobson, *English Pronunciation, 1500–1700* (Oxford, England: Oxford UP, 1968), 2:558–63; Charles Jones, *A History of English Phonology* (London: Longman, 1989), 246–47.

16. See, e.g., Robert J. Gregg, "The Scotch-Irish Dialect Boundaries in Ulster," *Patterns in the Folk Speech of the British Isles,* ed. Martyn Wakelin (London: Athlone, 1972), 109–39; Michael Barry, "The English Language in Ireland," *English as a World Language,* ed. Richard W. Bailey and Manfred Görlach (Ann Arbor: U of Michigan P, 1982), 84–133; and J. Y. Mather and H. H. Speitel, *The Linguistic Atlas of Scotland, Scots Section,* vol. 3: *Phonology* (London: Croom Helm, 1986).

17. The examples are adapted from Barry, "English Language," 111–14.

18. Barry, "English Language," 113.

19. See Dobson, *English Pronunciation,* 992; Charles Jones, *A History,* 298–300; Charles Barber, *Early Modern English* (London: Andre Deutsch, 1976), 305.

20. Montgomery, "Roots of Appalachian English," 181.

21. E. B. Atwood, *Survey of Verb Forms in the Eastern United States* (Ann Arbor: U of Michigan P, 1953), 28–29, 34–35.

22. Montgomery, "Exploring the Roots," 248–59; Montgomery, "Roots of Appalachian English," 182–88.

23. Peter Trudgill, *Dialects in Contact* (Oxford, England: Blackwell, 1986), 81–126.

24. Trudgill, *Dialects,* 95–96.

25. James G. Leyburn, *The Scotch-Irish* (Chapel Hill: U of North Carolina P, 1962), 169–79. See also Fischer, *Albion's Seed,* 606–10. Fischer argues that immigration was heaviest in the decade 1765–75, with perhaps two-thirds of the immigrants arriving during that period. However, according to estimates based on the 1790 census, immigration from all sources accounted for only 15 to 20 percent of the growth in the white population during the eighteenth century; see David Ward, "Immigration: Settlement Patterns," *Harvard Encyclopedia of American Ethnic Groups,* ed. Stephan Thernstrom (Cambridge, MA: Belknap P, 1980), 502.

26. See G. B. Adams, "Ulster Dialects," *Ulster Dialects,* ed. G. B. Adams (Belfast: Ulster Folk Museum, 1964), 1–4; Gregg, "Scotch-Irish Dialect Boundaries," 109–13; Crozier, "Scotch-Irish Influence," 312; Barry, "English Language in Ireland," 115–19.

27. Leyburn, *Scotch-Irish,* 191, 232–33, 270; John C. Campbell, *The Southern Highlander and His Homeland* (New York: Russell Sage Foundation, 1921), 51.

28. For early census figures, see John C. Belcher, "Population Growth and Characteristics," *The Southern Appalachian Region, A Survey,* ed. Thomas R. Ford (Lexington: U of Kentucky P, 1962), 37–53. In the ten years between 1790 and 1800, the total population of the Southern Appalachians increased from 175,189 to 293,584. In 1800, the mountain region of eastern Kentucky had a population of only 1,587. The upland sections of Georgia and Alabama had no recorded population until the census of 1820.

29. Trudgill, *Dialects in Contact,* 98–102.

Jim Wayne Miller

See volume 2, chapter 2, for biography.

Talk About Pretty

He said: I like to get me a sixpack, drop it in
the cooler, some bait—I'll buy beer but not these
two-cent crickets, or these nightcrawlers,
that's baiting your hook with a dime every time.
Bagworms, they're good when you can find some,
I usually can, or a big wasper's nest.
And I like to drive down past Lucas in my pickup,
catch me a mess of bluegills, some little channel cats.
I like a midnight supper, when it's cooler.
I've fished off the rocks there at the Narrows
when it was coming dark, moon already on the water
like a big print of butter. I recollect once
there was this cloud, big cloud, just as blue,
and soft as mole fur, reflection of it there
on the water, like a sea horse or something
you're apt to come on in a book. And I
like to drive back when the filling stations
have got their Pepsi and RC signs turned on,
sheet lightning off in the sky is pretty, too,
and drive past houses, see the tv's on,
sometimes the screens will have that peach color
of women's drawers, but they're every color now,
and farmers out driving along real slow
looking over corn and soybean fields
and the tail lights on their pickup trucks,
and mist down in the bottoms along the river
like a picture you're apt to come on in a book.
Chinese drawings? Japanese? You know about that.
And black cattle bunched in a pasture corner,
and—you take a rose, a rose is as pretty a thing
as ever you're apt to see, and a deer
standing in a field by a fencerow of an evening.

From *Vein of Words,* Seven Buffaloes Press, 1984. Reprinted by permission of the author and
publisher.

R. Chesla Sharp

R. Chesla Sharp is a native of East Tennessee. He attended Carson-Newman College, the University of Tennessee at Knoxville, the University of Chicago, and the University of Wisconsin at Madison, where he received the Ph.D. in English. He taught at the University of Massachusetts at Amherst before joining the faculty at East Tennessee State University, where he teaches courses in linguistics and American literature, and where for several years he directed the graduate program in English.

Sharp's essay "Teaching Correctness in Appalachia" is based on extensive experience in the classroom, a native's knowledge of the region, and extensive travels and study in other parts of the country.

Teaching Correctness in Appalachia

Recently while I was traveling along Interstate 70, I stopped at a restaurant in Green River, Utah. The restaurant was on a little river in what was otherwise a desert and was called Tamarish. On the wall was an etymological lesson on the name: "*Tamarach* is the local name for a wild bush growing along the river bank. In its travel west it was misnamed. It is correctly named *tamarish.*"

This tendency to assume that if there are two variant forms one is correct and one is wrong is fairly uniform. When my wife first met my father, he was telling her a story about lightning bugs, and when she mentioned sometime during his story that her term for the same bug was *firefly,* he responded that he was sure *firefly* was the correct term. When I deal with variant forms in my class in introductory linguistics, I now expect someone very soon to ask which is correct. Recently one of my older students told me that when she was growing up in northern Georgia, her family did not think of its speech as dialect, but simply a form of incorrect speech. I had experienced the same thing growing up in a small town in East Tennessee.

This focus on correctness works to the disadvantage of any dialect that is not mainstream. State and school authorities focus on national norms, and English teachers focus on the prescriptive tradition codified in the handbooks of their discipline. Students do not consider their language a subject of serious inquiry, since they always have been asked to change it because their language does not conform to the standard dialect.

Linguists usually have some intellectual discomfort with the concept of a standard form. This discomfort comes about because the concept of a standard involves the elevation of one form above that of another; from a nonelitist point of view, there is no good reason for this evaluation. Linguists

Printed by permission of the author.

think that any dialect is adequate for the community in which it functions. Problems of judgment enter the picture only when one dialect comes into conflict with another. The linguist is not comfortable being put in the role of a parent deciding between the claims of two children. Another problem that linguists have with a standard is that a standard wants to freeze the language in time. Linguists focus on the dynamic state of language. We like to say that language is in a state of change. The prescriptive tradition of the classroom often forgets this dynamic state.

About thirty years ago, as a young teaching assistant, I was working with foreign students on non-count nouns. I dutifully put the students through a pattern practice with *give me a piece of bread, a cup of coffee, a glass of orange juice.* I remember that one student asked if one couldn't say "give me *a coffee.*" I replied that one could not. Coffee was non-count and must have a dummy head. In those days students were outwardly respectful. So he said nothing. After class I went to a small cafe next to my classroom for breakfast and was horrified at what was happening to the language. Customers were ordering *a coffee* and waiters were screaming *two coffees coming up.* The foreign student obviously was listening to the English language more closely than his native-speaking teacher was, and the other native speakers of the language were blissfully destroying the distinction between two categories of nouns which were being so dutifully taught in class.

A possible objection to a standard can be raised on stylistic grounds. Standard, as taught in the public schools, often has produced at best a colorless speech and at worse an inflated circumlocutious form, as seen in the following press release from a college president: "These efforts need to go forth in tandem with those which will emanate from the scheduled visit of the chancellor to the campus. His purpose is to understand the specifics underlying the general issues communicated to him following last Friday's vote and then to make appropriate responses subsequent to that review."

Finally, the most serious objection to a standard is pedagogical. The focus of energy is so terribly misplaced. Wolfram and Christian hint at this objection when they talk about spending more time on essential skill rather than focusing on the correction of a child's dialect (162). If students spend all their time on correcting perceived errors in sentences already written, they will have no time to write sentences of their own. Standard and nonstandard forms have much in common. They have some differences, but these differences are usually in the surface structure and not the deep structure. The Appalachian *I have went home* differs from the standard *I have gone home* only in the lexical choice of one item. The two forms share the features of tense and aspect, verb placement, and phrasal rather than inflectional perfect form of the verb. A language program that discusses only the lexical choice leaves much about the verb system unanalyzed.

A language program that focuses only on mastery of the written standard is a deficient program. The College Board recommends that a language program should teach students that a language is a system, that the system changes over time, and that within the system there are dialectal and situational variations (23–24).

It is within these guidelines of the College Board that I suggest we treat the Appalachian dialect in the curriculum—as a dialectal variety of English that shows the characteristics of any form of language. The systematic nature of Appalachian English is seen in a-prefixing. Based on the work of Christian, Wolfram, and Dube (51–58), one can prepare the following distribution corpus:

A-prefixing occurs in the following:
1. He was a-beggin' and a-cryin' and a-wantin' to come out.
2. I knew he was a-tellin' the truth, but still I was a-comin' home.

A-prefixing does not occur in the following:
3. He likes a-huntin'.
4. The ten a-livin' children are at home.
5. She was a-eatin' the food.
6. She was a-enterin' from her house.

An examination of the corpus shows a fairly regular distribution of a-prefixing. It occurs only before the *ing* form of the verb and only when the *ing* form occurs as main verb of a verb phrase. It occurs only when the main verb begins with a consonant. Consequently, a-prefixing does not occur when the *ing* form is a gerund or an adjective or when the verb begins with a vowel. The nasal in *ing* in all forms is realized as an alveolar. Thus the speaker with the Appalachian dialect outlined will have the following forms:

1. He was a-cryin' to come out.
2. She was eatin' the food.
3. The ten livin' children are at home.

Change in Appalachian English is indicative of change in the language as a whole and in the change of grammar from one generation to another. Appalachian English changes to preserve what is perceived to be the dominant system or pattern in the language. Standard English has two ways of comparing adjectives:

1. *-er* and *-est* are added to words of one syllable or words of two syllables that end in a vowel:

taller	tallest
prettier	prettiest

2. In words of two syllables that end in a consonant and those of more than two syllables *more* and *most* are usually used:

more beautiful	most beautiful
more awful	most awful

Yet Appalachian English extends the *-er* and *-est* to words of more than one syllable that end in a consonant. Thus we get the following forms:

1. It was the awfulest mess.
2. It was one of the beautifulest pieces.

Historically, suppletive adjectives have formed irregular paradigms in Modern English:

good better best
bad worse worst

Appalachian English often gives each historically different form independent status and then forms regularized comparisons:

bad badder baddest
worse worser worsest

This tendency to regularize is seen in the Appalachian reflexive pronoun. Standard English has the following paradigm:

SUBJECTIVE	OBJECTIVE	POSSESSIVE	REFLEXIVE
I	me	my	myself
you	you	your	yourself
he	him	his	himself
she	her	her	herself
it	it	its	itself
we	us	our	ourselves
they	them	their	themselves

The rule generating the standard form calls for the possessive form to be added to *self* except in the third person pronouns *he* and *they*. Here *self* is added to the objective form.

But the Appalachian simply generalizes one rule for all forms. Add *self* to the possessive form:

SUBJECTIVE	POSSESSIVE	REFLEXIVE
I	my	myself
you	your	yourself
he	his	hisself
we	our	ourselves
they	their	theirselves

Analogical change resulting in regularization and simplification is a very common thing in both children's acquisition of their language and in the history of the English language. The child's grammar is simpler than that of the parents. This is obviously seen in a child's use of *foots* for *feet*. The Old

English principal parts for *help* were *helpan, holpe,* and *holpen* and this pattern extends through Chaucer's time in the description of Saint Thomas à Becket "That hem hath holpen whan that they were seeke" (18). By analogical change with the regular verb pattern in Modern English *help* has become *help, helped, helped.*

This analogical change has not taken place in all forms of the Appalachian dialect. Thus one hears from certain Appalachian speakers, largely older speakers, the following: "I holp him cut his 'bacco and he holp me put up my hay." The [l] in *holp* in not pronounced in this dialect. The [l] would not be pronounced in *palm, bulb, calm* and *help* either. This dialect systematically reduces consonants in certain phonetic environments.

The school child's learning that Appalachian English shows systematic features and patterns of change inherent in the language and in the child's development—in short, that Appalachian English shows certain language universals—should engender respect for the dialect. One would thus be achieving one of the objectives that Falk lists in "Social Dialects and the Schools": the removal of the linguistic and social prejudices behind many language judgments (404). Since, however, I cannot assume that any body of knowledge will automatically lead to a set of beliefs, I would suggest that the school study social responses to dialects and what these responses are predicated upon.

The best way to make this study is to examine particular social and linguistic solutions and to see the value system behind the solutions. A local mall is undergoing remodeling, and the story has it that the new owners are unwilling to renew the lease of any store that is not a chain. If the story is true, the new owners obviously see no value in regional ethnicity. They want a mall in Knoxville to look exactly like a mall in Lexington even down to the dreary colors of the carpet. A local council on tourism has partially succeeded in changing the name *Upper East Tennessee* to *Northeast Tennessee.* The last name, according to the council, is more descriptive of the location. It is also less unusual and exactly what any other state may have chosen. I am sure that the local tourism council, if it were to move to Massachusetts, would want to change the names of Northhampton, Southhampton, Easthampton, and Westhampton because some poor soul from Wichita couldn't find the nonexistent Hampton. The attitudes of mall owners and tourism councils need not be the only models presented to students; these attitudes hardly illustrate universal response. Along State Route 611 in Pennsylvania are three small towns called Lower Bethel, Bethel, Upper Bethel. This naming pattern seems to me to be a delightful way of looking at a new settlement. It is not new; it is just an extension of the old. As a child I always found churches called the Church of the Good Shepherd, the Church of the Blessed Virgin, the Church of Saint John infinitely more interesting than the pattern in my small town: First Baptist, Second Baptist, Third Baptist, Bell Avenue Baptist. My wife likes to go to a small country store because the owner offers her a poke for her groceries. For someone who calls a shoe repairman a cobbler, a poke is an interesting variation upon a paper bag. Regional and ethnic forms have appeal, and we should attempt to make this appeal obvious to students.

The school in any area that speaks a non-mainstream dialect should have some form of dialect maintenance built into the language curriculum. A study of the linguistic forms in the dialect and social responses to these forms should go a long way in this maintenance, but I think the school should provide storytellers who keep the rhetorical traditions alive, and the literature curriculum should include regional writers who speak with the voice and style of the area. My first teaching job was in a German town in Wisconsin. Almost all my students' parents were native speakers of German; some of my students spoke only German before they came to school. The local Lutheran Church had two services on Sunday—one in English and one in German. Yet the intent both in the school and in the community was total eradication of German. The old went to the service in German; the young, to the one in English. While I felt strongly that German-Americans needed to learn English, I saw no reason why German should not have been encouraged along with English. So should it be with a dialect—learning a new form should not destroy the old.

There are times when Appalachian students should be taught new forms. Obviously, they should be taught standard written English, but this is true for any school child. The written dialect and the spoken dialect are two different linguistic forms for all children, and part of becoming literate is controlling the written dialect. But speakers of a non-mainstream dialect face an additional task in the school. Many linguists working with the education of children think that when two different dialects come into contact the person speaking a nonstandard dialect may suffer from the linguistic prejudice of the standard speakers. Falk says that those who use some variety of nonstandard dialect in the classroom may receive low grades from a teacher who speaks a standard dialect. Similarly, adults who apply for a job involving contact with speakers of a standard dialect may be rejected if their own dialect is nonstandard (404). Educators have often suggested that one could solve the problem by having the speakers of nonstandard English learn a standard dialect (Shuy).

The attempt to teach a standard dialect has usually led to one of two strategies, dialect replacement or bidialectalism (Wolfram and Christian 145). In the first, the school attempts to totally eradicate the student's native dialect and replace it with a standard dialect.

In order to avoid the harshness and the implied class judgment involved in eradicationism, some educators have suggested that students learn a new dialect—a form of standard English—for school and work and retain their original dialect for home and play. These educators named this approach bidialectalism and were very pleased with themselves for their tolerance and value-free approach to education. Bidialectalism is not a viable strategy. It is a verbal construct to allow educators to continue to do what they have always done under the guise that they are not doing what they are doing.

Bright students are going to know that the school considers their dialect inferior to the teacher's if they are told to use the teacher's dialect at school and theirs at home. This is exactly what they had done with the teacher who told them their dialect was wrong.

But dialect replacement in its old-fashioned form or in its politically correct form of bidialectalism will not work for the majority of students. Children speak the dialect they do because they learned it from their parents, friends, and neighbors. And no matter what they are taught in school, children will continue to use their original dialect as long as they have community support. The school just does not have the time to redo all the speech patterns supported in the students' home environment. Also the school itself probably supports the original dialect more than it realizes, particularly if it hires locally.

But I don't see why the school ever attempted the impossible in the first place. The only reason that one would want to change a dialect is so one can move freely from one social group to another, from one region to another, and this movement probably doesn't take as much dialect modification as one might think. Joseph M. Williams, in an article in *College Composition and Communication,* asks why English teachers find so many errors in their students' themes. Williams's answer is that English teachers are looking for the errors (154). Williams contrasts this teacher mode of reading with the ordinary reading mode. In the ordinary mode, one reads for content and finds few errors. Based on one's response to error, Williams divides the rules usually treated in the handbooks into three groups (159): (1) rules if violated we will notice; if we don't violate we will not notice (Williams lists double negatives and nonstandard verb forms as examples); (2) rules if violated we do not notice; if followed we do not notice (Williams lists as examples the injunctions not to begin a sentence with a coordinating conjunction and not to end a sentence with a preposition); (3) rules if violated we do not notice; if followed we notice. Williams lists the split infinitive and the who-whom distinction as examples.

If Williams is correct about the two modes of perceiving errors, then the amount of dialect modification needed for ordinary social discourse is probably very small. I would expect a large number of the differences between Appalachian dialect and standard dialect to pass unnoticed in social interchange. I would expect the following functional shift to be one of these: "I'm doctoring my cold." And perhaps the completive *done* in the following sentence will also pass unnoticed: "I'm sorry I have done turned the grades in." Obviously, any feature that goes unobserved need not be modified.

Certain features of the Appalachian dialect may appear pleasing. In this category I would place Appalachian rhetorical devices of exaggeration and understatement and word coinage. Obviously, any feature which one gets credit for using shouldn't be changed, but should be cultivated.

Finally, there are certain features that, for whatever reason, get in the way of social interchange. Some Appalachian phonemes are often misunderstood.

The vowel sound in *pipe* is one. An Appalachian outside his dialect would have communication problems with the name *Ryan White.* Once to a question, "Do you have ice cream?" I was told that the store did not have cream that specialized. Certain semantic changes present problems. When I tell someone I will have a book read by next Friday, I always think I have a week longer than the person to whom I have made the promise thinks I have.

There are forms that present no communication problem but still elicit a negative response. These include forms which lack subject-verb concord, such as *it don't matter,* and forms of certain pronouns, such as *you'uns, his'n.* Features in this third category are limited and probably are capable of being changed. Whether they should be is a heated question. The book by Shuy quoted earlier in this paper is a report of a 1964 conference held on social dialects and language learning. At this conference there was an impressive list of educators and scholars who shared the belief that the school should work to change social dialects which are not mainstream. James Sledd, in "Bi-Dialectalism: The Linguistics of White Supremacy," blasts the idea. On the whole I agree with Sledd. People who react negatively to a dialect are reacting to the people who speak the dialect. Changing the dialect will not modify this negative reaction much.

But I can't agree completely with Sledd. I think the schools should provide training in dialect modification under certain conditions. The course needs to be optional. Research studies in learning a language have shown that students' success depends on their motivation to learn the language as opposed to their motivation to pass the course (Falk 363). Students then who would profit from a course in dialect modification are those who already want to speak a dialect more inclusive than their original one. Students who find their dialect totally adequate will see no reason to learn a new one and will not learn one. Second, the list of features should be very limited. The course must confine itself to a very limited number of items, which are arrived at by some empirical study of features which do in fact prevent good social interaction across dialect lines.

Linguistic patterns don't change without a lot of practice and reinforcement. Therefore, I think it is imperative that students hear dialects other than their own in school. If students were to hear dialects other than their own, much dialect modification might take place by osmosis. Even for those who do not want to change their dialects, the hearing of a different dialect would be good. It keeps students from being linguistically provincial. But for students to hear a dialect other than their original one, superintendents must change their practice of hiring exclusively from their own county.

Not much time should be spent on dialect modification. A good language program should focus on the structure of language, language functions, language change, dialects, and stylistic varieties. If the program has time to teach students new forms, these new forms should be Japanese, Spanish, or Arabic. Appalachian students already know how to speak English. Teach them how to use the forms they already know effectively and confidently, so that if their region is invaded again, they might better defend themselves than their grandparents did when the coal barons came into the area. If the school is uncomfortable with a political agenda, then teach the students how to spell Appalachian forms, for their word processor certainly will not.

Works Cited

Chaucer, Geoffrey. *Chaucer's Major Poetry.* Ed. Albert C. Baugh. New York: Meredith, 1963.

Christian, Donna, Walt Wolfram, and Nanjo Dube. *Variation and Change in Geographically Isolated Communities: Appalachian English and Ozark English.* Tuscaloosa, AL: American Dialect Society, 1987.

College Entrance Examination Board. *Academic Preparation in English: Teaching for Transition from High School to College.* New York: College Board Publications, 1985.

Falk, Julia. *Linguistics and Language: A Survey of Basic Concepts and Implications.* 2d ed. Glenview, IL: Scott, Foresman, 1978.

Shuy, Roger W. *Social Dialects and Language Learning.* Champaign, IL: National Council of Teachers of English, 1964.

Sledd, James. "Bi-Dialectalism: The Linguistics of White Supremacy." *English Journal* 58 (1969): 1307–15, 1329.

Williams, Joseph M. "The Phenomenology of Error." *College Composition and Communication* 32 (1981): 152–68.

Wolfram, Walt, and Donna Christian. *Appalachian Speech.* Arlington, VA: Center for Applied Linguistics, 1976.

Judy K. Miller

Judy K. Miller has done much to promote the literary arts in Appalachia by co-founding and chairing the Appalachian Center for Poets and Writers, based in Abingdon, Virginia, where she lives and writes. A graduate of East Tennessee State University, she is also on the board of directors of the Appalachian Writers Association and has co-chaired the Virginia Highlands Festival's Creative Writing Committee. In 1990, she served as Artist in Education through the Virginia Arts Commission and in 1991 was a fellow at the Virginia Center for the Creative Arts. Her poetry and prose have appeared in a number of literary journals and have earned her a number of awards, including the Appalachian Writers Association's Wilma Dykeman Award for nonfiction. Miller has given a number of readings throughout the region. Though she continues to write poetry, she considers the writing of longer fiction to be her lifetime challenge. Since she has been both student and teacher in Southern Appalachia, her poem "English 101" is well grounded in this dual experience.

English 101

I am one of thousands driven
from the hills and hollers
by Tom Brokaw and his evening reports
of a changing world, driven
into the halls of hallowed learning.

There I hear: "We will rid ourselves
of regionalisms.
We will not say ain't and hit.
We will not drop the 'i' glide in fire and tire.
Deaf is not deef here.
Such is the stuff of illiteracy."

Then I remember: "Hit's been quite a spell
since I seed airy one of them."
Grandmaw. The illiterate.
"I ain't got none."
Mr. PreBrokaw. Pre101.

Now I say: "I reckon I'll try and do better.
I will try to overcome it.
I shall overcome."
And Grandma notices: "What's got into you?
Are you getting above your raising?
Ain't we good enough for you anymore?"

Printed by permission of the author.

Tom Wolfe

Tom Wolfe was born in 1930, in Richmond, Virginia. He earned his B.A. at Washington and Lee University in 1951 and completed his Ph.D. at Yale University in 1957. Wolfe is recognized as a leader in the "New Journalism," which employs in nonfictional writing techniques heretofore confined to fiction. Wolfe's unique blend of "pop" language and creative punctuation became his trademark. He became a leading chronicler of American trends with his books *The Kandy-Colored Tangerine-Flake Streamline Baby* (1965) and *The Electric Kool-Aid Acid Test* (1968). Winner of the 1980 American Book Award, Wolfe's *The Right Stuff* (1979) is a popular history of the early years of the American space program. Unsure of his ability to write a novel, Wolfe produced *The Bonfire of the Vanities* (1987), an exposé of greed and corruption in New York City.

The Right Stuff (1979) takes a "warts-and-all" approach to the formerly sacrosanct space program but celebrates the qualities of the people involved. Individuals such as West Virginian Chuck Yeager, in Wolfe's view, had "the ability to go up in a hurtling piece of machinery and put his hide on the line . . . and then go up again the next day, and the next day." Yeager's success carried over into the language of the space age, as "*Pygmalion* in Reverse" illustrates.

Pygmalion in Reverse

Anyone who travels very much on airlines in the United States soon gets to know the voice of *the airline pilot* . . . coming over the intercom . . . with a particular drawl, a particular folksiness, a particular down-home calmness that is so exaggerated it begins to parody itself (nevertheless!—it's reassuring) . . . the voice that tells you, as the airliner is caught in thunderheads and goes bolting up and down a thousand feet at a single gulp, to check your seat belts because "it might get a little choppy" . . . the voice that tells you (on a flight from Phoenix preparing for its final approach into Kennedy Airport, New York, just after dawn): "Now, folks, uh . . . this is the captain . . . ummmm . . . We've got a little ol' red light up here on the control panel that's tryin' to tell us that the *land*in' gears're not . . . uh . . . *lock*in' into position when we lower 'em . . . Now . . . *I* don't believe that little ol' red light knows what it's *talk*in' about—I believe it's that little ol' red *light* that iddn' workin' right" . . . faint chuckle, long pause, as if to say, *I'm not even sure all this is really worth going into—still, it may amuse you* . . . "But . . . I guess to play it by the rules, we oughta *hum*or that little ol' light . . . so we're gonna take her down to about, oh, two or three hundred feet over the runway at Kennedy, and the folks down there on the ground are gonna see if they caint give us a *vis*ual inspection of those ol' landin' gears"—with which he is obviously on intimate ol'-buddy terms, as with every other working part of this mighty ship—"and if I'm right . . . they're gonna tell us everything is copa*cet*ic all the way aroun' an' we'll jes take her on in" . . . and, after a couple of low passes over the field, the voice returns: "Well, folks, those folks down there on the ground—it must be too early for 'em or somethin'— I 'spect they still got the *sleep*ers in their eyes . . . 'cause they say they caint tell if those ol' landin' gears are all the way down or not . . . But, you know, up here in the cockpit we're convinced they're all the way down, so we're jes gonna take her on in . . . And oh" . . . *(I almost forgot)* . . . "while we take a little swing out over the ocean an' empty some of that surplus fuel we're not gonna be needin' anymore—that's what you might be seein' comin' out of the wings—our lovely little ladies . . . if they'll be so kind . . . they're gonna go up and down the aisles and show you how we do what we call 'assumin' the position'" . . . another faint chuckle *(We do this so often, and it's so much fun, we even have a funny little name for it)* . . . and the stewardesses, a bit grimmer, by the looks of them, than *that voice,* start telling the passengers to take their glasses off and take the ball-point pens and other sharp objects out of their pockets, and they show them *the position*, with the head lowered . . . while down on the field at Kennedy the little yellow emergency trucks start roaring across the field—and even though in your pounding heart and your sweating palms and your broiling brainpan you *know* this is a critical moment in your life, you still can't quite bring yourself to be*lieve* it, because if it were . . . how could *the captain,* the man who knows the actual situation most intimately . . . how could he keep on drawlin' and chucklin' and driftin' and lollygaggin' in that particular voice of his—

Well!—who doesn't know that voice! And who can forget it!—even after he is proved right and the emergency is over.

That particular voice may sound vaguely southern or southwestern, but it is specifically Appalachian in origin. It originated in the mountains of West Virginia, in the coal country, in Lincoln County, so far up in the hollows that, as the saying went, "they had to pipe in daylight." In the late 1940s and early 1950s, this up-hollow voice drifted down from on high, from over the high desert of California, down, down, down, from the upper reaches of the Brotherhood into all phases of American aviation. It was amazing. It was *Pygmalion* in reverse. Military pilots and then, soon, airline pilots, pilots from Maine and Massachusetts and the Dakotas and Oregon and everywhere else, began to talk in that poker-hollow West Virginia drawl, or as close to it as they could bend their native accents. It was the drawl of the most righteous of all the possessors of the right stuff: Chuck Yeager.

Yeager had started out as the equivalent, in the Second World War, of the legendary Frank Luke of the 27th Aero Squadron in the First. Which is to say, he was the boondocker, the boy from the back country, with only a high-school education, no credentials, no cachet or polish of any sort, who took off the feed-store overalls and put on a uniform and climbed into an airplane and lit up the skies over Europe.

Yeager grew up in Hamilton, West Virginia, a town on the Mud River not far from Nitro, Hurricane, Whirlwind, Salt Rock, Mud, Sod, Crum, Leet, Dollie, Ruth, and Alum Creek. His father was a gas driller (drilling for natural gas in the coalfields), his older brother was a gas driller, and he would have been a gas driller had he not enlisted in the Army Air Force in 1941 at the age of eighteen. In 1943, at twenty, he became a flight officer, i.e., a non-com who was allowed to fly, and went to England to fly fighter planes over France and Germany. Even in the tumult of the war, Yeager was somewhat puzzling to a lot of other pilots. He was a short, wiry, but muscular little guy with dark curly hair and a tough-looking face that seemed (to strangers) to be saying: "You best not be lookin' me in the eye, you peckerwood, or I'll put four more holes in your nose." But that wasn't what was puzzling. What was puzzling was the way Yeager talked. He seemed to talk with some older forms of English elocution, syntax, and conjugation that had been preserved uphollow in the Appalachians. There were people up there who never said they disapproved of anything, they said: "I don't hold with it." In the present tense they were willing to *help* out, like anyone else; but in the past tense they only *holped*. "H'it weren't nothin' I hold with, but I holped him out with it, anyways."

Chapter 5

Sports and Play

Introduction

Although always prominent features of Appalachian life, sport and play are probably the least studied and least understood aspects of the region's past and present. The frontier was a new Eden, and Eden, before the fall, was the home of play. Sport literature and sport writing began with the humorous and sporting literature of the Old Southwest, with many contributions by writers from Appalachia.

Sport and play are easier to describe than to define. Whereas sports are invariably competitive, play is communal. In sports, participants seek cultural prizes; those engaged in play delight in play itself. In sport the goal is victory over others, over nature, or over one's self in a previous performance; in play, the goal is recreation or re-creation of the spirit within.

Selections in this chapter reflect enormous changes in sport and play that have occurred in the last century and a half—changes that have brought new leisure opportunities to the region's population, but new problems as well. Radio and television have helped to transform an amateur sporting heritage into organized athletics requiring a few highly disciplined participants and many spectators. The folk music heritage has been converted into a highly commercialized network of professional musicians. Tourism—a form of play—promotes Appalachia as an American playground where vacationers from outside the region engage in recreational and leisure activities while natives watch, wait, and serve. The history of sport and play in Appalachia, like the history of other aspects of life in the region, suggest nothing is constant but change.

Robert J. Higgs

A native of Lewisburg, Tennessee, Robert J. Higgs graduated from the U.S. Naval Academy. After eight years of service in the U.S. Air Force, he resigned his commission as captain and entered the University of Tennessee at Knoxville, where he received his Ph.D. in English in 1967. He taught a year at Eastern Kentucky University before joining the faculty at East Tennessee State University. His main interests have been Appalachian literature and the literature of sports. With Ambrose Manning he edited *Voices from the Hills* (1975), and he is the author of *Laurel and Thorn* (1981) and *Sports: A Reference Guide* (1982). In 1994 he received the Cratis D. Williams Award of the Appalachian Studies Conference.

The following article, "Sports and Play in Southern Appalachia: A Tentative Appraisal," brings together two of the major themes which have engaged Higgs's attention over the years.

Sports and Play in Southern Appalachia:
A Tentative Appraisal

Wright Morris, in *The Territory Ahead,* says that no matter where we go in America today, we will find what we just left. As far as sports and play are concerned, I would not want to argue with that assertion. Once, not really so very long ago, sports and play in Appalachia were quite different from those forms found elsewhere, but not any more. Athletics and recreation are essentially the same across the American landscape, as are the problems, which, it seems, are forever increasing. In fact, writers from this region have been among the first to decry the now-familiar dehumanizing trends in sports, and they have continued to speak out on issues, as a few examples will make clear.

Sherwood Anderson, who made southwestern Virginia his permanent home, was one of the first American writers to regard the athlete as a cultural symbol and to suggest that sports are art forms providing the possibility of relief from the world of commerce. Like Johan Huizinga and others, he also saw the reverse occurring—the world of business encroaching upon the domain of sports and the athlete becoming a specialist and a celebrity.

Thomas Wolfe was witness to the same complex and shifting scene in American sports. In Nebraska Crane of *The Web and the Rock* and *You Can't Go Home Again,* he created an enduring hero of natural strength and virtue who could do what Wolfe himself could not, "remain detached from the fever of the times" and go home again. In Jim Randolph in *The Web and the*

From *The Impact of Institutions in Appalachia: Proceedings of the Eighth Annual Appalachian Studies Conference,* ed. Jim Lloyd and Anne G. Campbell, Appalachian Consortium Press, 1986. Reprinted by permission of the publisher.

Rock, he shows an opposite type of hero, one who is victimized by all the flattery that his athletic success has fostered, and he succinctly paints a devastating picture of alumni and fans who are all too ready to bestow praise, providing there is a victory, of course:

> They fill great towns at night before the big game. They go to night clubs and bars. They dance, they get drunk, they carouse. They take their girls to games, they wear fur coats, they wear expensive clothing. They are drunk by half time. They do not really see the game and they do not care. They hope their machine runs better than the other machine, scores more points, wins a victory. They hope their own hired men come out ahead, but they really do not care. They don't know what it is to care. They have become too smart, too wise, too knowing, too absurd to care. They are not youthful and backwoodsy and naive enough to care. They are too slick to care. It's hard to feel a passion from just looking at machinery. It's hard to get excited at the efforts of the hired men.[1]

Indeed, Arthur Miller was only echoing Wolfe a quarter of a century later when he said, "There doesn't seem to be any humanity left in big-time sports . . . people go to watch a machine operate. That wipes out the connection between spectator and team. The human side is out."[2]

Wilma Dykeman also suggests that the human side is out or perhaps going out. In a few pages in *Return the Innocent Earth* describing the big game between Jackson (read the University of Tennessee at Knoxville) and the University of Alabama, Dykeman identifies every reprehensible facet of the do-or-die game: the bromidic mentality of the alumni, the post-season bowl lust, the swelling arrogance sure to come with victory, and, most of all, "the dark malevolent growl" that "moves through the multitude." Is this, Dykeman seems to ask, sublimation of violence or incipient arrogance? Deborah Einemann (Dykeman's character), a Jew and citizen of the world, had "heard this crowd before"—in Germany, of course. So too had Nobel Prize winner Elias Canetti heard crowds before, as he makes clear in his unsettling book, *Crowds and Power.*

What type of men make up the machines that characters in Dykeman's novel witness? Dan Jenkins gives us his version, in his novel *Semi-Tough,* in his picture of T. J. (Torn Jock) Lambert:

> They say that when T. J. was in college at Tennessee, he kept a mad dog chained up in his room in the dorm and used to feed it live cats. They say that instead of going down the hall to the toilet, T. J. had a habit of taking a dump in his closet. And when it got smelling so bad in his room that even T. J. would notice it, they say he would throw a bunch of newspapers on the closet and set fire to the whole thing.[3]

Some would say that Jenkins surely jests and I suppose he does, yet in another sense he is right on the money in description of T. J. in college in the athletic dorms, for he has found the spot—second only to the frontier cat house—where anecdote and macho lore blur into fables of studliness. If one were to look for a character reminiscent of the world-beater and ringtailed-roarer out of the literature of the Old Southwest, there is only one place to turn, the athletic dorm at what Mark Harris called SSU (Southern State University). The picture of the athletic dorm at the University of Texas, in Gary Shaw's *Meat on the Hoof,* would tend to confirm this observation.

No doubt Lisa Alther is jesting too, to a degree, in a chapter entitled "Walking on the Knife's Edge, or Blue Balls in Bible Land" in her novel *Kinflicks,* but she has also zeroed in on the very real problem of muscular Christianity in our culture, which seems sometimes to be headquartered in the very heart of Appalachia. Note the following prayer of Brother Buck during the citywide Preaching Mission in the cavernous gymnasium of the Civic Auditorium in Hullsport as Ginny and Joe Bob obediently hold hands, "sweating and trembling":

> "Let us pray," Brother Buck instructed. "Father, our Coach, hep us, Father, to run Thy plays as Thou wouldst have them run. Knowing, Lord, that Christ Jesus Thy quarterback is there beside us with ever yard we gain, callin those plays and runnin that interference. Hep us, Lord, to understand that winnin ball games depends on followin trainin. Hep us not to abuse our minds and bodies with those worldly temptations that are off-limits to the teammates of Christ. . . .
>
> . . . and hep us, Celestial Coach, to understand that the water boys of life are ever bit as precious in Thy sight as the All-American guards. And when that final gun goes off, Lord, mayst Thou welcome us to the locker room of the home team with a slap on the back and a hearty, 'Well done, my good and faithful tailback.'"
> "A-man," Brother Buck added as an afterthought.
> "A-man," echoed the rest of us.[4]

This type of satire of muscular Christianity has become commonplace in the last few years, but it is timely and needed as long as evangelists insist upon the heretical notion that sports are the bridesmaid of religion and slant their proselytism accordingly. Jerry Falwell, Oral Roberts, and Billy Graham all acknowledge the power of sports in attracting converts, and Falwell has said that he wants to build "Champions for Christ." "Presumably," says Shirl Hoffman about the techniques of Falwell and Roberts, "the Lord likes to see his favorite team win, and trouncing the heathens from the state college up the road proves, in its own inexplicable way, that the institution's theology was right all along."[5]

What does all this mean for us in Appalachia today? It means that sports and play in Appalachia and elsewhere have become either ends in themselves or means of serving the goals of religion, patriotism, or commercialism. If we look at the last Superbowl game, watched by 115 million, and the half-time program put on by the Air Force as a recruiting effort and remind ourselves of all the links between sports and religion, we must admit, I think, the distinct possibility that we have become a leisure-class society characterized by the four occupations—sports, government, warfare, and religion—identified by Veblen in *Theory of the Leisure Class.* The rise of competitive sports and the decline of imaginative and unregulated play provide an index of the extent to which a society has moved toward a leisure class of what Veblen would call a barbaric culture.

Basically, the difference between sports and play is the difference between *paidia* and *ludus.* These terms, coined by Roger Caillois in *Man, Play, and Games,* represent principles which permeate all types of play. *Paidia* is a type of "uncontrolled fantasy, frolicsome, impulsive, or capricious"; *ludus* is the tendency toward "effort, patience, skill, ingenuity."[6] *Ludus* lends itself to rigid competition, complexity, and organization, and to easy alliance with the state; *paidia,* by contrast, is unstructured, simple, and highly individualistic in the sense that the player is not so tightly bound by rules, and even secretive in that the nature of the play depends to a large extent upon the imagination of a limited number of participants. In *ludus,* the player displays ingenuity in the method or technique by which he attempts to win highly competitive contests already well established within a particular culture. In *paidia,* ingenuity is displayed in the inventiveness of the player in creating new games or adopting variations; in his ability, as it were, to entertain himself. The principles of *ludus* and *paidia* are always bound together, but, as Caillois points out, they always move in any game—and, I would add, in any culture—in opposite directions. Again, what is true elsewhere is true of Appalachia, and the big switch seems to have begun in the 1920s, though much research is needed to document this tentative assertion.

The one thing we do know for sure is that things have not always been this way, if we trust the observations of earlier observers. The children, says Horace Kephart in 1913, "play few games, but rather frisk about like young colts without aim or method."[7] "The young people of the mountains," wrote John C. Campbell in 1921, "as a whole do not know how to play." Even when they do play, he says, they wish passionately to win and are inclined to take whatever means necessary to reach a goal. What is missing, says Campbell, in addition to sportsmanship, is organization, which organizations would provide:

> The Young Men's and the Young Women's Christian Associations might also find a special field of service in supplying and stimulating recreation. The young people of the mountains as a whole do not know how to play. They need to be directed into lines of wholesome vigorous activity. No definite program can be suggested. Here, as elsewhere, it will not be enough to supply the means. There must be definite fostering and supervision, and in places a traditional and religious opposition must be overcome, sympathetically and tactfully. The greater use of music—of community singing in particular—would be helpful, as well

as the encouragement of games in which all may take part, folk dancing, and sports of various kinds.[8]

It may have been true that "as a whole" the mountain children in 1921
did not know how to play, but as Pamela Henson showed in her unpublished paper "A Study of Children's Play in Appalachia," based on a survey
of numerous texts, it is certainly not altogether true. Mountain children did
know how to play to a significant degree. In her survey of games in Kentucky, Tennessee, and West Virginia, Henson

> found 277 games with distinctive titles, all collected since 1930. After
> classifying these games, Henson discovered that of those that could be
> identified, 136 used words, while twenty-eight were nonverbal. Eighty
> were exclusively played outdoors, thirty-five indoors, and forty-nine
> could be played either place. Perhaps the most interesting discovery is
> that thirty-four of the games required only one player, forty-two could
> be played with a minimum of two players, thirty with three, seventeen
> with four, fifteen with five, fifteen with ten players, and one required
> twenty-two.[9]

Henson's study is valuable since all of her conclusions on various games are
telling. In the case of jump rope, which is essentially a West Virginia game,
Henson found that "none of the 63 jump rope games . . . entailed competition between jumpers." Among her conclusions, Henson cites a "rarity of
competitive and team games, and games which entail assumption of roles."[10]
The games Henson surveyed reflect a clear divergence from the dominant
American culture (36).

The table makes it evident that children's games of all sorts, relatively
simple and unorganized, are, according to Caillois's classification, forms of
paidia. The games, and especially some of them such as counting-out rhymes,
are quite familiar to anyone raised in Appalachia and over, say, fifty years of age.
They are also disappearing, though I have no data to support that claim. Also
disappearing are the almost pure examples of *paidia* that Caillois calls "tumult," "agitation," and "immoderate laughter," which also helped to define
traditional Appalachian culture in the form of tall tales and practical jokes.
That tumult and agitation existed on a wide scale throughout the region, we
have on authority of one in whose honor this conference was established, and
in his discussion of George Washington Harris's Sut Lovingood, in whom
tumult abounded most gloriously:

> Sut's pranks, which belong to that low type of humor that derives its
> relish from the sight of gore and the infliction of pain upon others, are in
> the mainstream of mountaineer humor, which is preserved intact from the
> wild and boisterous frontier. That Sut's counterparts have not appeared in
> the fiction of the mountains to any marked degree merely indicates that

Classification of Games by Roger Caillois

	AGON (Competition)	ALEA (Chance)	MIMICRY (Simulation)	ILINX (Vertigo)
PAIDIA Tumult Agitation Immoderate laughter Kite-flying Solitaire Patience Crossword puzzles LUDUS	Racing Wrestling, etc. Athletics not regulated Boxing, Billiards Fencing Checkers Football Chess Contests, Sports in general	Counting out rhymes Heads or tails Betting Roulette Simple, complex, and continuing lotteries	Children's initiations Games of illusion Tag, Arms Masks, Disguises Theater Spectacles in general	Children "whirling" Horseback riding Swinging Waltzing Volador Traveling carnivals Skiing Mountain climbing Tightrope walking

Note: In each vertical column, games are classified in such an order that the paidia element is decreasing while the ludus element is increasing.

Source: From Roger Caillois, Man, Play, and Games, trans. Meyer Barash (New York: Free Press, 1961), 36.

polite taste excluded them. The pranks that Sut rigged on his enemies have been the stock in trade of his counterparts in the mountain country down to recent times. Such pranks as turning snakes and lizards loose in church, throwing nests of hornets among praying congregations, howling their sins at the mourner's bench, tying cans of lighted kerosene to dog's tails, mutilating cats, dogs and horses, luring preachers, sheriffs, candidates for office, and school teachers into compromising situations with women, and frustrating weddings have their local adaptations in the oral traditions of most mountain communities.[11]

Praise God, it might be said, that such forms of play and humor are no longer prevalent in the region, if extant at all, and enough has been said in a derogatory vein about such sadistic practices that it is not necessary for me to add another note of outrage. Edmund Wilson, remember, called Sut "not a pioneer contending against the wilderness but a peasant squatting in his own filth." He also acknowledged that the *Yarns* is "by far the most repellent book of any real literary merit in American literature." Sut's hatred,

Wilson contends, "is directed against anybody who shows any signs of gentility, idealism, or education."[12] "Hatred," I believe, is much too strong a word, reflecting a fundamental misunderstanding of the nature of play, or the ranges of play, on Wilson's part; he also fails to see, as others of Sut's detractors have, that Sut's pranks are directed for the most part against institutions or representatives of institutions, preachers, politicians, and teachers, and pretense in general. Indeed, one could easily imagine Sut letting loose a bag of lizards during the height of Brother Buck's sermon in the Hullsport auditorium in Alther's novel; or, for that matter, recalling the scene in *Return the Innocent Earth*, in a section of Neyland Stadium either during the pre-game prayer or during a heroic goal-line stand on which some commercial bowl bid depends. Can we not say, in fact, without being charged with absolute sadism, "Sut, where are you now that we need you?" The point I wish to emphasize and defend is not infliction of pain upon man and beast, but a sense of independence in forms of play and a refusal to blindly accept organized games that lend themselves so easily, especially given the promotional techniques of the modern world, to perverse relationships with commerce, religion, and the nation-state. There is a case, to be sure, for rules and structure, but how far do we go from the spontaneity of *paidia* that has always been a distinguishing feature of sports and play in Southern Appalachia? Note that unregulated athletics, racing, wrestling, etc., is a feature of *paidia,* and it is such forms of competition, indeed usually violent, that were a distinctive feature of the people who formed a very large part of the population of the region. I speak of the Scotch-Irish, whose contests are described by Reverend Edward L. Parker in *The History of Londonderry*:

> Their diversions and scenes of social intercourse were of a character not the most refined and cultured; displaying physical rather than intellectual and moral powers, such as boxing matches, wrestling, foot races, and other athletic exercise. At all public gatherings, the "ring" would be usually formed; and the combatants, in the presence of neighbors, brothers, and even fathers, would encounter each other in close fight, or at arms length, as the prescribed form might be; thus giving and receiving the well-directed blow, until the face, limbs, and body of each bore the marks of almost savage brutality. All this was done, not in anger or from unkind feeling toward each other, but simply to test the superiority of strength and agility.[13]

Note that in these contests there are no material prizes, and, apparently, little or no animosity between competitors or combatants; and though the bodily pain in boxing matches can easily be imagined, the injuries would appear to be minor compared to those in any ordinary football game in Southern Appalachia, where I have seen as many as eight people carried off the field in a single game. Still, the contests of the Scotch-Irish seemed brutal to observers, and no doubt that impression contributed to giving this group the image of being a "pernicious and pugnacious" people in the mind of easterners in the United States.

Benjamin Franklin, for example, regarded them as "violent, narrow-minded drunkards—white savages," as Ayers points out in *Vengeance and Justice: Crime and Punishment in the Nineteenth Century American South,* before going on to present this composite picture:

> A particularly virulent strain of violence entered the South in the culture of the Scotch-Irish, the majority of whom chose the South for their home in the eighteenth century. In Carl Bridenbaugh's language, the Scotch-Irish were "undisciplined, emotional, courageous, aggressive, pugnacious, fiercely intolerant, and hard-drinking." All observers agreed that the Scotch-Irish had little patience for legal forms and found quick recourse in their guns, knives, or fists. "It appears to be more difficult for a North-of-Irelander than for other men to allow an honest difference of opinion in an opponent," a contemporary and sympathetic biographer of Andrew Jackson argued, "so that he is apt to regard the terms opponent and enemy as synonymous." Southern mountain culture, indelibly dyed by the Scotch-Irish origins of so many early settlers, became famous for its sensitivity, as Horace Kephart observed, "to any disparaging remark or imagined affront."[14]

This is also a point made by Campbell in his 1921 call for reform of play in the mountains, without specific reference to the Scotch-Irish but referring to mountain youth in general:

> The Highland boy has, however, little knowledge of play as play. When he plays he plays to win. In contests of any kind, he wishes passionately to be the victor, and if he finds defeat threatens him he is too inclined to give up or take what means he can to reach his end. He is, moreover, very sensitive and swift to take offense. Ridicule, or the suspicion that someone is "throwing off on" him, he cannot bear, and he is quicker with the knife, or, when he is older, with the pistol, than with the fists. Thus he incurs the reproach of being, in popular parlance, a "poor sport," one who does not know the art of "playing the game to a finish," regardless of what it costs. It must not be inferred from this statement that he is a coward, although from a true sportsman's standpoint there is an element of cowardice in his failure to meet defeat squarely and honestly. In feats of daring, the mountain youth is brave to recklessness, and as has been indicated in a previous chapter, no man in the country makes a more valiant soldier. He needs, however, to learn the code of honest sportsmanship—the code of the "good loser"—which can best be taught through games which bring him in touch with his fellows in team-play and healthful competition.[15]

Without approving of quick recourse to gun or knife anymore than of cruel pranks on man or animals, can one not ask where the American Revolution itself would have been had the Scotch-Irish played the game of the British? Was not that spirited independence and suspicion of organizations, in whatever form, the very quality that made them, in the words of British historian Leeky, go "almost to a man on the side of the insurgents. They supplied some of the best soldiers of Washington."[16] Though I cannot prove it at this point, I believe the Scotch-Irish are the key to the understanding of the history of sports and play in the region. Even the celebrated Grandfather Mountain Highland Games, "America's Braemer," appears to be almost an imported event when viewed in terms of the traditional play of the mountains,[17] shaped so much, I suspect, by the proud and independent Scotch-Irish. Their descendants, however, have, like most of the rest of us, embraced with open arms all the mass forms of sports and play that now surround us.

Are there not corporate dangers in the present forms of sports and entertainment far outweighing those spontaneous, unregulated, and often violent forms of the older generations? Are there not dangers in crowds and hero-worship, the two requirements for spectator sports that now surround us? Ring Lardner apparently thought so, for in 1921, the same year that Campbell said the mountain children did not know how to play, Lardner voiced exactly the same complaint about the dominant culture. We do not know how to play in America, he said:

> because (1) we lack imagination, and (2) we are a nation of hero-worshipers. . . .
>
> But hero-worship is the national disease that does most to keep the grandstands full and the playgrounds empty. To hell with those four extra years of life, if they are going to cut in on our afternoon at the Polo Grounds, where, in blissful asininity, we may feast our eyes on the swarthy Champion of Swat, shouting now and then in an excess of anile idolatry, "come on, you Babe. Come on, you Baby Doll!"[18]

Over a decade later, Lardner was still disenchanted with the anile idolatry of crowds, as seen in his novel *Lose with a Smile.* The narrator, Danny Warner, is a busher from Booneville, Missouri, and in his letters home he tells his girlfriend what life is like in the Big Leagues:

> Some of the boys has got nick names like wear they come from like 1 of the pitchers Clyde Day but they call him Pea ridge Day because he comes from a town name Pea ridge and he was the champion hog caller of Arkansaw and when he use to pitch in Brooklyn last yr he use to give a hog call after every ball he throwed but the club made him cut it out because the fans come down on the field every time he give a call and the club had to hire the champion of iowa to set up in the stand and call them back.[19]

In such satire, the heritage of frontier humor is alive and well, and the object of attack, sports fans, seems as deserving of such treatment today as ever.

Here, then, is the familiar situation again. As in so many other aspects of Appalachian life, the effort in sports has been not to learn from the mountain culture but to transform it in imitation of mid-America. No doubt, in the 1920s many mountain kids profited from new teachers and coaches bringing to them new knowledge of new sports, but could not America then (and now) have learned just as much from the habit of mountain kids "who frisked about like young colts without aim or method"? A whole new series of books proposing alternative forms of play and non-competitive games[20] were in effect anticipated by children of Appalachia for over the past one hundred years. There is, in fact, or has been, an Appalachian physical education, if we care to look back and see. It is a way of play quite at odds with the modern sports industry, which reflects the same traits as the rest of modern society. The old ways were not perfect, by any means, but their virtues were hidden, not proclaimed and boosted as are the supposed ones of modern sports. To the degree that contemporary sports and play are reformed, they will in fact move back toward the old order, toward fun, simplicity, spontaneity, and naturalness, toward *paidia,* the spirit of childhood.

Notes

1. Thomas Wolfe, *The Web and the Rock* (New York: Harper, 1939), 122.

2. "Human Side Is Out of Sports—Miller," Knoxville (TN) *News Sentinel,* 13 Feb. 1986.

3. Dan Jenkins, *Semi-Tough* (New York: New American Library, 1972), 6.

4. Lisa Alther, *Kinflicks* (New York: Knopf, 1975), 42.

5. Shirl J. Hoffman, "Evangelism and the Revitalization of Religious Ritual in Sport," *Arete: Journal of Sport Literature* 2 (Spring 1985): 63–87.

6. Roger Caillois, *Man, Play, and Games.* Trans. Meyer Bararh (New York: Free Press, 1961), 13.

7. Horace Kephart, *Our Southern Highlanders* (New York: Outing Publishing and Macmillan, 1913; rpt. Knoxville: U of Tennessee P, 1976), 259.

8. John C. Campbell, *The Southern Highlander and His Home* (Russell Sage Foundation: New York, 1921), 319–20.

9. Bernard Mergen, *Play and Playthings: A Reference Guide* (Westport, CT: Greenwood, 1982), 208.

10. Pamela Henson, "A Study of Children's Play in Appalachia," unpub. paper, Georgetown U, Washington DC, 1973, 36.

11. Cratis Williams, "Sut Lovingood as a Southern Mountaineer," *Faculty Bulletin,* Appalachian State Teachers College, Boone, NC, 1966, 3–4.

12. Edmund Wilson, "Poisoned," *Voices from the Hills,* ed. Robert J. Higgs and Ambrose N. Manning (New York: Frederick Ungar, 1975), 414.

13. Quoted in Henry Jones Ford, *The Scotch-Irish in America* (Princeton, NJ: Princeton UP, 1915), 243.

14. Edward L. Ayers, *Vengeance and Justice: Punishment in the Nineteenth-Century American South* (New York: Oxford UP, 1984), 22.

15. Campbell, *Southern Highlander,* 126.

16. Quoted in Ford, *Scotch-Irish in America,* 208.

17. For a history of the Scottish games in North America, see Gerald Redmond's masterful study, *The Sporting Scots of Nineteenth-Century Canada* (Rutherford, NJ: Fairleigh Dickinson UP, 1982).

18. Ring Lardner, "Sport and Play," *Civilization in the United States: An Inquiry by Thirty Americans,* ed. Harold E. Stearnes (New York, 1922), 461.

19. Ring Lardner, *Lose with a Smile* (New York: Scribner's, 1933), 2.

20. In addition to the bibliography in Mergen, *Play and Playthings,* see George Leonard, *The Ultimate Athlete: Re-visioning Sports, Physical Education, and the Body* (New York: Viking P, 1978), 261–66; Jeffrey Sobel, *Everybody Wins: 393 Non-Competitive Games for Young Children* (New York: Walker and Co., 1983); and Nora Gallagher, *Simple Pleasures: Wonderful and Wild Things to Do at Home* (Reading, MA: Addison-Wesley, 1981).

Harry Brown

Harry Brown is a graduate of Davidson College. He received an M.A. from Appalachian State University and a Ph.D. from Ohio University. Since 1970 he has been a member of the English Department of Eastern Kentucky University, in Richmond, where he now teaches courses in modern American literature and poetry writing. His verse has appeared in publications such as *Kansas Quarterly, Southern Humanities Review,* and *Kentucky Poetry Review.* He was coeditor of *God's Plenty: Modern Kentucky Writers* (1990), and he has published two collections of poems, *Paint Lick Idyll* (1989) and *Measuring Man* (1989).

Hunting Reasons

Three of us climbed often through the hills.
One would walk a ridge,
The other follow hollows below,
Knowing the duplicity of squirrels,

From *From the Hills,* 1974; reprinted in *Measuring Man and Other Poems,* Lewiston, 1989.
Reprinted by permission of the author and the publisher.

How they circle hickory and oak
To make great fools of young hunting boys
Who do not always look at every side.
We didn't know the mountain land as yet
But still were trying ridges, fields, and hollows,
Slowly searching out good paths.
We seldom wondered why we killed,
And we were young and never considered lines
Or gave a second thought
To bending through two strands of wire.
Boundaries made no difference.
We never worried that a path
Might take us onto another's squirrel
That wouldn't properly be ours to kill.

After a few years passed each spent some hours
He might have hunted clearing ground,
Making fit a piece of deeded land
To hold a house and give a garden up.
And then he tacked some signs on trees along his line.

I, too, changed my ways, but changed again.
Embarrassed by boundaries,
I dug up long ago all my signs,
but when I turned my mind they reappeared.
Now I know to dig again each year.
And I have learned and left in fifteen years
As many paths,
Choosing one and then forgetting it
When squirrels and grouse grew sparse
Or when I found a better.
Reasons for change themselves have changed
But do so less each fall,
As if I were about to land upon
An absolute and perfect chart
That I might follow forever,
Some ideal map for hunters.
I would rather not,
And often leave a path to start another.

Thomas G. Burton

See volume 2, chapter 2, for biography.

While sports and play are usually characterized by "make-believe," they are nevertheless "real," occurring in actual times and places set aside for them. Thus, work and labor belong to the world of necessity, sports and play to the world of leisure. There is another side of reality, however, that differs from the bounded worlds of work and labor on the one hand and sports and play on the other, and this is what we call "emergencies," the sudden intrusion of dangers in our lives that are of a different order from those latent in our scheduled amusements and labors. It may be reductive to say that amusements and even athletic contests belong to the "toy department" or to the theological category of "apodropia" ("things indifferent"), but, with certain exceptions, such as mountain climbing and auto racing, they do not present challenges that are matters of life and death. The latter confront the young men in the following story while they are making merry in the mountains. In emergencies, the test of heroism—accepting the call for action, courage, and possibly sacrifice—occurs in the blinking of an eye and may never come again. In sports, opportunities for rites of passage are endlessly repeated but rarely intentionally entail the possibility that one may face tragic consequences at death's door. Sports and play may or may not build character, but, it would appear, they are seldom the final test of character, which seems to come outside the fields of play. It is good to remember that leisure, while an escape from labor, is no escape from hard and telling moral choices, which may loom up before us when least expected.

The Rescue

There were four of us at play in an awesome arena. David was behind the wheel, John up front, Don and I were in the back. We weren't intending to go anywhere really, just driving around, drinking, talking, being merry, with no Sherwood Forest, yet with more—big, powerful mountains, unemasculated by skis or fopped with lacy A-frames, mountains that were no nude Amazons on their backs, but bulky giants with massive deltoids, armpits engendering humans, Esau chests, shoulders and backs fleecy with rhododendron and laurel (or ivy as they used to say) and beards facing the sky—mountains through which we circulated on graveled roads, chased by plumy clouds that joined the mist where massive hemlocks thrust themselves into the circle overhead.

We came up by George's, David's brother's place; and since it was never too late there, we stopped for a drink. To our surprise he had neither red liquor nor white, though homemade beer, to justify our trouble; and while we sat around the table, George said he hoped we wouldn't take offense at being offered only home brew. David retorted, just ahead of John, "Perhaps a wooden rail or two, but not the whole fence." Don gasped, "God, that's the worst yet; once more, friend, and we'll stake you to an anthill and pour honey in your mouth."

About twelve we said goodnight, picked our way through the yard, across the creek, and drove aimlessly up the mountain. The road led to Beauty Spot, a bald on the crest some say is an ancient battleground, but according to Indian legend a section once burned off to guard against a monstrous bird ultimately killed by the Great Spirit. At that moment, however, our spirits were those instilled by George's.

As we ascended, someone noticed above a certain radiance that none of us could identify—a vehicle maybe, a campfire perhaps, or floodlights. We reasoned though that headlights would be moving, a campfire wouldn't be that intense, and there weren't any houses that far up.

Soon the glow became distinctly red; momentarily now and again we could see flames rolling upward and ebbing back like the surface of a star. Then we were there, at the top of the bald; and below us at least thirty yards, we could see what it was, though not clearly from the car. John and David leaped out: "Someone's slid off the road and caught fire." Don pushed the seat in front of him forward, blocking the one in front of me; his hand was grappling for the door post, but I couldn't wait for him to catapult his huge body through the breach. So I stuck my head through the V-shaped opening between the post and seat-back on my side and crawled out into the illuminated darkness.

The laurel was almost impenetrable, with enough thorns entwined to crown the world. One could have almost walked on top. I got down on all fours and made my way through the tunneled maze where there would have been no surprise, nor even fear, to meet some mythic monster. My nostrils extended in order that smell not be inferior to sight and sound, but I had not so much as a stick to put out carbuncled eyes, much less a byrnie to protect the bone-cage. There was, however, my old team jacket with skin thicker than mine cut into sleeves being gnawed at by millenary tiny teeth, a coat of thick wool from some ram, perhaps, which shivered on a distant mountain.

I followed the heat and light and finally reached the source, as did the other three. Flames were tearing the insides of a late-model Pontiac sports car, but besides us there wasn't a soul. "We better get back before the tank goes." "That's right." "But maybe we ought to circle the area first." "Right— someone could've been thrown clear or crawled out." We searched in ever-widening arcs, finding only ourselves, then gravitated back to the fire. There, all senses yielded to sight; and through the windows, the glass gone, we watched the glowing frame pulsate like a burning bush or a platter of crepes flambé. I moved to the front, where the opened hood was breathing flames, and saw that only the vital parts of the engine remained: arterial wires, hoses, and ducts had been consumed. Then it struck me that someone could be underneath; so I got down on my stomach, but saw only the body of the car being eaten through and its life's fluid gulped from the tank. It could have exploded at any moment; yet that wasn't the point, just as that no one had been in the conflagration—certainly not the owner who hadn't met his payments.

Other nights have come and gone, but since that day when spirits are high, old songs are sung, and tales are told, we cite the time we sought to save some folks from burning in a car.

Jeff Daniel Marion

Jeff Daniel Marion is a poet as well as a teacher, farmer, and printer. Marion took both undergraduate and master's degrees at the University of Tennessee at Knoxville. A resident of New Market, Tennessee, since 1966 Marion has taught English and creative writing at Carson-Newman College. In addition, he edited *The Small Farm,* an independent journal of poetry, from 1975 to 1980 and since 1983 has edited Mill Springs Press, a handprinting venture devoted to publishing Appalachian poets. His poetry has been widely praised and anthologized, and Marion has authored three books of verse, including *Out in the Country, Back Home* (1976), *Tight Lines* (1981), *Vigils: Selected Poems* (1990), and *Hello, Crow* (1992), a book for children.

Tight Lines

First read the water,
then cast toward pockets,
the deep spaces between
the cold print of rocks.

It's the flow that beguiles—
what's beneath that lures.

But when the line goes
taut,
a dark, waiting presence
will flash
and weave its way,
throbbing, into your pulse.

From *Vigils: Selected Poems,* Appalachian Consortium Press, 1990. Reprinted by permission of the publisher.

Charles R. Gunter, Jr.

Charles "Chig" R. Gunter, Jr., a native of Shelbyville, Tennessee, has taught at East Tennessee State University in the Department of Geography and Geology for three decades. He now spends half of his time as director of the Center for Undeclared Majors. He received a B.S. from Middle Tennessee State University and an M.A. from the University of Tennessee at Knoxville. Additional graduate studies were completed at the latter institution. His research and teaching interests include cultural geography, Latin America, Appalachia, and geographic education. He has published in the Appalachian Studies Conference *Proceedings, Tennessee Folklore Society Bulletin, Tennessee Cooperator,* and *Sports Place International.*

Cockfighting in East Tennessee and Western North Carolina

On the average, the [cockfighting] pit itself will have a diameter of sixteen to twenty feet. The size of the pit may vary according to the desire of the pit owner to accommodate more people. The pit floor frequently will be raised five to eight feet so that those people sitting on the first row will not obstruct the view of others sitting behind on the bleacher-type seats. A wall surrounds the pit floor, which may be composed of a claylike substance. Occasionally, this wall is made of glass to permit spectators to see better, but most likely the wall is made of plank or concrete block.

Both Sawyer and Hammer in a rather perfunctory manner tended to slight the preliminary activities such as matching and weighing game fowl, which must be accomplished before the cockfight begins. Nevertheless, their comments, plus those of Toole, do shed some light on these activities.

Hammer remarked that the chickens must weigh between four and six pounds. Let's say you are entering five gamecocks in a five-cock derby; you will put in five cocks and they will be matched with cocks of equal weight. If one of your entries weighs four pounds and twelve ounces, it will face another weighing four pounds and twelve ounces, or one within two ounces of it. Sawyer commented that six pounds and over is a pretty heavy rooster and that one rarely ever matches him to another rooster that heavy.

Once your game fowl have been weighed and matched with other roosters, Hammer observed that officials at the pit will begin calling the weights and will tell you which rooster you are supposed to "heel by band number." The banding of cocks is a very important phase of conducting a cockfight

From *Tennessee Folklore Society Bulletin* 44.4 (Dec. 1978). Reprinted by permission of the author and publisher.

and refers to placing a monogrammed band on each leg of the rooster. Since numbers rather than names are used on the bands, the matchmaker cannot be accused of deliberately matching certain entries.

A much more complete description of these preliminary activities before the actual fight was given by Toole. When the cockfighter reaches the pit after driving a few miles or five hundred miles, he is interested in getting his birds out of the car and into "scratch pens" or "exercise pens" so that these birds can pull themselves together. After flapping their wings, scratching, and crowing for thirty minutes or so, the roosters are put back into their carrying cases, and an effort is made to quiet them.

Should the cockfighter arrive at the pit location the day of the event rather than the night before, which is a more common occurrence, the first step would be that of weighing the birds and having them banded by the management. Once the band number and the weight of the cock are recorded, this information is given to the matchmaker and entry fees are paid.

Since the matchmaker must have similar information from all entries before he can begin the process of "blind-matching" the cocks, there is usually a waiting period. Frequently, cockfighters will engage in "hack fights" during the lull before the derby begins. Hack fights may be described as simply a fight between two birds arranged by two handlers. Usually a cockfighter brings more birds to a derby than will be entered. After a decision is made regarding which birds will be entered in the derby, the extra birds may be fought during these "hack fights."

"Heeling," as described by Sawyer, refers to putting the steel spurs (the proper name is "gaffs") on each leg of the rooster. Since the gaffs replace the natural spurs of the rooster, moleskin is placed on the rooster's leg and on his spurs. The gaffs, in turn, are so constructed as to permit these natural spurs to protrude through a hole in them. Pieces of leather are lapped over the gaffs and moleskin, and wax string is used to secure the gaffs on each leg. There is a degree of skill, apparently, associated with heeling.

After both cockfighters have either "heeled" their roosters personally or allowed someone else to accomplish this task, Hammer indicates that the birds are taken into the pit. Once they are in the pit, a lot of people think that something has to be done to make them fight. However, all that has to be done is to turn them loose. When they see another rooster they will fight. But the handlers always hold the roosters up in front of each other, allowing them to peck one another.

The referee, at the appropriate time, tells the two handlers to "get ready." When the referee says "pit," each handler sets his rooster down on scorelines which are drawn some eight feet apart. The handlers then step back approximately six feet from the birds and the fight begins. These scorelines usually are drawn with corn meal and need to be redrawn repeatedly.

Sawyer describes the cockfight like this: "The roosters fight until they hang, which means that one of these metal gaffs, which is needle-sharp on the point, has stuck in an opponent's rooster. It's up to the referee to order 'a handle,' and when he does so, if my gaff is in your rooster, you will take the gaff out of your own rooster. This rule would certainly prevent me from damaging my opponent's rooster."[1] Toole says that both handlers rush into the pit when the referee says "handle" and "pin the birds" to the floor so that they won't be shaking around and hitting each other. Sawyer says that twenty seconds elapse between "pittings" before the referee again says "get ready" and "pit." If both roosters reach the point of exhaustion after several "picks" or rounds, the referee may instruct the handlers to move to the "short line" or, as it is often called, the "center scorelines" which are drawn some sixteen to twenty-four inches apart.

Suppose you and I are contestants. We set our roosters down with one hand on the scoreline after the order to "pit," and if my rooster pecks at your rooster last, I say, "count me." The referee counts to ten; then he says "handle," which commences another twenty-second rest period. If my rooster never pecks or tries to fight, the count continues. One must have three ten-counts and one twenty-count to win a fight. The count can be broken if the cock being counted out fights.

According to Toole, if my rooster has the count, when I set him on the short score, I may tip him backwards just a little bit. Frequently, he is tired and he sinks to the floor. If I tip him the other way toward the other rooster, mine is likely to peck him, and I don't want him to since he already has the count. But, says Sawyer, a lot of times one doesn't go to the count. During the first "pitting" my rooster hits yours and it flops over just like it's dead—"He's just graveyard dead," pronounces Sawyer. You might not have to continue the count, but if there is still some life in the rooster, it is permissible to try to revive him.

The handler, according to Hammer, must know what to do for that rooster; he has to be a good first-aid man. There is some conjecture concerning putting the rooster's head into one's mouth and blowing on him, or covering portions of the rooster's body with cold water. Sometimes, by knowing what to do, the handler may win a victory rather than suffer defeat.

Winning or losing obviously would be of tremendous importance to someone like Sawyer, who makes his living from this sport. He does not consider himself a big fighter, but others have judged him to be pretty fair. Financially, he has the backing of a medical doctor.

The financial arrangements at various cockfights vary according to the entry fees paid by the contestants. For example, at Newport, Tennessee, earlier this year (spring 1978), Sawyer tied for the lead, but the entry fee was just $50. Three or four people split the pot, and he came home with only $800. If the entry fee had been $150, as it was a few weeks later, he would have made more money.

Additionally, side bets can be placed with the spectators or with the opposing handler. Sawyer's method is to holler out, "I've got $100 over here!" Usually somebody in the stands calls him. If a handler is confident, he sometimes gives odds.

Toole indicates that he doesn't know of another sport involving gambling where there is the same situation as in cockfighting. Frequently, in a crowd of several hundred spectators, there will be betting across the pit. Toole isn't sure whether it is a matter of tradition or what, but he says there is a tremendous amount of pride, integrity, and honor among cockfighters in that they will not welch on a bet.

Considered by many to be one of the oldest sports in the world, cockfighting today occurs under a wide variety of circumstances in the United States. Participation in this sport often is illegal, yet thousands are involved in cockfighting.

Note

1. Some minor rules of cockfighting vary from one region to another in the United States. Also, in a given region, house rules or pit rules may differ. However, rulebooks for cockfighting do exist. *Wortham's Rules,* published by *The Gamecock,* in Hartford, Arkansas, probably is the best-known publication containing modern tournament and derby rules.

Don Johnson

Don Johnson, a professor of English at East Tennessee State University, graduated from the University of Hawaii (B.A., 1964; M.A., 1966), where he also worked for one year as an instructor. He brings an interesting perspective to writing about Appalachia in his poetry, which focuses on moments and individual personalities that take on symbolic or metaphorical importance when transformed into verse. Johnson is also the author of *Watauga Drawdown,* a collection of verse, and numerous scholarly articles on topics ranging from Joseph Addison to "Hawaii Five-O." He serves as editor of *Aethlon,* a journal of sports literature. His poem "The Sergeant" (from his first volume of poetry, *The Importance of Visible Scars*) examines the permanent marks that experiencing the barbarities of war leaves on the individual.

Home Game

Heat lightning silhouettes the hills
beyond the worn-out pasture
where I lob slow pitches toward a flat rock
that no longer gleams like the white rubber plate
of the majors. My father taps soft liners

"Home Game" and "And the River Gathered Round Us" from *Watauga Drawdown,* Overmountain Press, 1990. Reprinted by permission of the author.

to my son. Professionally crouched
over burdocks, poised above the looped runners
of morning glories, the boy breaks
with each ring of the new metal bat, stumbles
through sedge and almost catches everything.

Wearing my tattered glove like a badge,
he dreams fences for the open field,
rags the old man to hit the long ball
he could climb the wall for like Yastrzemski.
He is out there where I have been

in the child's sweatless world of fame,
but I would have changed that thunder
building on the river to the first murmur
of applause that lived already as a faint twitch
troubling the sleep of boys throughout Virginia.

My father stole every sign and took my dream
to manage, ran it as he ran me in this very field
at dusk behind his tractor, crying "push, push, push,"
when I let up. In the listening air
his voice seemed to fade toward the waiting house,

to blend with my mother's calling us in
to supper. Now with clouds coming on
like middle age I want to tell my son
that dreams cost more than years,
that a bush league curve will earn

a lifetime's worth of nights in damp motels.
But I wave him back against a stand of pines
and turn in the rain's first spattering
to face my father, still crowding the plate
at sixty. The old game again. He knows

I mean to blow three quick ones by him, win
finally, before the night and the storm's dark
tarpaulin sweep in from deepest center field.
With the boy watching like a deer
from the tree line, I get two strikes clean,

then thunder booms overhead, the sound
of a high hard one splintering barn board
at my ear, bringing back his fatherly words:

"It's all in the delivery,
knowing when to bear down."

On the porch the women wave their white arms,
my mother, my wife, his wife, the boy's mother,
still calling us in as I wind up,
float the fat one down the middle, hearing
the ball peal off the level swing as I whirl

to track the high arc toward the clouds.
My son fades into pine boughs, bent on glory.
I stand here, face masked in rain, knowing
the old man stands at my back, his silver Adirondack
stuck into the storm, daring the lightning down.

And the River Gathered Round Us

After they wheeled away the town,
when the floodgates closed
and the river turned on itself,
we came back day after day
to watch the coves slowly fill up.

At the end of a week one road in
lay open. We drove it in three
Ford cars and a pickup towing
Wash Holt's rubber-tired wagon
that the boys from Mountain City rode.

It was not a Sunday. Most of us
had jobs, but we agreed to one more
game of ball before the smoothest
diamond in three counties
turned to lake bottom.

Water already lapped at the right field
fence where I killed a snake
before the first pitch, a fast ball
the batter himself called
a strike since we had no umpire.

Right went under with two out
in their half of the third
and we declared a ground ball

to that field an out. I played
barefoot and cheated toward

the infield, but it didn't matter.
Before the fifth was over,
water covered all but the mound
and the raked dirt at the plate.
By then, anything not a bunt

or fly ball was an out
and we were losing 6–2
when their pitcher called time
and said all three balls we had
were water-logged and that

he wouldn't ruin his arm
for no damn game in a lake,
so we brought him in half-way
where it was wet but close enough
to lob those melons in

with no pain. Then we lost
the bases, but ruled that running
in the right direction counted
if the runner didn't stop
until he made it home

or got out. We tied the score
on four straight hits to left
when a jon boat floated through
and blocked the fielder's way.
We called anything that hit

the boat a homer and it rained
that inning, the score tied
and water finally touching
the plate where both teams
congregated, soaked and up

to our knees in a field
without bounds, where everything
slowed and floated and nothing
sliding beneath the flood
would ever be forgotten.

Randall Norris

Of his own life, Randall Norris has written:

A child of the "hillbilly diaspora," I was born on December 13, 1949, in Lorain, Ohio. When I was twelve, my family moved to our ancestral home at Crossville, Tennessee. Since then I've spent most of my time just trying to stay alive. My struggle for survival is reflected in the themes I've chosen, or rather, those that have chosen me. My writing has always dealt with violence, both personal and cultural, as well as institutional violence, exploring why southerners are used as cannon fodder in America's wars.

I've always admired Russian literature. Tolstoy, Turgenev, and Gogol were my early favorites, and, later on, I developed a real love for Bulgakov, Pasternak, and Nabokov. I've learned what I know about short-story writing from Singer and de Maupassant, and my sense of the novel was first revealed by Faulkner, then expanded by García Marquez.

I've always wanted to write good fiction, and I sought out the best teachers I could find. At first, I studied in the fiction workshop at Bowling Green State University. While I was there, Phil O'Connor taught me about point of view, Robert Early taught me to trust my instincts, Richard Messer convinced me to believe in myself, and Steve Heller showed me how to edit a story. Ten years later, still unable to write fully realized fiction, I went to the Squaw Valley Writers Workshop, where I met Jim Frey, who taught me to write toward the fear. "The Rabbit Hunt," a chapter from my unfinished novel, *The Ice House,* is a product of that emotional journey. I am also the author of *Women of Coal* (1995).

The Rabbit Hunt

"I don't like the dark," Le Roy said.

He could hear his father fumbling with the lantern, but when he turned his head toward the sound, he couldn't see anything; black clouds hid the stars, wind-blown trees covered porch lights that ordinarily shined like giant orange fireflies stuck to the mountain, and he was standing so far under the hill he couldn't see the pale yellow glow from Grandpa Farley's kitchen window. Le Roy trembled.

Spotlighting rabbits seemed like a good idea this afternoon. He'd sat on the front porch, wiping his gun with an oily rag, while the bright fall sunshine warmed his face. Pa sat beside him, his big hands shining the small carbide lantern he'd borrowed from One-Eyed Gatty, an old coal miner who lived alone on top of Black Mountain, his only family a dozen redbone hounds. That was this afternoon.

Now, standing on the edge of a forty-acre hayfield, surrounded by woods

Printed by permission of the author.

and wild animals, with Pa towering over him in the darkness, it didn't seem like such a good idea. Only the .22-caliber rifle he clutched in his hands kept him from running.

"I don't like the dark," Le Roy said again, gripping the gun even tighter and holding it closer to his chest. The barrel felt cold against his skin.

"It'll be all right," Pa answered. "As soon as I get this lantern going."

Le Roy heard his father shaking the lantern up and down, mixing carbide and water together. When he stopped, he twisted the rusty knob until gas hissed, flipped the wheel on his Zippo and a long, thin flame shot out. He twisted the knob, narrowing the flame, slipped the lighter back in his pocket and put the miner's cap on his head.

Le Roy stood in Pa's shadow.

"Let's go," Pa said. He picked his gun up off the ground and started out across the field, his boots crushing the hay, his light shining back and forth.

Le Roy followed the light as much as he followed Pa, but now they were one and the same and he couldn't tell them apart. Then the light stopped.

"There he is," Pa said, pointing.

Le Roy looked. He could see two red eyes. He flicked the safety off with his right hand, raised the rifle to his shoulder, sighted carefully down the barrel, and pulled the trigger.

CRAAAACKKKK

The rabbit flipped over and lay still.

"You got him!" Pa said, running forward.

Le Roy followed close behind, barely missing the flying feet rising in front of him. His heart pounded and his breath came in short gasps. He couldn't remember being so excited. When they got to the rabbit, Pa stopped and looked down. The carbide lamp formed a puddle of light at his feet.

Le Roy looked around him.

The rabbit was lying on his side. Right between his eyes was a small, round hole. Blood trickled out of the hole and ran down his nose.

"Damn fine shot, Le Roy," Pa said, patting him on the shoulder.

Le Roy smiled when he looked down at the rabbit, and a small thrill of satisfaction ran up his back. He could still hear the crack of the gun and could see the rabbit flipping backwards.

When he flexed his hands the muscles were stronger, and the place on his shoulder where the gun went was hard. For the first time in his life he felt close to Pa.

Pa picked up the rabbit, tied a piece of twine around his hind legs, and handed him to Le Roy.

"You killed him," he said. "You carry him."

Le Roy reached out and took the dead rabbit, still soft and warm. He tied the twine around his waist and followed Pa across the field. Each time his foot hit the ground, he could feel the rabbit bounce against his leg.

After two more sudden stops, and two more shots, Le Roy was weighed down by three dead rabbits, each with a nice, neat, round hole between the eyes. They couldn't have been placed any better if he'd shot them from a foot away.

Le Roy felt taller, heavier and stronger. He was less afraid of the dark, and the gun in his hands was like a magic wand; wherever it pointed, a rabbit fell dead. He smiled. He was a crack shot, and it made him feel good.

"There he is, deadeye," Pa said, pointing once again at two red eyes.

Le Roy aimed, but this time his left hand dropped, and before he could raise it, he pulled the trigger. The shot went low, and instead of the rabbit flipping over backwards, dead, he sprawled out on the ground, turning first one way and then the other, squealing in pain.

"Come on, Le Roy," Pa said, running forward.

Le Roy hung back, his skin sweaty and clammy beneath his clothes. The light hurt his eyes, but that wasn't what held him back.

"Come on," he heard Pa yell again, a hint of anger in his voice. "Get up here and kill this rabbit!"

Le Roy's legs moved forward, drawn toward the rabbit by the sound of Pa's voice.

When he got there he looked down. The rabbit was trying to run, but he couldn't. The bullet had broken his back, and he was pinned to the ground in a circle of light. All he could do was push himself around and around, while blood poured from his mouth and nose and the hole in his chest. His eyes were swelled with fear, like he couldn't understand how his life had left, or where it had gone. He was caught in the confusion of dying.

Le Roy raised the gun to end his confusion, but Pa reached out and pushed it down.

"No sense wasting a shell," he said. "Just stomp his head."

Le Roy looked up at Pa, his eyes big as white silver dollars. All the power he'd felt quickly drained away.

"No," Le Roy said. "Let me shoot him." He tried to raise the gun, but Pa pushed it down again.

"Stomp his head," Pa said, an angry edge clearly in his voice. "I won't tell you again." He raised his hand above his head and held it there, ready to hit Le Roy if he didn't do as he was told.

Le Roy put his foot on the rabbit's head. The rabbit tried to move, but Le Roy pressed harder and harder, driving it deeper into the dirt, pressing more and more, and harder and harder, until it was too late to stop.

SNAP

The rabbit lay still.

His confusion was ended.

So was Le Roy's.

He stepped back, threw his gun on the ground, ripped the dead rabbits off his waist, and slung them as hard as he could. They didn't go far, because they seemed to weigh a thousand pounds. He turned and ran away.

"Come back!" he heard Pa yell, his voice no longer angry. "What's wrong? Everyone kills rabbits that way!"

"Not me," Le Roy yelled back.

He ran toward the light, leaving the darkness behind.

Dan Leidig

Dan Leidig grew up in southwestern Virginia. He has taught English language and literature at his alma mater, Emory and Henry College, Emory, Virginia, for thirty years. His courses in folk literature and poetry and his editorship of the *Iron Mountain Review* have contributed to the sustenance of regional voices and to critical assessments of Appalachian literature.

"Contrary Motions" is a perfect illustration of the form of playing known as *ilinx* (Greek for "whirlpool") or vertigo.

Contrary Motions

When you lay down on the wooden bridge
and stared at the water and willed it
the stream would begin to transport you backward

and in the twisting swing beneath the apple tree
you found that you could compel
the whirling backyard into drunkenness

and with an impious cross of the eyes
you could blur your mother into multiple images
even as she warned about lifelong disfigurement

and in due course you found that love
was a willing conjunction of contrary motions
and you knew it could move the earth.

But somewhere almost imperceptibly
you stopped imposing your will on the world
and began asking the motions to stop:

once on board a troopship still at anchor
in the night you felt yourself begin to move
implacably toward a distant unknown shore;

years later you sat on a train in a foreign station
clinging to your own unmoving reflection,
resisting the force of an unscheduled departure;

From *Now and Then* 9, no. 1 (Spring 1992). Reprinted by permission of the author.

and still later you simply stood up one day
to find the vertiginous planets realigning themselves,
insisting that it was all a temporary dislocation.

And now you are remembering your father's pale fists
clenching the bedsheet, trying to wring a pause
from the inexorable motions of his heart.

Patrick Sloan

Patrick Sloan was born and grew up in Weston, West Virginia. He received his bachelor's degree in psychology in 1969 from Fairmont State College, Fairmont, West Virginia, where he played varsity basketball. After serving in the United States Air Force, he received his M.S. and Ph.D. in clinical psychology from Ohio University in Athens, finishing in 1978. Since then he has lived in Johnson City, Tennessee, and served at the Veterans' Affairs Medical Center at Mountain Home as a clinical psychologist performing service, teaching, and research with veterans and medical and graduate students. A clinical associate professor in the Departments of Psychiatry and Internal Medicine, College of Medicine, East Tennessee State University, he has published articles in professional journals on neuropsychology, post-traumatic stress, and personality. His most recent publication deals with Appalachian Marine reservists who served in the Persian Gulf War. Sloan says sports have been a lifelong interest for him because they were such an integral part of his community and upbringing. Sports provided a sense of comradeship, play, and teamwork among people of a small town, he says, yet have served as a continuing source of satisfaction, interest, and communication in all the aspects of adult life, personal and professional, in the various places he has lived and traveled.

Sports Took Us beyond the Mountains
and Home Again

Whatever Appalachian values "Hot Rod" Hundley personified with his flair, Jerry West exemplified by stoic single-mindedness and determination, not to mention "fair" talent, as mountaineers wryly called it. Hundley's Kanawha Valley successor to the title as the state's greatest player, West is now enshrined in the Naismith Basketball Hall of Fame as one of a handful of undisputed best

From *Now and Then* 9.3 (1992). Reprinted by permission of the author and publisher.

players ever to wear a uniform. He is former coach and current general manager of the Los Angeles Lakers, the team for which he played for fourteen years and the most successful NBA franchise of the past decade. West expanded our horizons, perhaps because his games began to be televised, as the WVU Mountaineers surged into national prominence with a number one ranking and notoriety in the wake of Hundley in basketball, Sam Huff and Chuck Howley in football, and several other sports pioneers who joined the professional ranks beyond the mountains (such as Lew Burdette and Bill Mazeroski in baseball, Sam Snead in golf). Our home town of Weston's pioneer to "the pros" was the Huff team quarterback, Freddy Wyant, who played in the Canadian Football League for awhile before returning to Morgantown to become a successful businessman and National Football League referee.

West, who became nationally famous by his junior year in college, epitomized traditional rural life. He came from a large family in the tiny community of Chelyan, and displayed what he calls the "painfully shy" awkwardness of a country boy. But he was not awkward with a basketball and was perhaps more sensitive than many people realized. Collegian West seemed only slightly less embarrassed than I was, as I stood before him at age twelve in the kitchen of my friend Jim Kane, whose sister he was dating and would marry. Next to Jim, I was the second luckiest kid in West Virginia that summer day, but I was speechless and my stomach turned a flip-flop. Jerry seemed to sense my discomfort, so we went outside and passed a baseball. It seems ironic now, playing baseball with an All-American basketball player, but after all it was baseball season and I was carrying a baseball and fielder's glove. Later the following year, when Jerry returned to Weston, Jim and I played two-on-one basketball against him at my neighbor's dirt court, secluded from gawking crowds at Jerry's request. Here I had played hundreds of one-on-one games by myself, imagining I was alternately Jerry and Oscar Robertson, the two premier players of their day. There beside Town Run, I fantasized myself immortalized in his eyes by scrambling into the creek after a loose ball, because he complimented my desire at the time and mentioned the "dive" in later years, making me feel special, memorable, competent. He taught me how to make a quick step past a defender that day, and that maneuver later helped me earn a scholarship to Fairmont State. I best remember his serious intensity and how he was patient with our horsing around. In a telephone interview, he tells me he recalls that day and appreciates my recent letter reminding him of those encounters and what they meant to me. West says, "It's nice to hear things that might have been positive for some kid. That means a lot to me. Life, to me, is a collection of memories and experiences, both pleasant and unpleasant. Those help to build a whole person. I know I'm far from perfect, but I've been blessed with meeting some wonderful people, I think having an impact on some people, which obviously feels good." Perhaps it was my belief in our common roots that allowed me to call him now, over thirty years later. I remember our meeting my neighbor Herb while I was riding in Jerry's car that day, and I waved reluctantly, wishing Herb to see me but reverential, not wanting to violate Jerry's trust and privacy. It's funny, I felt the same about calling him now. When the voice on the telephone said, "Hello, Jerry West," my stomach was back in Jim's kitchen, but I knew it would be all right. We had a common history.

West told me:

> Growing up in West Virginia had a tremendous impact on my life. There's a quality of life, a quality of people in their ability to interact with one another in smaller communities that's much more personal, warmer, a much more secure feeling. I was always curious about how I might be able to function away from a very strong support group, very warm relationships with people I knew. I never lost my roots. I try to go back every year, just to slow down a little bit. What I miss most are the congenial people.

West Virginia is a rural state, but West grew up near Charleston, the state's largest city and capital, in the Kanawha Valley, which is industrialized if not urban. It's been said that industry can rob sport of its play because of its focus on competition and prizes, but industry also brought organization and facilities to the mountains. I mentioned this to West and recalled how impressed I was as a teenager at the quality of baseball parks in the Charleston area as compared to the more rural area around Weston where I lived. West says:

> I certainly didn't view myself as a city kid at all, because I never went to the city. Chelyan was only fourteen miles from Charleston, but we did not have a car, so it really wasn't accessible to me. If I would go, it would be by bus with my parents for an hour or two, and not very often. I always viewed myself as rural in nature but understanding that industry and cities are important to the welfare of the state and its people.

He is known for his humility, work ethic, and leadership. These values West believes came from his family and extended family. He says:

> I was exposed to a large family that depended upon each other for support, along with the same types of people in my neighborhood. These were the factors that made me feel secure. When you get out in the business world, you don't see that; it's a very competitive world. Americans are unbelievably competitive. Within that structure, there's going to be people who are not going to be supportive. Those are the people that you may relish competing against, because sooner or later those people can fail.

West is respected in the NBA as a masterful recruiter and polisher of players who are diamonds in the rough. His background helped shape his instincts in assessing character. General Manager West says:

All young people are not perfect. You have to look at where they come from and what their particular problems are. Many times when people have problems, they're selfish in nature, but if he can play in a team system, then you can work with him. You can steer him in directions that you will be proud of him when you put him on a basketball court. All of us are fragile in our personal feelings about how we live our lives, and we all want to be treated in a certain way. One thing I learned by living in West Virginia is that I treat people the way I want to be treated.

Richard Hoffer, in a *Sports Illustrated* article, described West as self-critical, gloomy, superstitious, and uncommunicative with family after a lost game. I asked West if this was true and if it is part of an Appalachian stereotype of stoicism, fatalism, and superstition. West places more emphasis on individual personality than cultural factors. He says:

The other (than cultural) aspects of a person's life reflect our personality. My personality is not based upon optimism. I'm not the most confident person in the world. I really think that in some respects that's a blessing. It pushes you, makes you want to excel more, and you won't give in. As far as not speaking to my family for weeks, that's simply not true. There were times I wanted to be left alone so I could concentrate on what I needed to do. It was important to me. I like to win. There was a time in my life when I felt my play dictated whether we won or lost. If I didn't play to my absolute maximum every night, there was a good chance we were going to lose. Knowing that and how I felt about this game, I just felt it was terrible—that if I left the floor and had anything left in me, it was wrong. Fans don't pay to see that. I was very difficult on myself, and that was one of the things I wish I could have changed. I'm sure I would have felt a lot better about myself as a player, instead of being so self-critical.

"But I've always felt in some respects that's a plus," he said emphatically. West seems to have resolved some of the ambivalence about his competitive strivings and his self-esteem. He says, "I've gotten to the point in my life where I like myself. Growing up, it seemed I was angry at everything. Even though outwardly I was not, inwardly I was. I'm not that way anymore. I like myself, but I'm still very, very competitive."

A college teammate of West's was Ronnie Retton, whose daughter Mary Lou also achieved fame as an Olympian gymnast. Retton discussed with me his family's consternation at his allowing Mary Lou to leave home at age fourteen to train in Houston at the invitation of Bela Karolyi, the Romanian coach who defected to the United States. He says:

She wanted to go, it seemed like a chance of a lifetime. We never dreamed it would turn out with her winning the Gold Medal, but we took a chance.

She called several times, crying, wanting to come home. We went to
Houston I don't know how many times, but she stuck it out. We had no
way of knowing what would come after the Olympics, all the publicity,
strangers coming to the house. We still get five or six letters a day, just
fan mail for her.

My brother-in-law Jimmy Priester tells me he chatted with Mary Lou recently while she was visiting family and friends in Fairmont. He described
her as genuinely friendly, "not uppity," traits admired by him and his Appalachian neighbors. Since Mary Lou, now married and residing in Houston,
was unavailable, I asked Ronnie what sage advice an Appalachian father offered
a future Olympic champion. He recalls, "I just told her the same thing I told all
five of my kids. Sports is like everything else in life, you get out of it what you
put into it. Be dedicated, always put into it your best." I also asked him what set
Jerry West apart from the other athletes Ronnie had observed in his experience
as a teammate and a professional baseball player. He says, "Jerry just kept getting better, in college and in the pros. That's what makes a great pro player.
Most guys reach their peak, but the great ones keep improving."

My coach at Fairmont State, Joe Retton, Ronnie's elder cousin and also a
native of Grant Town, made the same observation about West independently
in a recent telephone conversation. Joe Retton, himself an outstanding baseball player, became an exceptionally successful college basketball coach. He
is now a member of the NAIA Hall of Fame after being selected Coach of
the Year an unprecedented two times and having his Fairmont State teams
qualify for the national tournament twelve of his nineteen coaching years.
Under his tutelage, I was fortunate enough to become part of a highly successful team and was able to see beyond the mountains in many respects. My
first airplane ride was to the NAIA tournament in Kansas City in 1968. A
teammate from the coalfields was terrified to look out the plane's window;
another from a neighboring coal town was unmoved, showing me that one's
environment is not necessarily one's destiny. As I reflected on it recently, it
made me wonder why some West Virginians leave the mountains and hollows, and others do not. Given that perhaps the most outspoken West Virginia football player from that era, Sam Huff, was raised in a coal camp near
Fairmont, I called and asked his opinion.

Huff, the Pro Football Hall of Fame linebacker (New York Giants and Washington Redskins) and now vice president of special markets for Marriott Hotels
in Washington, D.C., was raised in Farmington (Number Nine coal camp),
where the mine explosion in 1968 buried some of his relatives among the
seventy-eight miners who died. His manner has been described as bombas-
tic, but I saw it as mountaineer candor without window dressing. Yet his
viewpoint was personal and more introspective than I expected. He said:

The New York Giants drafted me out of WVU to be part of a team.
That's different than my brother, a coal miner, going to New York and
getting a job. It's easy for me or somebody to say, "Go to New York,

Chicago, and get a job." But, for him to leave his culture, have no relatives there, no ties, it's too much to expect. Being part of a team is the greatest experience you can have. When you're in the huddle, that's the "comfort zone." It doesn't matter if you're black or white, Italian or Polish, you remember the value of cooperation. Teammates are friends for life, like family. When I left home for WVU, and then on to New York, I changed from one family into another. Being a part of something is really important. WVU belongs to every West Virginian, that's why WVU sports are so important to the people of West Virginia.

Huff, who once voiced his opinions in an unsuccessful bid for a U.S. congressional seat from West Virginia, was more critical than Jerry West of the performance of public colleges and universities in educating athletes and citizens. He said, "Colleges need to change. The West Virginias, Marylands, Penn States need to educate their own kids first, their own athletes first, and not just the A and B or out-of-state (non-athlete) students. It may be harder at first, but those kids will make good, productive citizens in the long run."

Huff's father was a coal miner. One of seven children, he says that "growing up in Number Nine taught me to be tough, not afraid of work, good work habits, basics that people in the city don't have. My father taught me how to survive in the outdoors, fish, hunt, change tires and oil. My own son doesn't know some of these things we took for granted. He can operate a computer, but can't change a tire. Appalachian people know how to survive." His upbringing did help prepare him to function in the professional and corporate worlds. Huff says, "Being from Appalachia gives you the basics," and he adds hopefully, "but you could span the world if you want to. Growing up, New York was a fantasy land to me. We had no television. We listened to 'Jack Armstrong' (the All-American Boy radio program) on the radio." But Huff made it to New York, went beyond the mountains, and is surviving quite well.

His experience is not common, however. Huff says, "I took my thirty-two-year-old son back to Farmington recently. My brothers and friends talk about when the mines reopen, they'll be the first to be called back. They can do anything with their hands, fix a car, build an engine, anything, but they won't leave. So, they survive day-to-day. It's their 'comfort zone.' It's hard to change a culture. I'd love to be there, but I can't do what I do there."

My father-in-law, Jim Priester, was reared in Number Nine a few years before Huff and preceded him in playing football at WVU. From his perspective as a former player, coach, and college professor, he has observed most of the local athletes who have come and gone since his playing days at Mountaineer Field. He cites the uniqueness of the environment and of certain individuals as factors in the development of mountain athletes. He says:

Deprivation sometimes seems to motivate those who have the mettle for it. Both Sam and Jerry were combative in their own way, persevering, persistent. Sam was more outspoken. He'd hit anything that moved. Jerry had quiet intensity. But both wanted to get to the top. Jerry reminded me of Stan Musial (the Baseball Hall of Fame member from the St. Louis Cardinals), delicate but very competent. In any sport, I have never seen a more courageous player in my life than Jerry West, playing hurt, with broken noses, over and over again. When deprived of things, they had a desire to better themselves, and they each had the support of many people. They were unique personalities, extraordinary individuals, each in his own way.

Judy K. Miller

See volume 2, chapter 4, for biography.

Widowed

Twelve oh five and all I can find
on my old television set is a team
of almost naked men throwing one another
from corner to corner in a roped-in stall.

And Estelle says the only relief she's found
from empty nights is a sweet old passage
from Psalms read over and again till she
falls asleep in the arms of scripture.

But I've never seen a Psalm bouncing back
and forth on thighs the size of Samson's
when Delilah took her scissors to his head
as if she was the Crusher and he Bojangles.

So I wrote me a letter to bouncing-thighs
Bojangles telling him I was sixteen
turned around backwards, a code for truth
which a muscled man is too slow to figure.
The picture he sent signed for sweet sixteen
and sealed with a kiss found its way to the only
frame in the house, the one holding Charlie
where he lay in his casket, eyes shut
and peace curling his lips.

From *Appalachian Journal* 15, no. 1 (Fall 1987). © *Appalachian Journal*/Appalachian State University. Used with permission.

Andrew Kozar

Andrew J. Kozar was an All-American fullback for the 1951 National Championship football team coached by Robert Neyland at the University of Tennessee at Knoxville. After graduation, Kozar earned the M.A. and Ph.D. degrees in
education at the University of Michigan. A popular speaker as well as a scholar,
Kozar is the author of several articles and books, including *The Sport Sculpture
of R. Tait McKenzie* (1992). He is the director of the Joseph B. Wolfe Collection of the sculpture of R. Tait McKenzie at UTK, where, since 1986, he has
been University Professor. Among several honors, he received the NCAA Silver Anniversary Award in 1978, presented to five former student athletes for
athletic achievement in college, baccalaureate degree, and career achievement.
In the following essay Kozar paints a picture of one of the most influential
individuals ever to come to the southern mountains.

R. R. Neyland: Engineer, Soldier, Football Coach

When Army Captain Robert Reese Neyland became head coach at the University of Tennessee in 1926, no one could have foreseen the enormous impact he
would have on the state and its people, nor how much his philosophies would
influence the game of football through so many of the men who played for him.

The story was buried on page ten of the *Knoxville News-Sentinel* on Christmas Eve, 1931, under the headline, "Chest Gets $18,582." The money had
been earned for Knoxville's Community Chest by the University of Tennessee football team's 13–0 win over New York University in a charity game
almost three weeks earlier.

The win over NYU completed an undefeated season. Carson Brewer,
popular columnist for the *Knoxville News-Sentinel,* recently noted that the
1931 charity game "was the first thing ever to mark East Tennessee with
greatness on a national scale." He emphasized his point by adding that this
"greatness preceded the creation of the TVA by two years and the establishment of the Great Smokies as a national park by three years."

The UT-NYU game was viewed by 40,860 spectators and by many of the
country's foremost sports writers. This was only one of the many non-bowl
postseason football games played between 1930 and 1934 as part of a nationwide effort to raise funds for the unemployed and other charities. It and
two Army-Navy games, all played in New York's Yankee Stadium, were
rated in the 1990 NCAA Guide as the most notable of all benefit charity
games because of the media coverage and their fundraising success.

People in the area had every reason for their pride in that 1931 team. Its
members, with few exceptions, were natives of the region, and the superstars

From *Now and Then* 9.3 (1992). Reprinted by permission of the author and *Now and Then.*

of that undefeated season were from the mountain South. Gene McEver and Beattie Feathers of Bristol, Virginia, and Herman Hickman, a native of Johnson City, are now enshrined in the National Football Hall of Fame. A fourth star of that team was Knoxville's Herbert "Deke" Brackett. They were all recruited, coached, and led by a native Texan, Robert Reese Neyland, an Army engineer-turned-coach who was building a football dynasty at the edge of the Great Smoky Mountains.

Prior to Neyland's appointment as coach in 1926, UT football was mediocre at best. Tennessee had won only two Southern Conference titles since fielding its first team in the 1890s. Neyland, an outstanding scholar-athlete at West Point, was the architect of the University of Tennessee football program that brought acclaim to East Tennessee and engendered pride throughout the state.

Interest in football was on the rise at the university and in the Knoxville area when Army Captain R. R. Neyland, assistant professor in the university's ROTC program and end coach of its football team, was named to succeed M. Beal Banks as head coach. Neyland quickly added two fellow West Pointers— William H. Britton, end coach, and Paul Parker, interior line coach—as assistants. Thus began the Neyland Era.

After six years as coach, his record stood at 51–2–4. The two losses were a 20–3 defeat by Vanderbilt in his first season and an 18–6 defeat by Alabama in 1930. Three of the ties were against Kentucky, and each wrecked the team's chances of winning the Southern Conference championship. Some believe that the 1931 stalemate with Kentucky killed an expected Rose Bowl invitation.

Neyland's success as a head coach in those first six years is incredible, considering the division of his time between university responsibilities and military assignments. His university obligations in the 1925–31 period included both football and ROTC; he also served after the football season as an engineer for the Army. The ROTC assignment ended in 1929, but he continued to split time between coaching and the Army, allowable under regulations of that day, until 1934. During that time he served the Army as district engineer, first at Chattanooga and later at Nashville.

Robert Reese Neyland was born on February 17, 1892, in Greenville, Texas, to Robert R. and Pauline Lewis Neyland. He established an outstanding record in academics and athletics at Greenville High School before attending Burleson Junior College for a year. He was studying engineering at Texas A&M when, through competitive examination, he won appointment to West Point at age twenty.

During his early years at the military academy, Neyland distinguished himself as an athlete, earning varsity letters in three sports. He was a starter at end on the 1914–15 football team, but his greatest athletic achievements came in boxing and baseball. He was West Point's heavyweight boxing champion in 1914–16, and once won twenty consecutive games en route to a 35–5 career record as pitcher on the academy's baseball team. He graduated near the top of his class at West Point, sharing in the top athletic award, and he received his second lieutenant's commission on June 4, 1916.

Neyland's initial assignment was with the First Regiment of Engineers at Brownsville, Texas, where he worked with construction and repair of levees, bridges, and roads. He later trained at the First Corps Engineer School at Washington Barracks before assignment to the First Army Engineering School in France during World War I. He returned to the U.S. before the war ended, eventually taking command of the training program for the Eighth Mounted Engineers at Fort Bliss, Texas.

Later Neyland studied mechanical and electrical engineering at Massachusetts Institute of Technology. He then returned to West Point, where he served as assistant and personnel adjutant and as education and recreation officer under General Douglas MacArthur, who was then Academy Superintendent. Neyland described MacArthur as "the nonpareil, who was unquestionably the greatest officer and man I ever knew. His incredible ability dwarfed all others by comparison."

Neyland absorbed and later expanded MacArthur's views on the significance of exercise and sports for cadets at the academy. He employed many of these lessons for the first time while serving as an assistant football coach during his academy tenure. After coming to Tennessee in 1925, he combined this experience with the West Point spirit to build one of the most respected football programs in America.

It was evident to anyone observing his relationship with athletes, whether in 1926 or 1952, that Neyland loved to command, whether dressed in a military uniform or in coaching togs. Neyland's personal notebook entries in 1926 filled only eight pages, but they reveal much about the man, showing him as a "commander-in-chief," plotting the season, setting a pattern he would follow throughout his coaching career.

Several pages of those entries dealt with team maxims, some borrowed from his Army coach, Charles Dudley Daly, and military-type verse from Rudyard Kipling, Marshal Ferdinand Foch, and others. All were applicable to football and outlined a path for team victory—"defeat of the enemy's forces," the first principle of war. Neyland applied these "team maxims" throughout his coaching career, and his former players can remember and quote them today.

The coach stressed team effort as the key to winning games and often cited this bit of verse to keep the value of teamwork uppermost in the minds of his players:

> It's not the guns or the armament,
> Or the money they can pay;
> It's the close cooperation
> That makes them win the day.
> It's not the individual
> Or the army as a whole,
> But the everlasting teamwork
> Of every blooming soul.

Coaching success can be measured in many ways. The most commonly used yardstick for success has always been a coach's win-loss record. Using that standard, Neyland's twenty-one-year figures are amazing. He won 32 of his last 37 games as a head coach, to bring his career total to 173 wins, 31 losses, and 12 ties.

Neyland's greatest achievement, perhaps, is evident in the number of his players who later became head football coaches, many in high schools in the mountain South and in major college programs across the country. Best known of this latter group was the late Bobby Dodd, a native of Kingsport, Tennessee, "field general" of Neyland's 1928–30 teams and a coaching legend in his own right at Georgia Tech. Through these men, Neyland's strong, martial approach has affected the game of football well beyond the mountain ridges of East Tennessee.

In an unpublished autobiographical manuscript, Neyland noted, "I am a Texan by birth, born of native Texans, and cherish the Texas belief that there is no place in the world to equal Texas." He may have been a Texan by birth, but his influence on the mountain South through long and outstanding leadership in Tennessee has been profound and permanent. The words "Neyland" and "Tennessee" have become inexorably linked for all time.

Harry Dean

Harry Dean, born in Cartersville, Georgia, in 1941, has been involved in Appalachian concerns for many years. A self-described "hill-country country boy," he was educated at Carson-Newman College (B.A.) and the University of Tennessee at Knoxville (M.A., Ph.D.). He has taught English at Cleveland State Community College, Cleveland, Tennessee, for twenty-two years. Dean has maintained his interest in writing since his college days, and in 1991 his chapbook of poetry, *A Sheltered Life,* was published. He describes his treatment of Appalachia as "a part of the larger world, thinking of people of Appalachia as having similar concerns as people worldwide."

Warren Peace

One year, my daughter's softball coach
was Warren Peace who had a wife
named Bitsy. He was a serious man

From *A Sheltered Life,* Rowan Mountain Press, 1991. Reprinted by permission of the author.

but she was a sight. She
once said he had been left
impudent by an automobile

wreck. But he could coach a softball team.
He could shout and throw and hit
infield and outfield practice and

Bitsy Peace said he did
all right for a fat boy.
Now my daughter plays piccolo

while her team-autographed softball
gathers dust high on a forgotten shelf.
Warren Peace died hitting infield,

defying a bad heart and fate,
impudent to the end.

Melinda Bollar Wagner,

Donna Lynn Batley,

Kai Jackson,

Bill O'Brien,

Liz Throckmorton

Melinda Bollar Wagner is professor of anthropology at Radford University. She received the B.A. degree from Purdue University and the Ph.D. from the University of Michigan in anthropology. The recipient of several grants, including awards from the Lilly Endowment and the National Science Foundation, Wagner served as chair of the Appalachian Studies Program at Radford from 1979 to 1982. She is the author of several articles and two books, *God's Schools: Choice and Compromise in American Society* (1990) and *Metaphysics in Midwestern America* (1983).

The following article was written following a class project in Appalachian culture taught by Dr. Melinda Bollar Wagner. The other four authors were students at Radford at the time (1986).

Appalachia: A Tourist Attraction?

Our study of the image of Appalachia as it is portrayed in tourist literature was born as a child of Wagner's (1981, 1982) theory that the image of Appalachia serves as an "alter ego" for urban American or middle American culture. Wagner's hypothesis is that America looks toward the image of Appalachia as its opposite, perhaps as what it once was and might be again. This hypothesis is borrowed from anthropologist Victor Turner's delineation of "community" and "communitas," which he says every society must have. "Community" is Turner's label for a society's social structure. It is a norm-governed, institutionalized, and abstract structure which delineates how people behave toward one another according to the roles they play. "Communitas," on the other hand, represents spontaneous, immediate, and concrete relationships among human beings, rather than as role bearers. Communitas suggests what "could be"; it is the crucible which holds human potentialities and universal human values. Turner sets forth the idea that society "needs" both: "Society seems to be a process rather than a thing—a dialectical process with successive phases of structure and communitas. There would seem to be—if one can use such a controversial term—a human "need" to participate in both modalities" (203).

Thus the image that "non-Appalachian America" has of Appalachia may serve as a "communitas." This image of Appalachia represents middle America's opposite—a less complex, community-oriented, rugged society. Like the American Indian, Appalachia is viewed in sentimental retrospect by an urban population which longs to free itself of its mechanized, computerized bonds and live in simplicity, at least for awhile. By looking toward its opposites, middle America may thus identify and appreciate itself through contrast. For example, if middle America is individualistic, then Appalachia is seen as collective. If middle America is task-oriented, then Appalachia is seen as person-oriented. If middle America's music is classical and rock and electrified, then Appalachia's music is "folk," "traditional," and acoustical. If urban America is concrete and pavement, Appalachia is mountains and trees.

We hypothesized that this desire to find "cultural difference" in Appalachia would be reflected in the literature of the tourist industry. By embarking on an analysis of the travel literature of each state, we set out to see if there is indeed an image of "cultural difference" displayed in this medium.

It is not surprising that we should look to *tourist* literature to see if the image we expected to find was "played out" there, for tourism *itself* may indeed serve a "communitas" function. Modern tourism, along with "much expressive culture such as ceremonials, the arts, sports, and folklore," serve "as diversions from the ordinary, which make life worth living." Tourism is "functionally and symbolically equivalent to other institutions that humans use to embellish and add meaning to their lives" (Graburn, "Tourism").

The most obvious example of this might be the pilgrimage, and we should

From *The Impact of Institutions in Appalachia,* ed. Jim Lloyd and Anne G. Campbell, Appalachian Consortium Press, 1986. Reprinted by permission of the publisher.

note that Batteau has identified the "pilgrimages" of outsiders into Appalachia during the troubled time of the 1930s and 1960s as one of the "forms that have figured prominently in the image-making of Appalachia" (along with myth, journalism, and, to a lesser extent, commodity) (Wagner, Batteau, Green 5–6).

As pilgrimage, as well as in its less serious forms, tourism is supposed to offer us "re-creation," a difference from the workaday world, a getting away from it all. "Tourism provides a . . . counterpoint to ordinary life" (Graburn, "Tourism" 24).

Tourism, then, is an "alternative state" (Graburn, "Comments" 470) wherein one may seek the opposite of his everyday "social-structural" world. Tourism thus is akin to rituals which embody communitas by carrying their participants through a "liminal" state (a state of transition, or marginality, or being on the "threshold") (Turner). For a tourist, just as a participant in ritual, is "out of the normal, everyday social-structural and cultural environment and beyond its social and moral constraints." The tourist is outside his normal space and outside his normal time (Akeroyd 468).

The history of tourism within Western civilization provides further fuel for our thought that an image of Appalachian otherness would be perpetuated in the tourist literature of today. In medieval Europe, travel was for religious purposes, as in pilgrimages or crusades. People of that day (who could afford to) traveled to religious retreats on spiritual quests for truth. This truth was to be obtained by reflection.

The Renaissance brought with it the view that "truth lay outside the mind and spirit" (Graburn, "Tourism" 24). Travel then turned away from seeking for truth as religiously understood toward exploration of facts as scientifically understood, and to an appreciation of the "high culture" of Europe.

The Industrial Revolution brought with it, among other things, safer and cheaper travel for the bourgeoisie. It also spawned "the romanticism that glorified nature and the countryside" (Graburn, "Tourism" 25). The aftermath of World War I had the effect of further loosening the hold of the aristocracy on tourism as a recreational activity.

During the 1920s, the aristocracy and its pleasures were further relegated to the realm of the "stuffy," and there was heightened interest in the lifestyles of common people. Ethnic or cultural tourism became popular; folk music and jazz were sought (Graburn, "Tourism" 26). Tourism as a product of industrial societies became a "search for the natural and the simple" (Pi-Sunyer 475).

This brief history of Western tourism shows that the motivations for tourism have evolved from the religious, cultural, historical, and educational to, more recently, a seeking after the themes of nature, recreation, and ethnicity. Thus we were expecting to see a commercialization of a longing for cultural difference in the tourist literature of the Appalachian area.

Another reason for choosing tourist literature as our medium is that tourism is a major activity in the region. It has been hypothesized that tourism "is quite likely to become the world's largest business by the end of the twentieth century" (Sutton 218), and the Appalachian region is no slouch in this regard. Since the 1950s, the Southern Appalachians have been considered one of the principal tourist areas of the country. Among national parks, the Great Smoky Mountains and the Shenandoah are annually ranked among the leaders in numbers of visitors. Related attractions such as the Skyline Drive and the Blue Ridge Parkway have a high volume of usage (Morris).

In monetary terms, Virginia has a 2.0-billion-dollar annual tourist industry, which is "as big an industry as agriculture and is more than equal to the combined dollar value of the industries of forestry, mining, and fishing" (MacCord). West Virginia sees 1.4 billion dollars a year in "direct travel industry expenditures," a figure that is "exceeded only by manufacturing" in that state ("Recreation and Tourism" 23–24).

To summarize what we expected to find, let us clarify what the tourist/seeker seeks. A common task in societies the world over seems to be an attribution of meaning through a process of defining "Culture" in opposition to "Nature." (This is the same process we go through when we seek to discover the meaning of any concept; we find out what it is *not*.) For the same reason, "communities" seek "communitas," in rituals or by imagining it or by seeking after it. Thus the highly "Cultured" city dweller seeks after Nature in two forms. One is to seek nature in the purest form, to get out "into" Nature, and the fewer people (bearers of Culture) around the better. But you can also get close to nature through Nature's "children"—the peasants of the world: "Interaction with them is possible, and their naturalness and simplicity exemplifies all that is good in Nature herself" (Graburn "Tourism" 27; see also Batteau, "American Culture," on Culture seeking after Nature).

The seeking after Nature in its purest form has been labeled "*natural tourism*" by those who study tourism; and of course, we expected to find this in the tourist brochures from the Appalachian region.

"Natural tourism" includes driving and hiking through mountains and countryside, sightseeing things like natural land formations. This kind of tourism is represented in the tourist literature by pictures of landscapes that look as though they were taken from cars on scenic highways, and by pictures of natural "oddities" like the Natural Bridge in Virginia.

As an example, we offer this ear-jangling put-together of down-home and media hype: "We've set aside some of the prettiest country you'll ever see. . . . We call 'em State Parks . . . and all in the middle of some of the prettiest country the good Lord ever made."

The kind of "cultural difference" image we expected to find has been labeled by those who study tourism as "*ethnic*" *or* "*cultural*" *tourism*. This is communing with Nature through her children or their artifacts. It includes the "picturesque, vestiges of a vanishing lifestyle . . . with old-style dwellings, horse-drawn carts and plows, and handmade rather than machine-made crafts." Activities may include meals in rustic inns and folklore performances (Smith 2). This kind of tourism includes the seeking after crafts, music, and dance.

To further explain what sort of cultural tourism we thought we would find, it is necessary to clarify that there are at least two constellations of images of Appalachia, which sometimes overlap. These "types" correspond to the distinction made by Batteau and Green between "stereotype," a popularized cartoon-like image; and "archetype," an image which relies on "some basic ideas within our cultural understandings," is akin to myth and legend, and harbors dichotomies like those included in the social structure/communitas model discussed earlier (Wagner, Batteau, and Green 4–8). The first might be called a "hard" image; these are the stereotypes which have been played out in cartoons, jokes, television series, and advertisements. This stereotype relies on the slouch hat, the moonshine jug, the rifle, and Snuffy Smith's junked-up cabin. The "softer" image emphasizes values that have been repeatedly attributed to Appalachia: a sense of beauty, modesty, self-reliance, pride, fatalism, collectivism (a person-orientation, as opposed to a task orientation), love of land, religiosity, family loyalty, and a slower, laid-back pace of life (e.g., Jones). Added to this should be artifacts and activities such as stringed instruments, folk and bluegrass music, clogging, quilts and quilting, and handmade wooden furniture, toys, and so on.

We did expect to find Appalachian "cultural difference" to be heavily commercialized by the tourist industry. We expected this commercialization to be of a "soft" type—i.e., using the more subtle images, such as bluegrass musicians, quilt makers, etc., as opposed to "hard" stereotyped images of lazy, moonshine-drinking hillbillies. Let us reiterate that we did *not* expect to find a "hard" exploitation of Appalachia through stereotypes such as the Li'l Abner character. At least, we did not expect to find this in the official literature of the state travel bureaus. We did not expect to find this, and we did not find it.

Before we tell you about our method and our findings, let us clarify the remaining types of tourism which students of tourism have identified. (The types of tourism discussed here have been adapted from Smith and from MacCord.)

"Recreational tourism" often features the beach, a package of coastline activities, and "sexy pictures and images" that attract tourists who want to "relax or commune with nature," but in a comfortable way, with the conveniences that a resort-type place can offer. This type of tourism also includes ski resorts and large, glamorous cities with a nightlife, like the "Big A" (Atlanta) shown in Georgia travel literature (Smith).

"Historical tourism" stresses the past, with tours of historical structures (like the "covered bridges" we found in abundance in the West Virginia literature) and reconstructions of past environments (like Williamsburg, Virginia).

"Industrial tourism" would include tours of factories, mines, mills, and the like. An example would be the Museum of Atomic Energy at Oak Ridge, Tennessee.

Thus, we thought we had good reason for looking for a commercialization—some might say an exploitation—of cultural difference in the travel literature, and we set out to see if it was indeed there. Keep in mind that our research is not aimed at determining whether the Appalachian region is *actually* culturally different from the rest of the United States. It has been "imaged" as if it were, and we wanted to see if this image prevailed in the tourist literature. Whether these cultural differences are actually to be found in the area is beside our current point. We simply wished to see if they were used as part of the "come-on" in the tourist literature of the Appalachian states. . . .

In general we found that commercialization of a soft "Appalachia is different" image was little in evidence.

Each state's literature has a particular theme. In no state was Appalachia—either its cultural or its natural attractions—the main emphasis in the tourist literature. For most of the states, the main emphasis was "VARIETY"—something for everyone. This was true even of West Virginia, which, of all the states, we expected to lean most heavily on its Appalachian heritage. Of the seven states, four (West Virginia, South Carolina, Georgia, and North Carolina) had "variety" or "something for everybody" as their theme. Tennessee had the theme of "recreation or outdoors." Virginia stressed "history." Kentucky's theme was "bluegrass."

The literature of the four "variety" states used all four types of tourism discussed earlier. All of the coastal states took advantage of their beaches as the major tourist attraction, while the land-locked states—Tennessee, Kentucky, and West Virginia—promoted outdoor recreation, including hiking, sightseeing, and a variety of other activities. Appalachia seems to become lost in the innumerable pages of golf, tennis, rafting, skiing, swimming, and other recreational activities, as well as the history and heritage of other sections in the states. Appalachian culture may be a tourist attraction, but to the states in which it lies, it is just one among a variety of choices for the potential vacationer.

All of the states except Tennessee and Kentucky sent us a main book (a "big beautiful book," as they advertised it), and many of them accompanied this with smaller brochures about particular places. These books were all divided into sections (ranging from three to eleven sections), each section emphasizing a different thing to see, thus underscoring the "variety" available within the state. Each travel section was given a name under which the activities, events, attractions, and accommodations in that area's vacation spots were listed, described, and illustrated.

In five of the states, these sections were geographically determined and labeled. For example, Virginia's book was divided into Northern Virginia, Tidewater, Eastern Shore, Central-Southside, Shenandoah, and finally, the Highlands. In North Carolina and Georgia, however, the books were divided and the sections titled by relating them to history or the type of people who live there or once lived there. For example, in North Carolina's literature, one of the sections was called "The Birthplace of English America," and another was called "The Land of the Sky," an area where many Indians lived.

Within these books, the placement of the section which would be considered Appalachian differed. For four states (Virginia, Kentucky, South Carolina, and West Virginia), it was the last thing in the book; in two states (North Carolina and Georgia), it was at the front.

In most of the literature, Appalachia appeared "historyless." There was little to indicate that any history had ever taken place here, other than a few references to Daniel Boone. In some of the states, history was a major part of the discussion of several of its areas, but was not mentioned at all in the Appalachian section of the state. One student noted that it seemed as though Appalachia had no people and no culture, just land and natural beauty.

We found that the word "Appalachia" was not much in evidence. No state used the word "Appalachia" to label the Appalachian region of its state; instead they used labels like "High Country," "Mountaineer Country," or "Highlands."

When the word "Appalachia" was found, it was used to refer to geological phenomena, or it was used as part of a proper name, such as the Appalachian Mountains, the Appalachian Plateau, or the Appalachian Trail. That is, it was very rarely used to refer to culture or to cultural traits. South Carolina did not use the word at all in its literature. Virginia used the word only once, to refer to the "Appalachian Plateau." In Georgia, the word Appalachia was used only when referring to the Appalachian Trail.

With the exception of South Carolina, all of the states portrayed some part of the traditional images of Appalachia in their travel literature. Thus, we found *some* emphasis on Appalachian culture in nearly all of the states, but not nearly as much as we had expected to find. The cultural aspects which we did find were quilting, traditional music, dancing, and festivals which featured all of these. Arts and crafts were the predominant form of "cultural" tourism.

The most popular Appalachian images included: mountain or Appalachian arts and crafts in general, quilts, and stringed instruments like the fiddle and the dulcimer (all found in five of the seven states); square dance, folk dance, flatfoot or clogging, and hillbilly or mountain costume (in three of the seven states), moonshine and stills, love of land, folk music, and a relaxed, rural atmosphere (in two of the seven states).

As an example, Virginia's literature, which made very little mention of Appalachian culture, did say: "And there's the Southwest Virginia Museum at Big Stone Gap, for a close-up look at mountain culture and customs. There you'll find . . . century-old quilts, b'ar guns, and a homemade still." Likewise, the Northeast Georgia Mountain region sports a "down-home atmosphere" with "rustic accommodations available from friendly people who are as widely known for their cleverly fashioned handicrafts as they are for their delicious country food."

Listings of things to do included many arts and crafts festivals and fiddlers' conventions, such as Tennessee's "Old Time Fiddler's Championship," with "flatfoot dance . . . and non-electric instruments."

The pictures also showed these particular facets of the image of Appalachian culture. In Tennessee, pictures depicted men with long white beards, men playing fiddles, old women quilting, and log cabins. One picture depicts a man in overalls with a mule; another is of a woman in traditional garb who is sewing on a quilt. Another shows some men sitting in front of a log house in flannel shirts and overalls playing music on banjo, guitar, and fiddle while a couple of other men watch and carve on pieces of wood. Virginia's "Highlands" section pictured a mill, a rocking chair, and a spinning wheel, a man making a dulcimer, a barn on a hill, a banjo player, a guitar player, and people on a porch. Kentucky's literature included a man playing fiddle, a picture of a chair in the woods with a shawl and some pottery sitting on it, and pictures of bluegrass musicians, log cabins, and a mill.

The travel literature of Tennessee, West Virginia, and Kentucky gave the strongest of these images of the Appalachian region(s) of their states, by including more pictures, phrases, and events that convey an "Appalachia as culturally different" image. But this still represented a small portion of all the images to be gleaned from the literature of the state. For example, in Kentucky's literature, the pictures described above were drowned in the overriding emphasis on "bluegrass." There were twenty-two pictures of horses in the literature, greatly outnumbering those with an "Appalachian" emphasis. "Bluegrass" was the most often used word in this literature, appearing sixteen times.

Much more in evidence were representations of natural attractions such as mountains, water, trees and other scenery. Mountains and scenery seem to be the universal symbols used to represent Appalachia. Our research showed a preponderance of beautiful pictures of the sun setting over rows of mountain ridges.

Morris, assessing tourism potential in Southern Appalachia, emphasizes the "diverse natural features" of the area, including mountains, ridges, gorges, valleys, rivers, caves, and forests. The only thing the area lacks is natural lakes, and the dams have taken care of that. All this is joined with mostly moderate temperatures and a comfortable relative humidity to make it nice for the tourist. A listing of the attractions Virginia has to offer says "Virginia is hard to beat for variety" when it comes to natural attractions. There are "waterfalls, natural tunnels and bridges, caves, cliffs, peaks, scenic overlooks, dunes, virgin forests, areas and streams for hunting and fishing, streams for canoeing, open water for boating and water-skiing, mineral and fossil deposits" (MacCord).

Thus, we thought we would find commercialization of cultural difference, and instead found largely an ignoring of cultural differences. We found a nuance of cultural tourism, drowned in other forms of tourism.

While our purpose was not to theorize why we found what we did, but rather simply to see what was there, we have given this some thought.

First, we have to consider what tourism is. It is, after all, an industry— "an organized industry, catering to a clientele who have time and money and want to spend them, pleasurably, in leisured mobility" (Smith 15). Areas thought to be the most profitable and best liked by vacationers may predominate in the literature of the state. Some of us have suggested that the tourist industry may not view communion with culture as lucrative, compared to communion with beaches, golf courses, restaurants, and motels. In other words, cultural tourism itself may not be considered profitable. (Although others of us have argued that it certainly is made much of in other areas; for example, Pennsylvania "sells" its Amish population to the point of genuine exploitation, and the literature we looked at used any Indian population as a "selling point" whenever possible.)

Second, we need to remember who produced the literature we used as our sample. This literature came from the Tourist Division of each state government. The few examples we had of a stereotyped negative image came from privately produced and distributed advertising of privately owned tourist traps. We may not find a commercialization of cultural difference in the state-produced literature for the same reason that Virginia has mandated that its plantations now be labeled "grand manor houses." (The state NAACP objected to this, saying it was a not-so-subtle way to rewrite Virginia history, and that a plantation should be called a plantation.) We call this a "blandifying" of the literature, a sanitizing of it to make it bland enough so as not to offend any particular group.

Some of the students to whom we have presented our findings have suggested that perhaps the makers of tourist literature themselves have only a negative stereotype of the Appalachian region, do not want to project this in the literature, and so project no image at all.

Third, since the Appalachian region is just one part of most of these states, it is logical that they would not give it more than its "quota" of notice in their travel literature.

Fourth, *perhaps,* after all, Appalachia is *not* actually different, and the tourist industry knows that better than we academics do. (This is not to be construed as a fact, but is offered merely as a "perhaps.")

A more theoretical argument, and one which might lay the foundations for our next paper, is that, if the cultured person is truly seeking Nature, any view of a culture to be found in that Natural setting (albeit a culture that is thought to be "different" from the tourist's own) only interferes with the Nature-seeking. If you want cultural tourism, you can go to "Amish Country" or you can hobnob with the natives in New Guinea. But Appalachia is portrayed as one of America's last bastions of uncultured *Wilderness* (which you can see from a car).

Note

Used throughout this paper but not cited specifically is the work of students in Radford University's 1984 class in Anthropology 411: Appalachian Cultures. Their contributions are available in *Appalachia: A Tourist Attraction* (Radford, VA: Appalachian Studies Program, Radford University, 1984). The authors and their chapters are: Marcia Cooper—ARC; Daphne Carr—New York; Barry Sites—Pennsylvania; Susan Finley—Maryland; Ben Steinberg—Ohio; Carl Rhodes—West Virginia; Liz Throckmorton—Virginia; Lorna Smith—Kentucky; Tami Stark—North Carolina; Bill O'Brien—Tennessee; Jeff Jarvis—South Carolina; Kai Jackson—Georgia; Lynn Batley—Alabama; Kelly Morris—Mississippi; Ana Sutphin—Blue Ridge Parkway.

Works Cited

Akeroyd, Anne V. "Comments on Anthropology of Tourism." *Current Anthropology* 22, no. 5 (Oct. 1981): 468–69.

Batteau, Allen. "The American Culture of Appalachia." Paper presented at the annual meeting of the American Anthropological Association, Cincinnati, Ohio, 1979.

Graburn, Nelson H. H. "Tourism: The Sacred Journey." *Hosts and Guests.* Ed. Valene Smith. Philadelphia: U of Pennsylvania P, 1977. 17–21.

———. "Comments on Anthropology of Tourism." *Current Anthropology* 22, no. 5 (Oct. 1981): 470–74.

Jones, Loyal. "Appalachian Values." *Voices from the Hills.* Ed. Robert J. Higgs and Ambrose N. Manning. New York: Frederick Ungar, 1975.

MacCord, Howard. "Your Locality and the Travel Industry." Richmond: Virginia Travel Council, 1981.

Morris, John W. "The Potential of Tourism." *The Southern Appalachian Region: A Survey.* Ed. Thomas R. Ford. Lexington: U of Kentucky P, 1967. 136–48.

Pi-Sunyer, Oriol. "Comments on Anthropology of Tourism." *Current Anthropology* 22, no. 5 (Oct. 1981): 474–75.

"Recreation and Tourism." *Appalachia* 7, no. 5–6 (May-Aug. 1984): 23–24.

Smith, Valene. "Introduction." *Hosts and Guests.* Ed. Valene Smith. Philadelphia: U of Pennsylvania P, 1977. 1–14.

Sutton, W. A. "Travel and Understanding: Notes on the Social Structure of Touring." *International Journal of Comparative Sociology* 8 (1967): 218–23.

Turner, Victor. *The Ritual Process: Structure and Anti-Structure.* Chicago: Aldine, 1969.

Wagner, Melinda Bollar. "America's Alter Ego." *Radford Magazine* 3 (Fall 1981): 2–5.

———. "Appalachia in America's Future: Alternative Cultural Forms." *Critical Essays in Appalachian Life and Culture.* Ed. Rick Simon. Boone, NC: Appalachian Consortium Press, 1982. 88–97.

Wagner, Melinda Bollar; Allen Batteau; and Archie Green. "Images of Appalachia: A Critical Discussion." *The Appalachian Experience: Proceedings of the Sixth Annual Appalachian Studies Conference.* Ed Barry Buxton. Boone, NC: Appalachian Consortium Press, 1983. 3–9.

Betty Williams

Betty Jennings Williams, born in Lone Mountain, Claiborne County, Tennessee, teaches English at East Tennessee State University, where she received the B.S. and M.A. degrees. Her major research has been on the poetry of Walt Whitman. She continues to write about Whitman as well as contemporary American writers, focusing on Anne Tyler, Toni Morrison, and John Updike. Her poems have appeared in *Modern Haiku, Tennessee English Journal,* and *Aethlon: The Journal of Sport Literature.*

A couple of notes on terms used in the selection: *ambeer* is a southern expression for tobacco juice; *Day's Work* is a brand of chewing tobacco.

His Lake

Norris Lake is half ambeer
they'd say when he fished there
Just in anticipation the flow would begin
down dual channels from the corners
of his mouth dripping from his chin
as he sorted plugs, tangle-checked lines
on reels, threaded rods
Then dressed in his moleskin fishing britches
he carried, dropped and dragged
his gear—the rods and reels, over-filled tackle box,
mismatched paddles, Johnson boat motor,
oil-soaked life-preserver cushion
(which preserved nothing but his bottom
against the boat's hard seat)—
to the 39 Mercury and spat a tributary
out car window and down path to boat and lake
Trolling he upped his spitting tempo
and accelerated it when he got a hit
into such a spluttering, splashing, splattering frenzy
that each bass and crappie he caught
broke surface through an amber froth
Thus he fished and spat
until he declared his catch
another good Day's Work day

When he was nearly ninety-two
and calling for tobacco
the nurse relented
He gummed the small chew
then spat a satisfying splatter
over the raised bed rail
—into Norris Lake

From *Aethlon: The Journal of Sport Literature* 9, no. 2 (Spring 1992). Used by permission of the author.

Joseph Barrett

Joseph Barrett was a native of Richwood, West Virginia. Though he attended Bethany College in Bethany, West Virginia, and Oxford University and was briefly a Poet-in-the-Schools and a youth worker, Barrett lived the life of a pure poet to a degree unusual in our day. He produced two books, *Roots Deep in Sand* (1969) and *Periods of Lucidity* (1975), then co-authored *Old Martins, New Strings* (1990) as one of the Mason-Dixon Trio (with P. J. Laska and Bob Snyder). He died unexpectedly while the book was in press, leaving behind *Blue Planet Memoirs,* a manuscript of his best poems.

Woman Playing a Jukebox

all evening she's danced
for three seedy men,
her ass a damp valentine
sagging in red slacks;
now only the broad feet
keep time,
baby blue sandals
tapping in sawdust
and spilled beer;

(O detroit city)

she must know
she is all the way home;
and turning from the machine
she carries her weight
through smoke
like a pregnancy
the slightest praise could father

From *Old Martins, New Strings* (Morgantown, WV: Soupbean Press, 1990). Reprinted by permission of Joan M. Barrett.

Chapter 6

Laughter and Humor

Introduction

If sports are the play of the body, then humor may be regarded as the play of the mind. Appalachian humor has several distinguishing characteristics, traceable mainly to the influence of the frontier and to a Calvinistic heritage. It is essentially a democratic humor that casts a skeptical eye upon human nature itself.

Davy Crockett, archetypal backwoodsman, "gamecock of the wilderness," "king of the wild frontier," represents one pole of Appalachian humor. On the other end of the see-saw of humor sits Crockett's East Tennessee antithesis Sut Lovingood, created by George Washington Harris. If Crockett suggests the limitless powers of the common man, Sut reminds us of human frailty and limitation. Instead of tracking bears, Sut is on the track of hypocrisy and pretense, his only weapon a ready wit. Where Crockett knows no fear, Sut depends on his long legs to carry him away at the first sign of physical danger. If Crockett is always on stage, Sut is under it, ready to create mayhem in some fashion. Crockett is romantic man *par excellence*, capable of bragging about his outsized exploits. In the comic vein, Sut represents the Judeo-Christian view of man who is "lost" without divine help. The comic absurdity of the *Sut Lovingood Yarns* reverberates in the fiction of Flannery O'Connor, Lisa Alther, and Lee Smith; it has survived on the commercial level in the humor of the Grand Ole Opry's Minnie Pearl, in the songs of Ray Stevens, and in the stories of Jerry Clower and Bob Murphy of Nacogdoches, Texas. While the tall tale as exemplified by Crockett persists, the comic absurdity of the tradition stemming from Sut Lovingood may well be the predominant form of Appalachian humor.

Anonymous

The mock sermon was a prominent form of humor in the antebellum South. While mock sermons were satirical, and in some instances anticlerical, several of them were written by ministers themselves. "Where the Lion Roareth and the Wang Doodle Mourneth for His First-Born" is one of the most famous of this genre. The source has not been identified, but scholars see it as representative of backwoods humor.

Where the Lion Roareth and the Wang Doodle Mourneth for His First-Born

I am an unlarnt Hardshell Baptist preacher of whom you've no doubt hearn afore, and I now appear here to expound the scriptures and pint out the narrow way which leads from a vain world to the streets of Jaroosalem; and my tex' which I shall choose for the occasion is in the leds of the Bible, somewhar between Second Chronicills and the last chapter of Timothytitus; and when you find it, you'll find it in these words: "And they shall gnaw a file, and flee unto the mountains of Hepsidam, whar the lion roareth and the wang-doodle mourneth for his first-born."

Now, my brethering, as I have before told you, I am an oneddicated man, and know nothing about grammar talk and collidge high-faultin, but I am a plane unlarnt preacher of the Gospil, what's been foreordaned and called to prepare a pervarse generashun for the day of wrath—ah! "For they shall gnaw a file, and flee unto the mountains of Hepsidam, whar the lion roareth and the wang-doodle mourneth for his first-born—ah!"

My beloved brethering, the tex' says they shall gnaw a file. It does not say they may, but shall. Now, there is more than one kind of file. There's the hand-saw file, the rat-tail file, the single file, the double file and the profile; but the kind spoken of here isn't one of them kind nayther, bekaws it's a figger of speech, and means going it alone and getting ukered, "for they shall gnaw a file, and flee unto the mountains of Hepsidam, whar the lion roareth and the wang-doodle mourneth for its first-born—ah!"

And now there be some here with fine close on thar backs, brass rings on thar fingers, and lard on thar har, what goes it while they're yung; and thar be others here what, as long as thar constitooshins and forty-cent whisky last, goes it blind. Thar be sisters here what, when they gets sixteen years old, bust thar tiller-ropes and goes it with a rush. But I say, my dear brethering, take care you don't find, when Gabriel blows his last trump, your hands played out, and you've got ukered—ah! "For they shall gnaw a file, and flee unto the mountains of Hepsidam, whar the lion roareth and the wang-doodle mourneth for his first-born."

Now, my brethering, "they shall flee unto the mountains of Hepsidam," but thar's more dams than Hepsidam. Thar's Rotterdam, Haddam, Amsterdam, and "Don't-care-a-dam"—the last of which, my brethering, is the worst of all, and reminds me of a sirkumstance I onst knowed in the state of Illenoy. There was a man what built him a mill on the north fork of Ager Crick, and it was a good mill and ground a sight of grain; but the man what built it was a miserable sinner, and never give anything to the church; and, my dear brethering, one night there came a dreadful storm of wind and rain, and the waters rushed down and swept that man's milldam to kingdom cum, and when he woke up he found that he wasn't worth a dam—ah! "For they shall gnaw a file, and flee unto the mountains of Hepsidam, whar the lion roareth and the wang-doodle mourneth for his first-born—ah!"

Now, "What the lion roareth and the wang-doodle mourneth for his first-born—ah!" This is part of my tex', my beseaching brethering, is not to be taken as it says. It don't mean the howling wilderness, what John the Hardshell Baptist fed on locusts and wild asses, but it means, my brethering, the city of New Y'Orleans, the mother of harlots and hard lots, whar corn is wuth six bits a bushel one day and nary a red the nex'; whar niggers are as thick as black bugs in spiled bacon ham, and gamblers, thieves, and pickpockets goes skiting about the streets like weasels in a barnyard; whar honest men are scarcer than hen's teeth; and whar a strange woman once took in your beloved teacher, and bamboozled him out of two hundred and twenty-seven dollars in the twinkling of a sheep's tail; but she can't do it again! Hallelujah—ah! "For they shall gnaw a file, and flee unto the mountains of Hepsidam, whar the lion roareth and the wang-doodle mourneth for his first-born—ah!"

My brethering, I am the captain of that flatboat you see tied up thar, and have got aboard of her flour, bacon, taters, and as good Monongahela whisky as ever was drunk, and am mighty apt to get a big price for them all; but what, my dear brethering, would it all be wuth if I hadn't got religion? Thar's nothing like religion, my brethering; it's better nor silver or gold gimcracks; and you can no more get to heaven without it than a jay-bird can fly without a tail—ah! Thank the Lord! I'm an oneddicated man, my brethering; but I've sarched the Scripters from Dan to Beersheba, and found Zion right side up, and hardshell religion the best kind of religion—ah! 'Tis not like the Methodists, what specks to get to heaven by hollerin' hell-fire; nor like the Univarsalists, that get on broad gage and goes the hull hop—ah; nor like the Yewnited Brethering, that takes each other by the slack of thar breeches and hists themselves in; nor like the Katherliks, that buys threw tickets from their priests; but it may be likened unto a man what has to cross the river—ah!—and the ferryboat was gone; so he tucked up his breeches and waded acrost—ah! "For they shall gnaw a file, and flee unto the mountains of Hepsidam, whar the lion roareth and the wang-doodle mourneth for his first-born!"

Pass the hat, Brother Flint, and let every Hardshell Baptist shell out.

H. E. Taliaferro

H. E. Taliaferro (1818–1875) is among the group of Old Southwest humorists that also included George Washington Harris. After working as a young man as a mill hand, farmer, and teacher, Taliaferro moved from North Carolina to Alabama, where he became a strongwilled Baptist preacher. During the Civil War, he rallied support for the southern cause as editor of the *Southwestern Baptist*. Taliaferro published only one book during his lifetime, *Fisher's River (North Carolina) Sketches and Characters* (1859). It contains a collection of anecdotes and descriptions of the language and behavior of the high-spirited people he met on the frontier. Between 1860 and 1863, he also contributed humorous sketches to the *Southern Literary Messenger*. Taliaferro's sketches are appreciated for their vivid characterizations, accuracy of dialect, and social and religious satire.

In "The Origin of the Whites," the speaker is supposedly a slave preacher in Surrey County, North Carolina, by the name of Charles Gentry. For Gentry, the pulpit is as good a place as any for the trickster to do his work, in this case to turn the tables on the Whites.

The Origin of the Whites

Beloved bredderin, de white folks ar clean out of it when dey 'firm dat de fust man was a white man. I'm not a-gwine to hab any sich doctering. De fact is, Adam, Cain, Abel, Seth, was all ob 'um black as jet. Now you 'quire how de white man cum. Why, dis a-way. Cain he kill his brudder Abel wid a great big club—he walkin'-stick—and God he cum to Cain, and say,

"Cain! where is dy brudder Abel?"

Cain he pout out de lip, and say, "I don't know; what ye axin' me fur? I ain't my brudder Abel's keeper."

De Lord he gits in airnest, and stomps on de ground, and say,

"Cain! you Cain! whar is dy brudder Abel? I say, Cain! whar is dy brudder?"

Cain he turn white as bleach cambric in de face, and de whole race ob Cain dey bin white ebber since. De mark de Lord put on de face of Cain was a white mark. He druv him inter the land ob Nod, and all de white folks hab cum from de land ob Nod, jis' as you've hearn.

From *The Humor of H. E. Taliaferro*, ed. Raymond C. Craig, The University of Tennessee Press, 1987.

Fred Millner

Fred Millner was born in Philadelphia, Pennsylvania, but migrated at an early age to the southern West Virginia coalfields with his parents, who were returning home. Ever since, he has considered West Virginia home, although he has traveled throughout the country. He is a former youth director of the Mercer County Economic Opportunity program. A lecturer in the Artists Series in West Virginia, Millner also has lectured on Appalachian subjects at the University of Kentucky and has conducted numerous poetry workshops. Living in Bluefield, West Virginia, he operates a construction company but maintains his interest in poetry and writing.

The following poem was written by Millner at Pompano Beach, Florida, when he was nineteen and a VISTA worker. He was inspired by the ethnocentric perspective of a minister attempting to bring spiritual guidance to migrant workers, including several from Kentucky, Tennessee, and West Virginia.

Amen (A Prayer for Niggers)

white Adam
white Eve
white Abel and Cain

only whites
on the ark
during the forty day rain

chosen peoples
that's the jew
stop praying nigger
god's a cracker too.

From *Soupbean: A Contemporary Anthology of Appalachian Literature,* Mountain Union Books, 1977. Reprinted by permission of the author.

Thomas G. Burton

and Ambrose N. Manning

See volume 2, chapter 2, for biography of Burton; volume 2, chapter 3, for biography of Manning.

This story was submitted by Virgie Love of Buchanan County, Virginia. It illustrates the flourishing raucous humor of the hunting stories and literature of the Southern Appalachian region, anticipating the wild hunting stories of Jerry Clower.

Hold Old Blue

An old farmer owned one of the best coon hounds around. It was a Blue Tick, so he called the hound "Ol' Blue." Often the old man and his men friends got together and went coon hunting. They never took any dogs except Ol' Blue because he was all that was needed. His owner had trained him to attack the coon sexually when it was shook out of the tree, and in this way he killed the coon. One night they all got together to go hunting. They hadn't gotten far into the woods before it began to drizzle rain, but this was no obstacle to them. Very shortly, Ol' Blue treed a coon. The old man climbed up in the tree to shake it out, but just as he was about to reach the coon, his foot slipped on the wet limb and he started to fall. Knowing how well he had trained his dog, he quickly yelled, "Somebody grab Ol' Blue. It's me coming down!"

From *A Collection of Folklore by Undergraduate Students of East Tennessee State University*, ed. Thomas Burton and Ambrose N. Manning (Johnson City: Research Advisory Council of East Tennessee State University, 1966). Used by permission of the editors.

Jeff Daniel Marion

See volume 2, chapter 5, for biography.

The Chinese Poet Awakens
to Find Himself Abruptly in East Tennessee

I have come home
heavy from the day's labor:
how the words of others fail
to bear up, droop their shoulders.
Even the mountains seem to sag
in this blue light.

Han-shan knew,
giving his poems to trees & rocks,
letting them stay home to weather
alone.

No escape:
everything settles into dust.

Suddenly from behind
the goat who has waited
all day to be fed,
charges—butts me forward.

I am moved.
The old bearded one knows his master.

From *Vigils: Selected Poems,* Appalachian Consortium Press, 1990. Reprinted by permission of the publisher.

Cormac McCarthy

Born in Providence, Rhode Island, Cormac McCarthy moved with his parents to Knoxville, Tennessee, at the age of four. He attended the University of Tennessee at Knoxville for four years before serving in the U.S. Air Force. Later he returned to school to concentrate on his writing skills. McCarthy has been compared to William Faulkner, Carson McCullers, and Flannery O'Connor, because his work exhibits the characteristics of the Southern Gothic mode: dark humor, intense characters, and violent plots reflective of universal themes. His first novel, *The Orchard Keeper* (1965), won the William Faulkner Foundation award for best first novel. Although best known for this novel, he has also written *Outer Dark* (1968), *Child of God* (1974), and *Suttree* (1979). His 1992 novel *All the Pretty Horses* won the National Book Award for fiction.

"Fighting a Gorilla" (title supplied) from *Child of God* reveals McCarthy's ability to interweave humor with the darkest Gothic themes.

Fighting a Gorilla

That reminds me of this carnival they had up in Newport one time. They was a feller up there had this ape or gorilla, ever what it was, stood about so high. It was nigh tall as Jimmy yonder. They had it to where you could put on boxin gloves and get in this ring with it and if you could stay in there with him three minutes they'd give ye fifty dollars.

Well, these old boys I was with they kept at me and kept at me. I had this little old gal on my arm kept lookin up at me about like a poleaxed calf. These old boys eggin me on. I think we'd drunk a little whiskey too, I disremember. Anyways I got to studyin this here ape and I thought: Well hell. He ain't big as me. They had him up there on a chain. I remember he was settin on a stool eatin a head of red cabbage. Directly I said: Shit. Raised my old hand and told the feller I'd try it one time.

Well, they got us back there and got the gloves on me and all, and this feller that owned the ape, he told me, said: Now don't hit him too hard out there cause if you do you'll make him mad and you'll be in some real trouble. I thought to myself: Well he's tryin to save his ape a whippin is what he's tryin to do. Tryin to protect his investment.

Anyways, I come out and climbed in the ring there. Felt pretty much a fool, all my buddies out there a hollerin and goin on and I looked down at this little gal I was with and give her a big wink and about that time they brought the old ape out. Had a muzzle on him. He kindly looked me over.

From *Child of God*, © 1973 by Cormac McCarthy. Reprinted by permission of Random House, Inc.

Well, they called out our names and everthing, I forget what the old ape's name was, and this old boy rung a big dinner bell and I stepped out and circled the old ape. Showed him a little footwork there. He didn't look like he was goin to do nothin much so I reached out and busted him one. He just kindly looked at me. Well, I didn't do nothin but square off and hit him again. Popped him right in the side of the head. When I done that his old head jerked back and his eyes went kindly funny and I said: Well, well, how sweet it is. I'd done spent the fifty dollars. I ducked around and went to hit him again and about that time he jumped right on top of my head and cramming his foot in my mouth and like to tore my jaw off. I couldn't even holler for help. I thought they never would get that thing off of me.

Dean Hunter
and Bobby Lawson

Dean Hunter and Bobby Lawson were school-dropout children in Mud Creek, Pike County, Kentucky. They wrote "Thomas Buckskin" while attending the Outpost school, taught by Mrs. Flem Messer, which used imaginative teaching techniques to stimulate interest and participation.

Thomas Buckskin

THOMAS BUCKSKIN was as big as a mountain and tall as a 60-foot pine tree. It took a thousand feet of lumber to make him a pair of shoes. Fried chicken was his favorite meal. He could eat 100 chickens at one sitting.
He let his hair grow very long. Also he had a long hanging moustache. He was a workingman. He was a good mechanic. He could pick up a car with one finger. He could put his toes around a boat and take it anyplace.
One day he was working on a car and he got his hair hung in the fan. When the car started, it pulled out his hair.
Come to find out his strength was in his hair. So now he was a weak man.
So he sat down on a mountain and began drawing checks.

From *Mountain Life and Work* 43, no. 1 (Spring 1967).

Richard Hague

and J. W. Williamson

Richard Hague was born and raised in Steubenville, Ohio, and educated in Cincinnati, where he teaches writing. He is the author of five volumes of poetry, including *Ripening* (1984) and *Possible Debris* (1988). His "Mill and Smoke Marrow" appeared in *A Red Shadow of Steel Mills*, edited by David Shevin and Larry Smith (1991). He has been a coordinator of the Southern Appalachian Writers Cooperative and a member of the poetry staff of the Appalachian Writers Workshop, Hindman Settlement School, Hindman, Kentucky.

J. W. Williamson is professor of English at Appalachian State University, Boone, North Carolina, and editor of the *Appalachian Journal*, which he has published since 1972. He was present at the famous Hindman Settlement School Appalachian Writers Workshop in the 1970s and early 1980s, when the best mountain storytellers held forth, including Cratis Williams and Richard Hague.

"An Appalachian Relic: Notes on 'Swarp'" was devised by Richard Hague as a cryptic history of one particularly notorious writers' week at the Hindman Settlement Workshop at Hindman, Kentucky. This apparently learned piece is a satire more of sterile scholarship than of anything regional. The actual author of this spoof is Richard Hague, and J. W. Williamson provided the notes.

An Appalachian Relic: Notes on "Swarp"

Editor's Source Note: The following manuscript was discovered by Richard Hague of Cincinnati, Ohio, in the Knott County, Kentucky, Public Library. Folded carelessly into a copy of *Chamber's Etymological Dictionary*, its nine longhand pages were unsigned though stamped with "Filson Philological Society, Dwarf, Kentucky." Though sketchy at best, lacking any conclusive ending, and filled with obscure allusions and topical references, the piece has enough interest, we believe, to merit publication even in so fragmentary a state. We have added some notes to the text in an attempt to clarify and to update the manuscript.

Preliminary study has connected "swarp" with the English word "swarf," which derives from the Middle English "swarff." Akin to the Old Norse "swarfa," the root thus seems to mean "to swerve," though a Scots cognate means "to swoon." C. D. Onions, in his seminal work, *Etymologies of the*

From *Appalachian Journal* 8.3 (Summer 1981), © *Appalachian Journal*/Appalachian State University. Used with permission.

Mountains,[1] maintains that the word, in its variant spelling "sworp," derives from a clever acronym devised in 1605 at the Plagued Dog Tavern in Cheapside, London, and that its letters are taken from the oft-repeated action of "standing while ordering repeated pints." Onions notes that it became a tradition at the Plagued Dog to hold an annual Sworp High Day, at which some unfortunate reveler, his name drawn from the lacquered skull of a murdered Papal Zouave, had to present some "dithering delight" for the amusement of his fellows.[2] In a rueful aside, however, Onions notes that the ritual lasted only one year, as the participants all "died miserably of the gout, or, like common wastrels and rogues, rotted in anonymous rural jails, defeated, forgotten, and bilious."

Not to be outdone, Professor Pissel Bush, in his work *Why We Don't Use Words We Never Use,* a popular revision of the earlier *Wamblies, Git-Fidgets, and Poltroons,* by Asa Middlehigh, the famous rival of Noah Webster, states:

> Though not a popular word, swarp nevertheless has enjoyed occasional currency in the isolated coves of Eastern Kentucky, where wild groups of snake-handlers, ginseng-hunters, and gum-cutters, as well as other unsavory types such as versifiers, prevaricators, and the inventors of riddles, use it as a euphemism for being "shitte [*sic*] drunk."

And in a footnote, Bush adds, somewhat moralistically:

> The word, with its sweet sibilant beginning, promising ease and beauty and grace, yet ends with one of the harshest sounds available in English: so too do the practitioners of swarping descend from the deceptive silken heights of their drunkenness to the foul charnel-house cellar of despair and crapulous degradation. "Swarping" is, indeed, a devil's word, and as such belongs in no polite vocabulary.

Despite Bush's objections, however, the word was recorded in at least semi-polite company in 1927. Cecil Wiley, the famous one-eyed sharpshooter mentioned in Ruben Sturgeon's *The Exploding Colt and Other Demises,* was invited to dinner at a well-known salon in Lexington, where a group of Bluegrass women had hoped to introduce him to Priscilla Furman Rockcastle, the grandniece of Annie Oakley.[3] As the evening progressed, however, it became apparent that Wiley was not to be marriage-matched. After being served his eighth sherry, he rose in his place at table, threw back his coattails, and extracted a pearl-handled derringer from his belt. Aiming at the young socialite, he cried, "By God, I'll not swarp with any woman who don't drink headbust!" and pulled the trigger. The gun, fortunately, failed to discharge, and Wiley fled the scene. But his use of "swarp" was repeated in a sensational headline the next morning, and can be found in the *Lexington Leader* for August 9, 1927.[4]

But it cannot be denied that the word "swarp," and its manifold regional variations, is primarily a lower-class term.[5] This fact was most dramatically illustrated in the long-forgotten study of the teaching of English in Appalachia entitled *Pigweed Participles, Pennyroyal Nouns,* authored by Rodney Longshanks. A pale, six-foot New Englander, Longshanks—so legend has it—was greeted at the forks of Hardscrabble Creek[6] by a bearded octogenarian leading a mule. When Longshanks inquired as to why the man was not riding his beast, the patriarch replied, "Why, hell's bangers, boy, cain't you see? This here mule's been hard-swarped, and won't be rid till his legs git straight."

More apropos of the matter at hand, however, is Longshanks's lengthy chapter on the Hardscrabble Settlement School's[7] organized effort to eradicate not only the word, but the despicable activities it described. One incident, taken from the chapter, will suffice.

Young Josiah Leathers, the first Kentuckian to graduate from Heidelberg University in Germany with a Ph.D.,[8] was apparently a troublesome chap in his youth. Sneaking from the dormitory one frosty night, he made his way down the right fork of Hardscrabble to the Drought County Courthouse.[9] No one was about, and the boy, eager to express his disdain towards those who supported the dismantling of his vocabulary, took from his slingpoke a cold chisel and hammer. Working swiftly, he carved the word "swarp" into the soft sandstone of the Court House steps.

Confronted the next morning by the director of the Settlement School, a sour-spittled woman with a long habit of chastity, Leathers defiantly cried, "I'll not unswarp myself for no quare woman, nor for the Lord God Hisself of these hills."

His recalcitrance won for Leathers the dubious distinction of being thrown into a sticker bush just outside the dining hall by a group of reactionary scholars led by a noxious youth named Dewars.

The Settlement School's campaign against "swarp" was, despite Leathers's considerable efforts, mostly successful. In most parts of eastern Kentucky today, the word is no longer heard, retired at last as a quaint archaism in the works of local yarn-spinners.

Notes

1. The "C. D. Onions" referred to here is clearly not C. T. (Charles Talbut) Onions, whose *Oxford Dictionary of English Etymology* is well known and respected. Raphaelson says that "C. D. Onions" was actually a mischievous pseudonym adopted by Sir James Augustus Henry Murray, whose *New English Dictionary on Historical Principles* (first published in 1888) would eventually be updated and revised by C. T. Onions. According to Raphaelson, Murray "resented, even twelve years before Onions's birth, the latter's intended revisions of the book that Murray had spent his entire life researching and writing," and so Murray created the "C. D. Onions" of *Etymologies of the Mountains* in order to "cast doubt and shame on the entire Onions clan." (See Carl Edgar Raphaelson, "Tears for the Onions: The Whole Sorry History of the English Etymology Industry," *Philological Quarterly* 47 [1953]: 347, 349–50.) This would seem to

cast some doubt on the reliability of *Etymologies of the Mountains* (which, according to the *Bibliography of Southern Appalachia*, is held in the Appalachian collections of several colleges and universities within the Appalachian Consortium). But Raphaelson also points out that Murray was too clever a forger and hoaxer merely to publish under the Onions name a list of spurious words with bogus histories; no (Raphaelson says), Murray's work was scholarly and thorough but littered here and there with misrepresentations and complete fabrications. Knowing which is authentic and which is bogus is part of the fun, Raphaelson contends. Clearly, our unknown Knott County lexicographer probably did not suspect that he had hold of the wrong Onions (and he seems to have missed entirely the point that the *mountains* referred to in the title were the Urals and not the Cumberlands). But this may be mere nit-picking.

2. Sworp High Day is indeed verifiable in the *Calendar of State Papers, Domestic Series, 1603–1625* (His Majesty's Stationers, 1867), 1:728. While the anonymous author of this present manuscript appears to associate Sworp High Day with anti-Catholic Protestants ("the lacquered skull of a murdered Papal Zouave"), the *C.S.P. Domestic* suggests just the opposite. In 1605, the Star Chamber, under the influence of Sir Robert Cecil, first secretary to James I and afterwards the Earl of Salisbury, undertook a full investigation of Sworp High Day to determine its possible connection with a gang of Catholic plotters who were attempting to introduce Continental pickled eggs into English alehouses. Cecil's investigation uncovered the apparently innocent circumstance that— only two weeks prior to the abortive attempt to blow up the houses of Parliament with gunpowder in November 1605—one Guy Fawkes had entered the Plagued Dog and called to the tapster for "a tankard for a yegg quiccke pickeled." This speech was recalled by the tapster, who was racked for his confession, and subsequently—as a result of Cecil's investigation—three Catholic recusants were hanged in Cheapside to a general acclamation, and the owner of the Plagued Dog had both his ears cropped and the tavern itself was pulled down, the ground plowed and sown with sea salt.

3. For another lively account of this episode, see Priscilla Furman Rockcastle's own two-volume biography, *The Things They Said about Me Are Not True* (New York: Semple P. Simon Publishers, 1930), 2:156–64.

4. On p. 10, col. 2.

5. See Fred A. Dudley, "'Swarp' and Some Other Kentucky Words," *American Speech* 21 (Dec. 1946): 272: "In the pple. form *swarping* only, the word has some currency in a sense roughly definable as wenching, hell-raising; or more mildly as skylarking, cavorting, playing: 'The boys was out swarpin' (or 'swarpin' around') last night. The occurrence of the opprobrious sense appears to be spotty; the word is used in the other senses freely and without embarrassment by native speakers who are distinctly modest."

6. Possibly Longshanks's fictional name for Troublesome Creek, though one should not be too swift in that assumption.

7. No such settlement school is known. It is not listed in Jim Stokely's *To Make a Life: Settlement Institutions of Appalachia* (Berea: 1977).

8. There is some reason to suppose that "Josiah Leathers" is Longshanks's thinly disguised portrait of Josiah Combs, who received a Ph.D. from the University of Paris. But in a communication from the archivist of Heidelberg University, we have learned

that, indeed, a Josiah Leathers of Kentucky was a student there between 1909 and 1911, though he took no degree of record. Improbably, Leathers was evidently intent on the advanced study of Sanskrit and "numerology." (*Numerologishergeschistekopfergehammerin*).

9. Knott County Courthouse?

Tony Feathers

A teacher of art at Greeneville Middle School in Greeneville, Tennessee, Feathers has also worked in advertising and as a news reporter. Born in Kingsport, Tennessee, he graduated from Tusculum College, Greeneville, Tennessee, and received his M.A. from East Tennessee State University.

Cartoons

Editors' Note

Nowhere is the theme of *Appalachia Inside Out* better illustrated than in America's cartoons and comic strips. "Li'l Abner" and "Snuffy Smith" are the most popular strips based on outside perceptions (or misperceptions) of mountain life. Cartoons also have a long history in Southern Appalachia, reflecting a give-and-take between the region and the surrounding cultures. The fictional Davy Crockett, "King of the Wild Frontier," was exploited as a popular exporter of backwoods braggadocio, as the cartoon on the cover of the 1836 *Crockett Almanac* illustrates. The legendary Crockett, a *miles gloriosus* or comic braggart, is seen wading the Mississippi on stilts and carrying his whiskey between his legs—the embodiment of the hardy, hard-drinking, gun-toting, all-conquering natural man (see fig. 1).

In the twentieth century, counterimages began to appear in urban America, with degrading cartoons of rural Appalachian life, as seen in the series by Paul Webb in *Esquire* magazine from 1935 to 1948. The cartoons show, in the words of Allen Batteau in *The Invention of Appalachia,* "themes of ignorance, squalor, poverty, animality, and sloth." Similarly, contemporary cartoons by Erich Sokol in *Playboy* extend the comedy to incest. Because of the heavy cost of permissions and our own modesty, we have not included examples of these types of cartoons.

From *Now and Then* 4, no. 2 (Summer 1987), and 5, no. 2 (Summer 1988). Reprinted by permission of the author and *Now and Then.*

Fig. 1.

The cartoons of Tony Feathers offer a view from inside out which draws upon a tradition substantially different from those of the *Crockett Almanacs* and of *Esquire* and *Playboy*. This is the tradition of the self-deprecating *eiron*, or comic trickster, best represented by George Washington Harris in *The Sut Lovingood Yarns,* which was illustrated by Justin Howard in the 1867 edition. Sut, who is always making fun of himself, is at the same time set against authority, especially the authority of his father. The latter runs bull-headedly into a nest of hornets while pulling the family plow, as son Sut watches the chaos unfold (see fig. 2). Says Sut's mother of her husband, "I know'd he cudent act hoss fur ten minutes wifout actin infunel fool, to save

Fig. 2. "Sut Lovingood's
Daddy Acting Horse," the
original illustration from
the 1867 Dick & Fitzgerald
first edition of *Yarns*.

CIVILIZATION ARRIVED ON THE BLUE RIDGE SOMETIME AROUND 1985.

Fig. 3.

Fig. 4.

Fig. 5.

John-Boy Wilson (aspiring writer) in search of the great Romantic Appalachian novel.

his life." Instead of "King of the Wild Frontier," Sut's pap is instead "King Fool." Sut calls himself a fool, but the difference between Sut and his sire and those other authority figures, rascal sheriffs and ministers, is that Sut is not self-deceived.

The cartoons of Tony Feathers are not so naturalistic as those of Sut Lovingood, but they reveal a sense of irony and depict a tension between cultural attitudes (see figs. 3, 4, and 5). Thus, while the *Crockett Almanacs* exported the comedy of the backwoods boaster and the urban press imposed an image of hapless buffoons and hicks, Feathers has eschewed simplistic versions by taking note of ironic detail where stereotypes collide. As in the Sut Lovingood tradition, Feathers' sketches reflect at once both self-deprecation and a suspicion, if not an outright rejection, of mainstream values.

Paul Curry Steele

See volume 2, chapter 2, for biography.

In the Midst of Death

I live next door to a mortuary.
The undertaker, embalmer, and funeral director
Is a pleasant, unemotional, friendly man.
He has a pretty wife busy with domestic matters
And two school-age children, a girl and a boy.
They live on the second floor of the mortuary,
In a cozy apartment furnished like rooms
In back issues of *Better Homes and Gardens*.
The bodies downstairs disturb them not at all.
I don't understand those alien people;
They might as well be Gypsies or Eskimos.
"How's business?" I ask the man with a smile.
"Dead," he replies, as he has for years.

From *Soupbean: An Anthology of Contemporary Appalachian Literature,* Mountain Union Books, 1977. Reprinted by permission of the author.

Elaine Fowler Palencia

Elaine Fowler Palencia, a freelance writer living in Champaign, Illinois, grew up in Kentucky and Tennessee. Her short stories have appeared in *Iowa Woman, Crescent Review, Appalachian Heritage,* and other literary magazines. A graduate of Vanderbilt University, she has been the recipient of two Illinois Arts Council Fellowships. First-place winner in the Appalachian Writers Association short story contest in 1985, Palencia received the John Ehle Award for Short Fiction from the same organization in 1990. Writing as Laurel Blake, she is the author of several romance novels and was a finalist for the Golden Medallion Award of the Romance Writers of America.

The Biggest Nation

This seat here? No, honey, it's not taken. Just set right down and rest. These malls make me paralyzed tired, don't they you? I'm so tired I'd have to make the walls come to me so I could bump into 'em. I'm Dreama McDonald, by the way, pleased to meet you.

Now, my husband, Floyd, is otherwise. Where clothes is concerned, he'll shop till he drops, and only for the best, that is, when we're in the money: cashmere coats, pinkie rings, silk ties, cuff links. I tell him he buys clothes like they're going out of style.

Floyd's not book smart like my brother Norton, but he's people smart. Wearing a suit and tie to work's kept him out of a lot of dirty jobs. Compared to him, everybody else on the line always looked strictly lower Basin Street. Over at Aeronica they'd see him standing around in a suit and they'd make him Inspector! Why, when I first knew him, people called him the Best-Dressed Man in Dayton, and he didn't even live there anymore. Of course, me, I'm a sale person, what with prices higher'n a Georgia pine. Every little bit helps, you know, as the old lady said when she peed in the ocean.

While I'm waiting for Floyd like this, I people watch. Most people aren't out here to buy anything. They're just sashaying, killing time because they accidentally woke up still alive this morning. I learned to people watch when we was with the carnival out west. Honey, you saw everything on the midway, freaks paying to see freaks. And Indians. I'm more of a hangbacker, but Floyd will get acquainted with anybody. There was one old squaw in New Mexico, tits as big as gallon cans, that wanted him to be godfather to her baby. Oh, he gets along with everybody. My powers of acquaintance isn't nothing compared to his, as you would instantly see if you met him.

Now look at that man down there, on the other end of the bench. *Look at*

From *Small Caucasian Woman,* © 1993 by the author. Reprinted by permission of the University of Missouri Press.

that receding chin and that hair combed straight back from such a low forehead. Don't he look like a possum? Hi there, Possum! No, it's all right, he
don't know I'm talking to him.

Mind if I smoke? If you do, you can move. When I was pregnant I quit
smoking for a year and a half, and the whole time I saw cigarettes as long as
my arm and twice as big around. They're my faithful friends. Who else
would get up with me at three in the morning when I get the creepy crawlies
from too much thinking? Most of us need all the friends we can get, and in
my opinion, whether cigarettes hurt more than they help is a mute point. As
Floyd says, you got to die of something. But, now, they didn't have nothing
to do with our baby not living.

Yes, I do shop here quite often, especially around the holidays when it's
so cheery. After we sold the business we could finally relax like this, but we
don't let no moss grow on us like some people. The couple across the hall
wears out two decks of playing cards a week on pinochle. Of course, at first
we went to the Eagles a lot, but like Floyd says, the trouble with whiskey is, it
gets in your stomach so bad. The world don't need two more retired alcoholics.

Later I tried to get him to go down to the Golden Agers with me.

"I ain't setting around with them old farts," says Floyd.

"Why not? You're an old fart," I said, but my logic didn't dent him.

Floyd's always been a party boy, see. You ought to hear him sing "Mammy."
One day after we retired, he went out in front of our apartment building and
glued a quarter to the sidewalk. Then we invited the couple in 2B over and set
at our window for three hours, laughing and watching everybody try to pick it
up. About once a month we go to the El Adobe. That Mexican restaurant over
on Twenty-fifth and Vine? Floyd doesn't care for foreign food, a steak is the only
eat-out food there is for him, but he'll go with me for the taco chips. He has this
little gray mouse made of rubber, and he'll put it about half buried in the basket
of chips. Then he'll call the waitress over, ask for more chips, and hand her the
basket. Taco chips all over the place! Most of the girls is good sports on account
of it's Floyd. You'd see right away he's a collector's item.

Now what's Possum laughing about? Look how tickled he is. Lord, they're
going to have to clean his seat!

Well, yes, I'd love for Floyd to meet you, too. When he's around, nobody
is lonely and you never know what'll happen—he makes things happen. Like
when we had our little business, he agreed to sponsor a Republican or a
Democrat bowling team, whichever party won. Right after that we got a
telegram from President Nixon asking for our support in the next election,
one of only a hundred thousand businesses that got one in the state of Ohio.
Floyd had it whatyoucall, xeroxed, and sent it to his brother Bob that thinks
he's shit ice cream and everybody wants a bite. Yes, we was quite up in the
world then, and we've always lived at nice addresses. Why, right now we
live on the same street as the mayor. He lives at number one-oh-one Grand
Avenue and we live at three thousand seventy-nine. That's exactly right, the
Mallview Apartments right across the highway from here. I can tiptoe over

here of a morning right when she opens. The Imperial's a beautiful car but such a gas hog, it's not worth it to crank her up. Oh, you better believe it's an Imperial. We bought that sucker eleven years ago. I never will forget, one afternoon Floyd come home with $10,000 in cash. "Ask me no questions and I'll tell you no lies," says Floyd, "but I think we better turn this into merchandise pretty quick." It's gorgeous, all white interior. When I'm riding in it I feel like I'm wearing a wedding dress. It's my friend too, like my cigarettes, and I baby it. I'd take it to bed with me if I could. My *God*, would you look at that woman. Now that's what I call a patriotic face: red lipstick, white powder, blue eye shadow. And she thinks it looks good. Well, as Floyd always says, the biggest nation is the imagination.

We got the car when we was living on Easy Street. No joke, there's an Easy Street in this town. Only two blocks long, which ought to tell you something about the good life. One time Floyd was drinking Seven and Sevens down at the Eagles and got acquainted with this lawyer. Pretty soon the lawyer couldn't hit the floor with his hat and he absolutely refused to believe there was an Easy Street. Floyd brought him right home. Oh, we had a big time. I fixed him my Jailhouse Chili, which what else would you feed a lawyer, and we got to drinking Reds, beer and tomato juice. Come to find out he was a real important dude and knew Johnny Bench.

We're getting along fine when all of a sudden this lawyer laughs right in Floyd's face. "*Tain't.* You said *tain't,*" he says.

Floyd comes right back at him, "Sure I did. You can't talk as good as me 'cause you didn't go to the same school I did. I speak three languages: literate, illiterate, and profane."

"What school is that?" says the lawyer.

"The school of hard knocks, you simple son of a bitch," Floyd says.

"That's right," I chime in, "we've went all over this great land of ours and known every kind of people: doctors, Mexicans, Mormons. We've got a piece of wood from the Petrified Forest and actual photographs of Mount Rushmore."

"Besides," says Floyd, "I did go through Ohio State. Lots of times, when I drove a delivery truck up in Columbus."

That lawyer just hee-hawed. "I know some people'd get a kick out of meeting you, Floyd. I'll have my secretary send you and your lovely wife an invitation to our family Christmas party," he says.

Which I bought a dress to go to, but the invitation never came. Now if that lawyer trotted up with the invitation, I wouldn't give him yesterday's ice water. Though I did make it my business to see where they lived and what his wife looked like. One time I saw her coming out of their big house, switching her bony little butt. The rich are all crooks anyway. You never have to pay somebody to watch your coat in a cheap restaurant, do you?

Now there goes some boys on cocaine. See the way they're sniffing like they've got a cold? That's how you can tell. Floyd taught me to recognize it. It's a shame what drugs are doing to our young people, and to think it all started with convenience foods. Why, hadn't you figured that out? When I was growing up, the only time we saw an orange was in the toe of our Christmas stocking, and we never had orange juice. I didn't have orange juice until after we was married and Floyd took me to Florida. Now you can buy it frozen for as little as eighty-nine cents a can on sale. Not only that, but you can buy any kind of frozen dinner—Chinese, Italian, French. Speaking of foreign cooking, imagine Floyd and I's surprise when we went to a fancy French restaurant in St. Louis one time and found out all those famous French sauces aren't nothing but gravies. I said, "Lord, honey, all the time we've been eating biscuits and sop, we was enjoying French gourmet food and didn't even know it."

But my point is that convenience foods got people to expecting their tastes to be satisfied too quick. Next come the fast food restaurants, and then the drugs. How many people do you think would snort it up their nose if they had to grow the durned stuff and render it? About as many people as would be eating bacon if they had to kill the hog and cure it. Oh, people are so lazy these days they wouldn't say "sooey" if the hog was eating them up.

That's why I try to do my bit at the holidays for the forgotten ones. Look how many people is sitting in this mall, not waiting for anybody but themselves. There is so many lost souls out there that no one is thinking of, which I decide on Thanksgiving who to invite to Christmas dinner. After they run the Shah of Iran out, and he was wandering from one place to another so sick, I invited him. I invited Nixon, too, one of those years when he was in disgrace. After all, he sent us that telegram when he was riding high. There's not no excuse for being lonely if you have a little bit of imagination. We had a big time, me and Nixon and the Shah.

Look, the mall's going to close pretty soon and like I said, I just live over the way. I've had such a pleasant time getting acquainted with you while I was waiting for Floyd. Why don't you come home with me and have supper? I've got some cabbage rolls made from an actual Polish recipe of a man we knew when we was in business. You can help me decide who to invite this Christmas. Pete Rose and Mayor Ed Koch are two I'm considering. And if you're an ax murderer, it don't make a bit of difference. Ax murderers have to eat too, and besides, I stopped worrying about that kind of thing a long time ago. Truthfully it was two years and seven months ago when Floyd was in the hospital for all them tests. We thought it was chronic indigestion due to an ulcer, and I'd been feeding him Maalox and ice cream by the bucketful, so we didn't go in till he couldn't keep nothing down for a week. Along about eight-thirty one night his doctor come by with the test results and called me out in the hall. He said this and that which I couldn't understand, and then he said a kind of cancerous word and I knew we were in for it.

I must have walked those hospital corridors for two hours before I thought I was calm enough to go back in where Floyd was, but the minute I tried it, my heart speeded up till it was ripping along like a lawn mower, and when I looked at him laying there so still, I commenced to cry. Floyd opened his eyes real slow, like raising heavy windows, and he smiled. It was a pale, white smile, like the faint little moon you see in the late afternoon sky sometimes in the winter.

"Come here, Dreama, and lay your head on my shoulder," he said, and I laid down along the edge of the bed and did like he told me.

"Now breathe when I do," he said, and I did, and after a while my heart and my breathing slowed down until they was calm and smooth as a whisper.

"Go to sleep now. Everything will be all right in the morning. I'm just so tired," Floyd said, and kissed my forehead.

And I've been coming here ever since.

Fred Chappell

See volume 2, chapter 3, for biography.

My Father's Hurricane

Like dust cloud over a bombed-out city, my father's
Homemade cigarette smoke above the ruins
Of an April supper. His face, red-weathered, shone through.
When he spoke an edge of gold tooth-cap burned
In his mouth like a star, winking at half his words.

At the little end of the table, my sister and I
Sat alert, as he set down his streaky glass
Of buttermilk. My mother picked her teeth.

"I bet you think that's something," he said, "the wind
That tore the tin roof on the barn. I bet
You think that that was some kind of wind."

"Yes sir," I said (with the whole certainty
Of my eleven years), "a pretty hard wind."

"Well, that was nothing. Not much more than a breath
Of fresh air. You should have seen the winds
That came when I was your age, or near about.
They've taken to naming them female names these days,
But this one I remember best they called

From *Wind Mountain* by Fred Chappell (Louisiana State University Press). © 1979 by the author. Used with permission.

Bad Egg. A woman's name just wouldn't name it."

"Bad Egg?"

       He nodded profoundly as a funeral
Home director. "That's right. Bad Egg was what
I think of as a right smart blow,
No slight ruffling of tacked-down tin.
The sky was filled with flocks of roofs, dozens
Of them like squadrons of pilotless airplanes,
Sometimes so many you couldn't even see between.
Little outhouse roofs and roofs of sheds
And great long roofs of tobacco warehouses,
Church steeples plunging along like V-2 rockets,
And hats, toupees, lampshades, and greenhouse roofs.
It even blew your aunt's glass eyeball out.
It blew the lid off a jar of pickles we'd
Been trying to unscrew for fifteen years."

"Aw," I said.

       "Don't interrupt me, boy,
I haven't told you half. Because the roofs
Were only the top layer. Underneath
The roofs the trees came hurtling by, root-ends
First. They looked like flying octopuses
Glued onto frazzly toilet brushes. Oaks
And elms and cedars, peach trees dropping
Peaches—splat!—like big sweet mushy hailstones.
Apples and walnuts coming down like snow.
Below this layer of trees came a fleet of cars:
T-models, Oldsmobiles, and big Mack trucks;
And mixed in with the cars were horses tumbling
And neighing, spread-legged, and foaming at the mouth;
Cows too, churning to solid butter inside.
Beneath the cars a layer of . . . everything.
What Madison County had clutched to its surface
It lost hold of. And here came bales of barb wire,
Water pumps, tobacco setters, cookstoves,
Girdles shucked off squealing ladies, statues
Of Confederate heroes, shotguns, big bunches
Of local politicians still talking of raising
Taxes. You name it, and here it came.
There was a visiting symphony orchestra
At Hot Springs School and they went flashing by,
Fiddling the 'Storm' movement of Beethoven's Sixth.

Following that—infielders prancing like black gnats—
A baseball game about six innings old.
The strangest thing adrift was a Tom Mix movie,
All wrinkled and out of order; Bad Egg
Had ripped the picture off the screen, along
With a greasy cloud of buttered popcorn."

                                          "Wait,"

I said. "I don't understand how you
Could see the other layers with all this stuff
On the bottom."

                    "I was coming to that," he said.
"If it was only a horizontal stream
It wouldn't have been so bad. But inside the main
Were other winds turning every which way,
Crosswise and cockeyed, and up and down
Like corkscrews. Counterwinds—and mighty powerful.
It was a corkscrew caught me, and up I went;
I thought I'd pull in two. First man I met
Was Reverend Johnson, too busy ducking candlesticks
And hymnals to greet me, though he might have nodded.
And then Miz White, who taught geometry,
Washing by in a gang of obtuse triangles.
And then Bob Brendan, the Republican banker, flailing
Along with his head in a safety deposit box.
Before I could holler I zipped up to Layer Two,
Bobbing about with Chevrolets and Fords
And Holsteins . . . I'm not bragging, but I'll bet you
I'm the only man who ever rode
An upside-down Buick a hundred miles,
If you call holding on and praying 'riding.'
That was scary, boy, to have a car wreck
Way up in the middle of the air. I shut my eyes . . .
But when I squirted up to Layer Three
I was no better off. This sideways forest
Skimming along looked mighty dark and deep.
For all I knew there could be bears in here,
Or windblown hunters to shoot me by mistake.
Mostly it was the trees—to see come clawing
At me those big root-arms—Ough! I shivered
And shuddered, I'll tell you. Worse than crocodiles:
After I dodged the ripping roots, the tails,
The heavy limbs, came sworping and clattering at me.
I was awfully glad to be leaving Layer Three."

"Wait," I said. "How come the heavy stuff's
On top? Wouldn't the lightest things go highest?"

"Hold your horses," he said, "I was coming to that.
Seems like it depended on the amount of surface
An object would present. A rooftop long
And flat would rise and rise, and trees with trunks
And branches. But a bar of soap would tumble
At the bottom, like a pebble in a creek.
Anyhow . . . The Layer of Roofs was worst. Sharp edges
Everywhere, a hundred miles an hour.
Some folks claim to talk about close shaves.
Let them wait till they've been through a tempest
Of giant razor-blades. *Soo-wish, sheee-oosh!*
I stretched out still on the floor of air, thinking
I'd stand a better chance. Blind luck is all
It was, though, pure blind luck. And when I rose
To the Fifth Layer—"

        "Wait," I said. "What Fifth?
At first you only mentioned four. What Fifth?"

"I was coming to that," he said. "The only man
Who ever knew about the Fifth was me.
I never told a soul till now. It seems
That when the hotel roofs blew off, Bad Egg
Sucked a slew of people out of bed.
The whole fifth layer of debris was lovebirds."

"Lovebirds?"
        "Lovebirds, honeypies, sweethearts—whatever
You want to call them."

                "J. T., you watch yourself,"
My mother interjected.

                "I'm just saying
What I saw," he said. "The boy will want
The truth, and that's the way it was . . . Fifty
Or sixty couples, at least. Some of them
I recognized: Paolo and Francesca,
And Frankie and Johnny, Napoleon
And Josephine; but most I didn't know.
Rolling and sporting in the wind like face cards

From a stag poker deck—"

                        "J. T.!" she said.

"(All right.) But what an amazing sight it was!
I started to think all kinds of thoughts . . ."

                        "Okay,"
I said. "But how did you get down without
Getting killed?"

          "I was coming to that," he said.
"It was the queerest thing—"

Michael Martin

Michael Martin lives under the shadow of Iron Mountain above Plum Creek near Glade Spring in Southwest Virginia. In a letter, he writes that he grew up forty miles from this site in Bristol. He traveled much as a young man, but after a quarter of a century returned to Southwest Virginia and built a shack in the woods, where he still lives.

The following verse is taken from a work entitled "Approaching History," a long poem printed in part in *The Iron Mountain Review* (Fall 1987). For Martin, approaching history is analogous to returning home, as his own life and his writing illustrate. Beulah, the speaker, is a visionary artist, potter, and storyteller with an excellent memory and sense of humor.

10–2 memory
Plum Creek, yesterday

talkingtoBeulah:complaining about Fall.andthe hotroads
how *hard* it was to keep antifreeze
in my little Datsun, these days . . .

                      Beulah says,

From *The Iron Mountain Review* (Michael Martin Issue), vol 4, no. 1 (Fall 1987). Reprinted by permission of the author.

—talking about how hard it is, and used to be, and all that:
during the war, this antifreeze
had a quota on it: government bought it all up . . .

now, those brothers: when they was driving school buses,
B. B. he'd put that wood alcohol in hisn 'n steam on off
with these pretty Plum Creek girls 'n leave Sylvester
still a pourin' water in hisn. Oh, he was a sharpster,
thought he was, yeah: thought he was a "dealer"
'n a wheeler too with his bright new yeller school bus
'n these rattle trap used cars a-rustin in his daddy's cow pasture.
I heard a few things about him and learned a few more
before I learned enough not to learn nothin' more.

He'd got in with Jack, down at "my shop," as he put it.
Well, one night in '44 when I got off work at the plant
I left my little Chevy coupe with 'em to boil out the radiator
'n instead of *my* antifreeze they slipped me this wood alcohol.
Next morning I started it up and went in for my coffee,
come out the door and it looked like a miniature steam plant down there,
smoke a pourin' out from under the hood. Red flames ready to shoot up.
The fire'd be a lickin' over that windshield any minute.
So I drove on over to B. B.'s. I looked at him level.
He had on his green shirt, pink polka dots, and this *striped* carrot,
strawberry-and-cream, *business* tie, about a foot wide.
Bee, I said, you be straight with me and I'll be straight with you.
Did you put antifreeze in that radiator or wood alcohol?
Well Bee looked right shocked, but he turned the other cheek.
Why Beulah, antifreeze, *antifreeze;* oh he was sly,
he was meek and humble, he was Christian, antifreeze,
you couldn't hear the last word, he wheezed it out so low,
like it was some kinda cuss word, nobody'd dare to breathe,
'cept me, maybe—me and the devil: *anti*freeze.
Antifreeze, Beulah rasps, whispering.

I said—Stand right there Bee, right in front of that hood there.
Started it up, lo and behold. Right up through Bee's shirt
a big cloud of smoke come a puffin like a steam locomotive.
Ol' B. B. vanished; disappeared. Yep Bee went up in smoke. Tie too.
I shut it off and just looked. Well Bee, I said very hard.
Well B. B. I looked very hard through that windshield,
'til poor Bee come out from under his cloud,
oh I looked at him hard. Beulah, he said, uh,
y'see, I put in antifreeze, 'n well, uh *uh* . . . ye see, Beulah . . .

                              —chain-smoking, one-lunged
Beulah, 70 years, 80 pounds
huddled in the doorway

broods, as the cigarette shortens:
as the red tip burns into her fingertips

she blunts it out in her palm, and rises, limber;
stabs it out on the woodstove; stabs it again;

stoops again to the sill,

one palm still full of ash, still smoldering,
one cupped, bare, open to the ceiling,

building the story with both, both hardly moving,
the potter in her is patient,

now sidelong, motionless,

looks across the linoleum
where Flo sits, massive, expressionless,
without response, on the sofa,

her hands on her knees, like a goddess,
a Mayan idol: her sister's
face somber, high-boned, masklike,

opaque in its fringe of grey,
its ghostly nimbus of plastic
shredded storm window on mountains.

Says, *I put in antifreeze*

Slowly Flo lowers her head
and raises her hands,
covers her leathery face
in both hands, trembling.

—Says, I put in antifreeze,

says Beulah, raising her pitch
to B.B.'s high treble
whispers her Bee-whisper.

Like a tremor of earth
passing under the sofa,
her shoulders shaking,
less sound than vibration,

Flo emits one low prolonged chuckle.

Gasping, doubled-over, struggling for breath,
her voice quavering with Bee-quaver, Beulah rasps

—Says I put in antifreeze, but it come out wood alcohol.

Flo lowers her hands, bares her dark face to the room
broken into a thousand wreathed lines.

—But it come out wood alcohol.

Laughter—Beulahn
laughter, Flo

laughter: doubled,
redoubled, trebled,

trembled over—

brimful—a jugful, a kegful—a drumful, a room full—

a bubbling room
with a spout

a living room's
small cauldron

a cunning, red
mountain pot

of the low, hushed
laughter

poured out, entire.

To raise it
to my lips
—to quench my thirst

. . . . .

to build a room
to make a room full
of that laughter

raised, though it be,

in Fall.

Loyal Jones

See volume 2, chapter 2, for biography.

Appalachian Humor

A good laugh is better than a dose of salts.
—Granny Morgan

Everything human is pathetic. The secret source of humor
itself is not joy but sorrow.
—Mark Twain

Nowhere else in the country is the tragic view of the human condition so
ingrained as in the South in general and the Appalachians in particular. Perhaps this is because we are closer to Calvinism than any other people. By
Calvinism, I mean the system of theological thought that perceives human
persons as flawed, unable to extract themselves from their own fleshly pursuits without the grace of God, that God alone decides who will be saved
and who not and that there is nothing we can do about it, that the God who

From *Laughter in Appalachia: A Festival of Southern Mountain Humor,* ed. with Billy Edd
    Wheeler, August House, Inc., 1987. Reprinted by permission of the author and
    publisher.

elects some of us to glory will keep us until the end, and that elected believers are equal. It is a grim system, but it has its attributes. Calvinists are rarely surprised and almost never astonished at our capacity to invent evil, and quite often they are pleasantly surprised that we are better than expected.

It is certainly true that the more optimistic gospel of the Methodists and others permeated the regions of the South, and many of us have tried to get the hang of perfectionism. We believe in God. We try to believe in goodness, in perfectibility, but underneath is the fear that we are going it alone in the world and getting euchred—flawed, unreliable, and absurd, pretending that we are worthy and in control. Yet we know that our dignity is a too-small hat in the winds of truth. All people know this, but here in this region, we keep it uppermost in our minds, so that the only reasonable thing to do about it is to laugh—at ourselves and at others who pretend, against odds, that all is well with the human enterprise.

It is easy to believe that such a view of life is passing from the American scene with the family farm, that urbanites would not be hounded by such. Yet, recently, in a review in the *Saturday Review,* Mark Zussman wrote: "The world is more or less as it must be, and the mature person approaches it with compassion, to be sure, but also with irony."

The mature person saves some compassion and most of the irony, or humor, for himself. This mature sense of things is a modest view. Such a person's humor is self-deprecating. It is also aimed at those who pretend to be what they are not, nor can be. Such a humor helps to create a proper perspective. It allows one to cope in a life that is often baffling and disappointing. It also comes from a defiant as well as a humble heart. No one can evade disaster and death, but we can escape the degradation of dreading and fearing the inevitable. That in itself is a victory.

Here in Appalachia, we have seen our loved ones die in hazardous occupations and from unchecked diseases. We have been bilked of land, minerals, and ballads. We have been gerrymandered, lied to, and done unto. But we have endured, partially at least, because we could laugh.

There is also, of course, the lighthearted banter, the rusties (pranks) that are pulled on one another. In every community there is the wag, the prankster, who lightens the day with his antics. Some of this humor has a barb in it, ruffles dignity, but most of it is gentle wit, not aimed at embarrassment. It is surface humor, light and yet concerned with the distempers of the human spirit.

Some comments on the characteristics of southern mountaineers may be in order. Their absorption with religion has been alluded to. I have made a case for the inherent Calvinistic nature of the belief system. This is supported by the Appalachian writer and raconteur Harry Caudill, who claims that we are all Baptists. "Oh, you'll find Methodists, but if you scratch one you'll find a Baptist underneath." Indeed, the old-time Baptist view of things does seem to explain Appalachians better than any other view. Many historians have given credit to Scotch-Irish Presbyterianism for shaping the character of those who settled the mountains, but Presbyterians tend to be middle-class and somewhat aloof from the common folks. Baptist theology attracts ordinary people, reinforces the leveling tendencies of mountaineers, and supports their basic radicalism. It seeps to the core, as Caudill suggests. I heard one fellow saying, "I used to be a Baptist." Another answered, "There is no such thing as an ex-Baptist!" There are probably more jokes about religion in the mountains than about any other subject. Why is this? In some parts of the country, people are afraid to make jokes about religion because they might be perceived as sacrilegious. Here even the preachers tell jokes about their foibles and the inconsistencies of the church. Perhaps it is because they have not been overly imbued with the perfectionist zeal. They see and comment on follies, even religious ones. A well-known story is this:

> A good Sister in the balcony of a church got happy and began to dance a little. She lost her balance and fell. However, her dress tail caught on a hanging light fixture, leaving her safely suspended but somewhat exposed. The preacher, thinking quickly, shouted, "The first man that looks upon this good Christian woman will be struck stone-blind."
> There was a long pause and then came a hoarse whisper from a man down front: "I think I'll risk one eye."

Modesty, already mentioned, is rooted in the idea of not taking oneself too seriously. Mountaineers are levelers, believing that each is as good as another but no better. Such people are quick to note tendencies in themselves for pretending to be what they are not, and they make a joke about it. They are even quicker to note the tendency in others. Again the joke, or quip—as when my friend from West Jefferson, North Carolina, called.

"With whom did you wish to speak?" I inquired with English-teacher stiffness.

"You, you stuffy bastard," he responded.

Mountain politicians are hesitant to claim too much in the way of talent and ideals. They walk a thin line between modesty and affirmation of ability to do the job at hand. The rural voters love the official who can tell stories on himself, who doesn't get above his raising. The best story to illustrate these qualities was told by Fess Whitaker, of Letcher County, Kentucky, when he campaigned for jailer of the county:

> You know, I was in Teddy Roosevelt's Rough Riders. I rode with him in the Battle of San Juan Hill in the Spanish-American War. I remember that day as if it was yesterday. Teddy and I rode stirrup to stirrup, our guns blazing and our sabers flashing in the sun, while off before us the Spaniards fled in a great cloud of dust. When we reached the top, Teddy reined up and said:
> "We've done a great thing here today, Fess, and one of us is going to be President."
> "You just go right ahead, Teddy," I said. "All I want is to be jailer of Letcher County."

Almost a contradiction of the value of modesty is the mountaineer's sense of independence and self-reliance, reinforced by a stubborn pride. These traits are illustrated by the following anecdote, said to be true:

> Several years ago there was a great snowfall in Western North Carolina, and many people were snowed in for weeks. The Red Cross came to help. Two workers heard of an old lady way back in the mountains, living alone, and they set out to see about her, in a four-wheel-drive vehicle. They finally slipped and skidded over the mountain and got into the high cove where she lived, got out and knocked on her door.
>
> When she appeared at the door, one of the workers said, "Hello, we're from the Red Cross," but before they could say anything else, she replied, "Well, I don't believe I'm going to be able to help you any. It's been a right hard winter."

Personalism is another trait of Appalachians. This means we think in terms of persons rather than degrees or professional reputations. We want to get you placed to see which Johnson you are. So we ask, "Whose boy are you?" "Are you from the Horse Hollow Johnsons?" "Do I know your Daddy?" "Are you the Johnson the tree fell on?" We tend to get sidetracked from abstract discourses if we have a good excuse to go off on a tangent and tell about some interesting person who may or may not be closely related to the discourse. Jeff Daniel Marion, the East Tennessee poet, captures this tendency with a poem, "In a Southerly Direction," a response to someone asking for directions:

> It's just
> over the knob
> there—
> you know the place,
> the one
> up there next to
> Beulah Justice,
> your mother's second cousin
> on her daddy's side.
> Or
> if you go in by
> the back road
> it's the farm across the way
> from Jesse's old barn
> that burned down
> last June
> with them 2 fine mules
> of his.
> Why hell, son,
> you can't miss it.[1]

The late Joe Creason, who wrote a column for the *Louisville Courier-Journal*, used to tell a story about his visit with a man in Pike County, Kentucky. They exchanged howdys and commented on the weather, and then the man asked, "Where are you from?" Creason told him he was from Louisville. There was a long pause, and then the man asked, "Who's the barber up there now?" The world of the traditional Appalachian is a warm one of persons that one knows or would like to know.

Appalachians have known more poverty and over a longer period than have most Americans. Therefore, hard-time jokes and allusions are a part of the fabric of life. The legendary invitations to hospitality were usually qualified with something like, "—if you don't mind staying with poor folks." My father told of being invited to dinner with a family who had only sorghum and cornbread, but with the host graciously inviting them to "just reach and get anything you want." My father overdid it with the sorghum. The hostess, seeing his plight, offered to wash his plate for him. Expecting another dish, he complied, but when she returned the plate, nothing else was put on the table. When asked what he would "like to have now?" he replied, "I guess some more sorghum." William Sturgill, coal man and banker from Hazard, Kentucky, told the story about a woman going to see the governor about getting her husband out of the penitentiary.

"What is he in for?" the governor wanted to know.

"For stealing a ham."

"That doesn't sound too bad. Is he a good worker?"

"No, I wouldn't say that. He's pretty lazy."

"Oh. Well, he's good to you and the children, isn't he?"

"No, he's not. He's pretty mean to us, if you want to know the truth."

"Why would you want a man like that out of prison?"

"Well, Governor, we're out of ham."

One place name is Gnaw Bone, indicating that the people had to get every bit of nourishment they could from the food they had available.

The place names of the mountains contain a great deal of humor and irony. Consider: Hell-fer-Sartain, Beauty, Lovely, Sodom, Gizzard, Matrimony, Affinity, Bulltown, Only, 'Possum Kingdom, Pinchem Tight, Relief, Razorblade, and Cheap. Place is very dear to mountain people. One fellow said he lived so far back in the hills that the sun set between his house and the main road.

Family is the functional unit of the mountains. It is extended, far-flung, made up of individuals of diverse dispositions but held together by affection, obligation, and tradition. One wag, commenting on do-gooders, professors, and the like who came to study mountaineers or do unto them, commented, "The typical mountain family is made up of a father, mother, six children, four grandparents, a bunch of aunts, uncles, cousins, a sociologist, and a family planning specialist."

One brother said to another, "You know, I've decided that Uncle Herman is a real SOB." The other considered this for a moment and replied, "Yeah, but he's our'n." Perhaps this attitude spawned the phrase "good old boy." One might say, "Jess is a good old boy" *even though* he drinks, beats his horse, or whatever. It is a tolerant acceptance of kin, warts and all. They are family. They can expect support when they need it.

My kinfolks represent generations of North Carolina mountaineers, a mixture of Welsh, Scotch-Irish, English, and Dutch (or German) stock, Baptist to the core. They did the best they could and then stood and took it. Grandpa Jones, a farmer and storekeeper, and Grandpa Morgan, a Baptist preacher-farmer, were both endowed with fiery Celtic tempers. Grandpa Jones was turned out of the church for fighting with his son-in-law over politics. It was said that they tore down a half-acre of corn, holding hands and kicking each other's tails in a merry-go-round of vituperation and retribution. Grandpa was an ardent Democrat, my uncle an ironclad Republican. Grandpa made terrible jokes about Hoover and the Republican Depression, asking my uncle if he knew that it was against the law to shoot up into the air before 9:00 A.M. When Uncle said he did not, Grandpa crowed, "Because you might hit somebody up in a persimmon tree getting his breakfast." This would nudge Uncle into a bitter and vindictive mood, because he was humorless when it came to politics. Grandpa Jones was a practical joker of the first water, always teasing children and leading adults into the bogs of his imagination.

Grandpa Morgan preached fiery sermons and was noted for the power of his rhetoric. He tolerated imperfections in members of his congregations until he could exhort them to mend their ways, but he had little patience with an errant horse or cow. He could blister the hair off the offending animal with his judgment on its intrinsic worth.

Humor around our house took the form of bantering, calling attention to inconsistencies and foibles. Practical jokes were in order. Gentle disparagement was used ironically—that is, really showing affection and approval even if the words indicated otherwise, as in: "You look like the hind wheels of hard time," or "You must have been behind the door when the looks were passed out." Sometimes, though, the ridicule hurt, as when my brother's prize fighting cock got out of its cage and was slain by my mother's Rhode Island Red rooster. The threat of such ridicule kept us out of trouble at times. Once I was goaded into making a bid on a hip-shot, spavined, ancient, and emaciated saddle horse, and I bid what I thought was a safe twenty dollars, which was accepted with gleeful alacrity. I fled in dismay amid derisive comments, but this was better than the treatment I would have had if I had brought that decrepit horse home.

In church we devised games to play during the long sermons. One was to read off the hymn titles and add the words "under the covers." Thus we came up with such provocative and stimulating titles as: "Just as I Am Under the Covers," "Guide Me Under the Covers," and "A Wonderful Time Under the Covers." Of course we imagined that our parents would skin us alive if they found out about our sacrilege, not knowing that they probably had played the same game in their time.

It is a joy when your own children take up some of the same interests and tastes as their parents. Our children like and make mountain music. They love stories and humorous anecdotes. Yet I see a hesitation and sometimes a strained laugh when the old rural jokes are told. Their experience is different from ours. A generation is a long time in the twentieth century. Across the country, a way of life, with references to agricultural terms, is passing. Just last month in the *Louisville Courier-Journal*, a journalist, obviously urban-spawned, reported that a federal judge, who grew up on the farm, was trying to decide which of two options in a legal case "was the easiest road to hoe." My friend Jim Wayne Miller, who hails from Buncombe County, North Carolina, says that if the back-to-the-land movement keeps growing, we'll be having reverse malapropisms, such as "hitting the row" or "on the row again." All this reminds me of the stories I heard as a child of other children's misunderstanding the words to hymns—for example, one boy's fondness for the "cross-eyed bear hymn" ("Gladly the Cross I'd Bear") and the one about "Round John Virgin" ("'round yon Virgin"). A great deal of humor involves misunderstanding of words. As culture and experiences and interests, as well as localities, change, the possibilities for misunderstanding increase. It is both humorous and disquieting.

But life and culture and values go on, always changing. As Raymond K. McLain and Heraclitus say, culture and tradition are like a river, which appears the same but is ever-changing. No one of us can ever step into the same river twice. Yet we, like a river, always have the same basic characteristics. Our atoms change. Our children are different from us parents, but they are of the same genes and culture. Their tendencies and needs and desires will be similar to ours. Human nature is as it is, and we must be what we are, learn to live with it, and, if we are to survive, laugh whenever we can.

Note

1. From *Out in the Country Back Home* (Winston-Salem, NC: Jackpine P, 1976), 13. Reprinted by permission of Jeff Daniel Marion.

...AND FOR A WHILE THERE WAS ONE LESS
BRIDGE IN MADISON COUNTY (NORTH CAROLINA)

Chapter 7

Education and Criticism

Introduction

While books and formal education may have been rare on the Appalachian frontier, they were often highly prized by pioneer leaders. But frontier conditions were such that the descendants of settlers sometimes could not read the classics cherished by their ancestors. Despite the humanistic and religious instruction offered by Presbyterian ministers who came to Appalachia in significant numbers before 1830, and despite the missionary and cultural work of the founders of settlement schools in the late nineteenth and early twentieth centuries, formal learning in Appalachia gradually yielded to the imperatives of a folk culture.

But if the folk culture did not emphasize formal learning, a number of writers and educators have argued in recent decades that Appalachia has as much to teach mainstream America as the region has to learn from the larger culture. This view has been most effectively expressed in the Foxfire books and the Foxfire educational program developed by Eliot Wiggginton, which treats the student's immediate community as an extended classroom. The novelist Wilma Dykeman is sympathetic to this approach when she observes that the search for knowledge may lead us into new realms, but the search begins with the self, often on native ground.

In the debate about Appalachian studies and the worthiness of Appalachian literature, the scholar's task remains that identified by Emerson: "To find similarities amid differences and differences among similarities." How does Appalachian literature relate to southern literature and to American literature? What themes are constant, and what themes are limited to the mountain region? How does the history of Southern Appalachia relate to that of the rest of the country?

What can Appalachia learn from the rest of the world, and what lessons can the story of the mountains offer to others?

With such powerful questions facing us, there seems every reason to study Appalachian literature, whether distinguished or only distinguishable. If the goal of education is, as Flannery O'Connor says, to find what one lacks, then the first step would be to turn to the mirror of understanding: the literature and history of one's region.

Jo Carson

See volume 2, chapter 1, for biography.

Storyteller

a First Amendment poem

Meaning what I say
is not saying what
I mean and yet I
do not always know
the difference.
I cannot speak
the unspeakable,
I say instead
those things
best left unsaid.
Life is short,
love is unrequited,
the dead do not
take questions.

I can tell this:
there is enough
of truth to offend
everybody.

From *Now and Then* 10.3 (Fall 1993); reprinted by permission of the author and the publisher.

W. H. Ward

W. H. (Bill) Ward was born in 1943 in Tuscaloosa County, Alabama. The county's southern portion lies along the Black Warrior River and in the 1940s supported a Black Belt culture, while its northern reaches remained essentially Appalachian in economy and topography.

Ward received the B.A. in English from the University of Alabama in 1966 and the M.A. and Ph.D. from the University of Tennessee at Knoxville, completing his dissertation in early American literature under Richard Beale Davis in 1971. Since then, he has been a member of the faculty of Appalachian State University in Boone, North Carolina, where he serves as associate vice-chancellor for academic affairs.

In addition to critical and scholarly publications dealing primarily with colonial and nineteenth-century American writers, Ward has indulged his keen taste for mountain music through numerous reviews of recordings and books in the *North Carolina Folklore Journal* and the *Appalachian Journal*.

The Rush to Find an Appalachian Literature

The current interest in the notion of Appalachian literature stems from two familiar impulses, one of them intellectual in character and the other basically emotional. First, there is the urge to classify and categorize, the Aristotelian prescription for bringing order to the apparently chaotic welter of things in which humanity exists. For American humanity in particular, this scheme has proved indispensable because it permits us to make at least partial structural sense out of the multiplicity of regional cultures that history and geography have evolved here; to explain how our *unum,* such as it is, has been achieved *e pluribus.* But when an area becomes aware of itself as a discrete entity, and especially when that area has sensed the disdain of supercilious outlanders, it finds itself in the quandary of a man who has just become convinced that he possesses an immortal soul: it is now obliged to *do* something with the fact. So like the American literati in the first flush of post-Revolutionary nationalism, the mountain clerisy are compelled by pride, the second and more intense of the forces behind the Appalachian literary boom, to demonstrate that they have produced, or can produce, a body of writing deserving of the world's respect as art. They have set about the task with considerable determination and, it seems to me, more enthusiasm than the situation warrants.

Voices from the Hills,[1] the anthology brought forth in 1975 by Robert J. Higgs and Ambrose N. Manning, is at once the most concrete evidence of the push for the recognition of Appalachian letters and the focal point for

From *Appalachian Journal* 5, no. 3 (Spring 1978), © *Appalachian Journal*/Appalachian State University. Used with permission.

discussion of the entire topic, as has recently been reflected by C. Hugh
Holman's largely negative review of the book and by the response of Higgs
and Manning to the review.[2] It is an obvious tribute to the collection's significance that it has become so closely identified with its subject. And, not-
withstanding Mr. Holman's critique (some of whose strictures I believe to
be misplaced), I am willing to suggest that *Voices from the Hills* is about as
satisfactory a single-volume gathering of Appalachian belles-lettres as could
be compiled (which is not so extravagant a compliment as it may at first seem).

But the problem of which belles-lettres may fairly and instructively be
regarded as "Appalachian" is a crucial one. If anything at all emerges from
the exchange between Mr. Holman and the editors on this point, it is that
no one knows where the boundaries of Appalachia lie—no one, that is, with
the exception of the Appalachian Regional Commission, which is persuaded
that the region is somehow bigger than it was ten years ago and reserves the
right to alter their maps without prior notice. Mr. Holman's solution is to
extend Southern Appalachia "so that it is seen as a part of the whole southern Piedmont. . . . " (Holman 78). To do this, however, would be to lose all
chance of understanding Appalachia by the logical method of setting it apart
from everywhere which definitely is *not* Appalachia. And that, as far as I am
concerned, includes the southern Piedmont. Messrs. Higgs and Manning, on
the other hand, despair of ever resolving the matter: "What is Appalachian
literature? It is the literature of Appalachia. What is Appalachia? Who
knows? We do not profess to have definitive answers. We are inclined to
agree with Lawrence Thompson . . . that Appalachia is a 'state of mind'; and
sometimes sadly we are inclined to agree with Wright Morris . . . that all the
regions are dead" (Higgs and Manning, "More on Appalachian Literature"
96). The foregoing hardly sounds like the position of men who would put
together an excessively "reductive" anthology, as Mr. Holman charges. It is
rather a philosophy which would lead them, in their loyalty to their home
region, to be less reductive and restrictive than they should be if their anthology were to be reserved for the work of writers clearly "Appalachian"
and thus to be the most precise instrument possible for the discovery of just
what Appalachian literature really is.

The best means of dispelling the confusion is to adopt something akin to the
eighteenth century's sense of the essential identity of things. We cannot say
where the edges of Southern Appalachia are, but we know very well the location
of its center: the mountains. And we obscure the canon and character of Appalachian literature by just so much as we diverge from the assumption that it is
writing about the southern mountains or writing which can plainly be shown to
bear the impress of those mountains and the kinds of life they have nurtured.

By this standard, for instance, James Agee's *A Death in the Family* is not in
any important respect "Appalachian," though it is easy to see how highland
scholars would be tempted by its stature to annex it as such. But to view it, a
book preponderantly about a household of urban Catholics, as an example of
Appalachian fiction will teach us nothing about the novel or the tradition

either. In contrast, the Sut Lovingood yarns of Agee's fellow Knoxvillian George Washington Harris, mainly narrated and populated by mountain characters and founded on situations growing out of the distinctive life beyond the town limits, are impeccably mountain in substance. To a degree (but only to a degree), the same is true of Thomas Wolfe. Though it would not likely occur to a flatlander to call Wolfe an "Appalachian" novelist, some parts of his books justify the designation under the criteria I have offered. I doubt, however, that there is much more to be gained from approaching him in this context than has now been presented in "Thomas Wolfe's Mountain Gloom and Glory" by Ruel E. Foster,[3] who teaches at the University of West Virginia. Nor does the fact that Samuel Clemens was "conceived in East Tennessee," as the editors of *Voices from the Hills* remind us (101), supply an Appalachian connection for Mark Twain. Again, one must suspect that this confusion of Clemens the fetus with Mark Twain the Great American Author proceeds from their patriotic desire to find another star for the crown of mountain letters.

What can we realistically expect to be accomplished by the establishment of Appalachian literature as an object of study? The unearthing of neglected masters and masterpieces would put the question beyond argument, but such estimable "undiscovered" fiction as does exist—notably James Still's *River of Earth* and Harriette Arnow's *The Dollmaker*—is scarcely on a par with that of Wolfe or perhaps even Harris, both of whom have regularly found their way into American literature courses without special benefit of regional puffery. In short, the Appalachian writers most deserving of recognition already have it.

Another sort of objective would be that stated in the introduction to the Higgs and Manning collection: "We seek to illustrate the wide range of images (of mountain people) in the hope that the recognition of this diversity will lead to a better understanding of the southern mountaineer and his native land, both on the part of himself and others." The main obstacle here, of course, is an abiding one in a great deal of regional writing still deeply tinged with local color: the tendency of characterization to run to stereotypes. It is easy enough to decry the stock figures in Murfree and Fox, those favorite whipping-persons for advocates of truer portrayals of *homo montanus*; yet even books which enjoy a substantially higher reputation than Murfree's and Fox's for fidelity to life are peopled with major characters whose creation has clearly been by formula. For example, the bestial Doke Odom of Anne W. Armstrong's *This Day and Time* is merely a latter-day version of the "lubbers" whose squalid inertia so disgusted William Byrd and who served as the prototype for the persistently negative image of the "hillbilly." Only less blatantly a conventional type is Ivy Ingoldsby, Armstrong's protagonist. Imbued with the humble pride of primitive democracy and a measure of moral strength so great as to make her seem single-handedly responsible for keeping her neighbors from perdition, Ivy is everything we would like not just the mountaineer to be, but ourselves as well. She is as angelic as Doke is diabolical, and no amount of circumstantial realism can lend either sufficient life to make them useful in effecting a "better understanding" of the people they supposedly represent. The very centrifugal extremes which they embody are unfortunately typical, however, so that the "range of images" is anchored at both ends by palpable untruths, and the "real" mountaineer, if there is one, remains lost somewhere in between.

It may strike some as perversely self-contradictory that I both complain about the predominance of stereotypes in Appalachian fiction and reject as "un-Appalachian" such works as *A Death in the Family*. My basis for the exclusion, however, is not merely that Agee's book avoids the very stock figures and situations which deaden so much of the belletristic writing about the southern mountains: such reasoning would be at best fallacious and at worst hypocritical. I insist, rather, that the essential Appalachia is no more to be found in downtown Knoxville than under John Fox's lonesome pine. And if, as I was recently told, the value of including urban novels in courses on Appalachian literature is to demonstrate that Appalachians are "like other people," I can only ask again, what is the point of isolating the literature by and about them as a distinct body of writing?

There is in the fiction a veritable Cult of the Mountain Female, possibly stemming from a perception of the Southern Highlands as a place where a form of the old frontier life goes on and which thus still harbors a favorite mythic American figure, the Pioneer Woman. A potentially powerful character in gifted hands, she is nevertheless only a two-dimensional cliché in those of the vast majority of writers, whether of the Appalachian school or not. On balance, her availability as a type has been more a curse than a blessing to the cause of mountain literature insofar as its proper aesthetic calls for the honest portrayal of human beings; for simply to take her as found—and to beset her with all the trials necessary for the display of her endurance—is to commit oneself to melodrama. Even competent artists, as Wilma Dykeman's *The Tall Woman* illustrates, succumb to the lure of her imposing outlines only to bring forth a sort of high-altitude *Perils of Pauline*. Indeed, until Arnow packs her off to Detroit, Gertie Nevels herself manifests all the predictable qualities of the mountain superwoman, freeing mired automobiles by main force and performing tracheotomies with hunting knives.

A final implicit hazard of Appalachian fiction—one cautioned against in Robert Penn Warren's "Some Don'ts for Literary Regionalists," which Higgs and Manning conscientiously include in their anthology—glares out from Mildred Haun's "Melungeon-Colored" (237–51). The story's worst defect is not that its plot hinges dubiously on a woman's superstitious refusal to tell a secret whose revelation would have saved two lives. Its broader failing grows instead from Haun's hyperawareness of the folk-milieu of her tale, so strong a consciousness of cultural idiosyncrasy as to make the narrative seem only a pretext for its catalogue of bad-luck signs and laboriously quaint expressions (on the order of "I made up my mind that I wasn't going to worry over a swinging foot-log till I was sure I would have to cross one"). Such stuff is "touristic regionalism," in Warren's phrase, and, while Haun's strain of it is admittedly extreme, one need only consider the literate mountaineer's fascination with the folkways of his people to understand why the mountaineer-as-writer (or, far worse, his sojourning cousin from the city) is constantly susceptible to overdoing them in print.

Anyone intending to write seriously about the Southern Appalachians would do well to study Beulah Childers's "Sairy and the Young'uns" (171–89). Unlike the generality of rustic caricatures who feud and fiddle their way to a richly merited oblivion, Childers's characters are people, mountain people, judging from their speech and habits, but most importantly just *people.* Where they live is entirely subordinate to their humanity, and the story in which they have their existence is a lesson in the literary art of suggesting the general through the particular. Virtually all fiction, as has no doubt been observed more often than necessary, is in some sense regional, for action has to be set somewhere. The writer's supreme challenge is to search out and treat human universals in terms of the limited area with which he is intimately familiar. Childers's presentation of the varying reactions of the Hale family to the coming of Sairy Pendergrast and her brood of preacher's kids is a study in the essence of human relationships and an affirmation of the influences lives have upon other lives in all times and places. But precisely because it is not distracted by the anomalies of the culture it depicts, the story is sadly an extraordinary one.

If recent Appalachian fiction has gravitated in the direction of realism, the poetry has remained unabashedly romantic, though the mode of its romanticism has broadened since the days of Jesse Stuart's effusions on the Kentucky landscape. At its thematic heart is the obsession with mutability: topographical, cultural, and personal. It is demonstrably possible to write good poetry about sad changes in the life of the region. Jim Wayne Miller does it in "Small Farms Disappearing in Tennessee" (350–51) by facing the inevitable with graceful humor instead of righteous anger and avoiding the polemical tone that can turn a sonnet into a rhyming editorial. One cannot escape a sense of falseness, however, when one hears Lee Pennington preach natural primitivism in "Robert Williams Sings His Song" (333), then resort to the vocabulary of the U.S. Department of Health, Education, and Welfare for "In the Field":

> Given equal opportunity
> And equal needs,
> Victory always comes
> To the fighting weeds.

The sheer number of cemetery poems (by such relatively good poets as Louise McNeill as well as some bad ones) suggests that the "mountain muse" is more given over to a funereal state of mind than is artistically or perhaps psychologically wise. To be sure, we have had our Graveyard Schools of verse before and can weather another if we must. We have even seen attempts to ground new literature on the theme of cultural evanescence—through the "dying Indian" and "loss of Eden" motifs, for instance. But it remains my opinion that one Philip Freneau was plenty.

The analogy between the present literary atmosphere of the Southern Highlands and that of America's Early National period is, I think, a legitimate and revealing one. However worthy an objective it may be to honor and adorn one's homeland before a misapprehending world, zeal may be a positive impediment to the generation of good writing, as the turgid epics of the 1780s reflect. Today Appalachia finds herself in a limbo between the passing of the oral culture which has been her chief glory in the past, and the firm establishment of the written one that she understands the modern world to require and which her loyal sons and daughters are hell-bent to create. They may do it in time if they can bring themselves to stop trying so hard. For the moment, though, the most formidable question with which the promoters of Appalachian literature must wrestle is not that of how distinguishable it is, but rather how distinguished.

Notes

1. Robert J. Higgs and Ambrose N. Manning, eds., *Voices from the Hills* (New York: Frederick Ungar, 1975). Hereafter, I cite references to this anthology parenthetically.
2. C. Hugh Holman, "Appalachian Literature?" *Appalachian Journal* 4 (Autumn 1976): 73–79. The response of the editors appeared in the succeeding issue: Robert J. Higgs and Ambrose N. Manning, "More on Appalachian Literature," *Appalachian Journal* 4 (Winter 1977): 93–98.
3. Ruel E. Foster, "Thomas Wolfe's Mountain Gloom and Glory," *American Literature* 44 (Jan. 1973): 638–47.

Albert Stewart

An East Kentuckian, Albert Stewart is the founding editor of *Appalachian Heritage* and the founder of the Appalachian Writers Workshop at the Hindman Settlement School. Students of Appalachia everywhere owe Albert Stewart a debt of gratitude for the contributions he has made as a poet, teacher, editor, and student of the region. His major collection is *The Untoward Hills* (1962).

Appalachian Studies (1)

For Leisa
(I hain't sugar ner spice ner nobody's honey.)
Here comes Leisa Francisco
With eyes bright as a bird's
Down from Pike County, talkin Appalachian
Saying *over thare* and *naow whurr?*
Saying *down-air* and *up-air*
And jabbing with Appalachian banter:
I kum to git married. Are you ready?
And telling tales of an Appalachian grandmaw
Superstitions and charms and cures
Until I wonder if she's a good witch
A magical grandmother in disguise
And I say: H'lo, Grandmaw Leisa.

How musical and un-Appalachian her name.
How lilting and Appalachian her ways.
How wonderful and mysterious her origin.

(Grandpaw had a rooster could talk, but nobody but
grandpaw knowed what he said. And he wudin tell.)

From *Appalachian Heritage,* Spring 1973, © *Appalachian Heritage*/Berea College. Reprinted by permission of the author and publisher.

Allison Ensor

Allison Ensor is a professor in the Department of English at the University of Tennessee at Knoxville. A native of Cookeville, Tennessee, he graduated from Tennessee Tech and took an M.A. at UTK and a Ph.D. at Indiana University.

Most of his scholarly writing has concerned Mark Twain, especially his book *Mark Twain and the Bible* (1969), and his Norton Critical Edition of Twain's *A Connecticut Yankee in King Arthur's Court* (1982). He has also published articles on Henry David Thoreau, Wallace Stevens, Flannery O'Connor, and the nineteenth-century Tennessee novelists and short-story writers Mary Noailles Murfree and Sarah Barnwell Elliott.. His current long-term project involves Mark Twain's interest in music and use of it in his writings.

American Realism and the Case for Appalachian Literature

The realistic movement in American literature followed on the heels of the romantic movement, as America again fell in line behind England and the continent of Europe. Realism sought to reproduce scene and character accurately and objectively. It was an attempt to show the world as it really is, not as we might like it to be. It was, as William Dean Howells said, "nothing more and nothing less than the truthful treatment of material . . ." (38). Art and literature, said Howells, are expressions of life and should not be judged by any test other than their fidelity to it. A writer should "report the phrase and carriage of every-day life" and try "to tell just how he has heard men talk and seen them look . . ." (12). Over and over Howells declared that literature should emphasize the "simple, natural and honest" (13) rather than the ideal, the heroic, the impassioned, the self-devoted, the adventureful. "Fidelity to experience and probability of motive," he said, "are essential conditions of a great imaginative literature" (15).

So there was to be no more fantasy or heroic derring-do. Literature was going to show what people were really like and how they really thought and talked and acted. The characters of novels and short stories were going to be real people, not allegorized or generalized figures. And they weren't going to be superhuman, either. There would be no more Natty Bumppo or Beatrice Rappaccini or Roderick Usher. Now it would be Silas Lapham, Editha, John Marcher, and Huckleberry Finn.

The three great realistic writers—so we always say—were Mark Twain, William Dean Howells, and Henry James. The great books of the realistic movement in America have usually been designated as *Adventures of Huckleberry*

Printed by permission of the author.

Finn, The Rise of Silas Lapham, and whatever James novel you wish to name—
Portrait of a Lady, The Ambassadors, The Golden Bowl, The Wings of the Dove.

What I have said so far leaves out Appalachia. What I have outlined is very much the way I was taught. Although I attended elementary school, high school, and college in one of the Appalachian counties of Tennessee, I heard virtually no indication from my teachers that the literature—or the history or culture—of Appalachia was of any importance at all.

Let me give the matter a little perspective. For years American colleges did not teach American literature. What was there to teach? There it was; one simply had to read it. Chaucer needed to be explained, Shakespeare needed to be explained, Milton needed to be explained—but surely not Poe or Hawthorne or Whitman and certainly not Mark Twain. Eventually American literature became an established part of the curriculum, though when it did, little attention was paid to the literature of the South. I think Flannery O'Connor's testimony concerning her experience at Georgia State College for Women (GSCW) is worth quoting:

> When I went to college twenty years ago, nobody mentioned any good Southern writers to me later than Joel Chandler Harris. . . . As far as I knew, the heroes of Hawthorne and Melville and James and Crane and Hemingway were balanced on the Southern side by Br'er Rabbit—an animal who can always hold up his end of the stick, in equal company, but here too much was being expected of him. (55–56)

In the forty-five or so years since O'Connor attended GSCW, southern literature has come into its own. Every national anthology includes selections from such writers as Faulkner, Tennessee Williams, the Fugitives and Agrarians, Eudora Welty, and Flannery O'Connor herself. Appalachian literature, on the other hand, is all too often neglected and ignored.

There has been a real need, I think, to emphasize more fully the fact that Appalachia has produced and is producing a significant body of literature. Much has been said recently concerning the "canon" of American literature. Most discussions have called for "opening the canon" to allow a greater representation of women, blacks, and other special groups within this country. If the canon is to be opened to Appalachia as well, then it seems appropriate that we deal with the way in which Appalachia participated in the great literary movements which swept the United States during the nineteenth century and which continue to make themselves felt today.

I need first to raise the question: when does American realism begin? Does it begin with Twain, Howells, and James? If so, then its starting date would seem to be somewhere in the 1870s, with the most significant works coming in the 1880s and in the decade or so following that time.

To my mind, however, American literary realism begins with the southern frontier humor of the early to middle nineteenth century. And although many of the major writers of this genre (Thomas Bangs Thorpe, A. B. Longstreet,

Johnson Jones Hooper, William Tappan Thompson) had no connection with Appalachia, there were at least two who did. The first of these, Davy Crockett, I will simply mention, as he soon left East Tennessee for parts west.

Much more significant for my purpose is George Washington Harris, the creator of Sut Lovingood. Harris, a native of Pennsylvania, came south while still a child and settled with his half-brother at Knoxville. He continued living in East Tennessee until shortly before the Civil War, when he moved to Nashville. The Sut Lovingood yarns appeared in Tennessee newspapers and in various papers around the country for a couple of decades prior to their publication in book form in New York in 1867. It is surely worth noting that Mark Twain was attracted by Harris's book and made favorable mention of it in one of his columns for the San Francisco *Alta California.* "The book abounds in humor," Twain reported, "and is said to represent the Tennessee dialect [as if there were only one] correctly." "It will sell well in the West," he predicted, "but the Eastern people will call it coarse and possibly taboo it" (*Travels* 221). Not only the "Eastern people" but a good many respectable southern people wanted to "taboo" the book as well, for the realism of its language, its sexual innuendoes, and its violent action were unacceptable to the Victorian sensibilities of the time.

Some of the best of the Sut Lovingood pieces, most of which are set in extreme southeastern Tennessee (the Copper Basin near Ducktown and Copperhill), are now included in the national anthologies, though I'm not sure how many teachers assign them. Students, especially those outside the South, have a hard time reading the Harris dialect, because he chose to alter the spelling of almost every word spoken by Sut. A fight seldom appears as "fight" but rather as "fite." To Harris, the latter is much truer to what his characters would really say. The characters' actions and thoughts—never any too genteel— also represent what Harris believes such people might really do and think— though he admittedly overemphasizes violence and suffering.

Every Sut story comes to us as an overheard conversation between Sut and "George," a city-oriented man who speaks standard English and who is sometimes as puzzled as we as to the meaning of some of Sut's phrasing. For instance, at the beginning of "Mrs. Yardley's Quilting," George's question as to what Sut has been doing receives the reply, "Helpin tu salt ole Missis Yardley down" (114). "What do you mean by that?" George asks, and Sut explains a bit further: "Fixin her fur rotten cumfurtably, kiverin her up wif sile, tu keep the buzzards frum cheatin the wurms." By now George has understood—even if we haven't— and he exclaims, "Oh, you have been helping to bury a woman." Sut confirms this and then comments on the contrast between George's and his own style: "That's hit, by golly! Now why the devil can't I 'splain myself like yu? I ladles out my words at random, like a calf kickin at yaller-jackids; yu jis' rolls em out tu the pint, like a feller a-layin bricks—every one fits" (114). Sut usually begins telling George about some recent adventure, ordinarily one involving plenty of fun, fighting, cursing, and general consternation, very likely with a hint of sex thrown in, all narrated in Sut's inimitable fashion.

As an example I will cite one of my favorite Sut stories, "Parson John Bullen's Lizards," in which Sut takes revenge upon a hypocritical backcountry preacher by sending "seven ur eight big pot-bellied lizzards" (54) up the parson's britches leg while he is holding forth at an outdoor meeting on the appropriate topic of "Hell-sarpents." When he first begins to feel the lizzards, Bullen slaps and scratches at them and then rubs himself against the pulpit. I'll let Sut take it from there:

> About this time, one ove my lizzards, scared an' hurt by all this poundin' an' feelin, an' scratchin, popp'd out his head frum the passun's shut collar, an' his ole brown naik, an' wer a-surveyin the crowd, when ole Bullin struck at 'im, jis' too late, fur he'd dodged back agin. The hell desarvin ole raskil's speech now cum tu 'im, an' sez he, "Pray fur me brethren an' sisteren, fur I is a-rastilin wif the great inimy rite now!" (55)

As the lizards proceed with their work, the parson begins to shed his clothes and then to run through the crowd nude, though not before crying out: "Brethren, brethren, take keer ove yerselves, the Hell-sarpints *hes got me!*" (56).

Noting that at Bullen's next appearance there were no women on hand to hear him, Sut comments to George: "Passuns ginerly hev a pow'ful strong holt on wimen; but, hoss, I tell yu thar ain't meny ove em kin run stark nakid over an' thru a crowd ove three hundred wimen an' not injure thar karacters *sum*. Enyhow, hits a kind ove show they'd ruther see one at a time, an' pick the passun at that." (57) Harris shocked some readers and delighted others with his tales, or "yarns," which surely contained some of the most realistic Appalachian writing of the entire nineteenth century.

One of the next writers after Harris to depict Appalachia in fiction was one who had never lived or traveled in Appalachia; what he knew of the region he had heard at second hand. I mention him chiefly because his stature as a writer surpasses that of anyone else who has written about Appalachia. The opening chapters of Mark Twain's novel *The Gilded Age* (1873), written in collaboration with Charles Dudley Warner, are set in what he calls "the Knobs of East Tennessee" (17; ch. 1) in the fictional village of "Obedstown." In their story of Squire Hawkins and his purchase of 75,000 acres of land in the Cumberland Mountains, these chapters reflect the experience of Twain's father and mother, who lived in Fentress County, Tennessee, for about ten years prior to their move to Missouri in 1835. Twain's portrait is anything but flattering, emphasizing as it does the laziness, ignorance, and poverty of the people of that area. The view of outsiders is summed up in Twain's observation that the place "had a reputation like Nazareth, as far as turning out any good thing was concerned" (17; ch. 1; cf. John 1:46).

I will also mention an earlier, ostensibly Appalachian piece by Mark Twain, "Journalism in Tennessee" (1869). Since the narrator is employed by a newspaper called the *Morning Glory and Johnson County War-Whoop*, the story apparently is set in Johnson County, though my guess is that Twain knew virtually nothing about the real Johnson County, Tennessee. The kind of vigorous journalism he depicts doesn't sound notably different from what he calls "Arkansas journalism" in *A Connecticut Yankee in King Arthur's Court.*

I studied a good deal about Mark Twain in my Tennessee schooling, but in all the discussions of *Tom Sawyer* and *Huckleberry Finn,* I do not remember that any teacher ever told us that Twain had written about our state or that his parents had once lived no more than twenty-five miles from my school, in the town of Gainesboro, Tennessee, and afterwards in Jamestown. Shouldn't teachers mention such local angles? I think they should.

Some scholars have recently sought the origins of American realism in the local color story which flourished so widely for several decades following the Civil War. It seemed as if every distinctive (I hesitate to say "peculiar") region of the country soon developed its store of local color writers, and Appalachia was among them. It was, in fact, at this point that the region made its first significant appearance on the literary map.

Mary Noailles Murfree, who was known to her contemporaries by her masculine pseudonym "Charles Egbert Craddock," was not the best qualified person to interpret the Tennessee mountains realistically to the readers of the *Atlantic Monthly* or to those who would buy the many novels and short story collections she published, usually in Boston. She was anything but a mountain woman, having been born into a prominent Middle Tennessee family. The Murfrees of Murfreesboro were Episcopalians and possessed sufficient wealth that they could send their daughter to Philadelphia to study at the Chegary Institute. Murfree did have some acquaintance with such mountain locales as Beersheba Springs and Montvale Springs, then fashionable Tennessee "watering places." Her most frequently reprinted story, "The Harnt That Walks Chilhowee" takes place near the latter.

I will not try to make a case for Murfree as an outstanding Appalachian realist. She probably didn't know enough to be thoroughly realistic in her portrayal of the mountain people, and if she had the knowledge, her genteel sensibility might have prevented her from using it. And then there is her inflated, florid, descriptive style, which contrasts so radically with the speech of her characters. In many ways she is a perfect example of what Appalachian realism is not.

Nevertheless, I do find in a story such as "Drifting Down Lost Creek" some elements of realism. Evander Price's rejection of the mountains and his eager embracing of technology is surely realistic. Riding in a railroad car for the first time in his life, he exclaims, "Ef this ain't the glory o' God revealed in the work o' man, what is?" (66). Set to work at a forge in the prison to which he has been unjustly sent, he is delighted and rejects his former life. A fellow inmate gives this report on him: "He war plumb welded ter his work—he sets more store by metal than by grace. He 'lowed ter me ez he wouldn't hev missed bein' thar fur nuthin'! 'Vander air a powerful cur'ous critter: he 'lowed ter me ez one year in the forge at the Pen war wuth a hundred years in the mountings ter him" (67).

Hired out to an iron works, Evander experiences a similar ecstasy: "He 'lowed ez he'd ruther see that thar big shed an' the red hot puddler's balls atrundlin' about, an' all the wheels a-whurlin', an' the big shears a-bitin' the metal ez nip, an' the tremenjious hammer a-poundin' away, an' all the dark night around split with lines o' fire, than to see the hills o' heaven!" (68)

During the time Evander is in prison, his sweetheart Cynthia Ware keeps working for his freedom, eventually presenting a clemency petition to the governor of Tennessee on the day he visits the county seat, Sparta. The romantic ending to the story of female courage and sacrifice—as well as wronged male innocence—would be a joyful reunion of the pair after Evander's release from prison, followed by their living happily ever after, somewhere in the hills of eastern White County, where Evander would take up moonshining and forget all about the industrial revolution. But Murfree's ending is strikingly realistic: the ungrateful Evander never even thinks to inquire as to the source of his pardon, marries someone else, and does not return to the mountains for the next ten years.

I wonder how many high-school students in White County, Tennessee, ever know that their county was the setting for a story by a nationally known writer, published in what was then America's most prestigious literary journal, the *Atlantic Monthly*. I grew up in an adjacent county with the impression that no one had ever written about our place and our people.

Murfree was by far the best known but certainly not the only nineteenth-century fiction writer presenting Appalachian characters and scenes. Will Allen Dromgoole was also a Tennesseean, also a woman with a masculine name—though in this case her own, also a writer of novels and short stories which she published in Boston and Philadelphia. It must be said, though, that Dromgoole was far too devoted to sentimentality and moralizing to impress us very much as a realistic writer, even when her central character is a historical figure such as Governor Robert Love Taylor in her story "Fiddling His Way to Fame." A third Tennessee woman local color writer, Sarah Barnwell Elliott, who lived at Sewanee most of her life, has received a good deal of praise for her portraits of mountain life in such novels as *Jerry* (1891) and *The Durket "Sperret"* (1898). Part of her achievement was to lead writers away from the excess of sentimentality which too often permeated the contemporary fiction about the southern mountaineer.

One of the clearest examples of early twentieth-century Appalachian realism is a little-known but nevertheless significant novel, Anne W. Armstrong's *This Day and Time* (1930). In his preface to a reprinted edition, David McClellan informs the reader that his maternal grandmother burned her copy of the book because it was too realistic—or, as he says, "its realism amounted to obscenity" (xvi). He reports that the novel was similarly treated in other families of East Tennessee as well. It was a kind of "underground classic," he says—a term which could accurately be applied to the much earlier yarns of Sut Lovingood. Realism obviously was not in great demand in Tennessee at that time, and readers were uncomfortable that Armstrong set out to portray the life of Tennessee mountaineers in its ugliness as well as its beauty.

A small sample of the novel's frankness may be seen in this paragraph about Ivy Ingoldsby, who was married at sixteen and then deserted by her husband shortly before their child was born: "'There hain't livin' man kin say I've give in to him, an' him speak truth,' she reflected now, in a matter-of-fact vein, but with grim satisfaction. 'Many's the one, sence Jim left, has named hit to me— good as named hit. But one thing's certain an' shore, Jim can't put no name o' whore on me ef he comes'" (41). (None of Murfree's characters ever talked like that—or even thought about sex, as far as the reader can tell.)

Still stronger is this conversation between Ivy and a Miss Dodd, about the sexual activities of one Shell Henson: "Shell, he's bigged Pernie, an' Pernie, she named it to him they orter marry, an' he denied her. But Pernie, she put son of a bitch on Shell, an' won't no man stand fer that" (67).

Though these examples may scarcely disturb us now, the genteel Tennessee readers of sixty years ago found them hard to accept. But however objectionable the novel may have seemed, many events portrayed in it would be familiar to anyone who knows rural Tennessee life: molasses making, churning butter, serving a big dinner, churchgoing, courting, gossiping. And surely many readers would have approved the way in which Ivy, the central character, affirms her love of the way of life she knows when she responds to a visiting senator who has spoken of the "tragically monotonous lives" of those living in the mountains and argued that they would be better off in the mill towns: "Law, Senator . . . I hain't never plowed, but I'ud a heap ruther to hoe an' to clear the filth off o' new ground as to work in ary factory on earth! . . . I couldn't never be satisfied in no town on earth. . . . Seems like nothin' don't never happen in town, like here" (167).

Ivy knows that life is for most people a mixed blessing. "Looks like there's so much to delight a body," she muses, "but oh, Lord, why does folks have to suffer so in this life?" (204). But in spite of all that happens to her, Ivy is still able to say to her son in the last sentence of the novel, "Law, Enoch, people is so good, hain't they?" (269). I believe that in Ivy Ingoldsby we have one of the earliest realistic portraits of an Appalachian woman.

A slightly later Appalachian writer was Mildred Haun, who grew up in Cocke County and used her county's ballads and songs as the material for her M.A. thesis, written under the direction of Donald Davidson at Vanderbilt in 1937. Haun's chief published contribution to Appalachian literature came in the form of her collection *The Hawk's Done Gone* (1941).

This collection of interrelated stories, quite realistic in some ways, has as its chief figure Mary Dorthula White Kanipe of Cocke County, Tennessee, who has, she tells us, "been Granny-woman to every youngon born in this district for nigh sixty years now" (7). "I've tied the navel cords of all the saints and sinners that have seen their first daylight in Hoot Owl District," she says, adding, "They all have bellies about alike. There's not much difference" (7). For eleven chapters she tells us the story of the various members of her family, with the twelfth chapter presenting her own story of how, at the age of fifteen, she became the lover of a Confederate soldier, bearing him an illegitimate son years before she married Ad Kanipe. (Nothing like that ever happened to the heroine of a Mary Noailles Murfree story.) Mary Dorthula lived into her nineties, finally dying in fall 1939, so that the last chapter is left to be told by her daughter Amy.

Like Murfree and the other local color writers, Haun worked into her stories much of the language, songs, customs, and superstitions of her place and time, but she is strikingly different from them in her realistic treatment of sex and violence. She is also more experimental in technique, as witness the moving final chapter of Mary Dorthula's narration, where, in a stream of consciousness, her thoughts keep moving back and forth between Ad and Linus Kanipe's selling her things to antique hunters and those nine nights during the Civil War when she and Charles were lovers. "That trundle bed," she says, "had been a part of every speck of bliss I ever had" (175).

The work of Harriette Simpson Arnow was not well known to most readers until the appearance of *The Dollmaker* in 1954, and many did not learn of the book until the 1984 television production starring Jane Fonda as Gertie Nevels. Gertie is a tough, strong-willed Kentucky hill-country woman who somehow finds the strength to cope with a husband, children, and conditions in the Detroit to which the Nevels—like so many from Appalachia— moved in hopes of finding better jobs and better pay. The television adapters could not resist giving Gertie's story the ending they believed it should have— i.e., a return to her native hills—though in the novel Gertie stays on in Michigan, as did Harriette Arnow. I think too that Gertie Nevels probably was not quite so attractive as Jane Fonda. But if the television version of *The Dollmaker* has a bit of romanticism in it, there are certainly many realistic elements in the novel, and one feels that here is a real story of an Appalachian woman whose experiences must have paralleled those of many women of that time.

I should say too that, although *The Doll Maker* is the only Arnow novel known to the general public, she wrote several others set entirely in Appalachia which are also significant, especially *Hunter's Horn* (1949), which takes place in the area of the Big South Fork of the Cumberland and involves Nunn Ballew's passionate pursuit of a wily red fox named King Devil. Though his obsession with hunting down and killing the fox will certainly remind readers of mythic hunts for such creatures as Melville's whale and Faulkner's bear, there is a good deal of realism in the novel's focus on the hardship and deprivation which Ballew's consuming desire brings to his wife and children. For all his perversity, though, Ballew does feel some guilt over what he has done to his family, and that is to his credit.

Arnow sprinkles her story with ample profanity and obscenity of the kind never used in Appalachian fiction until more recent times, and is sometimes so graphic in her descriptions, especially of childbirth, that she drew criticism from the reviewers of the late 1940s. Particularly objectionable to some was the scene in which Lureenie Cramer, a neighbor of the Ballews, dies in childbirth while her husband is away and while her father-in-law insists that to call in a doctor from town would be against the Bible (referring to the curse laid upon Eve, I suppose)—and too expensive, which is probably the more significant consideration. One long sentence from that passage will suffice:

> Suse [Nunn Ballew's daughter] had seen sick people and dead people
> and people in pain, but never a face like Lureenie's; it no more than the
> scream seemed to belong to Lureenie or have anything to do with the
> mounded belly under the dirty quilt or the blood on Sue Annie's apron or
> with anything that had ever been or would be again; among all the big
> people and framed in the masses of red-gold tangled hair, it seemed little,
> no bigger than a child's face, but the eyes staring straight up were not a
> child's eyes nor Lureenie's eyes as she remembered them. (390)

A few pages later, the distraught Suse curses Lureenie's father-in-law, her own
father, God, Christ, and the world. When Nunn Ballew protests that he has
done the best he could by her and her mother, Suse lashes out verbally at him:
"Aw, hell. You've always done th best you could to keep her in th family way.
An you do get worried when she ain't able to work an wait on you. . . . As fer
me, you'll marry me off to some little shaved-tail son of a bitch when th rest
gets big enough to work. You've not got money to keep me in shoes now" (394).

Nunn objects that he intends to send her to high school, but she says, "High
school, hell! You'll never have enough to send me in decent clothes to th post
office, let alone high school. You're always aimen; never finish nothen—" (394).
Hunter's Horn is a notably realistic treatment not only of fox hunts in the Kentucky hills but also of relationships between people, of what Faulkner called "the
human heart in conflict."

Some mention should of course be made of the most recent Appalachian
writers. I am sure that every reader has his or her favorites: one of mine happens to be Lee Smith, a native of southwestern Virginia who is now living in
distinctly un-Appalachian Chapel Hill and teaching at North Carolina State
University. In such novels as *Oral History* (1983), *Family Linen* (1985), and
more recently in *Fair and Tender Ladies* (1988) and *The Devil's Dream* (1992),
she chronicles the lives and concerns of people living in the mountains of
southern Virginia, both past and present. Part of Smith's concern has been
to be very realistic in her approach. In an interview in Richmond's *Style
Weekly*, Smith stated her desire to "write a book about an ordinary woman's
ordinary life," adding that she was "so tired of books that are not about the
way we really live" (Cleary 27). "Most of us don't really do anything much,"
she adds, "but everyone's life is just full of drama and fine feeling and sentiment and faith" (Cleary 27).

As Smith sees it, her southwestern Virginia heroine Ivy Rowe "lived as full a
life as it is possible to live" (Cleary 27)—a verdict which would seem ludicrous to
the inhabitants of New York, and perhaps of Chapel Hill and Richmond as well,
since Ivy never leaves the section of southwestern Virginia in which she lives.
(There is a striking resemblance at this point between her and Anne Armstrong's
Ivy Ingoldsby.) In her first letter, Ivy, then a teenager, writes: "I have nare seed
the ocean nor has anyone I know seed it althogh Daddy has been to the city too,
he did not like it with bad water and no air and no mountains like Bethel Mountain yonder, Daddy says he needs a mountain to rest his eyes aginst" (11).

Fair and Tender Ladies represents a resurrection of the epistolary novel. All of the letters are written by Ivy Rowe over a span of several decades, from World War I to the 1970s, though not all the letters were sent and some are apparently never received. As the story of Ivy's life from teenager to old woman unfolds, we hear much about the traditional stories and the songs of Appalachia as well as the harsher realities of life in the mountains. Coal mining, for instance, makes its appearance when Ivy writes about John Reno:

> He is a agent for one of them big coal companys that is bying up land all around here. It seems crazy to me as they is not even a railroad yet . . . so how culd you mine the coal? But Mister Reno is bying up coal land rigt and left, and everbody is getting rich! For *nothing* it seems, as he is not going to do a thing with it nor bother them that lives ther in any way. So this is free monney, it is like picking monney offen a monney tree. (94)

The naiveté expressed here is painful to read, representing as it does the illusion and short-sightedness of so many who failed to see what was to follow the sale of land and of mineral rights to outsiders: the coming of the railroads and the big coal companies, the destruction of the environment, the unsafe working conditions in the mines. Lee Smith gets a good deal of that in; all too soon Ivy reports that

> they are laying men off left and right, and working part weeks, and taking off shifts, and people don't know what to do with themselves. They have given up their land, those hardscrabble places we all came from, and they have noplace to go back to. They have lived here so long they have forgot how to garden anyway, or put up food, or trade for goods, or anything about how they used to live. So they have got nothing now. They have got nothing but what they owe to the company which is so much they will never pay it off. (159)

A 1926 mine disaster results in the death of nineteen men, and there is a strike, with the company bringing in what Ivy calls "thugs . . . with Gatling guns to protect the scabs" (185).

But coal mining is not the focus of Lee Smith's book. It is just one element of the life of the mountains she records in the novel. She is most concerned with the life of Ivy Rowe, and she has Ivy tell us everything. Like Mildred Haun's Mary Dorthula White, Ivy becomes pregnant by a man she knows only briefly; she then goes on to marry and have several children by another man, Oakley Fox, a survivor of the mine explosion. Ivy is not always faithful to Oakley, either. For a time she goes off and lives with a bee man with the unlikely name of Honey Breeding, but eventually she returns to her husband. "Life seems contrary to me, as contrary as I am," she says, offering a bit of her philosophy. "I feel like you never say what you ought to, nor do as you should, and then it is too late. It is all over. I have spent half of my life wanting and the other half grieving, and most often I have been wanting and grieving the same thing. There has been precious little inbetween" (275).

The plight of the coal miner, touched on by Lee Smith, becomes the central subject of Denise Giardina's *Storming Heaven* (1988). The novel is set in the coalfields along the border of West Virginia and Kentucky and is, as I see it, a kind of *Grapes of Wrath* transferred to Appalachia. Harsher, darker, and I suppose more realistic than Lee Smith's books, *Storming Heaven* is an angry, pro-labor, pro-union novel which focuses on the plight of those who lost their land to the big coal companies, on the miners who worked under extremely difficult and hazardous conditions, and on the struggle to organize the men as members of the United Mine Workers. The novel's climactic event is the "battle of Blair Mountain," in which U.S. Army troops are sent by President Harding to put down a rebellion by the miners. Giardina, a native of West Virginia, employs four narrators in a manner slightly reminiscent of Lee Smith's *Oral History,* though both probably derive from Faulkner's *As I Lay Dying.* The style, however, is far more straightforward and clear than Faulkner's. An "Afterword," dated 1987, ends with the sentence, "The companies still own the land" (312). One of the major goals of the period sixty-five years earlier had been to get the land back into the hands of the families who originally owned it. *Storming Heaven* is not a pleasant book to read, and it is not intended to be. The Appalachian songs and stories which obviously delight Lee Smith have some place here, but Giardina does not allow them to distract the reader she seeks to arouse to indignation.

My brief survey of realism in Appalachian literature will undoubtedly leave some asking, "But what about . . . (fill in the blank)?" I am aware that I have omitted some prominent names, names which should have been included, names such as Fred Chappell, John Ehle, James Still, Wilma Dykeman, Richard Marius. Others might reach a little farther back in time and mention James Agee, Thomas Wolfe, or Emma Bell Miles. The point I want to make is that the realism which came to have a prominent place in nineteenth-century American literature ultimately prevailed in Appalachia, too, in time supplanting the romanticism of such nineteenth-century writers as Mary Noailles Murfree; and that it continues to the present day in the work of such writers as Lee Smith and Denise Giardina, who seek to set before us the people of the region as they talk, as they live, as they love and hate—in short, as they really are. I urge anyone who teaches in the Appalachian region to gain some knowledge of its writers and their work and to pass on as much as is practicable of this knowledge to their students. New England's domination of American literature was broken after two centuries; the importance of southern literature was eventually established. Appalachian literature needs to come into its own, to be taken more seriously, to be studied more widely. Our students should realize that something of consequence does happen here and that significant literature has been written and is being written about the place where we live. As New York, San Francisco, and Los Angeles do not make up the whole of the United States, so Richmond, Charleston, Atlanta, Nashville, and Oxford, Mississippi, are not the whole of the South. Our teaching should not imply that they are.

Works Cited

Armstrong, Anne. *This Day and Time.* With a personal reminiscence by David McClellan. Johnson City, TN: Research Advisory Council, East Tennessee State University, 1969.

Arnow, Harriette. *Hunter's Horn.* New York: Macmillan, 1949.

Cleary, Ben. "The Power and the Story." *Style Weekly* [Richmond, VA], 29 Aug. 1989, 24–27.

Giardina, Denise. *Storming Heaven.* New York: Norton, 1987.

Harris, George Washington. *Sut Lovingood's Yarns.* Ed. M. Thomas Inge. New Haven, CT: College & UP, 1966.

Haun, Mildred. *The Hawk's Done Gone and Other Stories.* Ed. Herschel Gower. Nashville, TN: Vanderbilt UP, 1968.

Howells, William Dean. *Criticism and Fiction and Other Essays.* Ed. Clara Marburg Kirk and Rudolf Kirk. New York: New York UP, 1959.

Murfree, Mary Noailles. *In the Tennessee Mountains.* Ed. Nathalia Wright. Knoxville: U of Tennessee P, 1970.

O'Connor, Flannery. *Mystery and Manners.* Ed. Sally and Robert Fitzgerald. New York: Farrar, Straus & Giroux, 1969.

Smith, Lee. *Fair and Tender Ladies.* New York: Putnam's, 1988.

Twain, Mark, and Charles Dudley Warner. *The Gilded Age: A Tale of To-day.* Hartford, CT: American Publishing Co., 1873.

Twain, Mark. *Mark Twain's Travels with Mr. Brown.* Ed. Franklin Walker and G. Ezra Dane. New York: Knopf, 1940.

Rudy Thomas

Rudy Thomas is an educator as well as a poet and serves as superintendent of Berea Independent School District, Berea, Kentucky. The author of five books of poems, such as *The Ground of Memory* (1978), his works have appeared in three anthologies of Appalachian writers, including *God's Plenty: Modern Kentucky Authors* (1991). His poetry, essays, and short stories have appeared in numerous publications, such as *Appalachian Journal, Laurel Review,* and *Appalachian Heritage.* In 1978 he received the Jesse Stuart Award from the Kentucky Poetry Society.

Body Man

My father does not like
to read poetry
does not know
he has written his own verse
with a ball peen hammer,
banging rockerpanels and crumpled fenders
until he edits the flaws.
He does not realize
that I use his works
to judge my own.
He is master of perfection
I parody.

From *God's Plenty—Modern Kentucky Authors,* ed. Lillie D. Chaffin, Glenn O. Carey, Harry N. Brown, Penkevill Publishing Co., 1991, © 1991 by Rudy Thomas. Reprinted by permission of the author.

Wilma Dykeman

Wilma Dykeman has been described as a "spokesperson for the Appalachian region and for humane values everywhere." A native of Asheville, North Carolina, and a longtime resident of Newport, Tennessee, Dykeman is a Phi Beta Kappa graduate of Northwestern University. She holds two honorary doctoral degrees. She is a professor of English at the University of Tennessee at Knoxville, and in 1992 she was the Goode Visiting Professor in English at Berea College.

Dykeman's first novel, The Tall Woman (1962), has been in print continuously for over thirty years. Among her sixteen books are The Far Family (1966), Return the Innocent Earth (1973), and Explorations (1984).

Dykeman has received many awards, including a Guggenheim Fellowship, a Senior Fellowship from the National Endowment for the Humanities, the Thomas Wolfe Memorial Trophy, and the Chicago Friends of American Writers Award. A prolific lecturer who books more than thirty speaking engagements across the nation annually, Dykeman has also claimed the Hillman Award for the best book of the year on world peace, race relations, or civil liberties; and the North Carolina Gold Medal for Contribution to American Letters. "Seeking Knowledge" is appropriate wisdom coming from Wilma Dykeman.

Seeking Knowledge

A long time ago I became acquainted with a young man (who eventually became an older man and has since died) who was scholar in the truest sense of the word. He held a responsible position in one of the major oil companies but did not seek the highest executive positions—because "his" time, the hours and days away from his desk, were spent in studies of mathematics and the history of science and in enjoyment of music. His pleasure and great wealth was of the mind.

A few years ago I met a retired banker who had moved his residence from the Northeast to the Southern Appalachians. He appreciated—indeed, he loved—the mountains, and on any walk or hike I took with him he observed each plant and tree, moss and shrub, asking for names, habitat, characteristics. His curiosity was as boundless as his enthusiasm for his adopted place, and I often compared his concern with the apathy shown by many natives who did not know, nor cared to know, about the magnificent world around them.

A few days ago I encountered this sentence in a book I was reading: "The purpose of research in every field is to set back the frontier of darkness." Let us give the word "research" a broad and spacious interpretation. The

From Explorations, Wakestone Books, 1984. Reprinted by permission of the author.

doctor in his laboratory is pushing back the darkness of sick minds and bodies; the scientist at his calculations is pushing back the shrouds of space; but each of us, as well, when we sharpen our minds, respect the gift of our curiosity, and seek to know more about this world and this adventure called life—we are overcoming our own bit of the darkness.

As an English novelist once said, "I like to understand things because then I can enjoy them. I think knowledge should intensify our pleasures. That is its aim and object, so far as I am concerned."

How right he is! And yet how dreary many of us consider knowledge to be. Its acquisition is made laborious, when it should be joyous; we plod toward something called learning when we should run and skip and plunge, stumble and rise and run again. Not that research of any kind, and knowledge worthy of the name does not require work. But it is work repaid not only in earning of bread but in winning of our very spirit.

Perhaps we too often mistake facts for knowledge. As an eminent archeologist has pointed out, the kind of unrelated scraps of information one gets on a quiz program offer scant satisfaction:

> Bare facts by themselves do not fascinate us; they must be clothed with the play and counterplay which produced them. The defeat of the Spanish armada in 1588 is a bald historical fact. It takes on meaning when it is shown as the culmination of a play of forces and the clash of the opposing temperaments and philosophies of two nations, personified in the characters of Philip the Second and Elizabeth. To understand these antagonisms, one must know the cultural backgrounds, the ways of thought, and the conflicting traditions of the two peoples. One must study Torquemada and Chaucer, John of Austria and Latimer, the choir stalls of Toledo cathedral and the fan-vaulting of St. George's, Windsor, and even the dances and field sports of the protagonists.

All knowledge, then, is related. When we know more about the corner of the world where we live, we know more about the green and fragile planet which is home to all humans. Our own little spark of curiosity is a part of the immense mystery which surrounds all life.

To know! To seek to know! How dull and dead we are when we relinquish that right, that rapture in our lives. Whether it is in mathematics or music, woods-knowledge or earth-wisdom, or effort to understand ourselves and those around us—whatever the area of our knowledge, how satisfying to realize that truly "the purpose of research in every field is to set back the frontier of darkness."

Harry Brown

See volume 2, chapter 5, for biography.

Appalachian Education

Educators, politicians and preachers pity us.
We have failed to progress.
We haven't the modern way.
The trinity examines our mountain schools, houses and clothes.
The trinity speaks of the lofty virtues and values

of their better consolidated schools,
modular scheduling,
micro-teaching,
and team teaching.

The trinity speaks of their electrical appliances,

modern conveniences,
and technical advances.

All of which, the trinity allows, lead to ego strength,

ambition,
peer-group security,
autonomy,
dignity,
and better speech habits.

The trinity exhorts us to leave the mountains and enter into

Progressive America.
Into cities.
Into universities.
Into industries.

I tell the trinity that in the morning *Courier* I read about

From *Appalachian Heritage* 1.3 (1973), © *Appalachian Heritage*/Berea College. Reprinted by permission of the author and the publisher.

murders in Chicago,
race riots in Washington,
a heroin bust in a New York City junior high,
muggings on a Dallas campus,
Nixon holding up a sign in Progressive America saying,
"Hogs are Beautiful."

Educators, politicians, and preachers

want to help us so,
they say,
we can help ourselves.
The trinity tells us if we lose their welfare programs

we'll fold—
we'll starve.

I tell the trinity,

let me take a rope
and string it around about Appalachia
so that we can keep our coal,
limestone,
iron,
clay,
natural gas,
petroleum,
and timber—
all got through broad-form rape at fifty cents an acre—
and then we'll see who hangs.

David Whisnant

David Whisnant's work is frequently difficult to classify, as it combines sociology, mass psychology, history, and literary and social criticism in its wide-ranging analyses of Appalachian problems and proposed solutions. Born July 16, 1938, in Asheville, North Carolina, Whisnant received degrees from Georgia Institute of Technology (B.S.) and Duke University (A.M., Ph.D.). He has a prestigious record of publications, including three books on Appalachia. Two of these, *Modernizing the Mountaineer* (1981) and *All That Is Native and Fine* (1983), are among the most controversial works written about the region.

Modernizing the Mountaineer examines how agents outside Appalachia, particularly government-sponsored commissions, have made various efforts, forcible in many cases, to bring mountain society into line with "modern" standards. Whisnant's obvious distaste for what he considers hegemony has created some discussion. But his cogent and frequently powerful arguments merit serious attention.

Cannibals and Christians

That cultural intervenors may be on the whole decent, well-meaning, even altruistic people does not (indeed must not) excuse them from historical judgment. One may reasonably display great charity for the cross-purposes, confusions, and miscalculations of fallible individuals in difficult circumstances. But insofar as those people actively intervene in the cultural (or other) lives of large numbers of people, their failures and miscalculations, however "understandable," become a legitimate object of public concern. For the effects of what they do touch so many, and linger so long.

One can see that with some clarity in the current situation at both Hindman Settlement School and the John C. Campbell Folk School. Both have only recently acquired their first native-born directors, and each is struggling to find a useful contemporary role that is to some degree congruent with the institution's past (and—necessarily—therefore agreeable to established contributors). But since each school's program was in major respects so *in*congruent with the local social, economic, and cultural situation at every period, maintaining continuity is a decidedly mixed blessing. Thus a major barrier for each institution is precisely its own past and the inertias and pieties that attach to it.

Michael Mullins, current director of Hindman Settlement School, has searched diligently and with some success for a new role and new functions for the institution. As the school entered its ninth decade, the dormitories no longer echoed with archaic ballads and sword-dance tunes. Instead, there was a remedial learning program for dyslexic children, a National Women's Health Network meeting, an annual workshop for young Appalachian writers, a "visual arts week" which drew both local and outside artists as instructors, workshops on childbirth, credit unions, greenhouse construction, and an adult high-school equivalency program. These are all admirable efforts in themselves, all perfectly consistent with the practice of settlement houses as it developed ninety years earlier. And all several Anders hops beyond sword dances in their social utility.

And yet—one must reluctantly observe—they focus on the symptoms rather than the causes of social dislocations: on poor educational programs and housing and nutritional conditions, rather than on the coal-dominated social, political, and economic system of the area.

The reasons for this emphasis are not hard to understand. First, eastern

David Whisnant, "Cannibals and Christians," from *All That is Native and Fine: The Politics of Culture in an American Region,* © 1986 by The University of North Carolina Press. Reprinted by permission of the author and publishers.

Kentucky history is replete with dramatic and sometimes gruesome evidence of the cost of calling a spade a spade. From Harlan County in the 1930s to the strip-mining wars of the 1960s and 1970s, the cost has been clear; one may as well read the system and weep, for it will tolerate (personally or institutionally) only that which poses no real threat. Thus Mullins's choice is an agonizing one: sacrifice the school or steer it delicately between the channel markers placed by the industry, relieving as many personal hurts along the way as one can.

Second—and this harks back to the very beginning—the school's involvement with a safely defined "culture" gives it an arena of apparent legitimacy, connectedness, and usefulness which partly alleviates the sense of frustration and futility that might otherwise sweep over one and all. In Miss Watt's terms, the school has "successfully" avoided politics for eighty years; in Alfred North Whitehead's tougher terms, it has chosen a domain of misplaced concreteness as its major sphere of activity. It is as if the romantic version of local culture, introduced at the Forks of Troublesome by some Bluegrass ladies, now will not ever go away. Romantic "culture" and the myth of Uncle Sol are available for each new generation, and they blur the stark realities of life in eastern Kentucky.[1] Culture as "soft" legitimacy, as energy sink.

At Hindman, the cultural ghosts linger on in the form of dulcimer concerts, "folk evenings," handicrafts classes, and "family folk weeks" interspersed with GED classes and greenhouse workshops. The culture featured at the 1982 "family folk week" had about as much basis in local tradition as the culture featured at the school had ever had: two Ritchie daughters presenting what D. K. Wilgus recognized more than twenty years ago as a special settlement school version of mountain music; Morris Amburgey making the same dulcimers his father learned to make from Uncle Ed Thomas, who shipped most of *his* dulcimers to New York; a local bluegrass band; a Lexington, Kentucky, hammered dulcimer maker, and a player from the Midwest whose role in the mountains currently bears an intriguing resemblance to that of Richard Chase or John Jacob Niles a half-century earlier; the McLain Family Band, led by Raymond McLain, who guided the school through its most intense morris- and sword-dance period; and the daughter of a former Berea College president, who is the latest link in Hindman's historic tie to the Berea versions of mountain dancing, weaving, and ballad singing.

At Brasstown, the situation is both more and less complicated than at Hindman. Less in that Clay and Cherokee counties had no coal, and therefore were spared some of the more dramatic upheavals of Knott County, Kentucky. Less also in that, lacking such a concentration of money and power, the area has spawned no monolithic local system which the school must confront. But more, in the sense that throughout its history the folk school existed within a conceptual box that was even tighter than that at Hindman. Except for a brief (and surprisingly successful) foray into agriculture, the folk school focused most of its energies, programs, and facilities upon folk-revival enterprises of a romantic and essentially alien sort. Both its buildings and (more important) the people who take classes there and contribute money now reflect that focus; local people have very little to do with the folk school.

The dilemma for mountain-born director Esther Hyatt is acute: in order to maintain the staff and physical plant, donations and class fees must continue. But they will continue only if the programs preferred by benefactors and potential students are continued. And those programs remain rooted in the cultural vision of the Southern Highland Handicraft Guild, the settlement schools, Berea College, and the romantic cultural revivalism of the 1920s and 1930s. In effect, then, the school is a refuge from both local *and* national cultural reality. As such, it is more or less ignored by local people and frequented mostly by culturally dislocated middle-class visitors from other parts of the country. Local people are more likely to enroll at the tri-county vocational-technical school in Murphy—many of whose functions and emphases were vainly urged upon folk school trustees by Dagnall Folger and Howard Kester thirty years earlier.

In one way, then, the schools are reverse images: facing overwhelming needs, Michael Mullins has little freedom to act in Knott County; Esther Hyatt, having considerable freedom to act insofar as the local situation is concerned, is constrained by the preferences of her distant supporters and by the lack of a clear sense of precisely what local needs the school could at long last respond to.

≈

A final word, both serious and playful. In early seventeenth-century Virginia, Sheehan relates, it was a continual embarrassment to English colonizers—who considered themselves such admirable specimens of spiritual and cultural superiority—that so many of their number became convinced of the actual superiority of Indian life and "went over" to live with the "savages." It is perhaps perverse, but tantalizing, nevertheless, to speculate on what might have happened had more New England and Bluegrass ladies (and gentlemen) "gone over" to the enemy. The image of a shouting and slightly tipsy Lucy Furman riding hell-for-leather through the muddy streets of Hindman on an old-fashioned saturnalian (that is to say, "chair-flingin'") Christmas Eve is no doubt too far-fetched to contemplate, but had she sketched a scene in one of her novels of a recidivist Fighting Fult Fallon escaping in the nick of time—purple knee-britches and all—through the bushes with his mountain Nancibel in tow, it would at least have given William Aspenwall Bradley something disquietingly useful to ponder. Like the narrator of Tom T. Hall's country song "The Little Lady Preacher," he could have "sat and wondered who it was converted whom."

"The world," as the pagan Queequeg tells the New England idealist Ishmael in *Moby Dick*, "is a joint-stock company. Us cannibals have to help those Christians."

Note

1. For the most recent retreading of the Uncle Sol myth, see Mercy Coogan, "At the Forks of Troublesome Creek: Hindman Settlement School," *Appalachia* 14 (Mar. 1981): 33–40. *Appalachia* is the magazine of the state-federal Appalachian Regional Commission.

STEPHEN KING'S FIRST ATTEMPT AT APPALACHIAN MACABRE.

Helen Lewis and Rich Kirby

Helen Lewis is a sociologist, writer, and educator. She holds a Ph.D. from the University of Kentucky and has taught at East Tennessee State University, Appalachian State University, and Clinch Valley College of the University of Virginia in Wise. She has been a staff member at Highlander Research and Education Center, New Market, Tennessee, as well as director of Appalachian studies at Berea College, Berea, Kentucky. She is the author of numerous articles and books on Appalachian social and economic issues, coal mining communities, and families. She is director of the Appalachian Center at Berea College.

Rich Kirby is a graduate of Trinity College, Hartford, Connecticut, and holds a law degree and a master's degree in urban studies from Yale University. For a number of years he was self-employed as a musician and storyteller, and since 1990 he has been general manager of WMMT-FM, Appalshop, in Whitesburg, Kentucky. He has written extensively on land use in Appalachia, and as a musician he has made several contributions to albums for June Appal Records and served as producer of a number of recordings.

All That Is Native and Still Undefined:
A Response to David Whisnant

Modern history began rather suddenly for the southern mountains, in the years around 1900. What had been an isolated rural area began to confront the industrial revolution, as outsiders bought up coal and timber and began operating railroads, mines, and mills. Outsiders also mined the vivid and unique culture of the mountains, as the "local color school" of writers, led by John Fox, Jr., cranked out novels and pulp fiction filled with picturesque and rather savage hillbillies.

Those outsiders who stopped to think about it concluded that mountain people needed to be saved from something: usually from ignorance and primitivism, sometimes from obscure versions of Christianity, occasionally from other outsiders. Some of these folks, those who chose to work with (or on) the native mountain culture, form the subject of David Whisnant's *All That Is Native and Fine.* He concentrates on the Hindman Settlement School in Kentucky, the John C. Campbell Folk School in North Carolina, and the Whitetop Folk Festival in Virginia.

In 1900 Katherine Petit, May Stone, and some other women, all from bluegrass Kentucky, came to Hazard and began teaching. In a legendary confrontation, patriarch Solomon Everidge walked over from Hindman, observed, approved, and offered the women land and support. By 1904, the Hindman Settlement School had begun. It had a focus beyond simple education. Many missionaries felt that mountain people had "no culture" or a deficient one. Petit and Stone believed that the mountain culture—such as they conceived it—was well worth saving, and made this a priority at their school. For the next fifty years or so (the school still operates but has changed its focus), it promoted old ballads, woven coverlets, dulcimers, and a romanticized version of the "pure" mountain culture that included these things as well as various English country dances that were thought suitable for the Anglo-Saxon mountain youth. Their vision of the culture was narrow and selective, excluding rowdiness, traditional Christmas customs, and banjo music. After the visit of the pioneer folksong collector Cecil Sharp in 1917, Hindman Settlement School came—in the minds of many outside the region—to define what mountain music and culture was or should be.

Olive Dame Campbell of Massachusetts was more openly progressive and activist. Traveling through the mountains around 1908, she became drawn first to old ballads, then to the singers, then to their culture. Desiring to preserve "all that is native and fine," she turned to the Danish folk school movement as a model for an Appalachian institution which would educate, preserve folk culture, and provide an economic base. Named for her late husband and located in Brasstown, North Carolina, the John C. Campbell Folk School began in 1926 and continues today. It taught academic subjects and folk (more or less) music

Printed by permission of the authors.

and crafts, and promoted cooperative farms. The school declined for a variety of reasons, including the decline of small mountain farming and the school's odd emphasis on Danish songs and dances. As time went on, its focus changed to high-class handicrafts—it spawned today's prestigious and not very folky Southern Highland Handicraft Guild. Mrs. Campbell died in 1950.

In 1931 Mrs. Annabel Morris Buchanan became interested in a fiddlers' convention to be held on Whitetop Mountain in southwestern Virginia. A middle-class lady from nearby Marion, she held strong views regarding what was (Anglo-Saxon) and what was not ("Negroid") legitimate mountain music. The next year she teamed with a noted Virginia composer and avowed racist, John Powell, to present another event showcasing this material. The Whitetop Folk Festival became annual; it made history of a sort when Eleanor Roosevelt attended in 1933—ironically, her father had been the land agent who, forty years before, had bought the land for development. For the next few years, the festival insistently presented a version of mountain culture that was rigidly old and Anglo-Saxon. Participants were screened, sometimes tutored; morris-dance teams from the settlement schools were welcome, hillbilly string bands were not. Riddled with pretension and paradox, the festival dwindled and died after 1939.

All That Is Native and Fine tells the stories of these adventures with erudition, scholarship, and often biting wit. David Whisnant's account is grounded in strong views about what mountain culture is and what should or should not be done with it. In presenting his case, he raises both hackles and important questions.

In Whisnant's view, the efforts of these women—cultural workers were almost always women; it seems to have been their job to try to mitigate the harsh effects of industrialization—were silly at best. More than that, they represented a serious and destructive manipulation of mountain culture. The notions of "Elizabethan" speech and song, of "contemporary ancestors," were flawed and biased; dulcimers, for example, were seldom heard of until the settlement ladies came along. They changed the styles and designs of traditional crafts to fit an outside aesthetic Whisnant calls "traditional chic." Believers in a racist "Anglo-Saxonism," they systematically excluded a great deal, including the great black contributions of banjo and flatfoot dancing. And by virtue of their power and legitimacy in the larger society, they were able to make these definitions stick, not only in the outside world but also (he argues) in the mountains themselves. They failed, moreover, to take account of the vast social and economic dislocations going on around them (especially in Kentucky) or to challenge the new order to redress abusive treatment. Instead of trying to use culture to empower local people to resist, they settled for being "cultural first-aid stations."

This raises a fascinating array of questions. What is the role of culture in any society, particularly that of an exploited people? Who can or should define it, or play around with it? Was mountain culture, as Whisnant claims, so "malleable" to these intruders? Some of these questions are dealt with in the book; others are raised during one's reading of it.

One matter that pops up at once concerns the curious lack of testimony from the "other side," from the people whose culture was being interfered with. Whisnant's sources are the women: their letters, diaries, books, newspaper articles, and the like. Many of the native people who attended the schools and played at the festivals are still around; at least one of them recalls that banjos were far more common at Hindman than Whisnant implies. But these people are absent from Whisnant's account. Only a short interview with the late fiddler Albert Hash (who played at Whitetop) gives us any view of their experience—for Hash at least, a positive one. Those who have not found mountaineers depraved and deficient often have seen them as noble savages, admirable and unknowable. And so mountaineers remain in *All That Is Native;* their perceptions and personalities surprisingly don't make it into the book.

This also leaves the reader somewhat in the dark about the nature of the mountain culture which the women were manipulating. It comes across as a sort of brooding omnipresence to be taken for granted. In fact, it was more vital and more complicated. Mountain people (some of them, at least) were willing victims of the process he describes. Mountain people gave the women land and built houses on it, and attended the classes and festivals; some of them insisted that they ban banjos and clog dancing. This has to do, I think, with the class structure of communities like Hindman and Marion: the preindustrial mountains were not really a classless society, and the women seem to have sought out the support of the "better" people. Similarly, "settlement school music," if not the whole of mountain music at the time, certainly was a part of it. Rich's grandmother, Addie Graham, who grew up at that time about fifty miles from Hindman, sang both the Anglo-Saxon ballads and the black-oriented blues. And she clogged. Things are seldom simple, especially in Kentucky.

The mountaineers turned out, too, to be largely immune to this manipulation. The "malleability" that puzzles Whisnant turns out to be a sort of passive and polite resistance. The settlements failed to introduce or preserve their dances (outside Berea!); people moved away from the Brasstown area, despite the folk school's efforts to keep them there; Virginia musicians learned songs just to sing at Whitetop, and no doubt forgot them as quickly. The string band continued to evolve, banjo and all. The manipulating institutions failed or changed radically. In the meantime, people got what they wanted from the women—an education, a job, a chance to be paid for a musical performance—and ignored the rest. Who was manipulating whom?

Whisnant focuses on a phenomenon that ended, more or less, by 1940. But the issues involved resonate today, as Appalachian music is "revived" and Appalachia itself is studied in schools and colleges throughout the region. The mountains have proven able to digest cultural interference far greater than that of the women. Blacks were manipulators of great importance, to the lasting enrichment of the tradition. Bluegrass, undreamed of in 1910, is now entrenched as mountain music, and probably thirty years from now electric instruments will have a place in what is undeniably "Appalachian."

These changes have not come easily, or without criticism. One thinks of the Blue Sky Boys, the great and popular North Carolina musicians who retired rather than meet RCA's demands that they use electric instruments. Or of the thousands of old-time players who stopped playing during the early Elvis years, feeling suddenly awkward and out-of-date. In the last twenty years, there has been a considerable revival of traditional music, the impetus coming largely (at first) from outsiders. Critics have not been lacking to say that these too are cultural manipulators who have selfishly used mountain traditions for their own purposes. (This is how we read Whisnant's petty and gratuitous insult of John McCutcheon.) What of the academic programs that trade in mountain culture? What of the burgeoning Hillbilly Days–type celebrations in mountain communities, where undeniably native people dress up in "Li'l Abner" costumes and self-consciously wonder what it all means? Do we judge a person's music (or culture) by his good intentions, or birth certificate, or hair length? What is tradition? How do we take account of its propensity for change?

The questions are now coming into focus. The answers are not clear to Whisnant, to us, or to anyone we know. *All That Is Native and Fine,* with its invaluable scholarship and provocative insights, still does not settle matters. The book is marred by its contentiousness and tendency to overdramatize; for example, by comparing the women to the seventeenth-century English who exterminated the Indians of eastern Virginia. But it leads us onto the horns of a fascinating dilemma. We need to know our cultural history, to appreciate where we came from and who we are.

George Scarbrough

See volume 2, chapter 2, for biography.

Schoolhouse Hill

At the noon hour
She traipsed townward
To steal the creams and sticks
She bought her friends with:
From her coats and cuffs
Spilled the economies of love.

"Schoolhouse Hill" from *Invitation to Kim,* Iris Press, 1989; reprinted by permission of the author and publisher. "Early Schooling" from *Appalachian Journal,* 16, no. 2 (Winter 1989), © *Appalachian Journal*/Appalachian State University; used with permission.

Past love's savagery,
Larceny left her.
Abandoning contraband,
She drifted about Benton,
The metropolis of all our lives,
In pleasant rue.

Uphill again she flourished
In perfumes like bouquets,
Sweetened by her own sack:
Then, butterflies in sight,
She dropped down again
Into the yielding town.

I stole too for my moment
Of attractiveness. Pariah
Of ordinary hours, I stuck
To my desk at noontime, writing
Papers for the less authorial,
Great dumb brutes I loved.

Early Schooling

Retained for three years,
Plagued by plagues,
I read the same book
Until I had it memorized.

My father raged at contagion,
Declaring his conviction
That schools were profligate places,
Disease the wage of sin.

It was the law, he proclaimed,
That made his children sinners,
And took his gun to the truant officer,
Who left not to return.
Meanwhile, I chanted my book
Over again like a devotee
At text, but failed the glory
Of office. My mind ached and dulled

And fell far behind,
Disenchanted with chanting.
Then immunity came to the hill.
Plagues were eradicated.

I could return to the cloakroom
Library with its spare shelves,
Wearing the great black blister
Of smallpox vaccination,

Indebted to modern medicine
For my first full term ever,
My father's near apoplexy,
And a new reader.

Isabel Bonnyman (Bonny) Stanley

Isabel Bonnyman (Bonny) Stanley is an assistant professor of English at East Tennessee State University. She was born in Knoxville, Tennessee, and attended Roman Catholic schools in Knoxville and Washington, D.C. She holds a Ph.D. in English from the University of Tennessee at Knoxville. She has published articles on Barbara Pym, on Vera Brittain, and on children's literature by C. S. Lewis, Maurice Sendak, and Nina Bawden; and has contributed pieces to several books of creative nonfiction. Bonny Stanley was born and bred in the Briar Patch of Appalachia but reserves the right to be herself.

Slaying the Mythical Kingdom

Which of the following definitions of *Appalachian* (n.) is correct?

1. One born on a mountaintop in Tennessee, maker of moonshine, player of the dulcimer, slayer of the Queen's English (unless the queen is Elizabeth I), possessor of an eighth-grade education, member of a snake-handling religious sect. Or:

2. One born in a city who has always lived in a city, a Roman Catholic, one whose grandparents had college degrees, one who loves opera and isn't too fond of country music.

Most people from outside the region would say, "Number One, of course; Number Two is a carpetbagger who moved into the area to work at Oak Ridge or TVA." Wrong. I'm not too sure where Number One lives, except in the mythical kingdom of Appalachia Stereotypica. But, as a Two, born and bred in the Briar Patch of Knoxville, Tennessee, as were many of my relatives going back to the 1700s, I know there are many like me all over Appalachia. Most of my life I thought I was just an ordinary Tennessean.

From *Now and Then* 5.2 (Summer 1988). Reprinted by permission of the author and publisher.

There has been a more urban, educated side to Appalachia for a long time, just as there have been colleges in these hills for many years: the University of Tennessee, founded in 1794; Emory and Henry College, 1838; Sewanee, 1857; Knoxville College, 1863; East Tennessee State University, 1911. There has been religious diversity, too: the Roman Catholic Church of the Immaculate Conception, founded in Knoxville in 1855, is one of the oldest historical churches in the state; Jewish religious communities in Knoxville and the Tri-Cities date from the nineteenth century. Appalachians are a diverse group and have been from the earliest days. Yet misconceptions persist.

When I went off to school in Washington, D.C., in 1957, any number of people asked, "Are those your first pair of shoes?"

I answered, "No, do you have on your first pair?"

More recently, just two summers ago, I attended a National Endowment for the Humanities Institute at Duke University on the sixteenth-century French essayist Montaigne. After a while the questions arose: "How have you managed to travel so much coming from Tennessee?" "How in the world did you learn to speak French?"

I enjoyed answering, "My grandmother taught me French. She learned it as a child growing up in the hills of North Georgia. She used to read from her French Bible every night to keep up her proficiency."

"Well, you must be an exception to the rule where you live," they persisted.

"Not at all," I answered. "You're just thinking of Appalachian stereotypes. All of my friends are better educated and more cultivated than I."

A few had the grace to blush.

Amy Tipton Gray

A native of Johnson City, Tennessee, Amy Tipton Gray received her B.S. and M.S. at East Tennessee State University. She is currently the coordinator of the Writing Center at Caldwell Community College in Hudson, North Carolina, where she teaches classes in math, the arts, and country music history. Her poems have appeared in magazines such as *Now and Then*. In 1988 Gray's poem "Hillbilly Vampire" was awarded honorable mention by the Appalachian Writers Association in their annual competition. A collection of her poems under the same title, *The Hillbilly Vampire* (1989), satirizes the exploitation of the Appalachian South by ethnologists.

The Hillbilly Vampire Goes to Class

The hillbilly vampire
    did not have a well-developed sense of irony.

He did, however, have a horde of little ghouls
    who signed up for his classes and hung on his every word
    because he was so charming
    and gave such easy tests.

Never hearing the hiss of scale and claw
    itching to unfurl
    beneath the broadcloth and the tweed
    (his field clothes kept separate
    for his work in the vineyards of the night)
    never wondering why his moustache
    hung down so long over his lip

    —never around to hear how he complained
    about their stupidity to other professors (but
    what could you expect in such a cultural Gomorra?)
    wishing to god he could get good students for once
    who had grandparents he could use
    as subjects for research—

    they sat there
    long-necked and literal as geese
    and believed he was everything
    a teacher should be.

From *The Hillbilly Vampire*, Rowan Mountain Press, 1989. Reprinted by permission of Rowan Mountain Press.

Bill Best

Bill Best grew up in Haywood County, North Carolina. He attended Berea College (B.A.) and the University of Tennessee at Knoxville (M.S.) before earning his Ed.D. at the University of Massachusetts at Amherst. From 1966 until 1988, Best was director of Berea College's Upward Bound Program. He has been an associate professor of physical education and general studies at Berea since 1988. In addition to Appalachian studies, Best's interests include aesthetics, aquatic art, and comparative mythology. During summers he grows heirloom tomatoes and beans, which he sells to farmers' markets and restaurants. Best is author of *The Tragedy of Platitudinous Piety* (1982) and *The Great Appalachian Sperm Bank and Other Writings* (1986).

To See Ourselves

The best hope for developing an educational system which will allow Appalachian people to grow in ways appropriate for us is to build upon educational philosophies, such as Schiller's, which are congruent with thought and action modes already existing in the mountains. One beginning could be to seriously examine the implications of his statement: "Before the sensuous man can be made rational, he must first be made aesthetic."

It has been known for some time, both to us and to outsiders, that we are an emotional people. Children are fondled and cuddled and made the objects of affection of parents, uncles and aunts, grandparents, cousins, and siblings alike. There are exceptions to the general rule, but, as a whole, emotional bonding within families is a fact of life early in life. Such bonding, I am aware, is a mixed blessing; but it is, for most of us, very important in terms of our development and in terms of our identities. Let us seriously *study the significance of those processes.*

Likewise, we are emotional in the sense that the arts play important everyday roles in our lives. Music and poetic forms of thought and speech arrive in our lives early and are part of the basic fabric of the culture. However, the arts are not something which we purchase or set aside as something to occupy certain niches. The arts are organic, in that they are not thought of as being separate, or something "brought on," or something necessarily special or esoteric. One of the things that Cecil Sharpe discovered during his travels was that singing was just as natural as talking.

Our feeling for artistic form is also expressed in such things as quilting, laying out fields for planting or harvesting, conducting church services, or arranging a barn for the calving season. Artistic forms are expressed in special family and community ceremonies, or coon or fox hunting rituals, or whenever two or more are gathered to share their relationships with their world. *What do our arts say about us? Let us undertake to find out.*

As mentioned earlier, conceptual forms are not absent from the culture, but they are different from the conceptual forms of many other cultures. They are based on metaphor and anecdote and frequently on stories and parables from the Bible. Intuition is relied on heavily, and reasoning is often done by forming generalizations based on knowledge gained from actual life experiences. Deductive reasoning from abstract premises is very much a part of the culture, but it is not a dominant form of reasoning.

From *Mountain Review* 5, no. 2 (Oct. 1979): 1–6. Reprinted by permission of the author.

We can work toward gaining the "aesthetic state" of freedom by working to gain conceptual understanding of the artistic forms of communication and expression within our culture. This is a form of self-knowledge which can be liberating, in that one can begin to understand the reasons why one behaves in certain ways in given situations. A danger to be guarded against is that conceptual forms of understanding can be overplayed and can begin to substitute for actual experiences and in time divorce individuals from their feelings and obscure or even destroy the meanings of artistic forms of expression and communication. The curse of so much of modern education is this alienation from feelings, making necessary the compensatory courses in "Humanistic Education" to put students back in touch with personality attributes they never should have lost touch with in the first place.

Within the Appalachian family there are many implicit assumptions and agreements which govern relationships. Discipline of children is tied into those relationships, relieving parents of constantly prescribing and monitoring behavior in public situations. Body language takes over the task of communication in such situations, but observers are usually unaware of the communication patterns in force. Those who write about Appalachian family relationships usually misread the communication patterns in such situations and proceed to assert to an all-too-gullible public that mountain parents are "permissive" in their child-rearing practices because they don't give their children direct, overt, and continuous guidance. *Let us tell the world about the strengths of our ways of raising children.*

Many, if not most, teachers in our public schools have forgotten how sensitive their students are to implicit control and to the influence of body language. They have also forgotten how sensitive they (the teachers) were at one time before they were "educated." They proceed to offend and hurt their students, especially the younger ones, all the while wondering why their students are so nonresponsive.

The combination of shame, emotional sensitivity, and artistic forms of expression makes Appalachian children poor candidates for success in the public schools, where almost all such attributes are not valued and where very few of their strengths are perceived as such. It is no wonder that the very bright, the very sensitive, and the very artistic drop out at the earliest opportunity if they can't find ways to circumvent the school, go in their own directions, and gain their own education despite the system.

In fairness to our miseducated teachers and administrators, we should never forget that we have never really developed our own school systems. Unfortunately, we can trace that direct linkage to Horace Mann's attempts in the newly formed public schools to anglicize the non-Anglo-Saxon immigrants to New England in the nineteenth century. Our schools are traditional only in that they were conceived as part of the overall attempt permeating all settled sections of the country to make imitation Puritans of all the citizenry of the United States. Our schools have no organic base within the culture, since most teachers and administrators are counted among the up-

lifted and have forgotten how to understand and/or appreciate that which
they at one time held most dear.

In starting new, we need to develop the type of system which will allow
and encourage our children to understand themselves within the context of
their world and then branch out to understand the worlds of others without
feeling that they necessarily have to forsake their own in favor of others. We
will have to educate teachers who can be secure in their knowledge of who
they are and who have not lost the ability to feel what it is like to be a child
in a new and trying situation. The one biggest complaint I hear continuously about the schools is the gross insensitivity of so many teachers at all
levels, preschool through college.

Such a system would be quite drastically different from the present one in
many ways. I will offer some suggestions based on my work during the past
dozen-plus years in a program deliberately designed to be an alternative to
the existing system:

The arts should be given much more priority at all levels. Art classes can
allow children, in a noncompeting situation and nonthreatening environment, to explore and create using different mediums. They can work in their
own ways at paces appropriate to their own needs, interests, and aptitudes.
Such classes can relieve the stress produced in the more structured situations
such as reading and math classes. Ideally, the more structured classes are designed to add conceptual forms to the existing artistic forms in the repertoire of the students. However, the usual procedure is to have the conceptual
forms replace the artistic forms over time—which, in my opinion, is about
the worst thing we can do to our children. Children need an opportunity to
continue to re-create and reassess their world through the use of artistic
forms—forms which are closer to feeling than are conceptual forms. Artistic
forms can serve as a bridge between thinking and feeling, keeping the two
from becoming too estranged from one another.

Reading and language arts should begin where the children are, in the most
literal sense. It is not enough to have Dick and Jane passing through the mountains on their way to Florida from New England. Early readers should contain
stories about life as it is lived in the particular areas where the children live.
Children should learn and be allowed to appreciate the meaning of words and
language patterns they hear at home and not just those they hear at school.

One day, when my youngest son was in the third grade, he announced a
discovery he had made. He said he had discovered two "kinds of talk"—
"school talk and country talk." I asked him to describe the differences between
the two kinds of talk. His answer should be required reading for all teachers. He
described "school talk" as a particular kind of talk used only at school. It was to
be used when teachers and students talked with each other, but it was not good
anywhere else—at least as far as he knew at that time. In contrast, "country talk"
was what one used at home and in the rural community where we live. He said
that "country talk" was the better kind of talk because it allowed one to "tell
about feelings." He also said that "country talk" was better because "you can say

what you mean using country talk." I told him that "school talk" did have some uses and that he should learn to use "school talk" so that he could use it when necessary. I also told him to hold on to his "country talk" because he might continue to have feelings which he might wish to share.

The social sciences should begin early but should be handled with great care. Such classes can give students a way of distancing themselves from their everyday environments, but care should be taken that such distancing not alienate young students from their families and communities. Young children can learn the meaning of such terms as "the extended family," "nuclear family," "rites," "rituals," and other such sociological and anthropological terms without ceasing to appreciate their roles in such. The problem comes when negative value is placed upon the particular lifestyle of the student.

By the second or third grade (and often earlier), children are already thinking philosophically, but teachers are not trained to pick up on the natural philosophical inclinations of children and thus miss out on the earliest opportunities to strengthen and develop philosophic modes of thought. As students wander in thought, they are all too often brought back to the task at hand, which might include learning some tools which might be used in thought once they "grow up." Too much of such skill learning is like learning swimming strokes on dry land and never going near the water. One can learn all kinds of swimming techniques while on dry land and still drown upon entering the water, because the swimming techniques can only be learned effectively in the water where they are to be used. Likewise, it is good to practice thinking skills by actually thinking. Unfortunately, that is a radical idea which has not found its way into the schools.

By learning to think philosophically, children can begin to understand the biases built into the languages of disciplines. They can also learn about the biases built into the world views of the cultures in which they live and about the biases of the media, politics, and other institutions of the national culture. Admittedly, philosophical thought is subversive in terms of much of what schools are supposed to propagandize students into believing, but the schools can stand a little more creative tension, especially if such can result in the development of more competent and confident individuals.

There should also be time for physical education and play. The old idea of "play period" was not as bad as some modern educators have made it out to be, because it allows children a time to be spontaneous. Physical education activities allow for strengthening muscles and developing coordination, and allow for the development of a sense of self, for which there is no substitute. Physical education activities combined with art in the forms of dance, gymnastics, tumbling, or aquatic art can also be very personally liberating for many students. I have seen such activities motivate students who have never been motivated before to do anything for anyone, including themselves.

More than anything else, we need teachers who have a deep understanding of their own humanity and who can approach students as persons. We need teachers who can think and feel and create—teachers who, in one way or another, have achieved an aesthetic education. We need programs whereby our alienated teachers can rediscover the strengths and liberation gained by coming to terms with oneself. One never gets too old to be reborn.

We need to see ourselves reflected back by a looking glass that we ourselves have constructed. For too long, we have seen ourselves pictured like reflections in a fun house at a carnival. Our weaknesses are shown in the form of grotesque bulges, while our strengths have appeared as tiny dimples.

I do not underestimate the magnitude of the task I have set forth. It is so easy to "go with the flow," to blame the more than half of our young people who cannot survive the public schools, to ascribe the problems that mountain people have to genetic deficiencies rather than to inappropriate institutional supports, and to assert that all we have to do is organize and throw the bums out. Life is not so uncomplicated.

But I am heartened by much of what has happened in the last ten years. We are beginning to accumulate that missing knowledge that Emma Miles talked about. We are reassessing and redefining our strengths and weaknesses. Many of the uplifted have unchained themselves by reevaluating their heritage. We are talking to each other and celebrating our arts and traditions. Let us continue.

Dan Leidig

See volume 2, chapter 5, for biography.

From *A Field Guide to Poetics*

I have come to this field of fresh earth
where John Duncan plowed on Thursday.
He did not want pay from a neighbor.
What he sought was talk.

And not about furrow-straight sentences
or theory of line
or paradoxes about roots
withering in resurrection.

It was about the hurt in his broken ribs
got while bracing a pole
to close a gap to keep the cattle in.
"My bones are old and brittle," he said.

Printed by permission of the author.

Now in this turned dirt I try
to make a connection, to close a gap.
From under the next hill
the sound of John's tractor
Echoes in the March air
and I find no simile
for the dark and brittle pain
in every turning.

Laurie K. Lindberg

Reared as a Hoosier, Laurie Lindberg received her education at Ball State University in Muncie, Indiana. After receiving an undergraduate degree in English, she spent several years in Canada, where she helped to found and edit Canada's first feminist literary journal. After receiving her M.A. and then her Ph.D. at Ball State, she accepted a position teaching writing and literature at Pikeville College in Pikeville, Kentucky, where she is now an associate professor of English who specializes in women's and Appalachian literature. She has served on the steering committee of the Appalachian Studies Association and the Assembly for the Literature and Culture of Appalachia. Recently appointed to the board of the Kentucky Humanities Council, she considers herself no longer a Hoosier but a Kentuckian.

An Ethical Inquiry into the Works of Denise Giardina

Multiculturalism is an idea whose time seems to have arrived. Everywhere there are seminars on the works of Hispanic and Native American authors. Seldom, however, except within our own region, do we read or hear about literature produced by writers from this region called Appalachia. And this seems singularly unfortunate, both for the authors and for readers in general, because writers from the Appalachian region have been, and are, producing works of high quality that deserve a readership and criticism outside as well as inside the region.

    Within the area, scholars discuss and interpret Appalachian works in magazines and journals like *Now and Then* (East Tennessee State University),

Printed by permission of the author.

Appalachian Journal (Appalachian State University), and *Appalachian Heritage* (Berea College). Robert J. Higgs has pointed out that we in Appalachia inhabit what has been referred to by the critic Stanley Fish as an "interpretive community" of our own. However, Higgs continues, if Appalachian literature is ever to take its rightful place among other specialized literatures of high quality, it must be considered not only by "insiders," with their unique perspectives, but also by "outsiders" and their critical systems.

Whereas texts by writers from the Southern Appalachian region sometimes have been considered in the light of sociology or politics or economics, few works have been investigated in terms of what the "outsider" critic Wayne Booth calls "ethical criticism." This neglect is difficult to understand, for much of the body of Appalachian literature invites, even seems to insist on, evaluation from an ethical perspective, perhaps because the history of the region involves so much exploitation, so much prejudice against people from the hills. In their acceptance of oppression or their active fight against it, many Appalachians have learned to think in terms of justice and freedom and tolerance; they have had to demonstrate patience and courage and endurance. So Booth's ethical criticism is an ideal system within which to consider and evaluate Appalachian literature.

Booth's most complete expression of his ideas about ethical criticism are presented in his book *The Company We Keep: An Ethics of Fiction* (1988), in which he argues against some of the most familiar critical ideas about literature. He suggests, along with the reader response critics, that the "affective fallacy"—that is, the tendency to judge a work by its effect on a reader—is not so fallacious as some have thought. He claims that scholars and critics have been erroneously taught to analyze a work and evaluate it without reference to reality, to "political beliefs and gut reactions" (6). And he views the text/narrative/story/fiction (whatever we choose to call it) not as a puzzle to be solved, nor as a challenge to be met, nor as a text which has no meaning except that which each of us assigns to it. He views a fiction and its characters as friends in whose company we spend time while we read, and whose influence on us may last long after we part company.

This metaphor of friendship between the work and the reader Booth extends to the author, as well. The idea is not new; he traces the history of it in his book (*Company* 25–48). But Booth gives this old idea of friendship between reader and work a new dimension. Expanding on the basic premise of his groundbreaking work, *A Rhetoric of Fiction* (1961), Booth argues persuasively that all authors and works bear a rhetorical message for the friendly reader. Although most of what we would term "good" books are not openly didactic, with few exceptions all literature presents, and tries to persuade readers of, its creator's political, ethical, social, or philosophical agendas. Not all authors intend to do so, nor do all readers get the message, of course; but Booth claims that all works operate persuasively upon the *thoughtful* reader, and it has now become almost a commonplace regarding not just the works we might normally class as rhetorical, like essays and speeches, but also fictions.

Some critics disagree regarding the value—what Booth even considers the *inevitability*—of an "ethical" critical approach to literature. Whereas Booth claims that "no reading can be considered responsible that ignores the challenge of a work's fixed norms" (*Company* 152), others insist on evaluating works only in terms of their "aesthetic" value or form, even those in which the plots are created from the characters' dilemmas as they face moral and ethical choices. They have resisted asking the questions which Booth designates as vital to a "responsible" response to a fiction: (1) Is this work "morally, politically, or philosophically sound?" And (2) "Is it likely to work for good or ill in those who read it?" (*Company* 5). The definition of "ethical" in operation here is not a narrow definition limited to moral standards, honesty, decency, tolerance, and other qualities that most of us consider goods (though these are certainly included); but, for Booth, "ethical" has its classical meaning of "an entire range of effects on the 'character' or 'person' or 'self'" (*Company* 8). The question of artistic quality is important, but it is only one consideration that should operate when we evaluate a work. *All* of the effects on the reader must be carefully considered.

This range of effects operates not only while the book is being read but afterwards as well. If we question acquaintances who read widely about the influence books have had on their lives, we will almost always find that books and authors have affected or even determined careers, lifestyles, philosophies—all kinds of personal choices, sometimes made long after the work in question has been read. Some people report that certain characters or situations or beliefs become integral to their lives after they have encountered them in fiction, and this may be especially true of literature set in one's own region. But there is another way in which stories, like our human friends, may influence us: even if the effect doesn't last beyond the reading, we are involved more or less deeply *while* we are reading. Booth suggests that

> Perhaps we all underestimate the extent to which we absorb the values of what we read. And even when we do not retain them, the fact remains that insofar as the fiction has *worked* for us, we have lived with its values for the duration: we have been *that kind of person* for at least as long as we remained in the presence of the work. (*Company* 41)

> Each work of art . . . determines to some degree *how at least the one moment will be lived.* (*Company* 17)

When we find a writer whom we admire, when we say, "Yes, I really liked that book, those characters, that author" and seek out more works by that author, we act in this way usually because we agree with, or at least admire, the ethical perspective of the book. The characters, the narrator, and the author are those whose company we can enjoy—and perhaps with whom we can identify and from whom we can learn.

For a number of us "insider" scholars and readers of Appalachian literature, one of these most rewarding of authors is Denise Giardina. The Appalachian novels of Giardina are among those particularly appropriate for the sort of ethical inquiry which Wayne Booth believes is the responsibility of all thoughtful readers. Giardina's works welcome, even invite, questions about values, about ethics, about what "character" and "integrity" are. They challenge us to live up to her characters'—and our own—beliefs.

The first of Giardina's two novels set in Appalachia is *Storming Heaven,* published in 1987 to considerable acclaim. That year Giardina was chosen for the Joe Savage award as one of the year's most promising new voices, and her book received a W. D. Weatherford Award for the best work about the Appalachian South. *The Unquiet Earth,* published in 1992, won the 1992 Lillian Smith award for fiction that contributes to a better understanding of the South. Both books have been popular among students and teachers in Appalachian studies classes throughout the area. What kind of company are we keeping when we read Denise Giardina, when we spend hours in the company of the characters within her field of vision, when we close the book but find ourselves remembering the people and world view she has created? What are the values, the "fixed norms" upon which the books appear to be based? What do they persuade us to wish for?

Storming Heaven and *The Unquiet Earth* form a natural unit for discussion because together these two novels chronicle the lives of the residents of eastern Kentucky and western West Virginia, beginning around the turn of the century and continuing up to the present. They focus on the conflict between the coal mine owners and the miners, and Giardina is unashamedly, passionately committed to the side of the miners and the union. The books are a strong indictment of what outside forces have done to Appalachia in their drive for profit, as well as what Appalachians have done to each other. Giardina's fixed norms are not difficult to see; she values justice, individual freedom, love—and the fight to guarantee all of these liberties. It is easy to see why the book has proven a favorite with readers both inside and outside the region.

As is true in both books, the narration in *Storming Heaven* is accomplished by a variety of first-person speakers. As they tell what is happening and reveal who they are, they provide exposition, advance the plot and characterization, and imply Giardina's values and vision. C. J. Marcum, for instance, the first and oldest of the four narrators in *Storming Heaven,* recalls the days before the railroad had persuaded the local people to sell the property rights to their land, rights that were passed on within only a few years to the coal companies. Raised by his grandfather, who named him Cincinnatus Jefferson for "the two greatest men that ever lived" (*Storming* 16) and planned for him to study law in the town of Justice, West Virginia, C. J. learns as a boy how little justice there can be for those who are poor and powerless: his grandfather is murdered for refusing to sell his land to the railroads, and the local sheriff evicts C. J. and his grandmother. This early experience has a lasting effect on him, and he enters the fight against the oppressive companies. Although C. J. joins the Socialist party and tells us that he votes for Eugene

Debs, he is no intellectual. But he is an honest man who does what he believes is right, who even has the courage to change his ideas when he decides that his old ideas were wrong. The prejudice he had felt against blacks, for example, dissolves after he comes to know Doc Booker, another of the members of the Socialist Club and a dedicated physician who treats his patients without charging any fees because he knows they can't afford to pay. C. J.'s commitment to justice and tolerance makes him a friend anyone should admire.

Another of the book's narrators, Rosa Angelelli, has little to offer us in comparison to the high ideals of justice held by C. J. Marcum, but Rosa's situation certainly evokes our compassion. Rosa is a difficult character with whom to spend time, because even her early sections of the book reflect the fear and confusion she feels. Like Giardina's own ancestors, Rosa is from Italy, sent by a desperately poor father to marry a man who believes, like so many others, that he will become rich in the West Virginia coalfields. Wanting only to love and be loved, Rosa is abused by her husband and exploited by "Senore" Davidson, the mine owner who employs her as a maid; her beloved sons are killed in a mining disaster, and Rosa loses her mind. Showing us the miserably lonely, terrifying life of Rosa, Giardina illustrates the plight of some of the immigrant women who came to the coalfields expecting wealth and happiness and beauty but found themselves struggling against poverty, alienation, and hideous ugliness. Like the butterflies pinned behind glass in Mr. Davidson's study, Rosa is trapped, all freedom gone. Rosa is not a comfortable "friend" to have, but meeting her may elicit our compassion and show us an aspect of the history of the coalfields with which we may not have been familiar—the cruel prejudice against minorities which operated there, just as it did in other parts of the country.

The relationship between the other two narrators, Carrie Bishop and Rondal Lloyd, provides the major love interest in the novel. Although the two never marry, they live together and work together to bring in the United Mine Workers union, which they believe will guarantee justice for the miners of the Appalachian coalfields. The child they have together is truly a love child—and clearly, for Giardina, not a matter for shame but for happiness and pride. While a prudish reader may condemn the two for their relationship outside of marriage, Giardina approves, not necessarily because she advocates "free love" as a fixed norm, but rather because it seems right between these two characters. Some may disapprove of Carrie's and Rondal's actions, but the relationship that results in the birth of the baby Dillon is no casual affair. We have to acknowledge the strong and loving bond between them that results in the child (who, in turn, becomes the bridge to the next book).

Carrie Bishop is a feminist in the same style as many women in earlier times; without ever using the word or conceiving of herself as a revolutionary, Carrie defies the edicts of her time by insisting on the same right to "personhood" as Wilma Dykeman's woman protagonist demanded in her novel *The Tall Woman* (1964). Ignoring her father's orders to spend her time with the womenfolk in the kitchen, Carrie listens in on the men's conversation. When her father refuses to let her learn to hunt, she persuades her brother Miles to teach her. When her father warns her that she'll never find a man because she's not "deferrin'" enough, she worries a little, but not too much, for her two aunts, both once married, are strong, decisive women. And when she thinks that she has found the ideal man in Rondal, she gives herself to him unreservedly and refuses to regret her rash action the next day, even though she knows she is now a "ruined" woman, seduced and abandoned. (Later, she will insist on another man's knowing of her relationship with Rondal before she will even consider his proposal, because she cannot be less than completely honest.)

From Rondal Lloyd, Carrie has learned about the union and the efforts the company is making to prevent its establishment; when she has the opportunity, she joins the forces against the company, even wielding a machine gun on one occasion when a huge group of irate women takes over a company stronghold. Devoted as she is to family and grateful as she is to her brother for sending her to nursing school, she repudiates Miles when she realizes that he has "sold out" to the company. Her training as a nurse becomes invaluable when the strikers are evicted from their homes and must struggle to survive in their tent cities, and always we see her just as gentle and compassionate and committed to healing as she is fierce and brave when she encounters violence and injustice.

Rondal is probably the most single-minded and the least self-aware character in *Storming Heaven*. From the time his father takes him as a ten-year-old into the mines with him, Rondal knows hate and fear—not so much of the work underground or the heaviness of the labor, as of the dangerous conditions sanctioned by the company and the unfairly low salaries that make it impossible for a man, no matter how hard he works, to support a family. Giardina leads us to see Rondal's anger against the coal mine owners and managers as just, and the union as the only means by which to wrest power from the company that has stolen the land and made the people who lived there virtual slaves. Having been rejected by a mother who feared to lose him in a mining accident, Rondal has grown up afraid to love any woman and does not even know why; but he knows well why he must risk his life for the union—to help his father, his brothers, his people regain the freedom and the power over their own lives which they once had. Giardina clearly approves of his resolve, and, by presenting him as a hero, though a flawed hero, she solicits our approval of him.

Wayne Booth believes that a great deal can be determined about the ethics of a literary work by considering what it persuades us to wish for. *Storming Heaven* finds us hoping for the death of the gun thugs who are shooting at random among the people sleeping in their tent city along the tracks. It encourages us to wish that Malcolm Denbigh, the manager who had ordered a union organizer thrown alive into a roaring furnace, may face some similar fate. Normally we would not consider the desire to see people killed a positive effect of a work, but Giardina seems to believe that violence, though not a good, is in some cases necessary if one is to protect one's life and freedom. To shoot a gun thug who would shoot you first if he could is not murder but self-defense. She would urge us to join battle with the forces of justice, tolerance, freedom, and love against all who would try to exploit others and deny them their human rights. Giardina and her book are friends who encourage us to get involved, to fight for what we believe is right, regardless of the risks to our own safety or comfort.

Storming Heaven is an illuminating book in several ways. Giardina herself grew up in a West Virginia coal camp, the daughter of a nurse and a book-keeper there, yet she never heard of the Battle of Blair Mountain (the climax of her novel and the West Virginia miners' efforts to establish the UMW) until she was an adult. During this little-known battle, striking miners were subdued by state and federal forces, the government turning upon its own people at the behest of the wealthy mine owners who could not afford to allow a union to educate and represent the workers. Like many shameful episodes in our nation's history, this battle had been ignored in histories of the state and the nation. As Giardina began the careful, exhaustive research on which her novel is based, she was appalled at what she found about the coming of the coal industry to Appalachia, and her fiction invites us to join in her judgment of this portion of our country's history. We are urged to deplore with her and her characters the avarice that led the railroads and the coal companies to steal the land that had belonged to residents of the area for generations, the violence of the owners and operators and of the "gun thugs" they hired to protect their ill-gotten investments, the lack of respect for human beings that characterized the operation of the mines and made them intolerably hazardous. Some commentators on Giardina's novel have criticized her for presenting a picture that is all black and white, for showing only one side of the story. Giardina's response: There are some situations that actually *are* black and white. It is difficult, for example, to find anything good to say about the Nazi forces of Germany during World War II. It is difficult, as well, to find anything positive to say about the coal industry in Appalachia during the early part of this century.

In *The Unquiet Earth,* Giardina brings her history up to date and offers us some new companions. In contrast to the four speakers and twenty-three shifts in speaker of the previous novel, *The Unquiet Earth* has six narrators and sixty-six shifts. The result is a narrative more fragmented and less unified, perhaps reflecting the more complex, changing conditions of the second half of the twentieth century. The fixed norms that Giardina believes in, however, remain unchanged. She still privileges love and freedom, justice and integrity, and, most of all, courageous activism in the face of political and social oppression. As in *Storming Heaven,* she encourages us to hate, not the people so much as the greed, cruelty, and selfishness that motivate all too many of those who misuse power. If violence is necessary, she will advocate that, too.

The violence that dominates the first part of *The Unquiet Earth* is World War I, as Carrie and Rondal's son, Dillon, serves in the British army because of his eagerness to fight against fascism, and Carrie's niece, Rachel, serves as a nurse on a hospital ship in the South Pacific. Both survive the war, and what operates for Giardina and for us as a symbol of its horror, a "Jap" skull, is to Rachel's boyfriend a souvenir and a joke. We recognize the moral strength of Dillon and the weakness of Rachel in their differing responses to the skull, when she justifies her possession of it by saying "Fred gave it to me," and Dillon responds, "It was a person. You can't carry a person's head around like this. . . . You don't give part of a dead person's body as a present!" (*Unquiet* 72). Although Dillon fights in the war, he fights for a principle (just as he will later oppose both the mine operators and a corrupt union), not forgetting the humanity even of his enemy. Dillon's respect for the dead demonstrated here foreshadows his grief and outrage over the mining company's callous removal of his father's bones from their grave. We can only sympathize with Dillon and share his disgust at the lack of respect and the inhumanity of the company.

In updating the story of the coalfields, Giardina brings in a phenomenon of the 1960s that objectified Appalachia as never before in the history of our country: the War on Poverty. This war and its army, Volunteers in Service to America, are represented by Tom Kolwiecki, a social worker who becomes disillusioned when he performs his mission of organizing a co-op that is so effective in empowering the townspeople that the federal government threatens to imprison him if he will not leave Blackberry Creek. Giardina creates in the character Tom a visionary who is sincere in his desire to help others, but who is prevented from doing so by the political and social institutions that supposedly exist for that very purpose. Like Rondal of *Storming Heaven* and his son Dillon in *The Unquiet Earth*, Tom is a fighter, someone who sacrifices a great deal for his commitment to what he believes will restore some measure of human rights to those who have lost them and improve the quality of life for some who are suffering. One portion of what Tom gives up is marriage (though not love) with Jackie, Dillon and Rachel's daughter, who has loved him since she was a teenager. But Tom is committed to his theological and humanitarian mission in Honduras, and he risks everything for his beliefs, embracing what Higgs terms "the old verities: courage, honor, sacrifice, pity, and compassion" that inform the works and characters of Giardina's and so many other Appalachian authors, making them admirable company indeed.

The Unquiet Earth is particularly interesting in what it reveals about its author. Without making the error of assuming too many autobiographical elements in the novel, we may note a number of parallels between the character Jackie and the author Denise: both were born in the West Virginia coalfields, spent a year studying in England, worked as journalists, were connected with charitable activities, worked as assistants to politicians, and were involved in politics themselves. Both eventually settled in or near Appalachia (though Jackie cannot stay after the flood, patterned in the novel after the real Buffalo Creek disaster). They are about the same age. Like Giardina, Jackie initially assumes that Appalachia is a subject about which no one would want to read but ends up embracing that subject as her own. Unlike Jackie, Giardina is happy living in the region, having recently bought a house and settled herself in Charleston, West Virginia. In a recent interview, Giardina explained how she views her role as an Appalachian writer. "I'm telling a story, honestly, from the inside," she said. "It's important for people from here to tell their own stories."

In "Sut Lovingood and the Hard No in Appalachian Literature," Robert J. Higgs calls Thomas Wolfe "the prototype of the modern Appalachian novelist, . . . one finding his or her own voice and vision on native ground" (47). Giardina follows Wolfe's example. Her vision is in a sense pessimistic, for she envisions the hatred and cruelty and avarice in people, but she has not allowed that vision to destroy her pleasure in life, also writing of love and courage and compassion and generosity. In short, she celebrates and affirms life, like Wolfe; denies that life is meaningless, whatever its pains; and says "yes to the joy of being alive, no matter how troublesome the local condition." Her willingness to face and fight evil in the world while insisting nevertheless on the goodness and meaningfulness of life makes her a good role model for others of us who are fighters, and a good companion and friend for those who merely wish for reassurance that, in spite of everything, we can still love ourselves and others.

Works Cited

Booth, Wayne C. *A Rhetoric of Fiction.* Orig. 1961. 2d ed. Chicago: U of Chicago P, 1987.

————. *The Company We Keep: An Ethics of Fiction.* Berkeley: U of California P, 1988.

Giardina, Denise. *Storming Heaven.* New York: Ballantine Books, 1987.

————. *The Unquiet Earth.* New York: Norton, 1992.

Higgs, Robert J. "Sut Lovingood and the Hard No in Appalachian Literature." *Appalachian Heritage* 20, no. 4 (Fall 1992): 41–49; and 21, no. 1 (Winter 1993): 6–8.

James B. Goode

James B. Goode is the author of four books of poetry: *Appalachian Mountain Mother* (1969), *The Whistle and the Wind* (1971), *Poets of Darkness* (1981), and *Canaries in the Coal* (1993). The son and grandson of miners, Goode says that he himself would have been a miner had he not gone to college and become a teacher. After attending Southeast Community College in Cumberland, Kentucky, he graduated from the University of Kentucky and returned to Southeast Community College, where he is professor and director of the Appalachian Civic Leadership Project.

Laborers in the Field of the Muses

(For James Still)

I was but in the far flung genes,
Spinning along in fixed tracks
Toward a sure destiny,
When he carefully cleared the mythical field of muses
Weeding words and sentences
And sayings
Into honest rows of conversation
Heaped
And raked
And pulled
From a stubborn Earth with the liquid rhythm of his hoe.

Practical and careful—
Wary of the fragile, gripping roots
He hoed out between Dead Mare and Wolfpen,
To weave his way by the bare cabins dotting Little Carr Creek.

Following hollows
And circling, airy smoke
From the lichen colored chimneys,
He plowed paragraphs around ancient trees,
And hunkered in the cool evening hollow shade,
Forging links metaphors and context made.
With feather hammers striking true,
What he heard and said
Fell
Floating into form and place.

In the cool Appalachian mists
He became the plow,
The rhythmical hoe,
The chain connected . . .
Blow by blow
He became the field he made,
A laborer
In the rows and rows.

From *Across the Ridge: The Newsletter of the Appalachian Civic Leadership Project,* Winter 1993.
Reprinted by permission of the author.

Fred Waage

Fred Waage, a professor of English at East Tennessee State University, was born and raised in Ithaca, New York. He received his B.A. and Ph.D. in English at Princeton University. Waage then worked on the staff of the Huntington Library and taught English at Northwestern University, California State University, and Douglass College of Rutgers University. After relocating to the mountains of East Tennessee, he became the founding editor of the Appalachian magazine *Now and Then,* on whose editorial board he continues to serve. Waage's poetry and fiction have appeared in small magazines, and he has published in scholarly journals on topics such as Renaissance literature, popular culture studies, and environmental literature.

Teaching Environmental Literature in Southern Appalachia

As an immigrant to Appalachia with lots of living experience in urbanized areas of the U.S., I've been struck by a paradox of attitude which may not seem such to a native. The beauty and magnificence of Appalachian nature contrast violently to the lack of concern for the preservation of this nature, even among people whose lifestyles supposedly still rely on traditional activities requiring relations with nature unmediated by technology. Part of this insensitivity to nature is probably based on the historical situation of Appalachia as a latecomer to the economic development of the eastern U.S., and therefore as subject to more frenetic efforts to create industry, jobs, incomes, and places to buy things, particularly "authentic" Appalachian things ("folk culture exists for the consumption by an elite"—consisting of outsiders [Batteau, "Sacrifice" 104]). Also, though it seems simplistic, I feel that, while the natural world is taken for granted by long-term residents, it is seen as vulnerable by more recent immigrants who have witnessed environmental destruction elsewhere, and many of whom moved there in part to escape it.

A third cause of the paradox is that many "traditional" activities in rural mountain communities which involve interaction with, or "use" of, nature are considered *ab*use by people not dependent economically or socially on these activities. What was relatively benign when practiced in 1892 is, with population growth, wilderness loss, and technological advance, relatively malignant in 1994. Finally, the persistent—despite great changes—sense of Appalachia as a region apart, *sui generis,* a unique cultural space, makes it harder for its residents to visualize it as subject to, or even affected by, environmental circumstances outside its borders, than for people in more changeable, less homogeneous regions.

Printed by permission of the author.

Allen Batteau, in articles and in his *The Invention of Appalachia,* has brilliantly elaborated on this paradox of how the "poetic attitude toward Appalachia and nature, bordering on a religious attitude, has coexisted with a rapacious destruction of both" in a "symbolic process of sacrifice and victimage" (Batteau, *Invention* 7). To the extent that all writing about Appalachia, by natives or outsiders, involves the expression of these paradoxical attitudes toward the region as a whole (including Nature), the evolution of these attitudes can be traced in a great variety of writings of and about Appalachia.

Considering the above, effective environmental education is to be achieved in Appalachia, more than in other locales, by addressing and analyzing attitudes, values, and perceptions at least as much as actual environmental issues and problems—particularly since, as emphasized above, much of Appalachian consciousness does not accept such problems—for example, public access to wilderness areas—as problems in the first place. Therefore, environmental *literature* (imaginative writing), which emphasizes the attitudinal and subjective at least as much as the empirical and objective, may be material uniquely suited to environmental education in Appalachia.

ॐ

"Environmental literature" can be defined as writing about nature which embodies "a vital dialogue between imaginative and active, practical and contemplative, experience" (Waage xii–xiii). It may contain much objective material, but this is informed by a primarily subjective vision, using the means of art to mediate subjective vision and objective content. There are many shadings in this definition, and it allows for many degrees of closeness between writer and nature observed. Probably Thoreau's writings, particularly *Walden*, can be considered, if not the first, at least the archetypal works of American environmental literature. *Walden* might be paired with a contemporary masterpiece of American (and Appalachian) literature, Annie Dillard's *Pilgrim at Tinker Creek,* as works which are on the "subjective" end of the spectrum while containing much specific and accurate nature observation. On the "objective" end might be Rachel Carson's *Silent Spring,* and many of John McPhee's works, such as *The Pine Barrens* and *Basin and Range,* which are primarily conveyers of information, but which are informed with such passion and artistry that they engage any reader's subjective feelings and attitudes.

The above definition of environmental literature allows it to include, as material for teaching, a wide diversity of writings. Many works of imaginative literature—fiction, nonfiction prose, poetry—are not primarily "environmental" in subject matter, yet contain much that can be discussed in terms of the above definition. Likewise, children's literature, which can't go very deeply into environmental issues and problems, can present very forceful visions of nature rightly and wrongly used by humans. What is lacking in writing of and about Appalachia—imaginative texts taking the environment as primary subject—can be compensated for by what is found subordinately or indirectly expressed in writings with a different primary focus.

In my book *Teaching Environmental Literature,* I defined four primary pedagogical formats for teaching environmental literature. First, a particular syllabus of works in environmental literature may be taught in a traditional classroom situation. Next, a writing course, taught in the classroom and/or in the field, can involve actual nature writing enlightened by the reading of significant texts. Third, environmental literature can provide the backdrop for a substantial, structured field experience, such as a wilderness camping expedition. Finally, literature can be taught as part of an interdisciplinary course focused on "knowing" holistically an entire geographically or ecologically defined region—the examples discussed in my book are the Colorado River's Glen Canyon Dam, the Mississippi, and New England.

All of these formats are applicable to Appalachian literature, but in differing degrees. Based on the premise derived from Batteau that all writing of Appalachia can be seen as to some degree environmental, much is available for teaching in the traditional classroom. As before, this material can be divided roughly into that which is ideological, conceptual, empirical; and that whose primary emphasis is "literary"—involving human situations and psychological insight crafted to evoke the subjectivity of human relations with nature. An important consideration in using any writings in these categories is the author's position as an "outsider" or "insider" to Appalachia, or as somewhere in between. To a readership of relative "insiders," the author's degree of "insideness," as intuited from what she/he says, may have a powerful influence on his/her credibility. In fact, this is the nexus of difficulty and importance in Appalachian environmental literature: can the "outsider's" environmental concern be made credible, given the "insider's" paradoxical nonchalance about it?

In the following paragraphs I want to discuss the implicit environmental content in classic Appalachian texts, literary and nonliterary, which are not usually considered "environmental." It should be noted that their authors are former "outsiders" who have taken on the public role of "insiders" and address themselves to "outsiders." Read by "insiders" today, these texts may express a complex subjectivity.

In Horace Kephart's famous and influential *Our Southern Highlanders* (1913), environmental commentary is implicit throughout. In Kephart's third chapter, he describes his interest in "the mountains themselves" as "set against" his "human neighbors" and as "an Eden still unpeopled and unspoiled" (Kephart 50). Among the generally "natural history" attributes of this Eden, he includes its "mineral wealth," ingenuously adding, "for the present, it is a hard country to prospect in, owing to the thick covering of the forest floor" (73). So here, set against the implications of transience in the "still unpeopled," we find the assumption of "prospecting" as a natural activity not in the category "spoliation." In ambivalent contrast, we find Kephart as prophet listening to a cogwheel locomotive, seeing it despoiling the Tennessee forest. Slowly but inexorably, a leviathan was crawling into the wilderness and was soon to consume it. He says to his audience:

All this . . . shall be swept away, tree and plant, beast and fish. Fire will blacken the earth; flood will swallow and spew forth the soil. The simple-hearted native men and women will scatter and disappear. In their stead will come slaves speaking strange tongues, to toil in the darkness under the rocks. Soot will arise, and foul gases; the streams will run murky death. Let me not see it! (104)

The status of this prophecy, in terms of the way in which Kephart presents his "simple-hearted men and women" elsewhere, would reward study.

Emma Bell Miles's *The Spirit of the Mountains* likewise navigates between author's and subject's implied stances toward the physical environment. Often, as in the dawn-to-dusk description of farm life (25–35), she portrays a seamless weaving of humans' and nonhumans' activities. She insightfully defines the separate outdoor male realm and the indoor female realm (68–70), implying sex-defined attitudes of natives toward all Appalachian spaces. When she accompanies old Pap Farris "on a tramp around his land," she reveals the values expressed in *possession* of land (versus the "common" wild land that dominates and encircles it). In her discussion of "folk" music (146), she reveals indirectly the aesthetic similarities between it and the wild land—by contrast to more "domesticated" folk music of other regions.

Similarly, another classic Appalachian writer, Mary Murfree, in her socially focused novels, still conveys implicit and explicit environmental ethics and perceptions. For example, in *The Ordeal* (1912), there are explicit word-portraits of hostile or indifferent nature: "The winds were loosed and rioted through the lonely recesses of the craggy ravines and the valley with a wild and eerie blare" (151). At the same time, this winter scene is rendered emblematic by the bright coat of the vanished boy Archie caught on a bare bough. The topographical shape of the whole novel creates isolated islands of human activity in an overwhelming ocean of wilderness. The quest for Archie is implicitly a quest to overcome the power this vastness has to break the threads of human community. Of course, Murfree involves literal scenes of environmental transformation—the railroad is always being built—but most of her constructs are symbolic, with different social spaces implying different roles of nature in human lives. The old Indian fortune-teller who shelters Archie until he is eventually found has mystical connections with nature's power and thrives in the center of winter's ravages amid the blood-curdling howls of wolves.

Much more recent Appalachian fiction and poetry deal more explicitly with environmental issues and consciousness. Lyrical descriptions of natural beauty are woven throughout James Still's *River of Earth* (1940), but they are persistently presented in a context of environmental ethics. Fletch enjoys the pasture by grabbing a handful of partridge eggs, "broken and running between his fingers" (22); seeing them, Euly turns white and slaps his face. When Uncle Jolly was little, grandpap killed him a Kentucky redbird, and secretly replaced it and each subsequent dead bird with a newly killed one when the old one got maggoty. But he becomes disgusted with his own kill-

ing, telling Jolly it "hain't right to take a creature's life just to pleasure yourself. Mighty nigh like killing folks" (150). In Still's coal-mining country,
"The waters ran yellow, draining acid from the mines, cankering rocks in its
bed. . . . There were no fishes swimming the eddies, nor striders looking at
themselves in the waterglass" (189). Wilma Dykeman's *Return the Innocent
Earth* (1973) frames its human drama around corporate sponsorship of crop-
treatment experiments for the canning industry, revealing the linkage between
environmental destruction and commercial exploitation of Appalachia. Lisa
Alther's *Kinflicks* (1975) counterpoints the protagonist's family connection with
environmentally destructive industry and her own cabin life in a natural setting, focused on her efforts to save the lives of swallows nesting in her chimney.

It is in poetry that the most direct recent evocations of Appalachian environment can be found. Its domain may best be defined by the title of a book
by Cherokee poet Marilou Awiakta: *Abiding Appalachia: Where Mountain and
Atom Meet* (1978 [8th ed., 1994]). The most prominent writer in this group,
though his home terrain is marginally Appalachian, is Wendell Berry, whose
verse is most accessible in his *Collected Poems, 1957–1982* (1985). As a poet,
Berry gives sensory life to the agrarian ideal he dramatizes in his fiction and
defends in his polemical essays; Berry is not so much an environmentalist as
the advocate of a non-technological, environmentally sensitive human culture, congruent with "native" Appalachian culture as described by Kephart
and Miles but not necessarily embodying the paradoxes of this culture described at the beginning of this essay. Another nationally prominent poet
and novelist, Fred Chappell, in *Midquest* (1981) and *Source* (1985), also dramatizes Appalachian nature in its interaction with human cultures, as in the
double meaning of "blood" in "Here":

> The ditch twinkles now the rain has stopped.
> And the ground begins to puff and suck
> With little holes. A man could live down here forever,
> Where his blood is. (*Source* 8)

Another important Appalachian poet of nature is Robert Morgan, whose
earlier volumes such as *Red Owl* (1972) presented lyrical, unmediated visions
of natural objects themselves, while in the more recent *Groundwork* (1980)
he combines nature and culture. Two other important regional poets whose
work is environmentally aware are Jeff Daniel Marion (*Out in the Country,
Back Home*, 1976), and Jim Wayne Miller (*The Mountains Have Come Closer*,
1980; rpt. 1991). Miller's *Brier, His Book* also continues the environmental
concerns expressed in poems like those in the sequence *Country People*. His
play, *His First, Best Country*, based on the Gnomon Press chapbook by the
same title, has been presented in rotating repertory at Horse Cave Theatre
near Mammoth Cave National Park during summer 1992. It opens with
Billy Edd Wheeler's song, "The Coming of the Roads," and concludes with
Jean Ritchie's song, "Black Waters," and has environmental concerns as a

chief theme. Miller's recent collections, *Vein of Words* (1984) and *Nostalgia for 70* (1986) are published by Art Cuelho's Seven Buffaloes Press, Box 249, Big Timber, Montana 59011. Cuelho's contributions to environmental themes in Appalachian writing are found in such collections as *Harvest from the Hills* (1984) and *Step Around the Mountain* (1983).

Although poetry dominates explicitly environmental Appalachian writing, a few prose works approach the tradition of Thoreau and Dillard: G. Douglass McNeill, *The Last Forest: Tales of the Allegheny Woods* (1940); Rose Hutchins, *Hidden Valley of the Smokies* (1971); Wendell Berry, *The Unforeseen Wilderness: Kentucky's Red River Gorge* (1971); Charlton Ogburn, *The Southern Appalachians: A Wilderness Quest* (1975); and Harry Middleton, *On the Spine of Time: An Angler's Love of the Smokies* (1991) all involve subjective, literary vision and language to some degree. As environmental writing, the important works of Harry Caudill, most famously his *Night Comes to the Cumberlands: A Biography of a Depressed Area* (1963) are extremely significant in their analysis of the "curse of coal" (*Night* 346) and its effect on Appalachian nature and traditional culture. *Night* was one of the great environmental texts of the 1960s, inspiring the "Great Society"'s economic discovery of Appalachia by "outsiders" and its many consequences, and could be particularly valuable in field-related environmental courses. Equally important in our context is Wilma Dykeman's *The French Broad* (1955), in the "Rivers of America" series published by Holt, Rinehart and Winston. Her chapter "Who Killed the French Broad?" advocates a consensual law for its preservation: "A law is the logic of man, a river is the logic of nature: when the two are fused for the benefit of both, the result is one kind of beauty" (Dykeman 293).

ॐ

Two other ways in which actual field experience can be involved with Appalachian environmental literature suggest themselves. The writing students in a class can perform observation in any outdoor space as source of writing, from informal journal entries (as in Weldon Reed's course on the wilderness experience) to the studied lyrical prose epitomized by *Pilgrim at Tinker Creek*. The Southern Appalachians provide opportunity for all sorts of definitional structuring of such experience. Field experiences can be defined by locality and habitat, or by a sequence of these: the "balds," for example, or nature observation at a series of points of elevation. Most appropriate to this area, and often used to shape environmental writing, would be focus on a particular natural or unnatural feature: trail, river, stream, mountain, hollow. A human community—traditional to recent—could be observed in detail, in terms of its interaction of human and nonhuman nature. As Harry Caudill's works show, powerful nontechnical expository writing can be done on a "case study" of a particular environmental controversy or issue. Again, members of a class could each choose, observe over time, and write about a different natural species or phenomenon present in a particular limited ecosystem; or else each student could produce her/his own work on the same species or space, involving consciousness of the "I in Nature" concept to promote awareness of an environmental locale's subjective identity in human terms.

Weldon Reed's course, "Teaching Wilderness Literature in the Smoky Mountains," is an example of field experience as complement to a literature course. One variation could be a historically based course on nature in Appalachian literature (including, for example, works by Murfree, John Fox, Jr., Harriette Arnow, James Still); it could be structured around a sequence of visits to the same (or comparable) locales portrayed in their works and could thereby provide vivid contrasts, evoking insight into cultural and environmental change.

A most environmentally relevant concept advanced by Raitz and Ulack is "cognitive regions": different areas whose inhabitants—"insiders," "cognitive outsiders," "residential outsiders"—define themselves as within Appalachia or without. By extension, such cognitive regionalization also identifies varying attributes (as above) as being more or less "Appalachian" and more or less integral to the life of the individual (fictive or real) in question. In a subregionally structured course, literature defined broadly could provide the cognitive dimension of the content, since it specifically integrates subjective vision and external reality (Culture and Nature in interaction), while other disciplines such as geography, music, and sociology could provide more objectively based content. Thus an interdisciplinary Appalachian studies course centered on "cognitive regionalism" might be best suited to addressing, if not explaining, the "paradox of attitude" with which this piece began.

Note

1. The Appalachian periodical with the most environmental content is the *Katuah Journal,* Box 638, Leicester, NC 28748. Also very relevant is the American Indian literary magazine, *The Four Directions,* Box 729, Tellico Plains, TN 37385.

Works Cited

Batteau, Allen. *The Invention of Appalachia.* Tucson: U of Arizona P, 1990.
———. "The Sacrifice of Nature: A Study in the Social Production of Consciousness." *Cultural Adaptations to Mountain Environments.* Ed. Patricia D. Beaver and Burton L. Purrington. Southern Anthropological Society Proceedings #17. Athens: U of Georgia P, 1989. 94–106.
Caudill, Harry M. *Night Comes to the Cumberlands: A Biography of a Depressed Area.* Boston: Little, Brown, 1963.
Chappell, Fred. *Source.* Baton Rouge: Louisiana State UP, 1985.
Cuelho, Art, ed. *Harvest from the Hills.* Big Timber, MT: Seven Buffaloes P, 1984.
———. *Step around the Mountain.* Big Timber, MT: Seven Buffaloes P, 1983.
Dykeman, Wilma. *The French Broad.* 1955. Knoxville: U of Tennessee P, 1965.

Kephart, Horace. *Our Southern Highlanders*. New York: Outing, 1913.

Miles, Emma Bell. *The Spirit of the Mountains*. 1905. Rpt. Knoxville: U of Tennessee P, 1975.

Miller, Jim Wayne. *Brier, His Book*. Frankfort, KY: Gnomon Press, 1988.

———. *Nostalgia for 70*. Big Timber, MT: Seven Buffaloes Press (1986).

———. *Vein of Words*. Big Timber, MT: Seven Buffaloes Press (1984).

Murfree, Mary. *The Ordeal*. Philadelphia: Lippincott, 1912.

Reed, Weldon. "Teaching Wilderness Literature in the Smoky Mountains." *American Nature Writing Newsletter* 3 (1991): 1, 3.

Still, James. *River of Earth*. 1940. Rpt. Lexington: U of Kentucky P, 1978.

Waage, Frederick O., ed. *Teaching Environmental Literature: Materials, Methods, Resources*. Options for Teaching, #7. New York: Modern Language Association, 1985.

Chapter 8

Regional Identity and the Future

Introduction

Appalachian literature conveys a strong sense of place. Appalachian writers and the characters they create frequently identify strongly with the mountain region as their homeland. Displaced Appalachians, real or imagined, are often homesick. Inside the region, Appalachian writers often look back on a time and way of life that is past or passing.

Properly understood, this concern with the region's past is only part of a caring commitment which includes concern for the region's future; for a vision of the future that does not reflect an understanding of the past is not tenable. Some critics believe it is imperative that every aspect of Appalachia's history, culture, and heritage be reexamined and understood in a more realistic fashion. How, for instance, are we to understand Appalachian "otherness" or difference? Appalachian speech and its relation to other varieties of English? What has been the real role of women in Appalachian life, as opposed to the role found in stereotypical depictions? What are the implications for Appalachians of tourism, increased industrialization, and development? How can the region's history and heritage best be presented in museums, theme parks, literature, and films?

The marked sense of place in Appalachian literature nourished an emerging environmental consciousness in the region, and Appalachian writers, owing to their knowledge of the region's past and their deep concern for its future, are gaining in reputation outside the area as well as inside it. The frontier, as Frederick Jackson Turner wrote in 1893, occurs at the intersection of culture and nature, an observation no less true today. Thus the quality of the frontier as we move into the future will be determined not only by how much we learn about our cultural heritage and the natural world, but also by how much we care about the balance between them.

James Still

A native of LaFayette, Alabama, James Still graduated from Lincoln Memorial University and completed his master's degree in 1930 at Vanderbilt University. Still has worked as a librarian and as a freelance writer. For several years he was an associate professor of English at Morehead State University. Skilled in several genres, Still is among the best known and most respected of Appalachian writers. His first volume of poems, *Hounds on the Mountain* (1937), displays a sense of authenticity which has continued to characterize his work. The short story "Bat Flight" won the O. Henry Memorial Prize in 1939. Still's best-known work, *River of Earth* (1940), which won the Southern Authors Award, has been compared to *The Grapes of Wrath* for its accuracy in chronicling the demoralizing years of the Great Depression. Like his contemporaries Jesse Stuart and Harriette Simpson Arnow, Still continues to receive praise for his depiction of Appalachian life in prose and poetry.

Appalachia

Appalachia is that somewhat mythical region with no recognized boundaries. If such an area exists in terms of geography, such a domain as has shaped the lives and endeavors of men and women from pioneer days to the present and given them an independence and an outlook and a vision such as is often attributed to them, I trust to be understood for imagining the heart of it to be in the hills of eastern Kentucky where I have lived and called my home and where I have exercised as much freedom and peace as the world allows.

From *The Wolfpen Poems,* Berea College, 1986. Reprinted by permission of the author and publisher.

Roberta Herrin

Roberta T. Herrin is associate professor of English at East Tennessee State University, where she has taught since 1976. She holds an M.A. from ETSU and a Ph.D. from the University of Tennessee at Knoxville; her doctoral dissertation was a study of H. L. Mencken as a philologist. Her most recent research has been in the area of children's literature. From 1988 to 1992, Herrin directed two regional institutes in children's fantasy literature, funded by the National Endowment for the Humanities. In 1992, she was named a Howard Foundation Fellow at Brown University, which gave her a year-long sabbatical to compile an annotated bibliography of Appalachian children's literature. Among her numerous contributions to the promotion of Appalachian studies is her service as chair of the following: Appalachian Studies Association; board of directors, Appalachian Consortium; and advisory board, Center for Appalachian Studies and Services, East Tennessee State University, Johnson City.

The Child and Appalachia: Rethinking Two Major American Symbols

It is hard to imagine a time when children did not command the status, rights, and legal protection that they are afforded today. In an age when children sue their parents, when courts appoint child advocates, and when advertising agencies target children as primary consumers with power to influence the nation's economy, it is impossible to believe that the idea of the child is a recent phenomenon. The idea of childhood first appeared in thirteenth-century art and developed through the seventeenth and eighteenth centuries to become, in the nineteenth century, a major American literary symbol (Aries, Fiedler).

Coincidentally, a similar process occurred, though over a shorter time span, with reference to an entire geographical region—Appalachia. According to Henry Shapiro, Appalachia was invented in nineteenth-century travel sketches and local color literature, largely between 1870 and 1900 (Shapiro, Batteau). The "idea" of Appalachia was "that the mountainous portions of eight or nine southern states form a coherent region inhabited by a homogeneous population possessing a uniform culture" (Shapiro ix).

Though these two entities—the child and Appalachia—are assumed to have *a priori* existence, both are cultural "inventions" which first manifested themselves through creative artistic endeavor. Further similarities are striking: (1) Both were generated by outsiders. (2) Each is characterized by "otherness" and isolation. (3) Both ideas began as expressions of natural innocence and purity. (4) Individuals were asked to conform to the "reality" of the inventions. (5) Both inventions are now taken as *a priori* fact. (6) Both represent New as opposed to Old Worlds. (7) Both creations are vehicles for the rebellious and revolutionary impulse. (8) Both continue to be met with ambivalence and tension. (9) Both creations are contingent on a middle class. (10) Once these inventions became "realities," they became commodities.

It is the purpose of this paper to examine the discovery and invention of the idea of the child and the idea of Appalachia, with particular reference to their roles as symbols within American culture and literature, particularly

Printed by permission of the author.

Appalachian children's literature. I will argue that both inventions have come to symbolize the nation's ambivalence toward its self-identity. America invented Appalachia for the same reason that adult society invented the concept of the child: both symbols represent an "otherness" which generates the dialectic tension necessary for individuation. The unanswered question is whether that dialectic tension has led to a synthesis, either within the adult or within the nation.

According to Philippe Aries's now-famous work, *Centuries of Childhood* (1962), the "idea of childhood" did not exist in medieval society; there was no recognition of a "nature of childhood" as distinct from that of the adult (128). Says Aries, "Men of the tenth and eleventh centuries did not dwell on the image of childhood and . . . that image had neither interest nor even reality for them. . . . [C]hildhood was a period of transition which passed quickly and which was just as quickly forgotten" (34). To the end of the thirteenth century, "there are no children characterized by a special expression but only men on a reduced scale." Only in Greek art was the child depicted with an idealized "grace and rounded arms" or as "realistically" (34–35).

But around the thirteenth century, a concept of the child appeared which was somewhat similar to the modern idea of childhood; three types emerged, all with holy connotations: the angel, the infant Jesus, and the naked child (Aries 34–35). While real children were "scarcely ever" depicted as naked even into the fifteenth or sixteenth centuries (44), in the fourteenth century, the concept of the soul became associated with "childish nudity" (35). From the time of that association, "The theme of Holy Childhood would never cease developing in both scope and variety" (36).

Developing concurrently with this theme of infant holiness and innocence was the theme of feminine holiness in the person of Mary. According to Rougemont's classic, *Love in the Western World*, there was a movement in the Church, from the twelfth century onward, to "institute a worship of the Virgin" as counter to the popular convention of courtly love. Says Rougemont, "It is from that time that Mary has generally received the title of *Regina coeli*, and it is as a queen that from that time art has depicted her." Her ascendancy to this position had several manifestations. For example, monks became thought of as "Knights of Mary," and in the game of chess, which previously had been played with four kings, the queen was given "precedence over all other pieces, save the King, and the latter was actually reduced to the smallest possibility of real action, even though he remained the final stake and the consecrated figure" (111–12). Thus the symbols of Virgin and child became fused with the theme of holiness and innocence, a theme which would take further hold in subsequent centuries.

As the idea of childhood progressed through the fifteenth to the sixteenth and seventeenth centuries, children's clothing began to "mark" them as separate from adults, and they became known for their "sweetness, simplicity, and drollery" (extensions of holiness) and thus they became a "source of amusement and relaxation for the adult" (Aries 129). During this period, children began to be "coddled" (130), a practice to which "moralists and pedagogues" of the seventeenth century objected. They no longer regarded children as "amusing or agreeable" but were, rather, interested in their psychology and "moral solicitude" (Aries 131). Aries feels that the growing attention to the "faculty of reasoning" within children "marks the beginning of a serious and realistic concept of childhood" (152).

Aries goes farther, to make a very important distinction: "The first concept of childhood—characterized by 'coddling'—had made its appearance in the family circle, in the company of little children." The second view of childhood—which concerned itself with moralism and reasoning—had its source "outside the family" among the clergy (132). Their view of children as "fragile creatures of God" then passed into family life (133). The significant feature here is the influence of the outsider in shaping attitudes toward childhood and the Virgin Mary *for* the family.

While the idea of childhood was invented between the thirteenth and seventeenth centuries, Leslie Fiedler argues that it was the mid-eighteenth century when the child was moved "from the periphery to the center of art—and, indeed, to the center of life" (253). According to Fiedler, the "prophet" of this "major revolution" is Jean Jacques Rousseau (254). Finally, Sommerville points out that in the nineteenth century, scientists, under the influence of Darwin, "soon realized that they knew almost nothing of how children grew" (209). Thus began the close observation of the daily lives of children; men such as Charles Darwin and Bronson Alcott kept diaries of their children's behavior. The result of such focused attention on the child was the flowering of child psychology and children's literature in the nineteenth century—the "golden age" of literature for children.

As the idea of childhood was invented and children were acknowledged for their "otherness" by parents, scientists, philosophers, and psychologists, they also earned distinction as objects of abuse, which has been well documented in history and in literature and need not be discussed in detail here. By the turn of the century, local and national attention in America focused on the abuses of child labor and the "status of children in the South," particularly in coal mines and cotton mills (Shapiro 164–65). The 1900 census reported that 25,000 "operatives" under the age of sixteen made up nearly 30 percent of the work force in the cotton mills (Shapiro 164).

What do these two parallel but contradictory attitudes toward children mean? Mary Jane Hurst poses the interesting question of whether adults see children *as children* with needs of their own or, as with Humbert and Lolita, as "objects for the fulfillment" of their own needs (29). Says Hurst:

> The overwhelming number of children in our literature may reflect our cultural concern for innocence and the problem of lost innocence, key American themes, but our apparent ambivalence toward children, in literature as well as in life, suggests that the reasons behind their prominence in our literary tradition must be complex. (2)

This complexity is played out in our culture and in our literature in a multitude of paradoxes. On the one hand, as noted earlier, in no previous age have children been so protected and nurtured by law; on the other hand, in no previous age have their abuse and neglect been so highly publicized. (I cannot assess whether abuse and neglect are more *prevalent* today than in other ages.) On the one hand, literature for children is one of the most prolific and profitable genres marketed; on the other hand, that same literature has yet to receive the status and critical attention afforded literature for adults. The Modern Language Association did not formally recognize children's literature until the 1970s, and the first graduate program in children's literature was not created until 1992, at Hollins College (Gladden).

Perhaps one of the greatest paradoxes is that, for all the attention to children, few literary studies of the child exist. According to Leslie Fiedler, "We move through a world of books in which the child is so accepted a feature of the landscape that we are aware of him chiefly when he is absent" (251). His presence, however, does not move us to view him critically. Certainly, there is nothing in literary criticism to parallel the massive psychological studies such as the work of Robert Coles. And while *individual* literary children have been thoroughly scrutinized—Hawthorne's Pearl, Twain's Huck, James's Maisie—Hurst asserts that "comprehensive studies of the child in American fiction" (2) do not exist: "As a universal subject, literary children have previously been the focus of only six books," none of which deals exclusively with American literary children (Hurst 3). Hurst is speaking here of literature for adults, not *children's* literature. Suffice it to say that absolutely *no* critical studies of the child in American children's literature exist and certainly no studies of the child in Appalachian literature, let alone Appalachian *children's* literature. Neither do the major works on Appalachia address the cultural role of children or children's literature. While studies by Shapiro, Batteau, and others focus on problems such as child labor, the emphasis is incidental, not central, to the works. Even David Mielke's *Teaching Mountain Children* (1978) focuses less on the child than on the adult and the region at large.

Of course, the idea of the child and its subsequent complex cultural manifestations did not develop in isolation; it emerged alongside the developing concept of the family. Aries asserts that the family had "existed in silence" in the Middle Ages; it simply "did not awaken feelings strong enough to inspire poet or artist" (364). The "iconographic blossoming" of family representations in the fifteenth and sixteenth centuries merely mirrors the "blossoming" of the concept of the family (364). Aries argues that, as with the child, the revival of interest in education in the sixteenth and seventeenth centuries gave the family "a moral and spiritual function." Parents were seen as having power to shape "bodies and souls," to which, says Aries, "the iconography of the seventeenth century gave brilliant and insistent expression": thus, the emergence of the "modern concept of the family" (412–13). Aries notes that Erasmus can be credited with the very modern belief that "children united family," most specifically because of "the emotion aroused by the child, the living image of his parents" (364). For the purposes of this study, the emphasis on emotional connotations of the concept of the child is of paramount importance.

While the concepts of the child and the family are complex inventions which evolved over several centuries and the concept of Appalachia is more recent, their histories and symbolic functions nevertheless are similar. The idea of Appalachia, like the idea of the child, is often taken for granted as an *a priori* geographical fact; but the concept was not contemporaneous with the geographical discovery and exploration of the continent. Says Leslie Fiedler, "America may have been discovered for the geographers in the fifteenth century but it is discovered for the imagination in the eighteenth" (255). This discovery of America "for the imagination" extended into the nineteenth century and included the travel sketches and local color literature which spawned the notion of Appalachia. The "making of Appalachia in the period from 1878 to 1888," says Allen Batteau, "was a true act of creativity" (56).

Henry Shapiro traces the idea of Appalachia to Will Wallace Harney's journey to the Cumberland Mountains in autumn 1869, which led to the 1873 publication in *Lippincott's* of "A Strange Land and Peculiar People" (Shapiro 93). As Shapiro indicates, the "discovery" of Appalachia "rested on a perception of the otherness of mountain life" (4), and "it was through literature that the otherness of the southern mountain region was introduced as a fact in the American consciousness" (18). Shapiro cites Harney as the first to insist upon an "'otherness' which made the mountainous portions of eight southern states a discrete region, in but not of America, and which, after 1890, would seem to place Appalachia and America in radical opposition" (4).

Following Harney, a multitude of individuals shaped the idea of Appalachia in the collective American consciousness, but three stand out: Mary Noailles Murfree, John Fox, Jr., and William G. Frost. According to Shapiro, "90 sketches and more than 125 short stories published between 1870 and 1890" presented a "vision of reality" that had far-reaching consequences; they "became the basis for private or public action" (18). In short, the literary depiction became accepted as a geographical and cultural reality in much the same way that the idea of the holy child and Virgin (created outside the family) became absorbed into family life.

Shapiro credits Murfree with being the first to use "exotic mountain scenery" as the core of her fiction and not merely as a "neutral background," as did her predecessors. Instead, Murfree's stories "took the fact of Appalachian otherness as their donnée" (19). Allen Batteau goes one step further to argue that Murfree's writings "made Appalachia a national reality" (39). Murfree's version of the region was seminal: "with certain modifications and elaborations, all [subsequent versions] have been based on the structure she established" (Batteau 40). As Shapiro and others have noted, Murfree was an outsider to the region, as were Fox and Frost, both products of Harvard. Though Fox had grown up in the Kentucky bluegrass, he came to the mountains late. Fox, through works such as *The Kentuckians* (1897), *The Little Shepherd of Kingdom Come* (1903), and *The Trail of the Lonesome Pine* (1908), and Frost, as president of Berea College from 1892 to 1920, "created Appalachia as a totality" (Batteau 58). As the representative pedagogues and clergy—outsiders to the family—shaped a view of the child which came to be accepted as reality within the family, so these outsiders shaped a view of Appalachia which came to be accepted without and, perhaps more importantly, *within* the region.

Shapiro credits Frost with coining the phrase "Appalachian America," a term which gave credence to the idea that the region was homogeneous but separate—it was an "other" (119). Shapiro stresses Frost's use of the New World metaphor in an address before the Cincinnati Teachers' Club in 1894 and quotes Frost as saying, "We have discovered a new pioneer region of the central South just as our western frontier has been lost in the Pacific ocean" (119–20). Frost describes the region as a sort of "saving remnant" of desirable values which, when reintegrated into the American mainstream, would help stem the tide of "lackadaisical effeminacy" prevalent at the time (Shapiro 120). In short, Frost argues that the discovery of this region would weave an innocent and unspoiled strand into the moral milieu of the 1890s.

Is this not the same charge assigned to the child in modern culture and fiction? Popular modern psychology characterizes the "inner child," the child within the adult, as a "saving remnant," a path to wholeness. In Appalachian children's literature, the savior-child is a major theme, from early works such as William O. Steele's historical fiction and Vera Cleaver and Bill Cleaver's *Where the Lilies Bloom* (1969) to more recent works such as Katherine Paterson's *Come Sing, Jimmy Jo* (1985) and Cynthia Rylant's *Miss Maggie* (1983) and *Missing May* (1992).

Other parallels between the "discovery" of Appalachia and the discovery of childhood are striking. When Leslie Fiedler speaks of the "ubiquitous and symbolic" figure of the child in American literature, a figure which is "no mere reproduction of a fact of existence," and when Fiedler argues that the child is "a cultural invention, a product of the imagination" (251), he could just as easily be speaking of the "ubiquitous and symbolic" presence of Appalachia. When Fiedler speaks of the Cult of the Child, he could just as easily be speaking of an Appalachia whose presence in American culture and literature has almost become cultic. Consider the following:

> Where the artist is most firmly committed to bourgeois values, especially where there is no surviving aristocratic tradition with which he can identify himself . . . , there is available to him one safely genteel symbol of protest and impulse: the Child. It is possible to insist that the child is Father of the man, that he comes "trailing clouds of glory" which are dissipated in a world of duty and work, without seeming seriously to threaten the middle-class ethos, without, indeed, revealing one's own revolutionary intent. Do not all decent people, after all, love children? (Fiedler 256)

I would ask, do not all decent people love Appalachia? And I would argue that the artist has *two* "safely genteel" symbols of protest available to him—

the child *and* Appalachia. When Frost speaks of having discovered a New World, a segment of American geography and culture which would save the nation from itself, is he not invoking the same revolutionary spirit as the literary artist who utilizes the symbol of the child? Is not the intent of invoking the symbol of Appalachia both salvation and revolution?

The revolutionary and symbolic nature of *Appalachia* was made emphatically clear in the 1960s, during Lyndon B. Johnson's presidency. Appalachia has traditionally served the nation—in history and in literature—as ground for the revolutionary spirit. It is of no small consequence that Rosa Parks was trained in the heart of Appalachia at the Highlander Center or that VISTA workers opted for service in Appalachia as a means of rejecting a flawed America. But what is the revolutionary intent of invoking the symbol of the child in Appalachian children's literature?

The child is almost always depicted as inherently innocent and as having higher values and greater insight than the adult. Examples from the adult literary canon are readily apparent, both British and American: from E. M. Forster's "The Celestial Omnibus" and D. H. Lawrence's "The Rocking Horse Winner" to Faulkner's "Barn Burning," Anderson's "I Want to Know Why," and Roth's "The Conversion of the Jews." Perhaps the classic American example appears in Walt Whitman's simple, child-posed question in section 6 of *Song of Myself,* "What is the grass?" The poet-persona answers with a question: "How could I answer the child? I do not know what it is any more than he" (99–100). Then the narrator continues with a catalogue of guesses as to what the grass is—"the flag of my disposition," "the handkerchief of the Lord," "the grass is itself a child," "a uniform hieroglyphic," and "the beautiful uncut hair of graves" (101–10). Mary Jane Hurst comments:

> Not only does the adult not know the answer, he even suspects the child is better equipped than he to solve the riddle. By casting the child as a deceptively innocent inquisitor whose capacity to ask questions exceeds the ability of his elders to provide answers, Whitman is weaving with a primary thread of our nation's literary fabric. (1–2)

Hurst points out that beneath the innocent, simple, literal question "lurks a tangle of more complicated questions about reality and perception and understanding" (1).

A century after Whitman's death, George Ella Lyon's 1992 picture book *Who Came Down That Road?* poses a Whitmanesque question, making the point that writers still weave with this "primary thread of our nation's literary fabric." But, more importantly, it illustrates that this thread has now been woven into children's literature, too. Like Whitman's poet-persona, the mother in *Who Came Down That Road?* tries to answer the child's query by explaining that a whole catalogue of historical travelers came down that "old, old, old, old road": from "Soldiers in blue coats," to "Mastodons and woolly mammoths." The child is not to be satisfied, however, and with every answer poses a new question: "Who came before the soldiers, Mama?" and "Who came before the mammoths, Mama?" In the century between Whitman and Lyon, the adult has become no better equipped to satisfy the child and must ultimately admit her ineptitude, and thus the child's wisdom, with her final response:

> Questions!
> Questions crowded like a bed of stars,
> thick as that field of goldenrod—
> . . . . .
> the mystery of the making place—
> that came before this road.

Lyon's Appalachian mother is led to observe that the great first cause was a question—a mystery, if you will: a decidedly Whitmanesque observation and a clear illustration of Hurst's suspicion that "the child is better equipped" than the adult to "solve the riddle."

The example from Lyon is not an exception. Appalachian children's literature is rife with innocent, wise children. At the end of Jenny Davis's *Good-Bye and Keep Cold*, the main character Edda Combs quotes her friend Charlie as saying, "Everybody has to raise their parents." Edda then asks, "Is that true? He says the time comes for all of us when we have to kiss them good-bye and trust them to be okay on their own. I've done the best I could with mine. Good-bye, you all, and good luck. Good-bye and keep cold" (210). The ending and the title echo Robert Frost's narrator's admonition to his apple orchard to keep cold and not bud too soon, a strictly parental admonition.

The presence of this wise-and-holy-child theme in adult literature is perhaps more understandable than its appearance in children's literature. It is one thing for adults to remind themselves that they inherently "miss the moral point" of life, but it is quite another for them to remind their children. What do we hope to communicate to children when we show them *themselves* as more knowing and competent and wise than their parents? Is the proliferation of the wise, innocent Appalachian child a psychological thumbing of the nose at parents?

Are these books merely a warning to children that adult values have failed? If so, then much of children's literature is homiletic. Or is the message perhaps a more revolutionary one which says, though society will try to teach you otherwise, you have within you *now* all that you will ever need to reach mature wisdom and wholeness? Are Lyon and Davis saying, see yourselves in this fiction, and thus in life, as competent and wise and holy? If so, the fusion of the child symbol with the Appalachian symbol is traditional in its revolutionary intent.

In relation to the child symbol, Fiedler describes the age of revolution as a "time which prefers the New World to the Old because that World is its own invention" (254–55). Whether one speaks of Appalachia or of the American fondness for literary children, both are our own inventions; hence, through them we can reject old worlds and old adult values. But exactly what worlds are we rejecting? Are we rejecting adulthood in favor of the Phoenix-like childhood which arises anew with each child out of adult ashes? Through the image of the innocent child—holy and naked—one can reject her old self. Through William G. Frost's invented image of an isolated, unspoiled Appalachia, the nineteenth century could reject its old, tainted morality.

It is no mere coincidence, then, that critics speaking of the child and of Appalachia use much the same language. Says Batteau, "Appalachia is just as much a social construction as is the cowboy or, for that matter, the Indian" (16). Substitute *the child* for *Appalachia* in the above quotation, and it becomes essentially the same sentiment uttered by Fiedler with regard to the child. Or interject the idea of the natural Appalachian person into the following quotation, alongside Fiedler's dark-skinned natives, Indians, peasants, idiots, buffoons, and whores, and the quotation clearly articulates the nineteenth-century American need for the child *and* Appalachia:

> Images of impulse and natural virtue were found readily enough, where one would expect them, in the virgin forests of the newer worlds: in dark-skinned natives in general and in Indians in particular. But there were noble savages closer to home; one did not have to go abroad for counterimages to set against the corrupt figure of the European courtier. The peasant could be glorified over the city dweller; the idiot or the buffoon over the philosopher; woman over man—and within the female sex, the whore over the bourgeois. All such oppositions are dangerous, however; . . . they threaten a disruption of the social values by which bourgeois society lives. (256)

Both the Appalachian and the child provide clearly threatening possibilities to adult bourgeois society but are at the same time necessary to that society. And if Appalachians are merely another version of the noble savage, then one indeed "does not have to go abroad for counterimages to set against the corrupt figure" of nineteenth- or twentieth-century America.

One of the most infamous uses of the noble savage theme in Appalachian children's literature is *The Education of Little Tree* (1976), a book whose revolutionary intent became apparent when its author, Forrest Carter, was revealed to be none other than Asa Earl Carter, speechwriter for George Wallace and author of Wallace's famous "Segregation now! Segregation tomorrow! Segregation forever!" speech (Reid, Leland). Carter's main character Little Tree—an innocent, wise, Appalachian Cherokee child character—takes on multiple layers of complexity if viewed as a literary hoax, as having been created out of purely cynical, revolutionary intent. Carter's choice of symbols—an *Appalachian* and a *child*—cannot be overlooked or overemphasized.

The revolutionary power of both inventions becomes even more apparent when one acknowledges that these creations are contingent on the presence of a middle class; hence, the idea of the child *could not* have existed in the tenth or eleventh century, but could have evolved only as the middle class evolved. Aries argues that the "moral ascendancy of the family," with its attendant child, was "originally a middle-class phenomenon: the nobility and the lower class, at the two extremities of the social ladder, retained the old idea of etiquette much longer and remained more indifferent to outside pressures. . . . There is therefore a connection between the concept of the family and the concept of class" (413–14). Whereas the old society had tolerated the "juxtaposition of the most widely different classes," the new society, with the family and child at its center, began to retreat "in homes designed for privacy." The results were less tolerance for difference and an insistence upon homogeneity within the private, isolated group. Says Aries, "The concept of the family, the concept of class, and perhaps elsewhere the concept of race, appear as manifestations of the same intolerance toward variety, the same insistence on uniformity" (415).

The concept of Appalachia is also contingent on the presence of a middle class; Appalachia was invented at the very time in American history when the middle class began to swell, to be self-conscious, and to be the subject of scrutiny in the American realistic literary movement. A consequence of its invention was a very real class consciousness which is predicated on isolation and homogeneity. Appalachia must be depicted as isolated and "other" or it ceases to exist.

The tension which results from this isolation, otherness, and class consciousness is a central and necessary feature of both inventions. For example, Aries's observations regarding the invention of the child make clear that, in the medieval age, the human being before age seven was not characterized by "peculiarity." Once this "otherness" was established, however, a tension between the adult and the child was created which now manifests itself most strongly in adolescence (another fairly recent "invention" whose examination here space will not permit). It is now a psychological "given" that the rebellious tension between child and parent is necessary to produce a whole, integrated adult. Does Appalachia serve that same purpose for a nation of diverse peoples and disparate goals which seeks to individuate itself—to *know* itself and thereby become whole? Similarly, once Harney, Murfree, Fox, Frost, and others established the otherness and peculiarity of Appalachia, it was forever in conflict with the rest of the nation. Because Appalachia was invented as a region—to quote Shapiro, *in* but not *of* America—tension between the region and the nation is a congenital condition, a prerequisite for existence.

When Leslie Fiedler speaks of yet another aspect of the invented child, the similarities with invented Appalachia are uncanny. Says Fiedler, children came to be expected to conform to their created images "as no Indian was ever asked to live up to his image; but then one could not confine children to reservations or kill them in popularly sanctioned expeditions" (256–57). Children have been "recreated . . . into facsimiles of their literary representations, and were addressed as if they were really such monsters of virtue, both in life . . . and in literature" (257). The success of *invented* Appalachia rests on this same principle: Appalachians were (and are) expected to *live* the "reality" created for them in the fiction of Murfree and Fox. (And for all practical purposes they *have* been confined to a reservation.) Jim Wayne Miller's poem "The Brier Losing Touch with His Traditions" is a perfect articulation

of the phenomenon. Again, Fiedler's description of the process of inventing
the child is eerily evocative of the modern Appalachian's experience:

> Indians and peasants and village idiots were mercifully spared the
> ultimate humiliation of having to read descriptions of themselves that
> were in fact projections of nostalgia, in a time of oppressive taboos, for a
> life at once impulsive and virtuous; they did not come to measure them-
> selves against such projections and failing them, berate themselves, as (pre-
> sumably) did the children of Anglo-Saxondom. (257)

Nor, one might add, as did the Appalachians. No other region in the country has suffered so significantly from its invented reality.

The question to be asked now is, what have these two symbols come to
mean in the twentieth century, after a hundred years of proliferation in the
nation's literature, history, and social policy? Ultimately, there are two possibilities. One is that they have served the nation well, that the tension generated has moved us from thesis to antithesis to synthesis and, thus, one step
closer to wholeness and individuation. Beginning with Huck Finn and ending with Paterson's Jimmy Jo, we can argue that the child has indeed reminded us of our inherent godliness and wisdom, to the destruction of our
baser instincts: nineteenth-century romanticism at its best. We can argue
further that, aided by the symbol of Appalachia, the nation has rejected its
old weak materialism, of which William G. Frost was so conscious, in favor
of a vigorous new spirituality. We can argue that the nation is less ambivalent toward its identity today than it was a hundred years ago.

Sadly, I find more evidence to support a second possibility: that the sym-
bols have failed us, that they no longer serve a dialectic purpose, but have
become the static commodities of a middle class motivated by materialism.
Batteau says that "every reality becomes a commodity" (11). He believes that
"Appalachia is packaged and sold" both literally—folk crafts, Foxfire books—
and metaphorically—the 1982 Knoxville World's Fair Folklife Pavilion (12).
The child, likewise, is packaged and sold both literally—at McDonald's, at
Toys-R-Us, in movie theaters—and metaphorically—in the lucrative market for children's books. Says Batteau, "as experienced in the life of an individual, commodity fetishism is the seeking of human meaning in mass-pro-
duced goods, and the pursuit of social goals such as companionship, acceptance,
and prestige as objects that can be traded on the market" (11).

If the symbols of Appalachia and the child had served a dialectic purpose
over the last one hundred years, they would themselves have taken on new
shapes, a new significance, and new meanings in literature and in life—and
most specifically in the genre which melds the two, Appalachian children's
literature. The literature written today, however, does not use the symbols
to any new advantage. It does not reflect an awareness of the complexity of
the symbols, much less revisionist thought. Cynthia Rylant's Appalachia: The
Voices of Sleeping Birds (1991) epitomizes a literature that has more in common with Murfree's and Fox's invented Appalachia than with twentieth-cen-

tury realities. This book is a commodity; it sells the promise of human meaning and feeling through its presentation of invented Appalachian children. This book and countless others still insist upon an outdated homogeneity; readers are still subjected to reading "descriptions of themselves that [are] . . . projections of nostalgia . . . for a life at once impulsive and virtuous" (Hurst 257).

Essentially these two symbols—the child and Appalachia—now operate in a world which recognizes them primarily as commodities, but we are well reminded that they are only two commodities among myriad other "inventions" of civilization, such as the aristocracy, the middle class, manliness, feminism, and political correctness. Still another invention is the future, as Dennis Gabor instructed us several years ago, and the future we invent in Appalachia will depend in large measure on how critical we are of the prevailing myths and symbols. The same principle is applicable to current race relations, which demonstrate that Huck Finn, one of the wisest children in American literature, has not been heard in our culture; he has most recently become a Disney commodity. Future race relations will depend in large part on how critical we are of that commodity.

Inventions are "myths" or versions of truth, and finding the best myths to live by (to use Joseph Campbell's phrase), including new myths or combinations of old ones, is the task of scholarship and art. To perpetuate inventions when they become commodities is the work, for better or worse, of the world of commerce. The challenge of scholarship and art is not to sell but to seek; not to proselytize, but to probe.

Works Cited

Aries, Philippe. *Centuries of Childhood: A Social History of Family Life.* New York: Knopf, 1962.

Batteau, Allen W. *The Invention of Appalachia.* Tucson, AZ: U of Arizona P, 1990.

Davis, Jenny. *Good-Bye and Keep Cold.* New York: Dell, 1987.

Fiedler, Leslie A. *No! In Thunder.* Boston: Beacon, 1960.

Gabor, Dennis. *Inventing the Future.* New York: Knopf, 1964.

Gladden, Chris. "Serendipity and Kiddie Lit." *Roanoke (VA) Times and World News,* 16 Sept. 1992, extra 1, 6.

Hurst, Mary Jane. *The Voice of the Child in American Literature.* Lexington, Kentucky: UP of Kentucky, 1990.

Leland, John, and Marc Peyser. "New Age Fable from an Old School Bigot?" *Newsweek,* 14 Oct. 1991, 62.

Lyon, George Ella. *Who Came Down That Road?* Illus. Peter Catalanotto. New York: Orchard, 1992.

Reid, Calvin. "Widow of 'Little Tree' Author Admits He Changed Identity." *Publishers Weekly,* 25 Oct. 1991, pp. 16, 18.

Rougemont, Denis De. *Love in the Western World.* 1940. New York: Pantheon, 1956.

Shapiro, Henry. *Appalachia on Our Mind: The Southern Mountains and Mountaineers in the American Consciousness, 1870–1920.* Chapel Hill: U of North Carolina P, 1978.

Sommerville, John. *The Rise and Fall of Childhood.* Beverly Hills, CA: Sage, 1982.

Whitman, Walt. "Song of Myself." *Leaves of Grass.* Ed. Sculley Bradley and Harold W. Blodgett. New York: Norton, 1973. 28–89.

Parks Lanier, Jr.

See volume 2, chapter 1, for biography.

Appalachian Sunday Morning

                    (with no apologies to Wallace Stevens)
Complacencies of long johns, and late
Coffee and cigarettes in a rocking chair,
And the freedom of a bluetick hound
Upon a rug to dissipate
The evangelist on the radio.
Wide awake she feels the wretched
Condition of sinners but is as unable
As the dog to scratch the fleas
Of sin and would not, were she given
The gift, know how to dance in the spirit
With her dreaming feet to Palestine Baptist
Church, dominion of the blood and sepulchre.

Why should she tithe to those deep-water tadpoles?
The god of her dreams lives not in heavy oak
Pews or the imaginings of sweating evangelists.
Shall she not find in comforts of the sun,
A baked hay field, or the sharp spray
Of water against the mountain rocks
Things to be cherished like the thought of heaven?
In the mirror of her great-grandma's washstand
She might find religion within herself,
For had she not felt at the hoedown
Passions of rain and yearned for gusty
Emotions on wet roads on autumn nights?
All pleasures and all pains, remembering
How that boy could flat foot with the best:
These are the measures destined for her soul.

That gutless preacher don't know nothing;
No mother sucked him, no sweet land gave
Him a sense of what is good and right.
He moves among us muttering his pieties
Until our blood, commingling, virginal
Congeals like the streams on the mountain
In winter, she thinks. She is too young
To be so cold in Appalachia's spring.
Shall our blood fail? Or shall it become
The blood of paradise? And shall Sevier County
Seem all of paradise that she shall know?
Yea, verily, the mists are on LeConte
And Clingman's Dome, making Charlie's Bunion
A dividing and indifferent blue.

(to be continued)
(or perhaps not)

Emma Bell Miles

For biography of Emma Bell Miles and an analysis of her pioneering role in the raising of gender consciousness, see the essay by Grace Toney Edwards which follows "The Common Lot."

The Common Lot

The big boy in the doorway was hot and dusty, but not tired. It was impossible to be really tired with running free on a morning when all the earth was awake and trembling with the eager restlessness of young summer. His head was carried high, with a deerlike poise; the dark young profile with its promise of early manhood flung up a challenge to greet the world. His gait all morning had been the wolflike pace by which the mountaineer swings the roughest miles behind him.

The woman—she was hardly the mistress—of the big log house was tired, however; she could scarcely remember a time when she had not been so. Life had resolved itself, for her, into conditions of greater or less weariness, and she had learned to be thankful if the weariness were not complicated by rheumatism or other pain. Her day was always long, her night was short; she had no time to think of the sunshine and roses in her own dooryard.

From *Harper's Monthly Megazine* 18 (1908): 145–54.

"I come apast Mis' Hallet's," he explained his presence, "and she stopped
me to send word that she wants Easter to come and stay with her a spell. I've
got a note in my pocket, if I can find it."

Mrs. Vanderwelt read the penciled scrawl from Cordy Hallet, her married
daughter. "Allison," she began, a distressed frown puckering her lined forehead, "if you're goin' by the spring, would you just as soon stop and tell
Easter? She's churnin' down thar. Ye might as well carry her a pokeful of
cookies."

She filled the boy's hands with freshly baked saucer-wide cookies, scarcely
more than sweetened soda biscuit–cakes, and put some into a paper bag for
her daughter.

The young fellow might have chosen the high road, but the sun-dappled
path through the woods drew first his eyes and then his feet. Everything was
in motion there, tilting and waving in the light breeze; dewdrops glittered
still under the leaves; brilliant bits of insect life started out of the sun-
warmed loam and rustled with many-legged creepings in last year's dry leaves.
On the way he cut a length of hickory, from which the sap-loosed bark could
readily be taken, and walked on more slowly, shaping a whistle with his knife,
and thinking of Easter, and their days in school. She was not so old as he by
several years; perhaps she was not quite sixteen. He had scarce awakened to full
perception of her girlish comeliness, but he admired her nervous agility and
grace in play. She could run and climb, and play coo-sheepy and hat-ball, as
well as any of the boys; that was his way of putting it to himself.

The spring was a dark pool, walled with rock and housed with a structure
of logs and hand-riven clapboards. It had a shelf all round below the surface
level, on which jars of milk stood in perpetual coolness. Easter, having finished her task, was nowhere to be seen; her churn stood outside, and new
butter floated in a maple bowl of water, set on the rock to cool. Having
tested his whistle and found to his delight that it would pipe three or four
notes, the boy bent over the water for a while, his eyes caught first by the
reflection of his own face and then by the leaping and stirring of sand and
tiny pebbles where the vein rose through the bottom. He laid himself flat
and drank deeply of the bluish cold water; then, closing the door of the spring-
house against stray "razorbacks," he began to look about in the woods. Once he
called timidly, "Easter!" but the sound of her name in his own voice rather
frightened him, inasmuch as he was not sure he ought not to put a Miss, or some
such foolish handle, before it; and he proceeded uncertainly into the maple
thicket below the spring, not knowing where to search. Then a gleam of blossom flashed between the boles, and he guessed that she would be there.

It was a white-flaming mass of azaleas, delicately rosy as mountain slopes
of snow splashed over with the pink of dawn. In the midst sat a girl, drinking the overflowed sweetness of that dripping and blowing bank of flowers:
now fingering single branches that lifted into the tender foliage their crowns
and pompons, and now drawing all together down against her face in a sheaf
of cool, pure petals—drowning her young senses in perfume. She had taken

off her coarse shoes to plunge her feet into the dewy freshness of those ferns that in such maple-shaded hollows keep the azaleas company. Easter was too old to go barefoot, but not too old to delight in the feel of the ancient soil beneath her feet, and in the shining dewdrops on her instep's blue-marbled satin. In after years, when the burden of responsibility bore heavily on her shoulders, she remembered that intermission among the flowers as her last taste of care-free pleasure, her last moments of childhood.

Suddenly, with a soft crash of rending growth, the boy parted the underbrush and came toward her. She gathered herself together with a swift instinctive modesty, tucking her feet under her skirt. "Howdy, Allison?" she greeted him, and "Howdy?" he answered, thrusting the bag of cookies at her by way of accounting for his presence.

She smiled in an embarrassed fashion as she took the poke from his hand. The thought of her bare feet made her unable to rise. The big boy dropped to the ground beside her. He delivered his message and watched her read the note.

"Air you goin?" he asked, eagerly. "Hit's closer to our house. I ain't seen you since school broke up."

"I reckon so," the girl answered him. And then to relieve the situation she offered him cakes. At that he remembered some May-apples in his pocket and produced them with the awkwardness of big-boyhood. Each was still child enough to enjoy the tasteless fruit of the mandrake simply because it was wild; and to him, moreover, it had all the exaggerated value of a boy's trove. Easter shared her cakes, and theirs was a feast of Arcady. So, too, might the Arcadian shepherds have piped among their flocks; for he tried his whistle again, and she must needs have it in her hands to blow upon it also.

Directly she glanced up, and her face brightened. "There's a hominy-bird," she whispered ever so softly. Following her gaze, he, too, saw the tiny creature, swift and brilliant, a flying dagger, more like an insect than a bird. They turned to smile to each other, and as quickly turned away. It poised over flower after flower with a hum as of some heavy double-winged beetle; and ere it could be drunk with sweets a new sound possessed the stillness.

The morning had been vividly many-colored with bird notes. The thrush had waked first, his passionless strain cool as the very voice of dawn; the rest had all caroled of nests and mating, of their lives that were hidden overhead in that trembling world of semi-lucent leaves: keen struggle of life with hunger, brooding tenderness of care for the young, wooing, and quarreling and fighting, the thousand tiny tragedies and comedies unperceived by human eyes. But now it was a mocker who set the dim, deep-lit shadow a-ripple with the pulsing of his own great little heart, in such wild song as could only come from the wild soul of a winged life—a song of world-old passion, of gladness and youth primordial. Oh, troubadour, what magic is in your wooing? Is it the vast and deep desire of Earth for the returning Sungod— her joy in the year's unutterable glad release, her yearning to the most ancient of Lovers ever young? . . .

Allison drew himself nearer to the girl, and laid his hand over hers. The mating instinct awakens early in the young people of the mountains—cruelly early; we cannot tell why—as a sweet-pain that overtakes the exquisite shyness of childhood unawares. She neither looked toward him nor shrank away. Slowly her hand turned until its moist, warm palm met the boy's; and before he knew it he had kissed her—anywhere, any way.

A kiss is a mystery and a miracle. Easter sprang up, dazed and thrilled, regardless now of her bare feet—conscious only of a choking in her throat and an impulse to burst into the tearless sobbing of excitement. Allison, frightened perhaps even more than she, stood half turned from her, flushed and tingling from head to foot.

At last he found his tongue. "I won't do that no more! I just don't know what made me. . . . Easter, won't you forget hit?"

It was all he could say.

She barely glanced at him. "I won't tell hit," she murmured, and, snatching up her shoes and stockings, fled away, and left him standing so, rebuked, condemned.

Once alone, she flung herself on the ground and hid her face even from herself. This it was, then, to kiss a boy? "Oh dear, why is it like this?" she wept, and crept closer to the ground.

But she had not promised to forget.

When Easter Vanderwelt went to "stay with" her married sister, she planned to come home in time to enter school when it should open, the first Monday in August. There was the half-formulated hope of seeing Allison somewhere, sometime during the term, even if he did consider himself too old to attend. So she stacked her six or eight books in the loft room over the kitchen, with an admonition to her brothers not to disturb them in her absence. She had always kept them neat, and the boys should have them when she had learned them through.

But Cordy's baby was a fretting, puny thing; Easter finally consented to forego the summer school and stay on till frost, when, it was hoped, the little ones would improve; and the round of toil soon drove out every other thought. Or did it? Four-year-old Phronie and Sonnybuck, his father's namesake, scarcely out from underfoot, the ailing baby to be tended, preparing cow's milk, washing bottles, wrapping a quill in soft, clean rags to fit the tiny mouth—looking after these was the task of a wife and mother; Easter could hardly devote all day and every day to them without figuring to herself a future of such, shared with—whom?

The children fell ill and needed to be nursed. There were the walls to tighten against winter with pasted layers of old newspapers. Hog-killing time brought its extra burdens. Cordy, a fierily energetic housewife, would set up a pair of newly pieced spreads and get two needed quilts done against winter. In the midst of it all, she got an order for rug-weaving from a city woman, and begged Easter to stay through the cold weather, with the promise of a new dress from this source over and above her wage of seventy-five cents a week.

Easter's lot was little harder in her sister's house than at home, and there she had no wages; yet she was glad when at last she could shut the three dollars and seventy-five cents in her hard, rough, red little hand—she had accepted a hen and six chickens in part payment—and set her face once more toward her father's house. Catching the hen and chickens and putting them into a basket made her late in starting. The sun was high when she turned out of the shortcut through the woods into the big road, and she found herself already tired. If a wagon would come along now, with room for herself and her small belongings—and, sure enough, before she had walked "three sights and a horn-blow" along the road, a wagon did. Who but Allison on the seat, and all by himself! She felt rather shy, this being the first time they had met alone since the morning he kissed her, under the swamp honeysuckles: she wished he had been anyone else, but when he greeted her with, "Want 'o ride?" she clambered in over the wheel.

He stowed the basket under the seat. "What ye got thar?" he inquired, for the sake of conversation.

"Hit's a old hen that stoled her nest and come off with these few chickens," she answered. "What y' been a-haulin'?"

"Rails to fence my clearin'," he told her with pride. He had recently worked out the purchase of a piece of land. "Hit's got a rich little swag on one ind, and a good rise on the other, in case I sh'd ever want to build. Hit fronts half a acre on the big road, too," he added, shyly, looking from the corners of his eyes at the girl beside him.

Talking thus, as gravely as two middle-aged people, they rode across Caney Creek and into the ridges. "Gid up," he gave the command to the team from time to time; but there was no haste in the mules; their long ears flapped as they plodded, and the wheels slid on through the dust as though muffled in velvet. He began to tell her of his hopes and plans, tentatively, without once looking at her.

"If I'm so fortunate—maybe next winter . . . I've been spoken to about a position in a hardware store in town, and . . . ." He did not finish that sentence, but presently went on: "One man told me last week that he wouldn't hire a single man—said they was always out nights, and no good in the daytime."

Now Easter knew that Allison was never out at night to any ill purpose, and she smiled a bit wisely to herself. His favorite pose was that of the cosmopolitan, the widely experienced man; but that was pure boyishness. There was a rough innocence about him, despite his everyday familiarity with all the crimes that lie between the moonshine still and county court. What of evil there was in him seemed to have grown there as naturally as the acrid sap of certain wild vines or the bitterness of dogwood bark. The freakish lawlessness of even the worst mountaineer seems in some way different from the vice and moral deformity of cities, as new corn whiskey is different from absinthe.

Under her sunbonnet the girl inquired, demurely, "Why 'n't ye stay here?"

"Oh, I'm jist restless, I reckon. . . . I would stay if I had a home here."

That word "home" laid a finger on their lips for full five minutes. Again he ventured, flicking nervously with his whip at the roadside weeds:

"And Mavity wants me in his new saloon. I seed him when I was in Fairplay last week. The wages is good."

She spoke now quickly enough. "Don't go thar, Allison! I don't want to be—worried—'bout you."

He turned away to hide a swift change of countenance, slashed hard at the inoffending bushes, and jerked out, in a husky, boyish voice, "What makes ye care?"

She dared not be silent. "Because I know how good you air. Because I don't want to see—a boy like you go wrong."

"I ain't good!" he cried, almost roughly. Then he turned to find her looking at him serenely, silently—not quite smiling. . . .

That was all, but it was almost a betrothal to the two. From this moment she tried to imagine what life with him would be like. The picture she saw clearest was of a low-browed cabin in the dusk; through its doorway, glowing with red firelight, a glimpse of a supper awaiting a man's return.

Mrs. Vanderwelt was as glad to see her daughter home again as was Easter to rejoin the family, but that did not prevent her levying on Easter's wages. The dish-pan had gone past all mending, and the water-bucket had sprung such a leak that it was no longer fit for use except about the stable. The lantern globe was broken. So Easter reserved for herself only the price of eight yards of gingham.

"Ye're jist in time for the dance over to Swaford's," announced her younger sister, Ellender, when, after the supper dishes were washed, they sat down to tack carpet rags. "They're goin' to give one a-Sata'day night."

"You 'uns a-goin'?" asked Easter. Of course the boys would be there, and all the youngsters of the countryside—Allison, too. There are never enough girls to go round in a frolic in the mountains.

It transpired, however, that Ellender had no dress—at least, none that could appear beside Easter's contemplated purchase. So Easter was forced to consider the means of providing eight yards for her sister as well as for herself.

This was on Monday. The sisters walked the two miles to the store next day, and chose the double quantity of cheaper goods together. It was white with a small pink figure printed at intervals, coarse and loosely woven as a floursack. They stitched all day Wednesday, and finished the frocks Thursday morning. But on Thursday evening they received a letter recalling Easter to her sister's house.

Easter's trembling hands dropped in her lap.

"Cain't you go this time, Ellender?" she pleaded.

"Maw says I ain't old enough to do what Cordy needs. She says you ain't—sca'cely," the younger sister protested.

"You-all act like you wanted to git shut o' me," Easter almost wept. "Cordy can wait three days. I'm obliged to go to this dance."

But she knew it was not so. Only in her pain she struck at what was nearest.

Easter's return found an ominous tremor and strain in her sister's affairs. At first her girl's mind groped vainly for the cause. There was the endless toil of spring house-cleaning and truck-patch, of chickens and cows, with the ailing youngest to tend, and Jim Hallet going softly, outcast by his wife's displeasure, while poor Cordy sat at night mending and freshening all the coarse little garments, scarcely outgrown, putting them in readiness for an expected use.

Oh, it was hard, it was hard on Cordy, thought the girl, pondering this thing of which she had no experience. It was hard; but she had as yet only the outsider's point of view.

Next week she had a surprise. Allison brought his team on Saturday evening, and asked her, "provided she didn't mind ridin' a mule," to go to the dance with him. It was a long way to Swaford's Cove, and she would be fearfully tired to-morrow, but she was accustomed to pay dearly for every bit of pleasure, and did not hesitate. So he came again Sunday week to walk with her to the church at Blue Springs, and later took her to the close-of-school entertainment, where she had the pleasure of seeing Ellender speak a piece, clad in the frock that was the counterpart of her own.

In the midst of corn-planting time the baby died. The weak life flickered out one night as it lay across Cordy's knees. Such was her exhaustion that the physical need of sleep came uppermost, and her grief did not reveal itself till next day.

The little body, cased in a rude pine box, was taken in the wagon to the untended graveyard by the Blue Springs church. Easter and Cordy rode beside Jim on the seat, and three neighbor women were behind in the wagon, sitting in chairs. These, with the Vanderwelt boys, who had helped dig the grave, were the only persons present at the burying. Cordy asked that one of the women should offer a prayer, but they protested that they could not.

"I never prayed out loud—afore folks—in my life," said one. "I wouldn't know what to say."

"If one o' you 'll hold my baby, I'll try my best," faltered the second, after some hesitation. "He's cuttin' teeth, and may not let nobody tetch him but me."

So it proved; and the third, a poor creature of questionable reputation, burst into hysterical sobbing, and answered merely that she did not feel fit.

"I cain't have it so," whispered the poor mother, desperately. "I cain't have my pore baby laid away without no prayer, like hit was some dead animal. Ef nobody else won't say ary prayer—I will."

She stood forth, throwing back her sunbonnet, clasped her hands, shut her eyes tight, and gasped. One could see the working in her throat. They waited. Easter stared at the open grave, shallow, because its bottom was solid rock; the impartial sunshine on the crumbling rail fence, and the little group of workaday figures; the rude stones of other graves scattered through the tangle of briers and underbrush. Then Cordy drooped her head, and whispered, with infinite sadness:

"Lord, take care of my pore baby, and give hit a better chance than ever I had."

"Amen!" Hallet's deep voice concluded with a dry sob, and the three women whimpered after him, "Amen!"

The earth was hastily shoveled in, and the woman who had accounted herself unfit to pray began crying out loud. Presently Jim led his wife back to the wagon.

She spoke but once during the ride homeward. "An' I've got no idy the next 'll thrive any better," she said, dry-eyed. Easter, sitting in one of the chairs back in the wagon, held her peace; so this was what life might mean to a woman.

All next week the bereaved mother went about her work muttering and weeping, until both Jim and Easter began to fear for her reason. But presently the work compelled her thoughts away from her loss. She began to take interest in the milk and the chickens; and she noticed Allison and Easter. She told her husband one day that those two would make a good match.

Far from a match, however, was the present state of affairs in that quarter. The mountain people have an overmastering dread of attempting to cope with a delicate situation in words, insomuch that the neighbor who comes to borrow a cup of salt may very likely sit for half an hour on the edge of a chair and then go home without asking for it. And Allison had never kissed her again. But both knew, without having discussed the matter at all, that Allison wished to marry Easter, and that she, although Allison was undoubtedly her man of all men, could not obtain consent of her own mind to agree.

Why?

Cordy awaited her sister's confidence, and at last it came.

"I'm afeared," the girl said, and her eyelids crinkled woefully, her mouth twisted so that she was fain to hide her face.

"You don't need to be afeared," said Cordy, slowly, staring straight ahead of her. "You'd be better off with him than ye would at home, wouldn't ye? Life's mighty hard for women anywhars."

"Well, I don' know," said Easter, doubtfully.

But when, some days after, Allison did formally ask her in so many words, she gave him the same reason for her uncertainty.

"What air you 'feared of?" he demanded at once.

She was silent, terribly embarrassed.

"What is it you're afeared of—dear? Tell me. Won't you tell me?" He put his arms around her. She hid her face on his shoulder and began to cry. "You know I'd never mistreat you?"

"Hit ain't that."

"What, then?"

"I'm just afeared—afeared of being married."

He took a little time over this, and met it with the argument, "Would you have any easier time if you didn't get married?"

She tried to consider this fairly, but there was not an unmarried woman in all her acquaintance to serve as a basis for comparison. Most girls in the mountains marry between the ages of twelve and nineteen. She saw, however, that it was a choice of slavery in her father's house or slavery in a husband's.

Then Allison made a speech; his first, and perhaps his last. "Dear, dear girl, I'll just do the very best I can for you. I cain't promise no more than that. You know how I'm fixed. I've got nothing more to offer you than a cow or two, and a cabin, and what few sticks o' furniture I've put in hit; but that's more'n a heap o' people starts with. Hit's for you to say, and I don't want to urge ye again' your will an' judgment. But I've got a chanst now to go North with some men that 'll pay me better wages than I ever have got, and I won't git back till fall; and I—want—you," he said, "to be my wife before I go. I want to know, whilst I'm away, that you belong to me. Then, if I was to happen to a accident, on the railroad or anywheres, you'd be just the same as ever, only you'd have the cows, and the team, and my place. Won't you study about it?"

Easter thought of that for days, in the little time she had for thinking. But she thought, too, of the other side of the picture. Poor child, she had no chance for illusions. Sometimes she felt that she would be walking open-eyed into a trap from which there was no escape save death.

She thought of Cordy at that tiny grave. She dwelt upon her sister's alienation from her husband. Would she, Easter, ever come to look upon Allison in that way?

Yet the time drew near when Allison must go with those who had employed him. The thing must be decided. There came a heart-shaking day on which, clad in a new dress of cheap lawn made for the occasion, and a pair of slippers, Cordy's gift, she climbed into his wagon beside the boy, rode away, and came back a wife.

"But I mighty near wisht I hadn't," she said, thoughtfully, as she told her sister of the gayety of the impromptu wedding at home.

He wrote every week, some three or four pages—a vast amount of correspondence for a mountaineer. At the end of a month, he sent her money, more than she had ever had before. His pride in being able to do this was only equaled by hers as she laid out dollar after dollar, economically, craftily, with the thrift of experience, for household things. He had given no instructions as to how the money was to be used; so she bought her dishes and cooking-pots, a lamp, a fire-shovel, and, by way of extravagance, a play-pretty apiece for Suga'lump and Sonnybuck, and even a tiny cap for Cordy's baby not yet arrived.

Then, one day, taking the little boy with her, she went to Allison's cabin to clean house, put her purchases in order, and make the place generally ready for living in on his return.

She chose a fair blue day, not too warm for work. White clouds lolled against the tree-tops and the forest hummed with a pleasant summer sound. She brought water from the spring and scoured the already spotless floor,

washed her new dishes and admired their appearance ranged on the built-in
shelves across the end of the room, set her lamp on the fireboard, and then
spread the bed with new quilts. She stood looking at these, recognizing the
various bits of calico: here were scraps of her own and Ellender's dresses, this
block was pieced entirely of the boys' shirts, this was a piece of mother's
dress, this one had been Cordy's before she married; others had been contributed by girl friends at school. Presently she went to the door and glanced at
the sun. It would soon be time to go back and help Cordy get supper, but
she must first rest a little. Seating herself on the doorstep, she began to consider what other things were necessary for keeping house, telling them off on
her fingers and trying to calculate their probable cost—pillow-slips, towels,
a wash-kettle; perhaps, if Allison thought they could afford it, they would
buy a little clock and set it ticking merrily beside the lamp on the fireboard,
to be valued more as company than because of any real need of knowing the
time of day. Her mother had given her a feather bed and two pillows on the
morning of her wedding; Allison would whittle for her a maple bread-bowl,
and a spurtle and butter-paddle of cedar; and she herself was raising gourds
on Cordy's back fence, and could make her brooms of sedge-grass.

Thus planning, she felt a strange content steal upon her weariness. It was
borne strongly in upon her mind that she was to be supremely happy in this
home as well as supremely miserable. She ceased to ask herself whether the
one state would be worth the other, realizing for the first time that this was
not the question at all, but whether she could afford to refuse the invitation
of life, and thus shut herself out from the only development possible to her.

Little Sonnybuck toddled across the floor, a vision of peachblow curves
and fairness and dimples. She gathered him into her arms and laid her cheek
on his yellow hair, thrilling to feel the delicate ribs and the beat of the baby
heart. He began to chirp, "Do 'ome, do 'ome, E'tah," plucking softly at her
collar. Easter bent low, in a heart-break of tenderness, catching him close
against her breast. "Oh, if hit was—Allison's child and mine—"

On reaching home she kindled the supper fire and laid the cloth for the
evening meal of bread and fried pork and potatoes; and it was given to her
suddenly to understand how much of meaning these every-day services would
contain if illuminated by the holy joy of providing for her own.

She fell asleep late that night, smiling into the darkness, but was awakened,
it seemed to her, almost at once. Cordy stood before her, lamp in hand,
laughing nervously; her temples glistened with tiny drops of sweat, and her
eyes were dark and strange.

"It's time," said she.

When it was over, and they could, in the gray morn, sit down for a few minutes' rest before cooking breakfast, Easter saw Jim approach the bed on tiptoe. His wife smiled, and raised the coverlet softly from over a wee elevation.
Tears came into the girl's eyes, and she rose hastily and went to build a fire
in the stove.

Beside the wagon road that was the sole avenue of communication between the Blue Springs district and the outer world, Easter sat on the mossy roots of a great beech awaiting her husband's return. Her sunbonnet lay on the ground at her feet, and she was enjoying herself thoroughly, alone in the rich October woods. She was now almost a woman; her abundant vitality had early ripened into a beauty as superbly borne as that of a red wood-lily. She had walked a long way among the ridges, her weight swinging evenly from one foot to the other at every step with a swift, light roll; she was taking time for once in her life to rejoice with the autumn winds and the riot of color and autumn light. How much of outdoor vigor was incarnate in that muscular body of beech towering beside her! Easter's eyes ran up from the spreading base to the first sweep of the lower branches, noting the ropelike torsion under the bark. A squirrel, his cheeks too full of nuts even to scold her, peeped excitedly from one hiding-place after another, and finally scampered into safety round the giant bole. Then through a rent in the arras of pendent boughs she saw her man coming.

His grandfathers both had worn the fringed hunting-shirt and the moccasins; and though he himself was clad in the Sunday clothes of a workingman, he moved with the plunge and swing of their hunting gait. Such a keen, clean face as she watched it, uplifted to the light and color and music of the hour! His feet rustled the drifting leaves, and he sang as he came.

It seemed but a moment's mischief to hide herself behind a tree so as to give him a surprise; but the prompting instinct was older than the tree itself—old as the old race of young lovers.

. . . Suddenly they were face to face. He never knew how he cleared the few remaining steps, nor how he came to be holding both the hands she gave him. They laughed in sheer happiness, and stood looking at each other so, until Easter became embarrassed and stirred uneasily. He drew her hand within his arm as she turned, and, not knowing what else to do, they began to walk together along the leaf-strewn roadside, but stopped as aimlessly as they had started.

To him a woman's dropped eyes might have meant anything or just nothing at all. He scarcely dared, but drew her to him and bent his head. And somehow their lips met, and his arms were about her, and his cheek—a sandpapery, warm surface that comforted her whole perturbed being with its suggestion of man-strength and promise of husbandly protection—lay against hers.

That kiss was a revelation. To him it brought the ancient sense of mastery, of ownership—the certainty that here was his wife, the mate for whom his twenty years had been period of preparation and waiting. And the tears of half-shamed fright that started under Easter's lids were dried at their source by the realization that it was her own man who held her, that he loved her utterly, and that her soul trusted in him. She lifted her arms, and her light sleeves fell back from them as she pushed them round his neck.

"Oh, Allison, Allison, Allison, Allison!" she murmured, as she had said his name over to herself so many hundreds of times; only, now she was giving herself to him for good or ill with every repetition.

Before them lay the vision of their probable future—the crude, hard beginning, the suffering and toil that must come; the vision of a life crowned with the triple crown of Love and Labor and Pain. Their young strength rose to meet it with a new dignity of manhood and womanhood. In both their hearts the gladness of love fulfilled was made sublime by the grandeur of responsibility—by the courage required to accept happiness in sure foreknowledge of the suffering of life.

The squirrel ran down the beech and gathered winter provender unheeded; and yellow leaves swirled round them as through the forest came a wind sweet with the year's keenest wine.

Grace Toney Edwards

Grace Toney Edwards was born in Sunshine, a community nestled against Cherry Mountain, in Rutherford County, North Carolina. Moving at age five with her parents and six siblings a few miles east to Ellenboro, she grew up on a small cotton farm and attended all twelve grades of school in the same building. At Appalachian State Teachers College in Boone, North Carolina, she earned B.S. and M.A. degrees in English; there she sat in several classes taught by Dr. Cratis Williams, fondly remembered as "Mr. Appalachia." However, only after a stint of teaching at both Central Piedmont Community College in Charlotte and then back at Appalachian State University did Edwards discover her own ties to Appalachia.

With Cratis Williams as her mentor, she enrolled in 1974 in the Appalachian Studies Workshop at Berea College to study with leading scholars such as Loyal Jones, Richard Drake, Jim Wayne Miller, Wilma Dykeman, and Leonard Roberts. With that life-changing experience as incentive, she entered the University of Virginia, earning in 1980 a Ph.D. in English with a specialty in Appalachian literature and folklore. At Radford University, she helped to develop an interdisciplinary Appalachian Studies Program that she has chaired since 1982. In 1992 she became chair of the English Department. In July of 1994 she was appointed director of the newly established Appalachian Regional Studies Center at Radford University. Her research interests include Appalachian-Scottish-Irish connections, and women's roles in Appalachian culture, focusing particularly on pioneers such as Mary Draper Ingles and Emma Bell Miles.

Emma Bell Miles: Feminist Crusader in Appalachia

Emma Bell Miles of Walden's Ridge, Tennessee, is best known for her ethnographic book *The Spirit of the Mountains,* published in 1905. Some readers also know of her poetry because of the posthumously published collection called *Strains from a Dulcimore.* Few, however, think of her as a fiction writer; yet in the decade spanning 1907 to 1917, she published fifteen short stories in popular magazines of the day. Her settings were always in the Appalachian Mountain region she knew and loved, and her subject matter invariably addressed the relationships between characters, particularly male and female, and between characters and their environments.

A close examination of these interests suggests two labels that may be applied to the writings of Emma Bell Miles: feminism and local colorism. All of her writing belongs to the local color school, as it is commonly defined, though literary historians usually claim that the local color movement was in decline by the time Miles began to publish. In the decade following her death, a new regionalism reached fruition, its proponents sharing a strong sense of place with the local colorists but imbuing their fiction even more overtly than most of their predecessors with social motives. They "wrote to support theses rather than to photograph a group of people against a setting," according to editors Harry Warfel and Harrison Orians (xxiii). Miles's fiction and nonfiction stand between the two closely related impulses, her form and style taking their pattern largely from the nineteenth century, her purpose with its intense seriousness providing a bridge into the twentieth.

Miles is scarcely the lone exemplar of this position. Many local colorists shared her seriousness of social purpose and created half-fictional polemic to wage a crusade for one cause or another. Their intentions, then, were multifold: to present a particular locale in all its beauties, and sometimes its ugliness; to portray ordinary people of the region, the Wordsworthian common men and women, through their speech and daily activities, through their homes, families, and work—in a word, through their culture; and, most especially, to espouse a cause, to conduct a campaign, to exhort, or to persuade. The cause might be economic, political, or social, as with Hamlin Garland in *Main-Travelled Roads.* Or it might be a crusade for the illumination and liberation of women, as with Emma Bell Miles in virtually every prose piece she wrote, including her short stories.

Intentions of this sort require a different kind of reading than is usual for fiction. When the local colorists wrote half-stories, half-tracts lambasting the unfair social or economic conditions of their characters, critics were prone to condemn them for their melodrama, sentimentality, and failure to penetrate the minds of their characters. But perhaps critics should not be reading the pieces as conventional short stories at all, but rather as quasi-fictional exposition. As such, their surface sketches of character may be enough to illustrate

---

Printed by permission of the author.

the theses they argue, and their so-called sentimentality and melodrama may be justifiable means of conveying their moral convictions about life.

Emma Bell Miles's stories can be profitably measured by these standards, for her whole body of fiction is a crusade on behalf of women, fettered not only by their gender but also by poverty. Yet Miles is well aware that poverty alone does not hobble women; in her Appalachian Mountain culture of the early 1900s, as in most others throughout America, the traditions of the patriarchal society determined woman's place. It is no accident that the local color movement teemed with women writers. That their subject matter often centered on women's activities, ambitions, frustrations, and satisfactions comes as no surprise when we consider the long silences women had been forced to endure. That their stories sometimes became impassioned pleas to sanction or reform a lifestyle also comes as no surprise. If one dares risk a generalization about the crusade message of local color women writers who wrote about women, it might be worded thus: Let attention be paid to that half of humanity whose life has been lived in the other half's shadow.

Emma Bell Miles approached her subject matter at a time when the organized suffrage movement was still relatively new in the South, and virtually unknown in the Mountain South. In her stories, her vision of women and their utter dependence on marriage is localized to the southern mountains—in reality, to her own Walden's Ridge, Tennessee. Her writing had been preceded by and was contemporary with that of Mary Noailles Murfree, a fellow Tennessean who traveled from Middle Tennessee into the Cumberlands to produce a view of the mountaineer that fixed itself in the minds of Americans and to some extent remains there today. John Fox left the Bluegrass region of Kentucky for Big Stone Gap, Virginia, where he replicated Murfree's picture to become one of the most popular authors in the country soon after the turn of the century. Dozens of other writers flocked to the Appalachians to view the scenery and to poke and prod the natives—if they dared—in their research for their next piece.

Miles, however, did not have to go anywhere: she looked out her door; she listened to husband Frank, to Grandma Miles, to sister-in-law Laura, to Aunt Lucy, to her babies. She wrote about the Appalachian mountaineer from home, where the view differs considerably. In 1914, after she had already composed most of her fiction that came to print, she remarked to an unidentified correspondent, "To one who has lived the life, the ordinary novel of moonshine & rifles seems merely newspaper twaddle" (Letter 15 Jan. [1914]). Her fiction does not build from without, then, as does that of other writers about Appalachia in her time. It grows from within, showing respect for the traditional folkways that have sustained this mountain people, but at the same time crying out against the cultural bonds that restrict, limit, dehumanize the women. Her characters are mountaineers, but they are not peculiar or different from common people anywhere.

In her correspondence with Anna Ricketson, her beloved friend from New Bedford, Massachusetts, Miles recognized qualities in her own writing that seemed to her detriments to her success. She wrote, "[My stories] generally lack the keen interest of action and plot which 'The Circle' [prize competition] makes a first consideration" (Letter 31 Mar. 1907). A few days later she continued, "I think my stories will never be popular; they are too serious. . . . Perhaps I shall acquire a lighter touch as the children grow older and the daily stress is somewhat relieved" (Letter 5 Apr. 1907).

Two striking points emerge from this self-assessment. First, her awareness that her writing differs from "popular" fiction: at this stage in her career, she cannot recognize that the chronological mode of fiction, with its past-tense narrative of "what happened," is not sufficient for her purposes, which tend toward a more generalized present-tense analysis of "what happens." She wants to write fiction, but her world view demands exposition. Thus, she dubs her stories "too serious." Of course they are serious, because they carry her message to the world about the status of her sex; they are heavily laden with her moral conviction of wrong, which she cannot express openly, even to herself, and so must camouflage in fiction. The second emergent point is Miles's personal exemplification of the cause she crusades for. Attributing her seriousness to the daily stress of rearing children, she hopes for a "lighter touch" as they grow older. How many mothers, longing to create, have breathed a similar hope? In reality, however, the mountain woman's burden seldom lessened with the passing of years. She was expected to serve in a nurturing role, whether she was a maid of ten, a mother of thirty, or a grandmother of sixty. No alternative existed.

Miles's first published story, "The Common Lot," probes this very dilemma, as sixteen-year-old Easter Vanderwelt weighs the prospect of marriage against spinsterhood. With her married sister, Cordy, as her example, Easter watches and helps with the unceasing toil to meet the needs of the babies, the husband, the women themselves, the little house they live in. Frequent pregnancies, the rigors of childbirth, and the specter of infant death define Cordy's view of married life—and that of most mountain women.

With such a vision before her, Easter understandably fears marriage for herself. Practicing the restraint that her times required, Miles can only imply that Easter's fear is rooted in the sexual and biological demands of wifehood. She occupies the curious position, as many a rural child does, of having witnessed and assisted at births and deaths; she knows much of the elemental aspects of life. Yet the sex act and workings of her own body represent mysteries that she is not sure she wants to fathom. Although she never verbalizes the cause of her worries, she shares her concern with Cordy. The sister replies, "You don't need to be afeared. . . . You'd be better off with him [Allison, Easter's suitor] than ye would at home, wouldn't ye? Life's mighty hard for women anywhars" ("Common Lot" 151). From this discussion and her own long deliberation, Easter comes to see that the choice is "slavery in her father's house or slavery in a husband's" (151). Harsh as such an assessment may seem, it depicts a woman's view, unhampered by illusion, of what her culture has to offer. She ultimately chooses a husband and her own home, realizing that to refuse them means refusing the "invitation of life" and the "only development possible to her" (152). In so doing she has acknowledged the common lot of mountain women, and perhaps rural women everywhere, in 1908.

"The Common Lot," in both title and subject matter, can stand as Miles's battle cry in her crusade. Almost all of the other published stories are variations on its theme. As a crusader, however, she apparently felt compelled to half-stifle her battle cry and to raise her standard only in twilight. In her presentation of the mountain woman's experience, she runs the risk of uncovering the ugly, the lewd, even the tragic. To avoid those revelations, she steps into most of her stories and works the details into a seemingly happy ending. The reasons for her manipulation, as with many local colorists, are more complicated than mere reader expectation. She was a crusader with an ideal world view; in her personal life she summoned an eternally rebounding hope to help her cope with problems far greater than any she ever depicted in fiction. The stories, then, become her wish-fulfillment of satisfactory resolutions. In her fictional charges, she flaunts the privation, subservience, and limitations of mountain women; but in her retreats, she withdraws to the safety of compensations. The divisiveness in her self and fiction probably wells from two factors. The mountain culture truly does offer rewards to women through the giving and nurturing of life, as Miles allows Easter Vanderwelt to see, and after her a parade of female characters in other stories; the author cannot and does not wish to ignore this fact. And as spokesperson for her culture, she must bear in mind her personal relationship to the people about whom she writes; they are a proud and fiercely independent lot who look with suspicion at her work simply because it is what it is. "These here writers and typewriters," Grandma Miles had said, "will do to watch."

Surrounded by the culture-bound, class-bound, time-bound woman that Grandma Miles represents—indeed, one herself—Emma Bell Miles could scarcely choose any other subject matter for her prose. A teacher by inclination, a crusader by moral necessity, she devoted the bulk of her life's work to demonstrating how mountain woman's inevitable lot of "service and of suffering . . . refines as it is meekly and sweetly borne. For this reason she is never quite commonplace" (*Spirit of the Mountains* 66). Rejecting the "moonshine and rifles" that sent Murfree's and Fox's popularity soaring, she elected to deal with the serious, to advance a social criticism, though she felt compelled to camouflage it beneath her stories of romantic love. Perhaps she set out to portray the larger picture of southern mountain folk culture, but as she molded her material, one aspect of it continually pushed to the forefront. In her fiction, its dominance so controlled her form that she evolved something more than, or different from, fiction. I have chosen to call it quasi-fictional exposition, a kind of communication that draws from both literary and expository writing, but with a definite aim to convince and persuade. It is a record of the life of mountain woman, as Emma Bell Miles knew it and lived it.

Works Cited

Miles, Emma Bell.

———. Letter to Anna Ricketson. 5 Apr. 1907. Chattanooga Public Library Archive.

———. Letter to Anna Ricketson. 31 Mar. 1907. Chattanooga Public Library Archive.

———. Letter to unidentified correspondent. 15 Jan. 1913 [1914]. Hindman Settlement
    School Archive, Hindman, KY. [Facts within the letter and contextual evidence indi-
    cate the date should be 1914.]

———. "The Common Lot." *Harper's Monthly Magazine* 18 (1908): 145–54.

———. *The Spirit of the Mountains.* 1905. Knoxville: U of Tennessee P, 1975.

Warfel, Harry R., and G. Harrison Orians. "Introduction." *American Local-Color Stories.* Ed.
    Harry R. Warfel and G. Harrison Orians. New York: Harper and Bros., 1960.

Nancy Carol Joyner

A native of Asheville, North Carolina, Nancy Carol Joyner received her
B.A. degree from Meredith College, her M.A. from Columbia University,
and her Ph.D. from the University of North Carolina at Chapel Hill. After a
five-year stint at the University of Kentucky, she moved to Western Carolina University, where she is professor of English. Her longstanding interest
in Appalachian writing is reflected in several essays on the subject, including, most recently, a chapter in *The Poetics of Appalachian Space,* edited by
Parks Lanier (1991). In 1985 Joyner edited *Only When They're Little: The
Story of an Appalachian Family,* a posthumous novel by her aunt, Kate
Pickens Day. Among her projects is a study of Appalachian women's writing entitled *Truth to Tell: Lives and Literature of Appalachian Women.*

Appalachian Women's Writings
and Identity Theories

Loyal Jones of Berea College tells the story about the time Francis Hutchins,
then president of Berea, bestowed an honorary degree on his brother, Robert
Maynard Hutchins, then president of the University of Chicago. As the
guests were moving toward the dining hall following the ceremony, two
women struck up a conversation. One said, "I think this is a disgraceful occasion. Giving one's own brother an honorary degree is a blatant example of
nepotism." The other said, "Do you know who I am?" At the negative re-

From *Gender, Race, and Identity,* ed. Craig Barrow et al. (Chattanooga, TN: Southern
    Humanities P, 1993), 223–29. Reprinted by permission of the author.

sponse, she said, "I am Mrs. Francis Hutchins, Robert's sister-in-law." The other quickly responded, "And do you know who *I* am?" "No," Mrs. Hutchins said. "Thank God" was the reply.

It is usually easier to discover someone's identity, at least of the nominal sort, than that of the hapless speaker in the anecdote. Even so, determining the identity of others or of oneself is no simple matter, largely because of the widespread and often conflicting use of the term. While the psychologically based "search for identity" has become such a popular activity of the twentieth century that it is a generally understood concept, virtually every discipline defines the term in its own way, thereby challenging the assumption that we know what identity is. Defining the term, then, is a prerequisite to dealing with the two other qualifiers of my topic, gender and region. In this essay I shall use the definitions of identity offered by three disciplines, sociology, psychology, and literary criticism, as the organizational basis for an an interpretation of certain texts whose background is the distinctive geographical and cultural locus of the Southern Highlands, and whose foreground is the lives of women.

First, the definition of the most apparent, because it is the most external, kind of identity is, according to one source, this "sociological truism": "I am not what I think I am. I am not what you think I am. I am what I think you think I am" (Young, 22). In *The Presentation of Self in Everyday Life,* Erving Goffman argues that we are actors playing roles that have been socially prescribed (121–22). Identity can and must be based on such external considerations as race, class, culture, gender, and, I would add, region. One's identity is determined inevitably by the time, locale, and condition of one's place in society.

This place is put in sharp focus in a society recognized as "other," such as Appalachia. Henry Shapiro, whose seminal work, *Appalachia On Our Mind,* maintains that Appalachia is not so much geographical as it is ideological, a concept created in large part by late-nineteenth-century local colorists who published in Boston magazines (ix–x). His most prominent example is the local color writing of Charles Egbert Craddock, the pseudonym of Mary Noailles Murfree, which, Shapiro points out, was written by an outsider, a resident of a locale near Nashville, who summered in the Tennessee mountains. Further, the stories were written for outsiders, the readers of the *Atlantic Monthly* (18–19). The norms of a marginal society, as Appalachia surely was presented as being, are different from those in the mainstream. Consequently its "otherness" is emphasized. Similarly, Simone de Beauvoir, in *The Second Sex,* delineates societal expectations of public and private gender roles and sees women as the "Other":

> [Woman] is defined and differentiated with reference to man and not he with reference to her; she is the incidental, the inessential as opposed to the essential. He is the Subject, he is the Absolute—she is the Other.
>
> The category of the *Other* is as primordial as consciousness itself. In the most primitive societies, in the most ancient mythologies, one finds the expression of a duality—that of the Self and the Other. . . .

Thus it is that no group ever sets itself up as the One without at once setting up the Other over against itself. (xvi–xvii)

Appalachian women, then, are the Other, both in relationship to the primary culture and to men. Both region and gender are factors in marginalization.

Lucy Furman's novel, *The Quare Women* (1923), provides a useful glimpse of the other gender in the other society. It is the first of several of Furman's barely fictionalized accounts of the early days of Hindman Settlement School in Knott County, Kentucky, where a group of women from the "level country," or the Blue Grass, were "fotched on" to teach basic skills to the unschooled mountaineers. Early in the book, one of the local matriarchs, Aunt Ailsie Pridemore, has this conversation with one of them:

> ". . . how old air you, Virginny?"
> "How old would you guess?"
> "Well, I would say maybe eighteen or nineteen."
> "I'm twenty-eight," replied Virginia.
> "Now you know you hain't! No old woman couldn't have sech rosy jaws and tender skin!"
> "Yes, I am; but I don't call it old."
> "Hit's old, too; when I were twenty-eight, I were very nigh a grandmaw."
> "You must have married very young."
> "No, I were fourteen. That hain't young—my maw, she married at twelve, and had sixteen in family. I never had but a small mess of younguns,—eight,—and they're all married and gone, or else dead, and me and Lot left alone. Where's your man while you traveling the country this way?"
> "I have no man—I'm not married."
> . . . Aunt Ailsie stared, dumb, for some seconds before she could speak. "Twenty-eight, and hain't got a man!" she then exclaimed. She looked Virginia all over again, as if from a new point of view, and with a gaze in which curiosity and pity were blended. "I never in my life seed but one old maid before, and she was fittified." (11–12)

From Aunt Ailsie's perspective, an unmarried woman of twenty-eight was not only unheard of but was also an unacceptable role in the mountain society. As a woman she actively participated in proscribing woman's role, seeing an adult, rational (not "fittified") woman as having only one identity, that of wife and mother.

Aunt Ailsie soon commences a match-making scheme in which she tries to convince Jeems, a young widower with six small children, to find a wife among the fotched-on women, thereby taking at least one out of her misery. Things go awry, however, when Jeems observes that none of them can milk a cow. The cow being in clear need of milking, and all of the men refusing to do so, one of the women makes an unsuccessful attempt. At that, a twelve-year-old boy, Billy, admits to his ability: "I've holp maw milk a many of a time, and Lethie, too. I don't care if hit hain't a man's job, I've holp 'em

when they was sick or busy. Here, you fotched-on women don't know nothing; gimme that air bucket, and a apern and sunbonnet, and I'll show you.
Of course, she wouldn't lemme come a-nigh her in breeches" (103–4). Billy
manages to milk the cow, but Jeems gives up on the project of finding a wife
among the fotched-on women. He seems to be aghast when he reports the
scene to Aunt Ailsie: "Them women all allowed hit was a man's job, not a
woman's, to milk a cow brute; and one of them head-women said she was
aiming to teach all the women-folks in this here country not to milk nary
'nother time theirselves, but to make the men-folks do hit allus" (105–6).

This reversal of roles is confirmed in the work of Emma Bell Miles, whose
1905 study, *The Spirit of the Mountains,* describes the situation of the mountain people she observed after she married Frank Miles, a stereotypically
shiftless mountain man who was either unable or unwilling to provide for
his large family. In his introduction to Miles's book, David E. Whisnant has
noted the "profound biculturism" with which Miles wrote, thus providing a
balanced perspective lacking in other nonfiction accounts of the region (xvi).
She has a lot to say about the difficulties mountain women encounter, such as
"At twenty the mountain woman is old in all that makes a woman old—toil,
sorrow, childbearing, loneliness, and pitiful want" (Miles 64), and "It is a very
fortunate wife, indeed, who does not carry a considerable burden of duties
properly supposed to belong to masculine shoulders, such as bringing wood
and water, milking, and raising garden" (21). Her most telling observation,
though, has to do with the lack of communication between husband and wife:
"They are so silent. They know so pathetically little of each other's lives" (70).

While Miles ostensibly writes about the external roles that mark a woman's
identity, her subtext surely must be a reflection of her own situation, or an
interior view of a woman's life. Eric Erikson, who is credited with coining
the term "identity crisis," emphasizes in his classification of life stages an
interior rather than exterior locus of identity. Adolescents especially try to
"find themselves" because social structures and therefore strictures of the past
are crumbling. This identity search is so pervasive that Robert Langbaum in
The Mysteries of Identity says that "the theme of identity appears almost everywhere in modern literature" (21).

One notable female identity is Ivy Rowe, Lee Smith's letter writer in *Fair
and Tender Ladies* (1988). Ivy directs her first letters to a pen pal in Germany
and identifies herself by writing "I am a girl 12 years old very pretty I have
very long hair and eight brothers and sisters and my Mother and my Father,
he is ill. . . . I want to be a famous writter [*sic*] when I grow up, I will write
of Love" (21). Ivy writes of love, all right: her first lover, Lonnie, who left her
pregnant to go to war; Franklin, the mine owner's suicidal son, with whom
she had a casual fling; Oakley, her solid, stolid husband; and finally Honey
Breeding, the bee man who swept her off her feet and out of the house for a
brief extramarital affair. She writes of the love of her five children, her foster
child, and her grandchildren. Perhaps the person she loves best is Silvaney,
her retarded sister and the person to whom most of her letters are addressed.

She admits to her daughter that she wrote to Silvaney long after she knew she had died, because Silvaney was "a part of me, my other side, my other half, my heart" (312). Psychologist Judith Stillion interprets this letter writing to a dead sister as a kind of bibliotherapy and says that Ivy fits the profile of Erikson's final mentally healthy life stage, which he terms "ego integrity." When Ivy is near death in her seventies, she writes that she intends to leave the hospital because "I have lived like I wanted by God, I will die that way too" (311).

Ivy's attitude about her life stands in sharp contrast to that of her sister Beulah, who marries an upwardly mobile man and is desperate to rise socially herself. When Ivy is living with Beulah and raising her illegitimate daughter, she writes to a friend:

> Beulah wants *so much* that I don't know if there is enough in the world to satisfy her, I honestly don't. And also she is so scared, and ashamed of herself someway. Last week she got invited up to Mrs. Bolin's house to make an alter cloth for the church, this is the kind of thing that is so important to Beulah. But then she fretted and fretted so much that she would say the wrong thing, or do something wrong, that she ended up flat on her back with a sick headache, and missed it all. And yet to see her, you would think Beulah more of a lady than any of these. . . . Somehow it's like she is still playing party and doesn't believe it herself. . . .
>   I am *glad* I am ruint, and don't have to worry over such as that. (163–64)

In the course of the novel, Ivy is "ruint" several times over in the eyes of her society and culture, but internally, or psychologically, she is a definite, and to her readers a delightful, success. She illustrates the fully functioning personality that Carl Rogers describes in *On Becoming a Person*. Rogers borrows heavily from existential philosophy in his work, using, for example, a quotation from Kierkegaard, "To Be That Self Which One Truly Is," to develop his theory (166). We see Ivy as existentially becoming. Thus psychology is blended with phenomenological philosophy, the basis of much current literary criticism.

Identity is not only important to sociology and psychology; it has also become a prominent concept among literary critics. Norman Holland's essay, "Unity Identity Text Self," posits the reader-response theory that unity is to identity as text is to self. Or: "we can think of *unity* and *identity* as expressing only sameness or continuity while *text* and *self* show difference or change, or, more exactly, *both* sameness *and* difference, *both* continuity *and* change" (122). This insistence that the subject and the work must be seen as one and the same adds a new dimension to the word identity, namely that of relationship. It is the relationship of characters with each other, of characters with their past and present selves, of characters with their method of presentation, the words on the page, that provides identity. Both Heidegger's *Identity and Difference* and Derrida's "differance" have insisted that identity is dependent upon its relationship to something else. Current literary criticism sees identity in its broadest sense. A character's identity in a work is not merely determined by a sociological or psychological interpretation but involves philosophical, linguistic, and political approaches to the work and especially to the reader. The identity of the critic is inescapably part of the identification of the character.

Identity of both the character and the critic becomes, then, an issue in feminist literary criticism. Elaine Showalter uses the apt metaphor of women critics being both daughters of a male-dominated tradition and sisters of a new approach to critical inquiry, which she calls "gynocriticism" (271–72). Josephine Donovan also uses Showalter's gynocriticism, arguing that women's condition in our society leads to an "internalization of otherness" that results in a sort of cultural schizophrenia (100). Similarly, Rita Felski takes on what she calls "the status of female identity," describing the tension between dual attitudes seen in women's self-discovery narratives:

> on the one hand, a desire for integration and participation within a larger social and public community as a means of overcoming a condition of marginalization and powerlessness, on the other, an insistence upon a qualitative difference of cultural perspective as a means of articulating a radical challenge to dominant values and institutions, a stress on difference which resists assimilation into the mainstream of social life. (150)

In other words, the desire to succeed within the group and the desire to succeed without it are tandem elements of the identity search for women.

Gertie Nevels faces this dilemma in Harriette Arnow's *The Dollmaker,* the 1954 novel made more widely known when Jane Fonda produced and starred in a TV film version thirty years later. Gertie is in tension with her culture, which tells her that she must go with her husband to Detroit while he works in a factory, although she wants to stay in Kentucky and farm. She is in tension with her husband, toward whom she remains silent about her wishes, discovering only too late that he shares her dream of a farm. She is in tension with her children in multiple ways, most tragically in her guilt at the death of her child Cassie.

But Gertie is more than dutiful daughter, devoted wife, and dedicated mother. She is also a skilled woodcarver and eventually the breadwinner of the family. Her final tension, symbolized by a large block of cherry wood, is her need to maintain her artistic integrity and the simultaneous need to commercialize her gift. She had brought the block of wood from Kentucky with her, thinking she might use it to carve a statue of Christ. But financial exigencies force her to make money with her whittling, and she eventually is given a large order for which she needs a large quantity of wood. To keep food on her family's table, she takes the block to the lumber yard to have it sawed up into boards. Because it must be split to be sawed, the final scene shows Gertie raising an axe to the partially completed carving.

This conclusion is indeterminate to the point of deliberate ambiguity. Arnow seems to be requiring the reader to interpret the outcome of the text, an outcome inextricably tied to Gertie's identity. Not surprisingly, critics have differed radically on the meaning of the final scene. Lewis Lawson sees it as Gertie's ritual sacrifice, in which she has "brought to its end the block which has represented her life" (74). Joyce Carol Oates, who reads the novel as a continuous downhill journey for Gertie, says that she is "lyrically aware of the horror of the world in which she now lives" (607). Carole Ganim observes that Gertie "learns that she can live somewhat peacefully in the industrial, male-dominated world without surrendering her own identity totally" (269).

In spite of the radical changes in her life and the tensions and ambiguities surrounding it, however, Gertie knows very well who she is. In the first extraordinary scene of that novel, she takes on a nameless soldier who refuses her and her critically ill son a ride in his car. "Even in the man's work shoes, the long and shapeless coat, green tinged with age, . . . she held herself proudly, saying: 'You want my name; I'm Gertie Nevels frum Ballew, Kentucky'" (11). In the equally impressive final scene, Gertie has no need to assert who she is, but she does come to a recognition of her relationship to her family and her neighbors.

Unlike Aunt Ailsie Pridemore of *The Quare Women,* whose author identifies her in the most stereotypical way, or Ivy Rowe of *Fair and Tender Ladies,* whose author has her go through an identity crisis and thereby go against her "raising," Gertie Nevels is presented as a fully dimensional heroine, significantly defined by her background and status, surely, but nevertheless a strong, independent individual.

As an Appalachian woman reader, reading Appalachian women writers writing about Appalachian women, I am able to identify with and identify this literature as important. Identity may be approached through other methodologies than the three used here, but none is comprehensive. The complexities of our society and the plethora of perspectives by which to make literary assessments are both frustrating and fascinating, much like the identities of us all.

Works Cited

Arnow, Harriette. *The Dollmaker.* Afterword by Joyce Carol Oates. New York: Avon, 1972.

Benstock, Shari, Ed. *Feminist Issues in Literary Scholarship.* Bloomington: Indiana UP, 1987.

de Beauvoir, Simone. *The Second Sex.* New York: Knopf, 1953.

Donovan, Josephine. "Toward a Women's Poetics." *Feminist Issues in Literary Scholarship.* Ed. Shari Benstock. Bloomington: Indiana UP, 1987. 98–110.

Erikson, Eric. *Identity, Youth, and Crisis.* New York: Norton, 1968.

Felski, Rita. *Beyond Feminist Aesthetics.* Cambridge, MA: Harvard UP, 1989.

Furman, Lucy. *The Quare Women.* Boston: Little, Brown, 1923.

Ganim, Carole. "Herself: Women and Place in Appalachian Literature." *Appalachian Literature,* 13 (1986): 258–74.

Goffman, Erving. *The Presentation of Self in Everyday Life.* Garden City, NY: Doubleday, 1959.

Heidegger, Martin. *Identity and Difference.* Trans. Joan Stambaugh. New York: Harper, 1969.

Holland, Norman. "Unity Identity Text Self," *Reader-Response Criticism.* Ed. Jane P. Tompkins. Baltimore: Johns Hopkins UP, 1980. 118–34.

Langbaum, Robert. *The Mysteries of Identity.* New York: Oxford UP, 1977.

Lawson, Lewis A. *Another Generation: Southern Fiction Since World War II.* Jackson: U Mississippi P, 1984.

Miles, Emma Bell. *The Spirit of the Mountains.* 1905. Facsimile ed. Fore. Roger D. Abraham. Intro. David E. Whisnant. Knoxville: U of Tennessee P, 1975.

Rogers, Carl. *On Becoming a Person.* Boston: Houghton Mifflin, 1961.

Shapiro, Henry D. *Appalachia On Our Mind.* Chapel Hill: U of North Carolina P, 1978.

Showalter, Elaine. "Towards a Feminist Poetics." *Twentieth Century Literary Theory.* Ed. K. M. Newton. London: Macmillan, 1988.

Smith, Lee. *Fair and Tender Ladies.* New York: Putnam's, 1988.

Stillion, Judith. Personal interview. 16 June 1991.

Young, Lung-chang. "Identity, Conflict, and Survival Mechanisms for Asian Americans." *Different People: Studies in Ethnicity and Education.* Ed. Edgar B. Gumbert. Atlanta: Georgia State U. 21–47.

Julie Pennell

Originally from West Virginia, Julie Pennell now lives in Ohio.

Conflict

City reared,
Mountain heritage.

City society,
Country feelings.

Formal education,
Backwoods knowledge.

Acceptable speech,
Appalachian twang.

Controlled violence.
Mountaineer fighter.

Social grace,
Appalachian brash.

Who am I anyway?

Vicky Hayes

A native of Paintsville, Kentucky, Vicky Hayes studied creative writing at Berea College and Appalachian literature at Appalachian State University. For several years she reported on environmental and labor issues in the coalfields for weekly papers such as the *Troublesome Creek Times*. Her news research has won her first-place awards in competitions of the Kentucky Newspaper Association. Her poetry has appeared in *Appalachian Journal*, *Mountain Review* and *Kentucky Magazine*.

Wire Wizard

Hello. . . Hello. . .
Is there anybody awake
out in that cactus country?
This be the Greybeard
from Eastern Kentucky,
that hillbilly state.
Arizona? Nevada?
Shake! Shake!

We're tryin to get your way
but with all this rain
the skips rollin off the eastern coast.
It's been pourin here all day.
It's glistenin on the trees,
rollin off the ground
and hangin to the wires.
This be the Greybeard
comin your way.
My ears are wet. Shake! Shake!

There's no way I can get out,
no way to go anywhere
till you honkers
stop keyin up on that gold coast,
that California coast.
Talk to us Kentuckians
or clear the channel.

Printed by permission of the author.

This be the hillbilly from Eastern Kentucky
better known down this way
as the Greybeard, the Greybeard.
Flyin over these wires,
we can go anywhere
when the channels clear.
We're gonna back way down now.
We're gonna shut this box down,
sit back and listen
to this heavy rain,
to your voices runnin in the air.
Goodnight, you wire wizards.
This be Kentucky 529,
out of this coal town
closin her down.

Ode to My Mountain

This is an Ode to my
    Mountain home,
With peaceful streams and
    people too,
And pretty flowers under
    a sky so blue.
No, I ain't leavin' my
    mountain home.
Not even for a million bucks,
'Cause since I got my
    satellite dish,
I realized the rest
    of the world sucks.

Wendell Berry

Wendell Berry is a farmer, poet, philosopher, and professor. His career increasingly has turned to serving as a spokesman for common sense in conservation and agriculture through such books as *Farming: A Handbook* (1971), and *The Gift of Good Land: Further Essays Cultural and Agricultural* (1981). In his prose and in his poetry (*Collected Poems: 1957–1982* [1985]), Berry defends the role of the farmer as steward rather than master, a tradition still surviving among some in the Appalachians. Further, he places this doctrine in the context of religion and "adult community life," as noted in the essay by John Lang which follows this poem.

The Satisfactions of the Mad Farmer

Growing weather; enough rain;
the cow's udder tight with milk;
the peach tree bent with its yield;
honey golden in the white comb;

the pastures deep in clover and grass,
enough, and more than enough;

the ground, new worked, moist
and yielding underfoot, the feet
comfortable in it as roots;

the early garden: potatoes, onions,
peas, lettuce, spinach, cabbage, carrots,
radishes, marking their straight rows
with green, before the trees are leafed;

raspberries ripe and heavy amid their foliage,
currants shining red in clusters amid their foliage,
strawberries red ripe with the white
flowers still on the vines—picked
with the dew on them, before breakfast;

From *Farming: A Handbook,* © 1970 by Wendell Berry. Reprinted by permission of Harcourt Brace, Inc.

grape clusters heavy under broad leaves,
powdery bloom on fruit black with sweetness
—an ancient delight, delighting;

the bodies of children, joyful
without dread of their spending,
surprised at nightfall to be weary;

the bodies of women in loose cotton,
cool and closed in the evenings
of summer, like contented houses;

the bodies of men, competent in the heat
and sweat and weight and length
of the day's work, eager in their spending,
attending to nightfall, the bodies of women;

sleep after love, dreaming
white lilies blooming
coolly out of my flesh;

after sleep, the sense of being enabled
to go on with work, morning a clear gift;

the maidenhood of the day,
cobwebs unbroken in the dewy grass;

the work of feeding and clothing and housing,
done with more than enough knowledge
and with more than enough love,
by men who do not have to be told;

any building well built, the rafters
firm to the walls, the walls firm,
the joists without give,

the proportions clear,
the fitting exact, even unseen,
bolts and hinges that turn home
without a jiggle;

any work worthy
of the day's maidenhood;

any man whose words
lead precisely to what exists,
who never stoops to persuasion;

the talk of friends, lightened and cleared
by all that can be assumed;

deer tracks in the wet path,
the deer sprung from them, gone on;

live streams, live shiftings
of the sun in the summer woods;

the great hollow-trunked beech,
a landmark I loved to return to,
its leaves gold-lit on the silver
branches in the fall: blown down
after a hundred years of standing,
a footbridge over the stream;

the quiet in the woods of a summer morning,
the voice of a pewee passing through it
like a tight silver wire;

＊

a little clearing among cedars,
white clover and wild strawberries
beneath an opening to the sky
—heavenly, I thought it,
so perfect; had I foreseen it
I would have desired it
no less than it deserves;

fox tracks in the snow, the impact
of lightness upon lightness,
unendingly silent.

What I know of spirit is astir
in the world. The god I have always expected
to appear at the woods' edge, beckoning,
I have always expected to be
a great relisher of the world, its good
grown immortal in his mind.

John Lang

Professor of English at Emory and Henry College in Virginia, John Lang was born in Minneapolis, Minnesota, in 1947. He received his B.A. in English and philosophy from St. Olaf College and earned his Ph.D. at Stanford University in 1975 with a dissertation on the novels of William Styron. He has published a number of essays on Styron and other southern and Appalachian writers, including Wendell Berry, Fred Chappell, Ernest Gaines, John Ehle, and Robert Morgan. His essays and reviews have appeared in *American Literature*, *Southern Humanities Review*, *Renascence*, *Southern Literary Journal*, *Journal of Kentucky Studies*, *Appalachian Journal*, and *Shenandoah*. In addition to his teaching responsibilities at Emory and Henry, he edits the college's *Iron Mountain Review*.

Wendell Berry: Fronting the Essentials

In a recent essay on Edward Abbey, Wendell Berry notes the difficulty of affixing any particular label to Abbey. "He is not," says Berry, "a conservationist or an environmentalist or a boxable *ist* of any other kind; he keeps on showing up as Edward Abbey" (*What Are* 36). According to Berry, who invokes the example of Thoreau, Abbey is best understood as an autobiographer, someone who is putting his *character* on record. The same can be said of Berry himself: poet, novelist, essayist, teacher, and farmer, the author of more than twenty-five books published over the last thirty years. To label him a Transcendentalist is not the aim of this paper. But with Berry's reference to Thoreau as point of departure, I would like to indicate several significant ways in which Berry's recent essays, collected in *Home Economics* (1987) and *What Are People For?* (1990), mirror and extend issues addressed by Thoreau and his transcendentalist contemporaries.

The title of the first of these two volumes, *Home Economics,* provides one important link between Berry and the Thoreau of *Walden,* whose opening—and longest—chapter is entitled "Economy." Like Thoreau, Berry repeatedly challenges the assumptions that underlie America's economic order: its extravagance and waste; its overspecialized division of labor; its excessive reliance on machinery and its naive faith in technological progress; its attitude toward—and the quality of—the work it affords for citizens; its dependence on the principle of competition; and its apparent inability to value anything that cannot be quantified or reduced to monetary terms. The Thoreau who considered "the fall from the farmer to the operative [to be] as great and

Originally published in the 1991 *Proceedings of the Virginia Humanities Conference*; reprinted in *Journal of Kentucky Studies* 9 (1992). Reprinted here by permission of the author.

memorable as that from the man to the farmer" finds his contemporary counterpart in Wendell Berry, as does the Thoreau who proclaimed: "My greatest skill has been to want but little" (43, 47). Both writers raise fundamental questions about "the true necessaries and means of life" (Thoreau 5) in their critiques of the artificial needs created by a consumption-oriented economy—an economy which, as Thoreau argued, exists "not that mankind may be well and honestly clad, but, unquestionably, that the corporations may be enriched" (17–18). The number—as well as the frivolousness and shoddiness—of consumer "goods" has grown exponentially since the mid-nineteenth century. Thus, what Berry sees even more clearly than Thoreau is the threat such an economy poses not only to humanity's moral and spiritual values but also to the natural world itself.

Like most of the Transcendentalists, Berry distrusts modern technology and the industrial economy to which it has led. The material enrichment produced by that economy often has been achieved at the expense not only of nature but also of individual identity and a sense of community. "Men have become the tools of their tools," Thoreau remarked (25), a process that Berry sees accelerating in the twentieth century (*Home* 99). For Berry, as for Thoreau, "technological progress" is characterized by a division of labor that deprives workers of a meaningful relationship to the products of their labor. Workers cease to participate in a creative process that involves "making" and are reduced instead to a mechanical process that focuses merely on "doing" (*Home* 77, 166). As a result, workers become alienated from their labor, which is perceived as overspecialized, degrading, trivial, and tyrannical (Berry, *What Are* 184). The industrial economy reinforces this sense of alienation by setting up what Berry calls "its characteristic division between life and work" (*Home* 33), a division evident in our society's T.G.I.F. mentality and in the deteriorating quality both of the products we manufacture and of our human relationships.

To gauge the disparity between our traditional ideals and our current practice, Berry cites the prayer "For Every Man in His Work," which is found in the 1928 *Book of Common Prayer*: "Deliver us, we beseech thee, in our several callings, from the service of mammon, that we may do the work which thou givest us to do, in truth, in beauty, and in righteousness . . . to the benefit of our fellow men" (*What Are* 101). In the context of our modern economy, this prayer, as Berry notes, is a relic. Its principles sound quaint, at best, when measured against the economic "principle" that shapes the business world—namely, the "law" of competition. The question Berry asks is:

> Can . . . a nation *afford* this exclusive rule of competition, this purely economic economy? . . . Rats and roaches live by competition under the law of supply and demand; it is the privilege of human beings to live under the laws of justice and mercy. It is impossible not to notice how little the proponents of the ideal of competition have to say about honesty, which is the fundamental economic virtue, and how *very* little they have to say about community, compassion, and mutual help. (*What Are* 135)

Elsewhere Berry writes: "We assume that we can have an exploitive, ruth-lessly competitive, profit-for-profit's-sake economy, and yet remain a decent and a democratic nation. . . . This simply means that our highest principles and standards have no practical force or influence and are reduced merely to talk" (*Home* 169).

Such contradictions and disjunctions arouse Berry's wrath wherever he en-counters them. He sees in our increasing specialization a threat to the indi-vidual freedom, the healthy self-reliance, that was central to the transcen-dentalist spirit. Moreover, he views this specialization as undercutting our sense of responsibility for the goods we produce. In the specialization of the university, Berry finds an extremely pernicious instance of this abdication of responsibility. His essay "The Loss of the University" laments American higher education's failure to raise "the question of the truth of what is taught and learned," as well as questions about "the fate and use of knowledge in the world" (*Home* 90). As Thoreau inquired, "Where is this division of labor to end? and what object does it finally serve? No doubt another *may* also think for me; but it is not therefore desirable that he should do so to the exclusion of my thinking for myself" (31).

The continued expansion of the industrial economy, Berry fears, will mean the obsolescence of the individual, a prospect that also concerned Thoreau. Unlike Thoreau, however, Berry grounds individual identity *in re-lationships*, not in the isolated self. Throughout his work, Berry stresses the concepts of marriage and family, of neighborhood and neighborliness, and of membership in local communities. His essay "Writer and Region" numbers Thoreau among the American writers who have failed "to imagine a respon-sible, adult community life" (*What Are* 77). Yet, despite this significant dif-ference, both Berry and Thoreau recognize the threat to individual identity posed by an industrial economy. For Berry, the destruction of community that is implicit in the principle of competition destroys individuality as well:

> It is only in these bonds [of marriage, kinship, friendship, and neigh-borhood] that our individuality has a use and a worth; it is only to the people who know us, love us, and depend on us that we are indispens-able as the persons we uniquely are. In our industrial society . . . indi-viduals are seen more and more as "units" by their governments, employ-ers, and suppliers. They live, that is, under the rule of interchangeability of parts. (*Home* 118)

In such circumstances the sense of individuality shrivels away.

How is late-twentieth-century America to reduce its dependence on such an economy? The initial word in Berry's title, *Home Economics*, points the way. Like the Transcendentalists, Berry argues that individual acts take pre-cedence over national and global solutions. The phrase "late-twentieth-cen-tury America" is itself an abstraction on which we cannot afford to wait. For

Berry, the self and the local community are the chief agents of social change, for "the problems are our lives" (*What Are* 198). Consumers share in the exploitation and degradation of nature practiced by industry and agribusiness. As Berry readily concedes, the problems are complex, and solutions are difficult to achieve, but the solutions must begin, to a great extent, with personal initiatives, with (in Thoreau's words) "tinkering upon our *lives* to improve *them*" (62). "To refuse to buy what one does not need" (*What Are* 196) is one crucial measure of self-discipline, of character. And, Berry warns, to avoid ecological disaster, "We are going to have to learn to give up things that we have learned (in only a few years, after all) to 'need'" (*What Are* 196). In an economy like ours, founded upon the creation of artificial needs, "a man is rich," Thoreau observed, "in proportion to the number of things which he can afford to let alone" (55).

As a farmer, Berry is keenly aware of his ties to the natural world. Just as he strives to redefine our assumptions about economic life, so he seeks to instill in his readers an awareness of humanity's radical dependence on nature. The continued health of nature is one of Berry's primary themes in such essays as "Getting Along with Nature," "Preserving Wildness," and "Two Economies" in *Home Economics;* and "Nature as Measure" in *What are People For?* That health is jeopardized, of course, both by America's industrial economy and by our failures of imagination. The recovery of a harmonious relationship with nature likewise was a part of the transcendentalist impulse at work in the writing of Emerson and Whitman and Thoreau. What differentiates Berry's stance from that of these writers, however, is his insistence on what he calls, in the title of another essay, "A Practical Harmony"—a harmony grounded in *doing,* not in observing or contemplating (*What Are* 103–8). He is not the Thoreau of "The Bean Field," who describes his husbandry as "on the whole a rare amusement" and refers to his planting as motivated not by the desire for beans but "for the sake of tropes and expression, to serve a parable-maker one day" (108). Nor is Berry likely to share the pride Thoreau feels in having had, though only in imagination, "the refusal of several farms" (55). Yet Berry certainly does share Thoreau's criticism of his contemporaries, for whom husbandry, once a sacred art, "is pursued with irreverent haste and heedlessness . . . our object being to have large farms and large crops merely." "By avarice and selfishness," Thoreau continues, "and a grovelling habit . . . of regarding the soil as property, or the means of acquiring property chiefly, the landscape is deformed, husbandry is degraded with us, and the farmer leads the meanest of lives. He knows Nature but as a robber" (111).

Berry's critique of modern agribusiness rests both on its motive—greed—and on its effects—destruction of the soil, of the small farm, and of the local culture that nurtures vital communities. Many of the essays in *Home Economics* and *What Are People For?,* like those in his earlier collections *The Unsettling of America* and *The Gift of Good Land,* focus on the plight of the small farm and the need for sustainable agriculture. Underlying Berry's attack on what he terms "industrial agriculture" is its failure to recognize the limits of human power. Berry is a writer at pains to remind his readers that they inhabit a world they did not invent. The argument of his essays, he remarks, is "an effort to describe responsibility" (*Home* ix). "The made order must seek the given order, and find its place in it" (*What Are* 12). That "given order" Berry defines in the traditional religious term "Creation," a word he capitalizes in order to highlight nature's divine origins and its sanctity. Nature requires the kind of care that is possible, Berry contends, only with the intimate relationship between farmers and their land that can occur on family farms. The "advances" of large-scale agribusiness have meant the deterioration of the soil *and* a growing inability to perceive our fundamental dependence on nature. "The national economy has prescribed ways of use," Berry notes, "but not ways of care" (*What Are* 110). That economy has tended to view the earth as a repository of raw materials or inert natural resources, and people as "labor" or consumers (*Home* 168). It has thus demeaned both nature and human beings. Its thrust is toward depletion, not replenishment.

And yet, as Berry insists, "we can live only in and from nature, and . . . we have, therefore, an inescapable obligation to be nature's students and stewards and to live in harmony with her" (*What Are* 104). While Berry echoes Thoreau's call for "the tonic of wildness" (Thoreau 209), he stresses, as Thoreau did not, the vital link between human health and the right use of *domesticated* nature. Berry's persona, the "mad farmer," in such works of poetry as *Farming: A Handbook* and *The Country of Marriage,* reinforces the impression of wholeness—of integrity of both vision and character—that distinguishes his work.

His confidence that such wholeness or order or pattern underlies nature provides another link between his work and that of the nineteenth-century Transcendentalists. As his "Letter to Wes Jackson" in *Home Economics* reveals, for Berry the term "random" refers not to "a verifiable condition" but to "a limit of perception" (3). His faith lies in "the natural integrities and processes that precede and support the life of the farm" (*Home* 188) and hence human lives everywhere. The Emerson of "Each and All" finds a contemporary expositor in Berry's emphasis on the interdependence of humanity and nature, the ultimate inseparability of the human *part* from the natural *whole* that precedes and circumscribes us. The current alienation from nature of most human beings in industrial societies only increases the importance and the urgency of Berry's writing. Our destruction of nature results from ignorance and greed. But that destruction is also a form of suicide—as Berry and others in the ecological movement, whose roots were nurtured by Transcendentalism, have observed. The etymology of the words "humus" and "human" bears witness to Berry's claim that human health cannot be separated from the health of the soil.

Like Thoreau, then, who defined the "cost" of a thing as "the amount of what I call life which is required to be exchanged for it, immediately or in the long run" (20), Berry analyzes the natural and human costs of our current "productivity" in agribusiness and industry. And, like Thoreau, he finds that the human losses outweigh the material gains, especially in the debts we are thoughtlessly imposing on future generations. The fundamental question raised by both writers is the one that serves as the title of Berry's latest book: What are people for? For neither author can that question be satisfactorily answered by the economic motive that dominates modern life.

Berry's advocacy of the traditional family farm is an effort to move agriculture away from an economy based on "the career of money" (*Home* 144). Moreover, since "good use of property requires the widest possible distribution of ownership" (*Home* 106), Berry views his agricultural and economic proposals as means of sustaining America's commitment to democracy, surely one of the central impulses of the transcendentalist spirit as it is manifest in the writing of Emerson and Whitman and Thoreau. For Berry,

> The question of survival of the family farm and the farm family is one version of the question of who will own the country, which is, ultimately, the question of who will own the people. Shall the usable property of our country be democratically divided, or not? If many people do not own the usable property, then they must submit to the few who do own it. (*Home* 165)

This emphasis on freedom and independence pervades Berry's work. It is always balanced, however, by his insistence on responsibility: to nature, to the human community, and ultimately to God.

In his introduction to *Selected Writings of the American Transcendentalists,* George Hochfield characterizes these thinkers as, among other things, "the most thoroughgoing critics of society that had yet appeared on the American scene" (xviii). He also notes how these writers questioned specifically the impact of a growing industrialism that created new class differences, a spirit of intensified competition, and a new dependence on machinery (xxiv–xxv). That Wendell Berry shares these—and other—transcendentalist concerns should now be evident. He is a legitimate heir of the spirit of American rebellion best exemplified, perhaps, among the Transcendentalists by Thoreau. Few readers of both *Walden* and Berry's essays can fail to hear echoes of Thoreau's substance and style, as in Berry's advice to "Think Little" (*Continuous* 71–85), or in his recommendation of "wakefulness in this world" (*What Are* 138). And certainly the *example* of Thoreau is a major source of Berry's own critical stance towards contemporary American values.

Yet in *What Are People For?* Berry remarks, "I want to argue with Thoreau" (41)—no doubt for various reasons. One of them, as I have already indicated, is Thoreau's tendency to overvalue the individual at the expense of community. Another, surely, is Thoreau's tendency to deprecate physical labor. Insofar as Thoreau adopts what Berry calls "the modern doctrine of the preeminence of the mind" (*What Are* 105), his ideas must strike Berry as misguided.

More than Thoreau—and certainly more than Emerson—Berry embraces "the principle of incarnation," of "embodied life in this world" (*Home* 117, 120). The Emerson who writes, "No object really interests us but man" and "The world is nothing, the man is all" (qtd. in Abbey 211, 214), is clearly at odds with the careful regard for the world in Berry's thought and action. For Berry, the body and nature do not reside in the Emersonian back alley of the "NOT ME." Nor is Berry's ideal the lofty hawk of Thoreau, soaring companionless "as if it had never set foot on *terra firma*" (Thoreau 209). Ultimately, according to Berry, "the test of imagination . . . is not the territory of art or the territory of the mind, but the territory underfoot" (*What Are* 83–84). And thus Berry strives to help his readers recover a right relation to that particular territory, to reexperience "the silence in which words return to their objects" (*Home* 79).

In the essay on Edward Abbey cited at the beginning of this article, Berry says that he reads Abbey "for consolation, for the comfort of being told the truth" (*What Are* 47). Surely we feel that same quest for integrity at work in Thoreau and Berry. While we must, of course, read all three writers prepared to argue with them, they share one final, crucial legacy of the transcendentalist spirit: a commitment to the imagination's ability to create alternatives to the economic and political and cultural assumptions that operate in our society. They teach us to question. They remind us that it makes a difference "whether we . . . live like baboons or like men" (Thoreau 62). It is the legacy of dissent in the name of what Thoreau terms "Higher Laws" that Berry's fiction and poetry and essays so ably cultivate.

Works Cited

Abbey, Edward. "Emerson." *One Life at a Time, Please.* New York: Holt, 1988.

Berry, Wendell. *A Continuous Harmony: Essays Cultural and Agricultural.* New York: Harcourt, 1972.

————. *Home Economics.* San Francisco: North Point Press, 1987.

————. *What Are People For?* San Francisco: North Point Press, 1990.

Hochfield, George, ed. *Selected Writings of the American Transcendentalists.* New York: New American Library, 1966.

Thoreau, Henry David. *Walden.* Ed. Owen Thomas. New York: Norton, 1966.

Robert Morgan

See volume 2, chapter 2, for biography.

Volunteer

Praise what survives
its season of domestication
and sprouts along the margin,
among next year's crop.

Aggressive species ignore
fences and the boundary lines
of rotation to emigrate.

Praise blooded varieties returning
to the wild.

Spontaneous replanting be praised. Let
self-sowers reverdure the earth.

Let every garden and tiergarten and
sunken eden leak
breeds that multiply
to the limits of resource.
Praise all escapes
and trailing shrubs, runners that
spill out of culture
and reseed themselves.

Let volunteers find accommodation.

From *Land Diving*, © 1976 by Robert Morgan. Reprinted by permission of Louisiana State University Press.

Jim Wayne Miller

See volume 2, chapter 2, for biography.

Nostalgia for the Future

Robert Penn Warren reminds us that "literary regionalism is more than a literary matter."[1] If we treat our literature as "just literature," it loses much of its value for us. Genuine literature is valuable to us because it springs from reality and experience. It is valuable not only to the individual, for private reasons, but also because it has its public uses and speaks to people collectively.

Much of our past and future—who we were and who we will be—can be found in our language. And future events and actions are often prefigured in language. "Quite often in history," Eric Hoffer says, "action has been the echo of words. An era of talk was followed by an era of events."[2]

Those of us involved in Appalachian studies, whether as action folk or creative people, need to listen to those voices in the region that are legitimate expressions of the region—of its history and collective experience. Both the past and the future—the past condensed and distilled, the future intimated—can be found in the language of the region's imaginative writers. Listen with me to some of these voices for evidence of the past life that is lost forever if it is not somehow caught in language, and for that "long knowledge," as Wendell Berry called it, "that is the potency of time to come."

Here is James Still, in a poem called "Heritage," expressing a determined attachment to place, something found in so much of the region's writing:

> I shall not leave these prisoning hills
> Though they topple their barren heads to level earth
> And the forests slide uprooted out of the sky.[3]

In strip-mined areas of Appalachia, the hills *have* toppled their heads to level earth; the forests *have* slid uprooted out of the sky. But many people feel what James Still has here expressed: an attachment to place, in spite of what has happened.

I think I am right in maintaining that this attachment to place is not just a literary posture. I think it is a genuine feeling widely held. People who have never thought of themselves as poets, and who have no connection with literature, when they express their feelings, say something quite similar to what Still says. The young poets repeatedly confront the devastation and

From *The Kentucky Review* 8.2 (Summer 1988). Reprinted by permission of the author and publisher.

damage, the scars and the blight, which belong to the region's history. In "Affliction," Robert Morgan condenses much of the region's history into a poem which finds a symbol in the chestnut blight:

> On the slopes where the old
> blighted years ago
> new
> chestnuts sprout and
> thrive until the age of saplings, then
> blossom and die.
>   . . . .
> after decades still trying to break through
> and establish hold. . . .
>   . . . .
> Like us straining to ascend,
> immortal
> only in dirt.[4]

Robert Morgan sees the people of the region as trees rooted in the earth, blighted but still trying to be well.

The effort to break through, to ascend, is central to Mike Henson's lyrical novel, *Ransack*. The novel's central character is a young man whose people come from Appalachian Kentucky to Cincinnati, where they now live in the Over-the-Rhine area. The young man looks out over houses at night, past the radio tower with its red blinking light, and thinks of all the people in the houses, behind their white squares of light. And he remembers: "Back home they were digging a well and they turned up in the red clay, one, then another, then a handful: the white sleeping locusts. And he thought of how they lay all through the fields, waiting for their year. Deep in the ground each whitely waiting to drill upward together all through the fields and hills at once . . . and sing."[5] Here again we see the close identification with earth—the locusts are buried in the earth—and the determination to work up from the ground, much like the chestnut saplings in Morgan's poem.

Mary Joan Coleman writes of a past and a way of life which, though it blighted *her* life in a way, she nevertheless prefers to what she finds in a drug-addicted representative of affluent America. Coleman writes of deprivation and irreparable harm done, in a poem called "Survivor":

> when i was ten, my skin waxed yellow
> we had meat once a month, drank canned milk
> no one sent a Care package, but on Halloween
> when i lay parched with scarlet fever
> town children knocked, "trick or treat for UNICEF"[6]

Cruel and harsh as this background was, Coleman can suggest strengths and benefits derived from it, and pit these, in a critique of a more affluent America, against the "heritage" of a drug-addicted student, a "Sweet Child of Hunger":

> a dying child
> who rubbed the needlepoint work on his gaunt arms,
>   * * *
> the petulant student of thirty-one
> mother and father send personal checks from miami
>   * * *
> desperate face of a boy lost at the fair
>   * * *
> i heard the whisper of death seep
> out of the wasp wounds in his flesh
> knowing that for all the real hungers of my past
> i never starved from a denial as cruel as his.[7]

Thus she affirms what she calls elsewhere her "deep-shafted heritage," takes a stand in that heritage, knowing her strength is in it, as the life of the chestnuts, though they are blighted, is in the earth. And like Henson's white sleeping locusts, she breaks through to a kind of song.

Richard Hague does not look at the region's past through rose-colored glasses, either. He does not try to soften or paint over the blight and affliction of the region. He knows the past and confronts it, but he does not dwell on it. There is no sentimentality or nostalgia for the past in "Finished With the Poetry of Coal":

> Too long, now,
> the trail of ashes
> from my grandfather's grave
> I will not wander back
> among the broken ties and ballast
> leading to the Mingo Roundhouse
> where he stoked his locomotives
>
> I will not think of coal train brakemen
> weeping in the chemical dark
> of Weirton,
> nor of Hambone McCarthy,
> who came to my grandmother's funeral
> almost crazy
>
> I will not think of the deep connections with fire
> that scarred me
> even before I'd grown into pain.

I will climb into light
that shines on the earth before me,
my body shedding its grit
of anger and cinders.

Even death has its ending.
Let me vine like a new brier
tough over blackened land.[8]

Here again is the connection with the earth—Hague thinks of himself as a brier—found in Still, in Robert Morgan's chestnut tree image. Here, too, the depiction of devastation, blight, affliction, scarring—of land and people—found in the poems examined here. Here again the coming to terms with the past, but certainly no nostalgia for it. If there is nostalgia for anything, it is (as Chicago's Mayor Daley put it in one of his famous lapses) a nostalgia for the future.

The past is present in this writing, in condensed, interpreted form. In Morgan's blighted chestnuts, in Mary Joan Coleman's "Survivor," in Henson's novel, which deals symbolically with the ransacking of a place and a people, I find symbols of the historical affliction and blight and ransacking of the Appalachian region. But what I hear in this writing also is an attachment to and identification with the earth—in this case, Appalachian earth—no matter what. I hear an affirmation of what is positive and good in traditional Appalachian life. I sense movement from sickness to health, from darkness to light; a refusal to dwell on the scars and afflictions of the past; a determination to grow and change. I think, in connection with this writing, of Wolfe's line: "The alexin of our cure grows by a mountain rock."[9]

What is literature good for? Appalachia's literature and its literary tradition—the love of telling, the love of a good story—can be a common meeting place for scholar and nonscholar, and, beyond that, the literature can be useful in revealing and building that sense of community that can be cultivated in the ground of the region's history. Our literature can help reveal the common life, history, and culture of the region. Appalachians have been deprived of a knowledge of their history by a complicated set of circumstances. For the most part, Appalachians have only suffered their history, the way we endure a dull pain whose cause we do not know. Our literature is full of doors and entrances into what the historian Carl Degler has called Appalachia's "triple history"—our history as Americans, our history as southerners, and the history that is peculiarly ours in this region.[10] Our literature is a common ground where the scholar, the man or woman of learning, can stand with the people of the region and begin to learn and understand our complicated and interesting triple history. In a place and among people the historian Wertenbaker called a "test laboratory of American civilization,"[11] both scholar and nonscholar can begin to participate in and influence that history, instead of simply suffering it.

Our region's literature is useful in getting on with those tasks Cratis Williams outlined when he said we need to "learn and write our history . . .

define our identity, write our own books . . . solve our own social problems . . . manage our own institutions, and build our own economy."[12]

Over two hundred years ago, Boone stood in the Cumberland Gap. And soon the people followed and settled the country beyond the gap. The people involved in Appalachian studies, whether action folk or creative people, are trying to find the gap to Appalachia's future so people can pass through and settle that country. The Appalachian people, Cratis Williams tells us, have migrated at least four times. Many moved to the border country between England and Scotland during the time of the Roman Empire. Many migrated to northern Ireland in the seventeenth century, to the American colonies and into Appalachia in the eighteenth and early nineteenth. Several millions migrated from the region to urban industrial centers in the Midwest in this century.[13]

We have moved many times, and I believe we can find the gap and migrate to the future as a people with a common history and heritage. Our history, which is our burden and our affliction, is also a source of strength. Our past has a future. In his history of the Scotch-Irish, James Leyburn tells how the Scots reacted to Calvinistic theology. Protestantism, Leyburn says, "for the first time in their history," had given these people "something to think about, seriously and deeply. Calvinistic theology invested the individual with primary importance. . . . Such attention the people had never known, and they responded warmly to it."[14] I believe a knowledge of our history and heritage, of our common interest and problems, is capable of giving the Appalachian people—many of whom are descended from these Scots who later came to be known as Scotch-Irish—something to think about, seriously and deeply. And I believe people will respond warmly to it. They are already doing so.

Our literature is one of the resources we have in providing something to think about. The nostalgia for the future found in it can be used as a means of possessing the future. Our imaginative literature can be used to enable people all over the region to say, "I have a place"; to think of themselves not as "citizens of nowhere" but rather as "citizens of somewhere"; to think of the region as a place (as Wendell Berry puts it) "whose possibilities I am one of."[15]

In working toward that goal, our relationship, as representatives of intellect, learning, and thought, to the region and its people ought to resemble what we find at the end of James Still's "Journey to the Forks." The sun is setting, it is getting dark. Dan, the younger brother, who has fingers missing—who like his region has been mangled and bears the scar—is acting as if he might turn back. "'I ought never thought to be a scholar,' Dan said. His voice was small and tight, and the words trembled on his tongue. He caught my hand [the older brother, the narrator, says] and I felt the blunt edge of his palm where the fingers were gone. We started down the ridge, picking our way through stony dark."[16]

We have thought to be scholars. As we move to the future of Appalachia, we have to take people by the hand and go on, and admit that, for all of us, the journey will be like picking our way through stony dark.

Notes

1. Robert Penn Warren, "Some Don'ts for Literary Regionalists," *Voices from the Hills,* ed. Robert J. Higgs and Ambrose N. Manning (New York: Ungar, 1975), 364. Copublished with Appalachian Consortium P, Boone NC.
2. Eric Hoffer, *The Passionate State of Mind* (New York: Harper and Row, 1955), 48.
3. James Still, *Hounds on the Mountain* (New York: Viking, 1937), 55.
4. Robert Morgan, *Land Diving* (Baton Rouge: Louisiana State UP, 1976), 4.
5. Mike Henson, *Ransack* (Cambridge, MA: West End P, 1980), 66–67.
6. Mary Joan Coleman, *Take One Blood Red Rose* (Cambridge, MA: West End Press, 1978), 5.
7. Coleman, *Take One,* 26.
8. "Mill and Smoke Marrow," in *A Red Shadow of Steel Mills,* ed. David Shevin and Larry Smith (Huron, Ontario: Bottom Dog P, 1991), 42.
9. Thomas Wolfe, *Look Homeward Angel,* intro. Maxwell C. Perkins (New York: Scribner's, 1957), 3.
10. Carl Degler, *The Other South* (New York: Cooper Square Publishers, 1963), 219.
11. Thomas Jefferson Wertenbaker, *The Old South* (New York: Cooper Square Publishers, 1963), 219.
12. Cratis Williams, "Appalachia," *An Encyclopedia of East Tennessee,* ed. Jim Stokely and Jeff D. Johnson (Oak Ridge, TN: Children's Museum of Oak Ridge, 1981), 14.
13. Cratis Williams, lecture, Appalachian Studies Workshop, Berea College, Berea, KY, 1976.
14. James G. Leyburn, *The Scotch-Irish* (Chapel Hill: U of North Carolina P, 1962), 57–61.
15. Wendell Berry, *Openings* (New York: Harcourt, Brace, 1968), 21.
16. James Still, *Sporty Creek* (New York: Putnam's, 1977), 125.

Jesse Stuart

Jesse Stuart (1908–84) was born in W-Hollow, near Riverton, Kentucky. In high school he discovered his love for literature, especially the poetry of Robert Burns, Carl Sandburg, and Walt Whitman. He graduated from Lincoln Memorial University in 1929 and returned to his native Greenup County to teach school in the 1930s. Heeding the axiom "Write what you know," Stuart wrote poetry and fiction which depicted the dialect, manners, and values of the Appalachian people. His first major publication was a volume of sonnets entitled *Man with a Bull-Tongue Plow* (1934), which was followed a decade later by *Album of Destiny,* a volume that presented the contrast between the rural life of the past and the urbanity of life in the twentieth century. The autobiographical *The Thread That Runs So True* received a "best book" citation from the National Education Association in 1949. Stuart was named poet laureate of Kentucky in 1954 and received a Pulitzer Prize nomination in 1975 for *The World of Jesse Stuart.* Stuart's world has long been a familiar one to readers of Appalachian literature. A pioneer in Appalachian poetry, Stuart is noted for fidelity in representation of folklore and his fierce love of his native land, which makes the poem "Our Heritage" all the more meaningful.

Our Heritage

We are a part of this rough land
Deep-rooted like the tree.
We've plowed this dirt with calloused hand
More than a century.

We know each cowbell's ringing here
Which tells the time of day.
We know the slopes to plant each year,
What our folks do and say.

We know the signals of each horn
And the messages they send
At set of sun or early morn
Upon a blowing wind.

When we lie down in bed at night
And hear a foxhorn blow,
We often rise, take lantern light,
Untie our hounds and go.

We like to follow hounds that chase
The fox until the morn
Then go back home with sleepy face
And on to plow the corn.
There is not one who does not love
A field and farming ground,
With sky and stars a roof above
And a companion hound!

From *A Jesse Stuart Reader* (McGraw Hill, 1963; rpt. 1988 by the Jesse Stuart Foundation). Used by permission of the Jesse Stuart Foundation, P.O. Box 391, Ashland, KY 41114.

We love this land we've always known
That holds us and our dead—
The rugged slopes with scattered stone
That grow our daily bread.

We love the lyric barking hound
And a piping horn that trills.
We love our high upheavaled ground,
Our heritage of hills.

James Still

See volume 2, chapter 8, for biography.

Heritage

I shall not leave these prisoning hills
Though they topple their barren heads to level earth
And the forests slide uprooted out of the sky.
Though the waters of Troublesome, of Trace Fork,
Of Sand Lick rise in a single body to glean the valleys,
To drown lush pennyroyal, to unravel rail fences;
Though the sun-ball breaks the ridges into dust
And burns its strength into the blistered rock
I cannot leave. I cannot go away.

Being of these hills, being one with the fox
Stealing into the shadows, one with the new-born foal,
The lumbering ox drawing green beech logs to mill,
One with the destined feet of man climbing and descending,
And one with death rising to bloom again, I cannot go.
Being of these hills I cannot pass beyond.

From *The Wolfpen Poems*, Berea College, 1986. Reprinted by permission of the author and publisher.

Selected Bibliography

Nonfiction

Allen, Barbara, and Thomas J. Schlereth, eds. *Sense of Place: American Regional Cultures.* Lexington: UP of Kentucky, 1990.

Bailyn, Bernard, and Philip D. Morgan, eds. *Strangers within the Realm: Cultural Margins of the First British Empire.* Chapel Hill: U of North Carolina P, 1991.

Barker, Garry. *The Handcraft Revival in Southern Appalachia, 1930–1990.* Knoxville: U of Tennessee P, 1991.

Batteau, Allen W. *The Invention of Appalachia.* Tucson: U of Arizona P, 1990.

Baughman, Ernest W. *Type and Motif Index of the Folktales of England and North America.* The Hague, Netherlands: Mouton, 1966.

Beaver, Patricia D. *Rural Community in the Appalachian South.* 1986; rpt. Prospect Heights, IL: Waveland, 1992.

Berry, Wendell. *The Unsettling of America: Culture and Agriculture.* Jackson, CA: Sierra Club, 1986.

Best, Bill. *The Great Appalachian Sperm Bank and Other Stories.* Berea, KY: Kentucke Imprints, 1986.

Blair, Walter, and Hamlin Hill. *America's Humor: From Poor Richard to Doonesbury.* Oxford, England: Oxford UP, 1978.

Blethen, Tyler, and Curtis Wood. *From Ulster to Carolina: The Migration of the Scotch-Irish to Southwestern North Carolina.* Cullowhee, NC: Western Carolina U, 1983.

Borman, Kathryn M, and Philip J. Obermiller, eds. *From Mountain to Metropolis: Appalachian Migrants in American Cities.* Westport, CT: Greenwood P, 1994.

Bradshaw, Michael. *The Appalachian Regional Commission: Twenty-Five Years of Government Policy.* Lexington: UP of Kentucky, 1992.

Brosi, George. *The Literature of the Appalachian South.* Richmond, KY: Eastern Kentucky U Bookstore, 1992. Distributed by Appalachian Mountain Books.

Brown, James S. *Beech Creek: A Study of a Kentucky Mountain Neighborhood.* Berea, KY: Berea College P, 1987.

Brunvand, Jan Harold. *The Vanishing Hitchhiker: American Urban Legends and Their Meanings.* New York: W. W. Norton, 1981.

Burton, Thomas. *Serpent-Handling Believers.* Knoxville, TN: U of Tennessee P, 1993.

Burton, Thomas G., and Ambrose N. Manning, *Folklore: Folksongs.* Johnson City, Tn.: The Research Advisory Council of East Tennessee State University, 1967.

———. *Folklore: Folksongs II.* Johnson City, Tn.: The Research Advisory Council of East Tennessee State University, 1969.

Cadle, Dean. "Man on Troublesome." *Yale Review* 57 (Dec. 1967): 236–55.

Campbell, John C. *The Southern Highlander and His Homeland.* Lexington: UP of Kentucky, 1969.

Campbell, Joseph, with Bill Moyers. *The Power of Myth,* ed. Betty Sue Flowers. New York: Doubleday, 1988.

Caskey, Jefferson D. *Appalachian Authors: A Selective Bibliography.* West Cornwall, CT: Locust Hill P, 1990.

Caudill, Harry. *Theirs Be the Power: The Moguls of Eastern Kentucky.* 1983; rpt. Urbana: U of Illinois P, 1990.

Cavender, Anthony, ed. *A Folk Medicine Lexicon of South Central Appalachia.* Johnson City, TN: History of Medicine Society of Appalachia, 1990.

Christian, Donna; Walt Wolfram; and Nanjo Dube. *Variation and Change in Geographically Isolated Communities: Appalachian English and Ozark English.* Publication of the American Dialect Society No. 74. Tuscaloosa: U of Alabama P, 1989.

Coles, Robert. *Migrants, Sharecroppers, and Mountaineers.* Boston: Little, Brown, 1972.

Corbin, David Alan, ed. *The West Virginia Mine Wars: An Anthology.* Charleston, WV: Appalachian Editions, 1990.

Council, Bruce R.; Nicholas Honerkamp; and M. Elizabeth Will. *Industry and Technology in Antebellum Tennessee: The Archaeology of Bluff Furnace.* Knoxville: U of Tennessee P, 1992.

Cunningham, Rodger. *Apples on the Flood: The Southern Mountain Experience.* Knoxville: U of Tennessee P, 1987.

Dickey, James. *Wayfarer: A Voice from the Southern Mountains.* Birmingham, AL: Oxmoor House, 1988.

Dorgan, Howard. *The Old Regular Baptists of Central Appalachia: Brothers and Sisters in Hope.* Knoxville: U of Tennessee P, 1989.

Dunn, Durwood. *Cades Cove: The Life and Death of a Southern Appalachian Community, 1818–1937.* Knoxville: U of Tennessee P, 1988.

Egerton, John. *Generations: An American Family.* 1983; rpt. New York: Simon and Schuster, 1986.

———. *Shades of Gray: Dispatches from the Modern South.* Baton Rouge: Louisiana State UP, 1991.

Ehle, John. *Trail of Tears: The Rise and Fall of the Cherokee Nation.* New York: Doubleday, 1988.

Eller, Ronald D. *Miners, Millhands, and Mountaineers: Industrialization of the Appalachian South, 1880–1930.* Knoxville: U of Tennessee P, 1982.

Ergood, Bruce, and Bruce E. Kuhre, eds. *Appalachia: Social Context Past and Present,* 3d ed. Dubuque, IA: Kendall-Hunt, 1991.

Farr, Sidney Saylor. *More Than Moonshine: Appalachian Recipes and Recollections,* 1983; rpt. Pittsburgh: U of Pittsburgh P, 1990.

Fine, Elizabeth C., and Jean Haskell Speer, eds. *Performance, Culture, and Identity.* New York: Praeger, 1992.

Fischer, David Hackett. *Albion's Seed: Four British Folkways in America.* New York: Oxford UP, 1989.

Fish, Stanley. *Doing What Comes Naturally: Change, Rhetoric, and the Practice of Theory in Literary and Legal Studies.* Durham, NC: Duke UP, 1989.

Fisher, Stephen L., ed. *Fighting Back in Appalachia: Traditions of Resistance and Change.* Philadelphia: Temple UP, 1993.

Foster, William Stephen. *The Past Is Another Country: Representation, Historical Consciousness, and Resistance in the Blue Ridge.* Berkeley: U of California P, 1988.

Frazier, Claude A., with F. K. Brown. *Miners and Medicine: West Virginia Memories.* Norman: U of Oklahoma P, 1992.

French, Laurence, and Jim Hornbuckle. *The Cherokee Perspective: Written by Eastern Cherokees.* Boone, NC: Appalachian Consortium P, 1981. Contains Cherokee stories and poems.

Frome, Michael. *Conscience of a Conservationist.* Knoxville: U of Tennessee P, 1989.

Frye, Northrup. *Anatomy of Criticism.* New York: Atheneum, 1966.

Galbraith, John Kenneth. *The Culture of Contentment.* Boston: Houghton Mifflin, 1992.

Gates, Jr., Henry Louis. *Colored People.* New York: Alfred A. Knopf, 1994.

Gaventa, John; Barbara Ellen Smith; and Alex Willingham. *Communities in Economic Crisis: Appalachia and the South.* Philadelphia: Temple UP, 1990.

———. *Power and Powerlessness: Quiescence and Rebellion in an Appalachian Valley.* Champaign: U of Illinois P, 1980.

Godbold, E. Stanly, Jr., and Mattie U. Russell. *Confederate Colonel and Cherokee Chief: The Life of William Holland Thomas.* Knoxville: U of Tennessee P, 1990.

Goforth, James A. *Building the Clinchfield.* Erwin, Tennessee: Gem Publishers, 1989.

Goodrich, Frances Louisa. *Mountain Homespun.* Knoxville: U of Tennessee P, 1990.

Green, Archie. *Only a Miner: Studies in Coal-Mining Recorded Songs.* Urbana: University of Illinois Press, 1972.

Green, Ely. *Ely: An Autobiography.* Athens: University of Georgia Press, 1990.

Halperin, Rhoda H. *The Livelihood of Kin: Making the Ends Meet "The Kentucky Way."* Austin: U of Texas P, 1990.

Hannum, Alberta Pierson, *Look Back with Love: A Recollection of the Blue Ridge.* New York: Vanguard P, 1969.

Harney, Will Wallace. "A Strange Land and Peculiar People." *Lippincott's Magazine* 12 (Oct. 1873): 429–38.

Harrison, Elizabeth Jane. *Female Pastoral: Women Writers Re-Visioning the American South.* Knoxville: U of Tennessee P, 1991.

Herzberg, Nancy, ed. *From Roots to Roses: The Autobiography of Tilda Kemplen.* Athens: U of Georgia P, 1992.

Higgs, Robert J., and Ambrose M. Manning. *Voices from the Hills.* New York: Ungar, 1975.

High, Elessa Clay. *Past Titan Rock: Journeys into an Appalachian Valley.* Lexington: UP of Kentucky, 1984.

Hiscoe, Helen B. *Appalachian Passage.* Athens: U of Georgia P, 1992.

Horton, Myles. *The Long Haul: An Autobiography.* New York: Anchor Books, 1990.

Inge, M. Thomas. *Comics as Culture.* Jackson: UP of Mississippi, 1990.

Inscoe, John C. *Mountain Masters, Slavery, and the Sectional Crisis in Western North Carolina.* Knoxville: U of Tennessee P, 1989.

Jacobs, Wilbur R., ed. *The Appalachian Indian Frontier: The Edmond Atkin Report and Plan of 1755.* Lincoln: U of Nebraska P, 1967.

Jones, Loyal. *Minstrel of the Appalachians: The Story of Bascom Lamar Lunsford.* Boone, NC: Appalachian Consortium P, 1984.

Jones, Michael Owen. *Craftsman of the Cumberlands: Tradition and Creativity.* Lexington: UP of Kentucky, 1989.

Joslin, Michael, and Ruth Joslin. *Mountain People, Places, and Ways: A Southern Appalachian Sampler.* Johnson City, TN: Overmountain P, 1991.

Keef, Susan Emley, ed. *Appalachian Mental Health.* Lexington: UP of Kentucky, 1988.

Kephart, Horace. *Our Southern Highlanders.* 1922; rpt. Knoxville: U of Tennessee P, 1976.

Kincaid, Robert. *The Wilderness Road.* Harrogate, TN: Lincoln Memorial UP, 1955.

Lambert, Walter N. *Kinfolks and Custard Pie.* Knoxville: U of Tennessee P, 1988.

Lampell, Ramona, and Millard Lampell, with David Larking. *O, Appalachia: Artists of the Southern Mountains.* New York: Stewart, Tabori and Chang, 1989.

Lanier, Parks, Jr., ed. *The Poetics of Appalachian Space.* Knoxville: U of Tennessee P, 1991.

Ledford, Lily May. *Coon Creek Girl.* Berea, KY: Berea College Appalachian Center, 1980; rpt. 1991.

Lee, David. *Sergeant York: An American Hero.* Lexington: UP of Kentucky, 1985.

Lemaster, J. R., ed. *Jesse Stuart on Education.* Lexington: UP of Kentucky, 1992.

Levy, Builder. *Images of Appalachian Coalfields.* Philadelphia: Temple UP, 1989.

Lewis, Helen, and Suzanna O'Donnell, eds. *Remembering Our Past—Building Our Future.* Ivanhoe, VA: Ivanhoe Civic League, 1990.

Lewis, Helen; Linda Johnson; and Donald Askins, eds. *Colonialism in Modern America: The Appalachian Case.* Boone, NC: Appalachian Consortium P, 1978.

Linn, Karen. *That Half-Barbaric Twang: The Banjo in American Popular Culture.* Urbana: U of Illinois P, 1991.

Lofaro, Michael A. *The Life and Adventures of Daniel Boone.* Lexington: UP of Kentucky, 1986.

———, ed. *Davy Crockett: The Man, the Legend, the Legacy, 1786–1986.* Knoxville: U of Tennessee P, 1985.

Long, Priscilla. *Where the Sun Never Shines: A History of American's Bloody Coal Industry.* New York: Paragon House, 1989.

Lornell, Kip. *Virginia's Blues, Country, and Gospel Records 1902–1943: An Annotated Discography.* Lexington: UP of Kentucky, 1989.

Lunt, Richard D. *Law and Order vs. the Miners: West Virginia, 1906–1917.* Charleston, WV: Appalachian Editions, 1992.

Lutwack, Leonard. *The Role of Place in Literature.* Syracuse, NY: Syracuse UP, 1984.

Mallory, William E., and Paul Simpson-Housley. *Geography and Literature: A Meeting of the Disciplines.* Syracuse, NY: Syracuse UP, 1987.

Malone, Bill C. *Singing Cowboys and Musical Mountaineers: Southern Culture and the Roots of Country Music.* Athens: U of Georgia P, 1993.

———. *Southern Music/American Music.* Lexington: UP of Kentucky, 1979.

Manley, Roger. *Signs and Wonders: Outsider Art Inside North Carolina.* Raleigh: North Carolina Museum of Art, 1989. Distributed by U of North Carolina P.

Maurer, B. B., ed. *Mountain Heritage,* 1980; rpt. Parsons, WV: McClain Printing Co., 1989.

McCaig, Donald. *An American Homeplace.* New York: Crown, 1992.

McDonald, Michael J., and John Muldowny. *TVA and the Dispossessed: The Resettlement of Population in the Norris Dam Area.* Knoxville: U of Tennessee P, 1982.

McKinney, Gordon B. *Southern Mountain Republicans, 1865–1900: Politics and the Appalachian Community.* Chapel Hill: U of North Carolina P, 1978.

McNeil, Nellie, and Joyce Squibb, eds. *A Southern Appalachian Reader.* Boone, NC: Appalachian Consortium P, 1988.

McNeil, W. K., ed. *Appalachian Images in Folk and Popular Culture.* Ann Arbor, MI: UMI Research P, 1989.

———. *Ghost Stories of the American South.* New York: Dell, 1985.

McWhiney, Grady. *Cracker Culture: Celtic Ways in the Old South.* Tuscaloosa: U of Alabama P, 1988.

Miller, Wilbur R. *Revenuers and Moonshiners: Enforcing Federal Liquor Laws in the Mountain South.* Chapel Hill: U of North Carolina P, 1991.

Mitchell, Robert D., ed. *Appalachian Frontiers: Settlement, Society, and Development in the Preindustrial Era.* Lexington: UP of Kentucky, 1991.

Montell, Lynwood. *The Saga of Coe Ridge: A Study in Oral History.* 1970; rpt. New York: Harper and Row, 1972.

———. *Killings: Folk Justice in the Upper South.* Lexington: UP of Kentucky, 1986.

Montgomery, Michael. "Exploring the Roots of Appalachian English." *English World-Wide* 10, no. 2 (1989): 227–78.

Mooney, James. *History, Myths, and Sacred Formulas of the Cherokees.* Rpt. Asheville, NC: Historical Images P, 1992.

Morgan, Robert. *Good Measure.* Baton Rouge: Louisiana State UP, 1993.

Moss, Gary, and Bettie Sellers. *The Bitter Berry: The Life of Byron Herbert Reece.* Atlanta: Georgia Humanities Council. Distributed by U of Georgia P, 1992.

Mullen, Patrick B. *Listening to Old Voices: Folklore, Life Stories, and the Elderly.* Urbana: U of Illinois P, 1992.

Murray, Kenneth. *Footsteps of the Mountain Spirits . . . : Appalachia: Myths, Legends, and Landscapes of the Southern Highlands.* Johnson City, TN: Overmountain P, 1994.

Neely, Sharlotte. *Snowbird Cherokees: People of Persistence.* Athens: U of Georgia P, 1991.

Obermiller, Phillip J., and William W. Philliber, eds. *Too Few Tomorrows: Urban Appalachians in the 1980s.* Boone, NC: Appalachian Consortium P, 1987.

O'Connor, Flannery. *Mystery and Manners.* New York: Farrar, Straus and Giroux, 1969.

Offutt, Chris. *The Same River Twice: A Memoir.* New York: Simon and Schuster, 1993.

Peacock, James L., and Ruel W. Tyson, Jr. *Pilgrims of Paradox: Calvinism and Experience among the Primitive Baptists of the Blue Ridge.* Smithsonian Series in Ethnographic Inquiry No. 17. Washington, D.C.: Smithsonian Institution Press, 1989.

Perdue, Charles L., Jr. *Outwitting the Devil: Jack Tales from Wise County, Virginia.* Santa Fe, NM: Ancient City P, 1987.

Perdue, Theda. *Cherokee Editor: The Writings of Elias Boudinot.* Knoxville: U of Tennessee P, 1983.

———. *Slavery and the Evolution of Cherokee Society, 1540–1866.* Knoxville: U of Tennessee P, 1979.

Perrin, Alfred H., ed. *Seeking a People Partnership: Eleven Speeches by Perley Ayer.* Berea, KY: Appalachian Center, Berea College, 1991.

Portelli, Alessandro. *The Death of Luigi Trastulli and Other Stories: Form and Meaning in Oral History.* Albany: State U of New York P, 1991.

Quillen, Rita. *Looking for Native Ground: Contemporary Appalachian Poetry.* Boone, NC: Appalachian Consortium P, 1989.

Raglan, FitzRoy Richard Somerset. *The Hero.* Westport, CT: Greenwood P, 1975.

Randolph, Vance. *Pissing in the Snow and Other Ozark Folktales.* Urbana: U of Illinois P, 1976.

Ritchie, Jean. *Singing Family of the Cumberlands.* 1955; rpt. Lexington: UP of Kentucky, 1988.

Roberts, Leonard. *South from Hell-Fer-Sartin: Kentucky Mountain Folk Tales.* 1955; rpt. Lexington: UP of Kentucky, 1988.

Savage, Lon. *Thunder in the Mountains: The West Virginia Mine War, 1920–21.* Pittsburgh: U of Pittsburgh P, 1990.

Scarborough, Dorothy. *A Song Catcher in Southern Mountains: American Folksongs of British Ancestry.* New York: Columbia U. Press, 1937; rpt. New York: AMS Press, 1966.

Shackelford, Laurel, and Bill Weinberg, eds. *Our Appalachia: An Oral History.* 1977; rpt. Lexington: UP of Kentucky, 1988.

Shapiro, Henry D. *Appalachia on Our Mind: The Southern Mountains and Mountaineers in the American Consciousness, 1870–1920.* Chapel Hill: U of North Carolina P, 1978.

———. *Ethnic Diversity and Civic Identity: Patterns of Conflict and Cohesion in Cincinnati since 1820.* Champaign: U of Illinois P, 1992.

Sharp, Cecil, and Maud Karpeles. *Eighty Appalachian Folk Songs.* Winchester, MA: Faber and Faber, 1983.

Sheppard, Muriel Earley. *Cabins in the Laurel.* 1935; rpt. Chapel Hill: U of North Carolina P, 1991.

Shifflett, Crandall A. *Coal Towns: Life, Work, and Culture in Company Towns of Southern Appalachia, 1880–1960.* Knoxville: U of Tennessee P, 1991.

Sisco, Eugene. *Looking In.* Pikeville, KY: M. F. Sohn Publications, 1990.

Slone, Verna Mae. *What My Heart Wants to Tell.* Lexington: UP of Kentucky, 1979.

Speer, Jean Haskell. *The Appalachian Photographs of Earl Palmer.* Lexington: UP of Kentucky, 1990.

Steel, Edward M., ed. *The Speeches and Writings of Mother Jones.* Pittsburgh: U of Pittsburgh P, 1988.

Sullivan, Ken, ed. *The Goldenseal Book of the West Virginia Mine Wars.* Charleston, WV: Pictorial Histories Publishing, 1991.

The Cratis Williams Symposium Proceedings: A Memorial and Examination of the State of Regional Studies in Appalachia. Ed. Barry M. Buxton et al. Boone, NC: Appalachian Consortium P, 1989.

Thompson, Stith. *Motif Index of Folk Literature.* Bloomington: Indiana UP, 1989.

Tillson, Albert H., Jr. *Gentry and Common Folk: Political Culture on a Virginia Frontier, 1740–1789.* Lexington: UP of Kentucky, 1991.

Tribe, Ivan M. *Little Cities of Black Diamonds: Urban Development in the Hocking Coal Region, 1870–1900.* Athens, OH: Athens County Historical Society, 1988.

Trotter, Joe William, Jr. *Coal, Class, and Color: Blacks in Southern West Virginia, 1915–1932.* Urbana: U of Illinois P, 1990.

Turner, Frederick Jackson. *The Significance of the Frontier in American History.* New York: Holt, Rinehart and Winston, 1962.

Turner, William H., and Edward Cabbell, eds. *Blacks in Appalachia.* Lexington: UP of Kentucky, 1985.

Verghese, Abraham. *My Own Country: A Doctor's Story of a Town and Its People in the Age of AIDS.* New York: Simon and Schuster, 1994.

Waage, Frederick O., ed. *Teaching Environmental Literature: Materials, Methods, Resources.* New York: Modern Language Association, 1985.

Wagner, Melinda Bollar. *God's Schools: Choice and Compromise in American Society.* New Brunswick, NJ: Rutgers UP, 1990.

Ward, William S. *A Literary History of Kentucky.* Knoxville: U of Tennessee P, 1988.

Wecter, Dixon. *The Hero in America.* Ann Arbor: U of Michigan P, 1963.

Weller, Jack. *Yesterday's People.* Lexington: UP of Kentucky, 1965.

Whisnant, David. *All That Is Native and Fine.* Chapel Hill: U of North Carolina P, 1983.

————. *Modernizing the Mountaineer.* Boone, NC: Appalachian Consortium P, 1981.

Wigginton, Eliot. *Sometimes a Shining Moment.* Garden City: Anchor, 1986.

Wigginton, Eliot, and Linda Garland Page, eds. *Aunt Arie: A Foxfire Portrait.* Chapel Hill: U of North Carolina P, 1993.

Williams, Cratis D. "The Southern Mountaineer in Fact and Fiction." Diss. New York University, 1961.

————. *Southern Mountain Speech.* Ed. Jim Wayne Miller and Loyal Jones. Berea, KY: Berea College Press, 1992.

Williams, Michael Ann. *Homeplace: The Social Use and Meaning of the Folk Dwelling in Southwestern North Carolina.* Athens: U of Georgia P, 1991.

Williamson, J. W. "Appalachian Poetry: The Politics of Coming Home." *Southern Exposure* 9, no. 2 (1981): 69–74.

Williamson, J. W., and Edwin T. Arnold, eds. *Interviewing Appalachia: The Appalachian Journal Interviews, 1978–1992.* Knoxville: U of Tennessee P, 1994.

Wilson, James R. *Landing Zones: Southern Veterans Remember Vietnam.* Durham: Duke UP, 1990.

Wimsatt, Mary Ann. *The Major Fiction of William Gilmore Simms: Cultural Traditions and Literary Form.* Baton Rouge: Louisiana State UP, 1989.

Withers, Alexander. *Chronicles of Border Warfare.* Cincinnati, OH: Stewart and Kidd, 1920.

Wolfe, Margaret Ripley. *Kingsport, Tennessee: A Planned American City.* Lexington: UP of Kentucky, 1987.

————. *Daughters of Canaan: A Saga of Southern Women.* Lexington: UP of Kentucky, 1995.

Wolfe, Tom. *The Right Stuff.* New York: Farrar, Straus and Giroux, 1979.

Wolfram, Walt, and Donna Christian. *Appalachian Speech.* Arlington, VA: Center for Applied Linguistics, 1976.

Young, Malone. *Latchpins of the Lost Cove.* Johnson City, TN: Latchpins P, 1987.

Fiction and Poetry

Agee, James. *A Death in the Family.* New York: Bantam, 1971.

Allison, Dorothy. *Bastard Out of Carolina.* New York: Dutton, 1992.

Alther, Lisa. *Kinflicks.* New York: Dutton, 1977.

Arnow, Harriette. *The Dollmaker.* 1954; rpt. New York: Avon, 1989.

Awiakta, Marilou. *Abiding Appalachia: Where Mountain and Atom Meet.* 8th ed. Bell Buckle, TN: Iris Press, 1994.

Awiakta, Marilou. *Selu: Seeking the Corn-Mother's Wisdom.* Golden, Co.: Fulcrum Press, 1993.

Ball, Bo. *Appalachian Patterns.* Atlanta: Independence, 1989.

Ball, Bonnie. *Red Trails and White: The Mysterious Life of Caty Sage.* New York: Exposition P, 1955.

Barker, Garry. *Mountain Passage and Other Stories.* Berea, KY: Kentucke Imprints, 1986.

Benedict, Pinckney. *The Wrecking Yard and Other Stories.* New York: Doubleday, 1992.

———. *Town Smokes.* Princeton, NJ: Ontario Review Press/Persea, 1987.

Berry, Wendell. *The Collected Poems of Wendell Berry.* Frankfort, KY: Gnomon P, 1985.

Best-Loved Stories Told at the National Storytelling Festival. Little Rock, AR: August House, 1991.

Bridgers, Sue Ellen. *Sara Will.* New York: Harper and Row, 1987.

Byer, Kathryn Stripling. *The Girl in the Midst of the Harvest.* Lubbock: Texas Tech P, 1986.

———. *Wildwood Flower.* Baton Rouge: Louisiana State UP, 1992.

Carson, Jo. *Stories I Ain't Told Nobody Yet: Selections from the People Pieces.* New York: Orchard Books, 1988.

———. *The Last of "The Waltz Across Texas" and Other Stories.* Frankfort, KY: Gnomon P, 1993.

Carter, Forrest. *The Education of Little Tree.* Albuquerque: U of New Mexico P, 1986.

Chappell, Fred. *Brighten the Corner Where You Are.* New York: St. Martin's P, 1989.

———. *I Am One of You Forever.* 1987; rpt. Baton Rouge: Louisiana State UP, 1990.

———. *The Fred Chappell Reader.* New York: St. Martin's P, 1987.

Chase, Richard. *Grandfather Tales.* 1948; rpt. Boston: Houghton Mifflin, 1991.

Crabtree, Lou V. *Sweet Hollow.* Baton Rouge: Louisiana State UP, 1984.

Currey, Richard. *The Wars of Heaven.* New York: Random House, 1991.

Davis, Donald D. *Listening for the Crack of Dawn.* Little Rock, AR: August House, 1990.

Depta, Victor. *A Doorkeeper in the House.* Memphis, TN: Ion Books, 1993.

———. *The House.* New York: New Rivers P, 1978.

Dykeman, Wilma. *The Far Family.* 1966; rpt. Newport, TN: Wakestone Books, 1988.

———. *The Tall Woman.* Newport, TN: Wakestone P, 1982.

Ehle, John. *The Road.* New York: Harper and Row, 1967.

Fox, John, Jr. *Trail of the Lonesome Pine.* Cutchogue, NY: Lightyear, 1976.

Giardina, Denise. *Storming Heaven.* New York: Norton, 1987.

———. *The Unquiet Earth.* New York: Norton, 1992.

Giles, Janice Holt. *The Enduring Hills.* 1950; rpt. Lexington: UP of Kentucky, 1988.

Giovanni, Nikki, and Cathee Dennison, eds. *Appalachian Elders: A Warm-Hearth Sampler.* Blacksburg, VA: Pocahontas P, 1992.

Goode, James. *Up from the Mines.* Ashland, KY: Jesse Stuart Foundation, 1993.

Gray, Amy Tipton. *The Hillbilly Vampire.* Blacksburg, VA: Rowan Mountain P, 1989.

Grubb, Davis. *You Never Believe Me and Other Stories.* New York: St. Martin's P, 1990.

Hague, Richard. *Ripening.* Columbus: Ohio State UP, 1984.

———. "Mill and Smoke Marrow." *A Red Shadow of Steel Mills.* Ed. David Shevlin and Larry Smith. Huron, Ontario: Firelands College, Bottom Dog P, 1991.

Hamilton, Virginia. *M. C. Higgins, the Great.* New York: Macmillan, 1974.

Harris, George Washington. *Sut Lovingood: Yarns Spun by a "Nat'ral Born Durn'd Fool."* New York: Dick and Fitzgerald, 1867.

Haun, Mildred. *The Hawk's Done Gone and Other Stories.* Ed. Herschel Gower. Nashville: Vanderbilt UP, 1985.

Huddle, David. *Stopping by Home.* Salt Lake City, UT: Peregrine Smith, 1983.

Johnson, Don. *The Importance of Visible Scars.* Green Harbor, MA: Wampeter P, 1984.

———. *Watauga Drawdown.* Johnson City, TN: Overmountain P, 1990.

Jones, Loyal. *The Preacher Joke Book: Religious Anecdotes from the Oral Tradition.* Little Rock, AR: August House, 1989.

Jones, Loyal, and Billy Edd Wheeler, eds. *Curing the Cross-Eyed Mule: Appalachian Mountain Humor.* Little Rock, AR: August House, 1989.

———. *Laughter in Appalachia: A Festival of Mountain Humor.* Little Rock, AR: August House, 1987; rpt. New York: Ivy Books/Ballantine, 1988.

Joyce, Jane Wilson, and Meredith Sue Willis. *Quilt Pieces.* Frankfort, KY: Gnomon P, 1991. Contains "The Quilt Poems" by Jane Wilson Joyce and "Family Knots" by Meredith Sue Willis.

Kay, Terry. *The Year the Lights Came On.* Boston: Houghton Mifflin, 1976; rpt. Athens: U of Georgia P, 1989.

Kinder, Chuck. *Snakehunter.* Frankfort, KY: Gnomon P, 1991.

Koger, Lisa. *Farlanburg Stories.* New York: Norton, 1990.

Laska, P. J. *The Day the Eighties Began: Poems, 1980–1990.* Bedford, NH: Igneus P, 1991.

Lyon, George Ella. *Borrowed Children.* New York: Orchard Books, 1988.

———. *Catalpa.* Lexington, KY: Wind Publications, 1993.

———. *Red Rover, Red Rover.* New York: Orchard Books, 1989.

Lyon, George Ella; Jim Wayne Miller; and Gurney Norman, eds. *A Gathering at the Forks: Fifteen Years of the Hindman Settlement School Appalachian Writers Workshop.* Wise, VA: Vision Books, 1993.

Madden, David. *Bijou.* New York: Crown, 1974; rpt. New York: Avon, 1976.

Marion, Jeff Daniel. *Hello, Crow.* New York: Orchard Books, 1992.

———. *Vigils.* Boone, NC: Appalachian Consortium P, 1990.

Marius, Richard. *After the War.* New York: Knopf, 1992.

———. *Bound for the Promised Land.* Nashville, TN: Rutledge Hill P, 1993.

———. *The Coming of Rain.* Nashville, TN: Rutledge Hill P, 1991.

McCarthy, Cormac. *The Orchard Keeper.* New York: Echo P, 1982.

McCrumb, Sharyn. *If I Ever Return, Pretty Peggy-O.* New York: Scribner's, 1990.

———. *The Hangman's Beautiful Daughter.* New York: Scribner's, 1992.

McFee, Michael. *Sad Girl Sitting on a Running Board.* Frankfort, KY: Gnomon P, 1991.

McNeill, Louise. *Hill Daughter: New and Selected Poems.* Pittsburgh: U of Pittsburgh P, 1991.

———. *The Milkweed Ladies.* Pittsburgh: U of Pittsburgh P, 1988.

Miles, Emma Bell. *Spirit of the Mountains.* Knoxville: U of Tennessee P, 1975.

Miller, Jim Wayne. *His First, Best Country.* Frankfort, KY: Gnomon P, 1993.

———. *Newfound.* New York: Orchard Books, 1989.

———. *The Mountains Have Come Closer.* Boone, NC: Appalachian Consortium P, 1980; rpt., 1991.

More Best-Loved Stories Told at the National Storytelling Festival. Jonesborough, TN: National Storytelling P, 1992.

Morgan, Robert. *At the Edge of Orchard Country.* Middletown, CT: Wesleyan UP, 1987.

———. *The Blue Valleys.* Atlanta: Peachtree Publishers, 1989.

———. *Green River: New and Selected Poems.* Hanover, NH: UP of New England and Wesleyan UP, 1991.

————. *The Hinterlands.* Chapel Hill, NC: Algonquin P, 1994.

————. *The Mountains Won't Remember Me.* Atlanta: Peachtree P, 1992.

————. *Sigodlin.* Middletown, CT: Wesleyan UP, 1990.

Murfree, Mary Noailles. *In the Tennessee Mountains.* Rpt. Knoxville: U of Tennessee P, 1982.

Norman, Gurney. *Divine Right's Trip: A Novel of the Counterculture.* 1971; rpt. Frankfort, KY: Gnomon P, 1990.

————. *Kinfolks: The Wilgus Stories.* Frankfort, KY: Gnomon P, 1989.

Offutt, Chris. *Kentucky Straight.* New York: Random House/Vintage, 1992.

Palencia, Elaine Fowler. *Small Caucasian Woman.* Columbia: U of Missouri P, 1993.

Pancake, Breece D'J. *The Stories of BREECE D' J PANCAKE.* Boston: Little, Brown, 1983.

Quillen, Rita. *October Dusk.* Big Timber, MT: Seven Buffaloes P, 1987.

Roberts, Elizabeth Madox. *The Great Meadow.* Southern Classic Series. Nashville, TN: J. S. Sanders, 1992.

Rylant, Cynthia. *Appalachia: The Voices of Sleeping Birds.* San Diego: Harcourt Brace Jovanovich, 1991.

————. *Missing May.* New York: Orchard Books, 1992.

Scarbrough, George. *A Summer Ago.* Memphis and Atlanta: Iris P, 1986.

————. *Invitation to Kim.* Memphis and Atlanta: Iris Press, 1989. Distributed by Peachtree Publishers.

Schenkkan, Robert. *The Kentucky Cycle.* New York: Plume/Penguin, 1993.

Secreast, Donald. *The Rat Becomes Light.* New York: Harper and Row, 1990.

Sellers, Bettie. *Liza's Monday and Other Poems.* Boone, NC: Appalachian Consortium P, 1986.

Settle, Mary Lee. *Charley Bland.* New York: Farrar, Straus, Giroux, 1989.

————. *The Beulah Quintet.* 5 vols. New York: Macmillan, 1988.

Shelby, Anne. *We Keep a Store.* New York: Orchard Books, 1990.

Showell, Ellen Harvey. *Our Mountain.* New York: Bradbury P of Macmillan, 1991.

Sinclair, Bennie Lee. *The Endangered: New and Selected Poems.* Greenville, SC: Ninety-Six P, 1993.

Smith, Effie Waller. *The Collected Works of Effie Waller Smith.* Introduction by David Deskins. New York: Oxford UP, 1991.

Smith, Lee. *Cakewalk.* New York: Ballantine, 1986.

————. *Fair and Tender Ladies.* New York: Putnam's/Ballantine, 1990.

————. *Me and My Baby View the Eclipse.* New York: Putnam's, 1990.

————. *The Devil's Dream.* New York: Putnam's, 1992.

Stewart, Albert. *The Holy Season: Walking in the Wild.* Berea, KY: Berea College P, 1993.

Still, James. *River of Earth.* 1940; rpt. Lexington, KY: UP of Kentucky, 1978.

————. *Rusties, Riddles, and Gee-Haw Whimmy-Diddles.* Lexington: UP of Kentucky, 1989.

————. *The Wolfpen Notebooks: A Record of Appalachian Life.* Lexington: UP of Kentucky, 1991.

————. *The Wolfpen Poems.* Berea, KY: Berea College P, 1986.

Stuart, Jesse. *A Jesse Stuart Reader.* 1963; rpt. Ashland, KY: Jesse Stuart Foundation, 1988.

————. *Taps for Private Tussie.* 1943; rpt. Ashland, KY: Jesse Stuart Foundation, 1992.

West, Don. *In a Land of Plenty: A Don West Reader.* Albuquerque, NM: West End, 1982.

Wilson, Leigh Allison. *From the Bottom Up.* Athens: U of Georgia P, 1983.

Wolfe, Thomas. *The Complete Short Stories.* Ed. Francis Skipp. New York: Macmillan/Collier, 1989.

————. *The Short Novels.* Ed. C. Hugh Holman. New York: Macmillan: Hudson River Editions, 1989

Films

Reference

"Appalachian Film List." Comp. Laura Schuster and Sharyn McCrumb. *Appalachian Journal* 11, no. 4 (Summer 1984): 329–83.

"Films and Filmstrips." *Blacks in Appalachia.* Ed. William H. Turner and Edward J. Cabbell. Lexington, KY: UP of Kentucky, 1985.

Williamson, J. W. *Southern Mountains in Silent Films.* Jefferson, NC: McFarland & Co., 1994.

Films

Agee. 1985. Directed by Ross Spears. James Agee Film Project of Franklin Lakes, NJ. Contact James Agee Film Project, 316 East Main St., Johnson City, TN 37601.

Carson Springs: A Decade Later. 1983. Produced by Thomas Burton and Thomas Headley. East Tennessee State U. Contact Thomas Headley, Dept. of Communications, ETSU, P.O. Box 70667, Johnson City, TN 37614.

Fat Monroe. 1990. Directed by Andrew Garrison. Appalshop, Inc., Whitesburg, KY, 41858.

Fixin' to Tell About Jack. 1975. Directed by Elizabeth Barrett. Appalshop, Inc., Whitesburg, KY, 41858.

Following the Signs: A Way of Conflict. 1986. Produced by Thomas Burton and Thomas Headley. East Tennessee State U. Contact Thomas Headley, Dept. of Communications, ETSU, P.O. Box 70667, Johnson City, TN 37614.

Four Voices: Stories of Community Based Education. 1987. Produced and directed by Pamela Yates (Skylight Pictures) for the Association for Community Based Education, 1806 Vernon Street, N.W., Washington, D.C. 20009.

Harriette Simpson Arnow: 1908–1986. 1988. Directed by Herb E. Smith. Appalshop, Inc., Whitesburg, KY 41858.

Morgan Sexton: Banjo Player from Bull Creek. 1991. Directed by Anne Johnson. Appalshop, Inc., Whitesburg, KY, 41858.

Soldier Jack. 1988. Directed by Tim Davenport. Davenport Films, RR 1, Box 527, Delaplane, VA 22025.

Strangers and Kin. 1984. Directed by Herb E. Smith. Appalshop, Inc., Whitesburg, KY, 41858.

The Bitter Berry: The Life of Byron Herbert Reece, Poet/Writer/ Farmer/Teacher. 1988. By Gary Moss and Bettie Sellers. Film Ideas, 3565 Commercial Ave., Northbrook, IL 60062.

The Electric Valley. 1983. Directed by Ross Spears. James Agee Film Project, 316 East Main Street, Johnson City, TN 37601.

The Journey Is Home: A Film About Nelle Morton. 1989. Ecufilm, 810 Twelfth Ave., South, Nashville, TN 37203.

They Shall Take Up Serpents. 1973. Produced by Thomas Burton and John E. Schrader. East Tennessee State U. Contact Thomas Headley, Dept. of Communications, ETSU, P.O. Box 70667, Johnson City, TN 37614.

To Render a Life. 1992. Directed by Ross Spears. James Agee Film Project, 316 East Main Street, Johnson City, TN 37601.

Traditional Springs: Violence in the South. 1985. Produced by Thomas Burton and Thomas Headley. East Tennessee State U. Contact Thomas Headley, Dept. of Communications, ETSU, P.O. Box 70667, Johnson City, TN 37614.

Index